THE **PUZZLE** OF THE
SOVIET CHURCH

An Inside Look at Christianity and Glasnost

KENT R. HILL

MULTNOMAH

Portland, Oregon 97266

in cooperation with the
Institute on Religion and Democracy

Edited by Al Janssen, Steve Halliday, and Rod Morris

Cover design by Krieg Barrie

THE PUZZLE OF THE SOVIET CHURCH
© 1989 by Kent R. Hill
Published by Multnomah Press
Portland, Oregon 97266
in cooperation with the
Institute on Religion and Democracy
Washington, D.C. 20005

Multnomah Press is a ministry of Multnomah School of the Bible,
8435 Northeast Glisan Street, Portland, Oregon 97220.

Printed in the United States of America

Library of Congress Cataloging-in-Publication Data

Hill, Kent Richmond.
  The puzzle of the Soviet church.
  Bibliography: p.
  Includes index.
    1. Soviet Union—Church history—1917-   2. Persecution—Soviet Union—
History—20th century.   3. Church and state—Soviet Union—History—1917-
4. Communism and Christianity—Soviet Union—History—20th century.
I. Title.
BR936.H55   1989   323.44'2'0947   89-12334
ISBN 0-88070-320-2

89 90 91 92 93 94 95 96 97 98 - 10 9 8 7 6 5 4 3 2 1

In memory of
Christopher Aaron Hill
my first son

In honor of
the Solovky Bishops
models of discretion and valour

In appreciation of
Janice
my wife and best friend

CONTENTS

FOREWORD

*T*he last two years have witnessed extraordinary changes in the life of the churches in the Soviet Union. It is no exaggeration to say that, in the formal sense, they have made more progress towards religious liberty and acceptance as an integral part of Soviet society than in the whole of the previous seventy years since the Revolution.

Kent Hill's book brings to the general reader extensive background to this change, basing himself throughout on the very best recent sources of scholarship, brought together here for the first time in a single comprehensive volume.

Particularly valuable, and perhaps the most original sections of the book, are the chapters on Marxism and religion and the particular application of this theoretical background to conditions in Russia after the Revolution. No one should enter into a Christian-Marxist dialogue without taking the cold shower which Kent Hill's analysis provides.

The Puzzle of the Soviet Church also underlines the fragility of the recent improvements for Soviet believers. This will persist at least until the promulgation of new laws on religion, which are still the subject of controversial discussion at the time when the author draws his line and submits the work to the publisher. On April 8, 1989, Mr. Gorbachev personally signed a decree introducing new and severe penalties for the political offenses of publicly calling for ''the overthrow of the Soviet state and social system or for its change by methods contrary to the Soviet Constitution.'' Believers in several republics have, over the last year, played a key role in demanding greater independence from Moscow for their national group. The new law could see them imprisoned for three years—or for seven, if they use printing equipment to disseminate their views, or for ten, if they collude with anyone from abroad.

Whether the Soviet system now goes forward or backward, this book provides a balance sheet under which the future positives and negatives can be recorded. The author rightly urges that many, many more believers worldwide should be personally involved in the process. Whether or not it closes in the future, the door is open at the moment for far more contacts than the churches are exploiting.

This leads me to mention the most sobering section of the book: a consideration of the role played over the last few years by the World Council of Churches, the U.S. National Council of Churches, the Assemblies of God, the Baptist World Alliance, and Billy Graham. This is the first comprehensive survey of a highly sensitive subject, which is likely to arouse emotion and defensive reaction by the bodies named. Each has a record which, to varying degrees, is deficient both in informing its constituency of the true nature of Soviet policy towards religion and in evolving any consistent way to support the cause of those who have undergone limitless suffering for their faith over many decades. The reader who has come this far with the author will applaud both his bravery in not flinching from a task which is bound to result in personal criticism, but also his avoidance of animus, leading him to set out his case clearly and with charity.

Kent Hill's work places him in the very front rank of American experts on a subject which is of potential concern to millions. Those who read it should find themselves ready to express that concern.

Michael Bourdeaux
General Director
Keston College
England

INTRODUCTION

*I*t was a cold, crisp February Sunday morning in Moscow. My wife, Janice, and I were returning from our first visit to the British Embassy directly across the Moscow River from the Kremlin. We had just attended a Protestant service for English-speaking foreigners at the British compound. The year was 1978 and what was about to happen would begin a transformation in our lives.

With the golden domes of the Kremlin sparkling behind us, we headed towards a bus stop. Just then a short, stocky, red-haired man, missing a couple of front teeth, approached us and demanded in Russian, "Where were you? You promised to meet me to give me the Bibles."

Surprised and somewhat taken aback, I responded: "I'm sorry, you must be mistaken. I don't know what you are talking about."

Raising his voice, the fellow fired back: "It's not nice to make a promise and not keep it. You promised to bring me the Bibles. Where are they?" By this time, others waiting for the bus were obviously uncomfortable and began to step back.

In an effort to escape this inexplicable confrontation, I responded, "I don't know what you are talking about, and I have never seen you before in my life!"

As we pushed by him on the sidewalk, the man half grinned and said under his breath in perfect English: "Good luck."

For the next seven months I was scheduled to do research in the Soviet Union for my doctoral dissertation on a Russian Jew who had emigrated to France in 1920. Jan and I had not brought Bibles to give away, knew nothing of those who did, and had no contacts with either the government-registered churches or the underground churches.

Many weeks passed before we understood more clearly the mysterious, belligerent redhead. The Soviets had done their homework. The purpose of the elaborately staged event was simply to let us know that they knew we were Christians and to inform us that if we did intend to contact the underground church, they were watching. Indeed, it was unnerving.

Another episode two months later is also etched vividly into our memories. It was near midnight before Easter and we wanted to attend the Yelokhovskaia Cathedral—the seat of the Russian Orthodox patriarch. However, the cathedral was cordoned off by plainclothes security men for two blocks in every direction.

For several moments we argued: I insisting that we be let through, they gruffly requiring a special pass. Only when I pulled out our American passports did the mood shift. A security supervisor, looking somewhat nervous, stepped out of the shadows and gave the command to let us through.

As we approached the cathedral, we noticed a long line of Soviet citizens waiting to enter. Up and down the line strode an aggressive, hostile, antireligious propagandist. "There's no point in waiting," he shouted. "It's already full inside, and besides, it's all just superstitious nonsense anyway." The huddled faithful were undeterred from their patient vigil.

When the authorities around the cathedral realized that we were Americans, they immediately ushered us to a side entrance reserved for foreigners. Though it was crowded, we managed to squeeze in and immediately found ourselves in another world. The bright colors of ancient icons, the gold of the iconostasis, the richly embroidered robes of the priests, the scent from the priests' censers, the rhythmic chant of the ancient liturgy, and the incredibly deep resonance of the Russian bass voices were a feast for our senses. Lost in a sea of Russian *babyshki* (old women), we did our best to avoid the mass of candles which threatened at any moment to ignite the clothes of the pressed-in humanity. It is impossible to attend such a service and entertain any doubt that religious faith is intensely alive in this so-called capital of scientific atheism.

Then there was the Bible study, hosted by Paul Roush, an American naval attaché at the U.S. embassy, and his wife Annette. I'm surprised we went, because I was not much inclined toward such things. In fact, I thought Bible studies were frequented by people who gave simplistic answers to tough questions.

But we went anyway, and the people we met were genuine. They were committed to God and to each other. There was a wholesome comradery to the group which was infectious. A young Marine, two Canadian embassy employees, a military attaché, a young graduate school couple, and assorted other embassy employees comprised the group. What none of us knew in the spring of 1978 was that we were establishing bonds of trust and friendship that would become essential for dealing with a crisis thrust on the American embassy at the end of June.

On June 27, a group of eight Christians from Siberia arrived at the gates of the American embassy in Moscow following three days of travel from their distant home. They only wanted to talk with American consular officials about the possibility of emigrating. The Soviet guards, however, refused to let them enter. In frustration, the group rushed by the startled militia. Seven succeeded, but sixteen-year-old John Vashchenko did not. The last the two families saw of John, a burly militiaman was choking him, then dragging him away.

And so the saga of the Siberian Seven began. An anticipated three-hour stay in the embassy turned into a desperate plea for asylum. The ordeal did not end until five years later, when thirty-one members of the two families were finally allowed to emigrate. But in June of 1978 none of us knew that we were witnessing the opening scenes of a protracted struggle between the superpowers over two simple peasant families from Siberia. We only knew that they were in trouble and that we ought to try and help.

Every member of the Bible study had a role to play. I became the interpreter for the Pentecostals. One Bible study member let me use his apartment in the embassy compound during the day so that I would not have to take sensitive documents of the Siberian Seven back to Moscow State University where Jan and I lived. Other members took the lead in providing food and fellowship, while still others were able to give critical advice on the developing stalemate between American and Soviet authorities.

After dozens of hours of personal interviews and study of the materials the Seven had brought to the embassy, I realized that we were dealing with one of the best-documented cases of persecution to emerge from the Soviet underground. It stretched from the days of Stalin's forced collectivization in the early 1930s to the most recent acts of the Brezhnev era. The stories I translated were filled with systematic and brutal treatment: imprisonment, labor camp, psychiatric hospitals, mysterious deaths, the forceful break-up of church services, and the kidnapping of Christian children by Soviet officials.

By the time Jan and I left the USSR in late August 1978, I was deeply involved in the effort to publicize the case of the Siberian Seven. During the course of the next seven months, I translated several hundred pages of Russian manuscripts for John Pollock. On the basis of this research, John's book *The Siberian Seven* was published.

So in the space of just six short months, from that first encounter with the red-haired man near the British embassy to our train trip out of the Soviet Union in August, we had become deeply immersed in the plight of believers in the Soviet Union. For the next five years, while I completed my Ph.D. at the University of Washington and began teaching at Seattle Pacific University, I was involved in speeches, radio and television interviews, testimony to committees of the United States Senate and House of Representatives, and many behind-the-scenes meetings concerning the Siberian Seven case.

During this period, I discovered a surprising fact: Christians in the West were often misinformed or apathetic about the fate of Christians in the USSR. It was not easy to get the oldline churches or the National Council of Churches excited about taking concrete action on behalf of Christians in the Soviet Union. There were problems among evangelicals in this regard as well, including the Pentecostals. In contrast to our Jewish friends, Christians were far less effective and united in their work for their co-religionists in the USSR. It is one of our great shames as a Christian community.

American Christians have been confused by two very different images of religion in the Soviet Union. For years parishioners in oldline, NCC-related churches were told that, though the situation was far from perfect, there was considerable religious freedom in the USSR. Those who argued to the contrary were dismissed as "cold-war warriors" and "reactionaries." In contrast, parishioners in other church denominations were led to believe that to be a Christian in the Soviet Union meant almost certain imprisonment or worse. No wonder American Christians have been perplexed by the diverse accounts of religion in the Soviet Union.

Rarely did I encounter a presentation which explained the differences between registered and unregistered believers, and the corresponding distinction between being discriminated against and being persecuted. A sensitivity to the unique difficulties of both church groups was almost never demonstrated. Tragically, Western Christians often chose to defend one group, but not the other; to embrace compromise or confrontation. What usually was missing was a balanced approach which recognized the need to support both registered and unregistered Christians, and to employ a flexible combination of quiet diplomacy and firm public protest.

It was some of these issues that helped me decide to accept an invitation in 1986 to become the Executive Director of the Institute on Religion and Democracy in Washington, D.C. The IRD works for renewal in both the oldline church world and the evangelical community. It seeks to help all parts of the religious spectrum by providing competent analysis of critical foreign policy questions. In the spring of 1987 I helped found a new organization: the Coalition for Solidarity with Christians in the USSR. This interdenominational, inter-ethnic coalition of eighteen organizations represents a hopeful new sign of ecumenical cooperation and responsible engagement by Christian organizations.

Of course, the biggest question on everyone's minds as the 1980s draw to a close is how to assess the amazing and enigmatic events which have occurred in the Soviet Union since Mikhail Gorbachev came to power in March 1985. Some argue that Gorbachev has inaugurated a new era of openness which has substantially and permanently improved the lot of believers in the USSR. Others assert, however, that the changes are only cosmetic and, in fact, designed to mislead the West.

How are we to know whom and what to believe? The answer lies in a careful study of reliable materials on the topic and, when possible, on first-hand interviews inside the Soviet Union.

In the spring of 1988 the Institute on Religion and Democracy, in cooperation with the Slavic Gospel Association, organized a two-week tour to the USSR. The occasion for the tour was the millennial anniversary of the conversion of Prince Vladimir of Kievan Rus' to Byzantine Christianity. Our group included representatives from the United Methodist, Presbyterian, Catholic, Nazarene, Baptist, Pentecostal, and Episcopalian communities. It was also our intent to talk to as many Christians as possible within the Russian Orthodox, Protestant, and Catholic fellowships. We sought contacts with both registered and unregistered believers. And we tried to facilitate frank and extended dialogue with Soviet officials on matters involving religious policy and practice. We traveled to the Russian and Ukrainian republics, as well as to the republics of Estonia and Latvia in the Baltic region. Principal cities visited included Moscow, Leningrad, Kiev, Tallinn, and Riga.

There is no simple answer to the question of the status of religion in the Soviet Union. Circumstances vary widely from region to region, and even from city to city. Sometimes the laws restricting and regulating religious practices are assiduously followed. Other times local authorities are much harsher or lenient than the legal statutes would require.

Furthermore, in the seventy-plus years of Soviet rule there have been definite cyclical patterns of repression and relaxation to which believers have found it necessary to respond. Is the present *glasnost* simply a brief respite from a general pattern of persecution? Or does it herald lasting changes supportive of true religious freedom?

In 1938 Winston Churchill commented that Russia "is a riddle wrapped in a mystery inside an enigma." There is certainly much truth in that remark. Yet, there also is a great deal that can be learned from serious study.

A basic thesis of this book is that Christians must fully acknowledge the positive changes which are occurring in the Soviet Union without succumbing to an unjustified judgment that religious freedom has now been achieved in this troubled land. Sober, dispassionate analysis is needed if we are to act responsibly in the days ahead. My hope is that this study will help Western Christians come to grips with the complex history and current realities of believers in the Soviet Union. Ultimately, the book is designed to be a kind of guidebook for prudent and effective action.

We will begin our study with an analysis of the Siberian Seven drama. I was in a position to experience or observe much of what happened in this momentous story between 1978 and 1983. This specific personal experience is intended to set the scene for the subsequent sections of the book which span back many decades before the Siberian Seven story began and up to the present since their emigration.

Section II introduces the reader to the relationship of Marxism to Christianity, both in its classical German form and in its Soviet embodiment.

Section III provides valuable historical background for understanding the present situation of believers in the Soviet Union. It is devoted to the history of Church/State relations from the Bolshevik Revolution in 1917 to the beginning of the Gorbachev era in 1985. Changes in 1917 are placed in a broader context of religion in Russian society in previous centuries. Readers who are well informed in these areas may choose to skim over these chapters. However, I strongly recommend that if you are not familiar with these materials you invest the time to acquire the necessary background this section provides. The Gorbachev era is still a short blip on the historical screen, and the legacy of the past—even in the most optimistic of forecasts—will certainly have its impact on the future.

Section IV addresses one of the most important issues in the book: the relationship between Soviet disinformation efforts and the all-too-often deficient response of the Western church. If we hope to do any better in the future, we first have to face what we have done wrong in the past.

Section V tackles the meaning and significance of *glasnost*. We will briefly discuss the political and economic forces which have helped shape the *glasnost* period. We will examine the encouraging cracks which are appearing in the information control system, and the signs of new life in Soviet culture. We will analyze a new public attitude towards religion which can be found in the press and in what the Council for Religious Affairs (which monitors religious groups for the Kremlin) is saying. We will review the positive impact of *glasnost* on believers. Releases from prison, expanded permission to emigrate, a less restrictive religious legal framework, increased opportunities for religious activities (evangelism, more control of internal church matters), greater availability of religious literature, reopenings and increased registrations of churches, and the right to volunteer for charitable activities are discussed.

However, it is critical that Westerners remain aware of problems which persist for believers even during *glasnost*. While there have been improvements, there have also been disturbing reverses and the continuation of serious interferences with religious liberty. Thus, we must review Gorbachev-era examples of discrimination and persecution which remind us of the need for structural changes in Soviet law to provide long-term protection for believers. We also must confront the thorny problem which the nationalities question poses for religious freedom.

Finally, we will address the question of whether *glasnost* and Gorbachev are here to stay. Can democracy, fundamental economic reform, and genuine religious freedom hurdle the obstacles of ideology and empire which threaten the future of *glasnost*? The final chapter provides advice for Western Christians on how we can most effectively respond in the months and years ahead to the unique needs and opportunities of believers in the USSR.

One of the most important parts of the book is the series of appendices. An effort has been made to collect in a single reference section items which have not appeared together previously. The reader's attention is particularly called to Appendix A, ''What Western Christians Can Do to Help.'' Here can be found a description of organizations which provide information on and opportunities for helping believers in the USSR, a guide for mailing religious literature into the Soviet Union, and suggestions on aiding those who choose to emigrate.

Appendix B provides the relevant sections of Soviet legislation restricting religion. This is important for understanding Church/State relations for most of Soviet history, and it provides a reference point for assessing Gorbachev-era changes in this legislation. Appendix C gives the key sections of international laws and agreements related to religious freedom.

While this book is written by a Christian primarily for fellow Christians, it includes information which should be useful for other faith communities and for human rights activists in general. This book is based on both firsthand experience (four trips to the Soviet Union) and more than a decade of study and reflection on the relationship between believers and the State in the Soviet Union. As such, the book is both deeply personal and the product of considerable research and study. If it helps Western Christians respond more responsibly to the special needs of their co-believers in the Soviet Union, then a major objective of this book will have been achieved.

This book would not have been possible without the help of many people. Valuable research assistance and/or comments on various portions of the manuscript was provided by Michael Bourdeaux, Michael Rowe, Mark Elliott, Bohdan R. Bociurkiw, Dmitry Pospielovsky, Anita Deyneka, Alan Wisdom, Theofanis Stavrou, Catherine P. Henry, Alice Young, Paul Mojzes, Victor Hamm, Michael Roshak, Serge Duss, Lloyd Billingsley, Robert Nichols, Paul and Annette Roush, Ray Barnett, Kathy Kersten, Amy Sherman, David Bovenizer, Helen Hill, Wayne Kenney, George Weigel, and Vasilij Alexeev. I am particularly grateful to the Institute on Religion and Democracy (IRD) for its allocation of staff and resources in support of this project. The detailed appendix is largely the work of Randy Tift, Father Stan DeBoe, and Lisa Gibney. As my research assistant, Lisa was very competent in tracking down information and footnotes. Slavic Gospel Association and Open Doors provided helpful information for parts of Appendix A, and Christian Solidarity International allowed me to use parts of their brochure on international laws for Appendix C. Diane Knippers, IRD's Deputy Director, served double duty during the writing of the book by both covering for me at work during several weeks of my writing and by being a perceptive critic of my manuscript. I was extremely fortunate to have in Al Janssen a very capable senior editor, and in John Van Diest a supportive and enthusiastic publisher. Multnomah Press has worked extemely hard to get this book out in a timely fashion. Special thanks are also due to the Bradley Foundation, the Elmer Bisbee Foundation, and George E. Luce who have provided financial support for the IRD's work on religious liberty. Needless to say, the errors in fact and judgment which remain in the book are the responsibility of the author.

Finally a special thanks to my family, who put up with me disappearing into my basement den night after night. I am very grateful, however, that the book did not interfere too much with my Saturday walks with Jennifer, my late afternoon soccer scrimmages with Jonathan, and my evening talks on the front porch with Janice. Some things, after all, ought not to be put off.

The transliteration system used is a version of that recommended by the Library of Congress. Modifications used here include: the Russian letter "e" at the beginnings of words is transliterated "ye," and "ii" at the end of a word is "y." However, consistency is not possible since many names have become part of the Western vocabulary in forms based on other transliteration systems.

Let me conclude with a passage from the apostle Paul which friends in the Soviet Union long ago asked that I share with their brothers and sisters in the West:

> Let us not become weary in doing good, for at the proper time we will reap a harvest if we do not give up. Therefore, as we have opportunity, let us do good to all people, especially to those who belong to the family of believers (Galatians 6:9, 10).

June 2, 1989
Washington, D.C.

THE SIBERIAN SEVEN:

A Case Study

CHAPTER 1

THE DRAMA
UNFOLDS

*T*here is a solitude in the hours before dawn which lends itself to reflection. As the overnight train from Leningrad to Moscow cut through the July night in 1978, I marveled at all the past five-and-a-half months in the Soviet Union had given us. We had spent three weeks in Central Asia, two weeks in the Caucasus, several days in the heartland of medieval Russia (Suzdal, Vladimir, Rostov), many weeks living in Moscow, and three weeks in Leningrad. Hundreds of slides had been taken and countless experiences recorded in preparation for my future university teaching of Russian history and culture.

In another month Janice and I would be in Paris to continue my doctoral research on Lev Shestov—a Russian thinker and philosopher who was obsessed with questions of faith and reason. I hated the thought of becoming a narrow specialist, so I had decided to pen a biography about someone who wrote about philosophy, theology, and literature. Thus, I was an intellectual vagabond, a cultural historian who was in love with all things Russian.

As the train pulled into Moscow that mid-July morning, I thankfully had no premonition of the adventures of the coming days and years. All we wanted to do was get to the embassy as soon as possible. For three weeks we had not heard from our relatives or friends, and we wanted to pick up our mail. The taxi driver kindly agreed to stop at the embassy on the way back to Moscow State University where we lived. I jumped out of the cab, flashed my American passport to the Soviet militia guarding the gates, and bounded up the steps to the consular section.

It was necessary to walk through a waiting room to reach the mail room. I had no sooner opened the door than I encountered seven figures dozing on the chairs and couches in an otherwise empty room. The seven were obviously Russian. There was a short man, slight of build, in his mid-fifties; two women in their fifties; three young women in their twenties; and one teenage boy. Before I reached the mailroom, the man said in Russian: "It is too early. The mailroom is not yet open. You will have to come back." Of course, I should have known it was too early. I thanked him and made my way back to the waiting taxi cab. It took a few more minutes for my mind to register how strange it was to see Russians in the consular waiting section so early in the day.

Several hours later, Jan and I returned to the embassy. A friend of ours, Annette Roush, wife of an American naval attaché, took us aside as soon as we entered the American compound. "Do you know who these seven people are?" Annette queried.

"No, we just returned from Leningrad early this morning," I responded.

Annette's tone was hushed, her manner intense as she told us what little was known at that time about the seven strangers in the waiting room. It was her hope that Jan could talk to the young women, and that I could perhaps learn a bit more about who the Seven were and their experiences.

It turns out that on the day Jan and I had taken the train to Leningrad—June 27—a group of Siberians had arrived at the gates of the embassy. Peter and Augustina Vashchenko, three daughters (Lida, 27; Lyuba, 25; Lila, almost 21), and one son (John, 17) had made a three-and-a-half day train trip from Chernogorsk in Siberia. Maria Chmykhalov and her sixteen-year-old son Timothy had accompanied the Vashchenkos. The purpose of the trip was to discuss with the Americans the possibility of emigrating. The Vashchenkos had recently (and miraculously) received through the mail a formal invitation to emigrate from Rev. Cecil Williamson (Presbyterian) of Selma, Alabama.[1]

Despite the fact that the USSR had signed a Consular Convention agreement which guarantees the right of Soviet citizens to visit the American embassy, the pledge had been routinely violated. The Soviet militia which guarded the two gates of the American embassy were not really there to protect the foreign compound, as they always claimed; they were there to prevent as many Soviet citizens as possible from gaining access to American officials. That was the case with this group from Siberia. John, however, tried to run by the guards. While the two militiamen pounced on him, the other seven members of the group scampered to safety inside the embassy compound. It must have been a frightening experience for them to see the next-to-youngest of their group being pummeled, yet not be able to rush to his assistance. To try and help John would mean only that his fate would become theirs as well.

UNEXPECTED LINK WITH THE PAST

What particularly added to the mystery of the Siberian Seven was an old book which had come into the possession of the Roushes just a few days before the Seven arrived at the embassy. It was titled *The Faith of the Russian*

Evangelicals, by the English biographer John Pollock, and it had been published fourteen years earlier, in 1964.[2] Pollock described a gripping episode
which occurred at the American embassy many years before.

It was January 3, 1963, and a light snow was falling when a group of
thirty-two Pentecostals approached the American embassy on Tchaikovsky
street.[3] Six men, twelve women, and fourteen children who wanted to emigrate had made the long train journey from Chernogorsk in order to plead for
help from the Americans. En masse they rushed by the startled Soviet militia.
What had driven them to this desperate act? The answer can best be summed
up in one phrase: the state kidnapping of Christian children.

Thumbing through the book, Annette Roush noticed a number of references to a family named Vashchenko. Wasn't this the name of one of the
families sitting down in the waiting room? Annette wondered if possibly, after
fifteen years, a remnant of the original "32" had returned to the embassy, still
seeking emigration.

It was indeed the same family, and Augustina was one of the famous
"32" Siberians. My research later revealed the heartrending details of their
story.[4] Unusually aggressive ideological attacks on believers constrained a
number of families to withdraw their children from the state schools. Beginning in late 1961, local authorities decided to deprive these particularly
troublesome believer parents of their "parental rights." The alleged legal
basis for this aggression against Christians came from Article 227 of the
Russian criminal code, which prohibited the practice of religion that harmed
other people. During 1962 ten children, from three different Chernogorsk
families, were taken from their parents: three from Peter Vashchenko, three
from Peter's brother Khariton, and four from the family of Anatoly
Shevchenko. Two of the three Vashchenko children taken, Lida and Lyuba,
would eventually become members of the Siberian Seven.

The abductions did not occur without a struggle. In February 1962, Peter
took his three oldest daughters (Lida, almost eleven; Lyuba, nine; and Nadya,
seven) and hid them with friends in the country. But on June 15, the authorities finally tracked Lida down. A month later the younger girls were apprehended as well.

By September the girls were in a boarding school (*Internat*) in Achinsk—
approximately 280 miles to the north by train. The parents were not told where
the girls had been sent. For many weeks Peter and Augustina had no contact
with their three daughters, and it might have continued even longer had not a
cook taken pity on the young girls. One day the cook heard the Vashchenko
girls crying. When she learned that they had been forcibly separated from their
parents, she wrote a neighbor of the Vashchenkos and told them where the
girls were.

For the next few years, Peter and Augustina alternated each week making
the arduous eighteen-hour pilgrimage by train to Achinsk for secret meetings

with their daughters. It was not until 1967 that Lida and Lyuba managed to return home. Nadya made her way back the next year.

In October 1962, Peter, Augustina, his five remaining children, and his brother's wife and baby went to Moscow. They wanted to complain to the Soviet authorities about the abduction of their daughters. They did talk with Soviet Kremlin officials and ended up in custody for questioning. At one point a registered Baptist leader was brought in to question them and find out what they wanted. The Protestant leader expressed surprise that they wanted to emigrate: "After all, you are free to believe in God here."[5]

BROKEN PROMISES

It was in this strained atmosphere of fear and distress that the thirty-two Pentecostals from Siberia showed up at the American embassy in early 1963. There were an estimated five hundred from their area that sought emigration to Israel, and they were simply the advance party. Peter was not among this group; he had been arrested in mid-December. However, Peter's father, mother, a cousin, and a brother, as well as Augustina and three of their children were all among the thirty-two. Many of the families represented had relatives in prison or children in state orphanages.

The delegation told embassy officials and the foreign Moscow press corps of the violent persecution of believers in the Soviet Union. Officials from the Soviet Ministry of Foreign Affairs showed up and expressed amazement at the stories of the Siberians. As Soviet official Kuznetsov put it: "We have no idea why the American embassy was chosen for this demonstration. As is well known, religious freedom is guaranteed in the Soviet Union. . . ."[6] Soviet officials promised the Americans and the Siberians that a special commission would be set up to investigate the charges of persecution (including the disruption of church services with fire hoses), and that those arrested would be freed, the abducted children sent home, and their request for emigration given serious consideration.

With those assurances, a bus was driven up to the embassy, and the thirty-two were invited to board. Again they were promised that there would be no reprisals for their coming to the embassy. Though the group was divided about what to do, finally all boarded the bus and disappeared into the Moscow maze. Back home in Siberia, the familiar routine of harassment and persecution was soon resumed.

The number three ranking American at the embassy in January 1963 was Richard Davies, who later became U.S. Ambassador to Poland. He urged the Siberians to come to an agreement with the Soviets because there was nothing the Americans could do to help them and they could not stay in the embassy. Davies now looks back on the events of that day with considerable regret. With bitterness Davies recalls that "the Soviet Foreign Ministry broke every one of the provisions of the agreement." Twenty years later Davies would testify before a Senate committee that the American embassy in 1978 also did not do nearly enough to help the unexpected Siberian guests.[7]

And thus the Siberian Seven drama began. American authorities were anything but happy about the presence of the seven Pentecostals. Violence at the entrance to the American compound transformed what was intended to be a two- or three-hour visit to the embassy into an extended stay. Their presence inconvenienced the Americans, and what was worse, it was not clear how long they would stay. American officials continually expressed to the Siberians that they had virtually no way of helping them. According to the consular officials, their fate lay in the hands of the Soviets, and the best thing the Seven could do was simply leave the embassy.

The Siberians expressed a willingness to go, if only John were returned to them unharmed. But at first the Soviets pretended to know nothing at all about what had happened to John. Then on July 10 the Vashchenko family in Chernogorsk called and was allowed to talk with their relatives in the embassy. Yes, John had finally been returned home by the KGB, but he had been badly beaten. He was so weak he could not come to the phone. The Chernogorsk family begged them not to leave the embassy. "If the KGB would do this to a minor, what would they do to you?"

By the time Jan and I arrived on the scene it was clear that the Siberian Seven case was not going to be resolved quickly. And yet from day to day it was unclear what would happen next. The Seven remained in the waiting room. They had no access to shower or bath facilities, though there was a toilet and sink they could use. embassy friends brought them food, but everyone lived in daily fear that they would be evicted from the embassy.

THE TRAGEDY OF AARON

The Seven had brought with them a pile of documents regarding their experiences in Siberia. However, embassy officials simply returned the materials to the Seven, apparently without studying them closely or even making copies. About a week after Jan and I first met the families, I became aware of this treasure trove of information. Naval attaché Paul Roush told me about the materials and said he was extremely curious about some handwritten journals, particularly one which included pictures of a house which had been broken into and a baby in a coffin. Paul asked me to try and decipher the handwriting and explain the troubling pictures.

It was not easy to find a place in the Moscow American embassy where sensitive work could be done. At that time there were approximately two hundred Soviets working in the U.S. facility. They were supplied by the Soviet government, and everyone understood that these secretaries, barbers, and motorpool employees reported to the Soviet security services on what they observed at the embassy.

(I once asked an American diplomat at a reception in Moscow why such a state of affairs was allowed to persist. He responded: "It is really much cheaper to hire Soviets than to bring Americans over. And besides there are not enough living accommodations for Americans as it is." The explanation struck me as unconvincing. The Soviets would not permit such a bizarre situation to occur in their embassy in Washington, D.C. They would laugh at the very notion of employing dozens of Americans within their compound.)

Thus, it was necessary to find a place away from the prying eyes of Soviet employees to do an examination of the journal in question. Paul took me to a secure floor of the embassy and left me alone to try and make sense of the materials. What I discovered in the next few hours still sends chills down my back. By the time Paul returned at the end of the day to check on my progress, I had learned enough to know that the people sitting down in the visitor's room had experienced a lifetime of suffering—not just under Stalin, but also under Khrushchev and Brezhnev. The journal I studied was one of the most gruesome chapters in their story.

It was the spring of 1975 and Lida, twenty-four years of age and a committed believer, was working as a nurse's aid in a maternity ward. Across the street abortions were performed routinely. As it was not uncommon to perform abortions very late in pregnancies, occasionally babies were born alive. In such situations, the newborns were carried across the street to where Lida worked. Lida was appalled to discover that no special attention was paid to these premature victims of abortion. Often, they were simply left to die.

On March 31, 1975 a baby boy was brought in—the victim of an abortion in the seventh month. Contrary to all expectations, the little baby lived, even though for days he was barely cared for. Lida took pity on the boy and obtained permission from the natural mother and hospital authorities to adopt the child. An official birth certificate, which I translated, listed Lida as the mother of the boy Lida named Aaron Vashchenko.

Aaron survived, then thrived in the warmth and love of the large Vashchenko family. There were already thirteen children, but the generous Christian family made room for one more precious child from God. However, certain city officials were not pleased when they learned that the Vashchenko family, with whom they had had conflicts for years, had adopted a child. Plans were made to deprive Lida of her "parental rights." This was a tactic that the Vashchenkos understood all too well. The memories of what had happened to Lida, Lyuba, and Nadya in the 1960s were still fresh.

The authorities were absolutely unscrupulous in their efforts to "save" this little child from the clutches of believers. They compelled the natural mother to say she feared that the Vashchenkos intended to "sacrifice" Aaron. Faced with the prospect of losing Aaron by force, Lida went into hiding. When she eventually returned home, authorities broke in, beat her, and stole

Aaron. Aaron was in perfect health on July 17, 1975 when he was abducted. It was the last time the Vashchenkos saw him alive.

I could hardly believe what I was reading in the carefully penned words of Lida's journal. Was this a dream? After all, this was an account of 1975, not 1935. Just three short years ago. And how did it happen that I was reading this? What was happening to the future Russian history teacher interested in taking pictures of twelfth-century churches? I knew virtually nothing about the persecution of believers, and here I was reading firsthand accounts not of discrimination, but of extreme persecution.

A HEARTBREAKING SEARCH

I broke out in a cold sweat. I knew enough to know that relations between the Soviets and the Americans were getting more tense. I also knew that an account such as I was reading was considered "anti-Soviet slander." It was dangerous to be associated with such materials, and it was especially dangerous to have written them. But I had to read on. I had to know what had happened to Aaron.

All of Lida's initial efforts to discover where Aaron was were futile. However, she did learn that the natural mother, Valya, refused to keep the child once the charade of taking Aaron back was accomplished. The authorities rewarded her with a nice apartment.

On August 24, Lida, her father, two brothers, and a sister went on an outing to pick wild berries. On the way back, while riding on an open freight car in the middle of the night, soaked to the skin by a relentless drizzle, the group was overwhelmed by a feeling of horror. As Lida described it:

> All of us were overcome by such fear that several of us began to cry, especially me. When they asked me what was the matter I answered: "I'm afraid." I did not know who or what I was afraid of, but I felt as if there was a gigantic force crushing down on us in the car. When I tried to creep towards my father I realized that he too sensed something and probably was crying, because he hid his eyes and would not admit that he too was frightened and had a foreboding of something bad. Each person wrapped himself up in his raincoat and quietly prayed.[8]

Several weeks later they discovered that Aaron died on this very night.

When Chernogorsk officials informed Lida that Aaron had died, she was driven by an indomitable will to find out if this were indeed true and, if so, what had happened. Lida and her father visited the local cemetery. To their great sorrow, they learned that a few days earlier the authorities had brought a little boy in for burial. He had reportedly been found in a field, abandoned by his parents.

The rest of the story read like a haunting mystery. Not only was the tragedy itself gripping, but Lida wrote with the passion and spirit of a poet. It was impossible to read her journal without weeping.

> Early on the morning of September 16, well before the break of day, we went to the cemetery to dig up the grave. . . . As we dug up the grave there were already women driving the cows out to pasture and a shepherd was standing on a hill and looked down at the visitors who had come to the cemetery so early. He couldn't understand what was going on. The child had been placed in an adult's grave, so it was necessary to dig around with the shovel in order find out in which corner of the grave the coffin was.
>
> We opened the coffin in order to make sure that it was him. . . . Without a doubt it was him and we took him home in order to bury him according to Christian ceremony. We had to fill the grave back up quickly because it was already getting light. The wind rustled the paper wreaths. The metal monuments were gleaming and the tin wreaths knocked about giving off a monotonous sound. It seemed that everything was alive, moving according to its own imperceptible laws.
>
> It was cold and all of this created an atmosphere that was so frightening that one's hair stood on end. Everyone was breathing very loudly and everything sounded noisy in the midst of this eternal quiet, although we worked very carefully and quietly, and hurried so as not to be caught at the grave. But the fact that before me was really a dead baby, that I had not mistaken him for my son, that he lay in this coffin disfigured—this feeling of grief was stronger than any feeling of fear.[9]

Having studied the pictures of Aaron in his coffin and read the detailed accounts provided by Lida, all that could be said with any certainty was that little Aaron was at least neglected to death. An operation had been performed sometime near the end of his life and a piece of rag stuffed in the incision. His body was covered with needle marks. His chest bore the scabs of being scratched by his long and untended fingernails.

But the Vashchenkos were truly believers. As horrible as this awful moment was, more powerful yet was their faith. Lida wrote:

> The infant had not lived long enough to do anything bad or good. His torments were undergone for God because he ended up in a family of believers and had it been a family of nonbelievers, then he would have lived and grown up. From this it follows that he bore his suffering for God, although he was unconscious of this fact because still a baby. He will inherit life eternal among the firstborn. Those

who abducted him do not believe in life beyond the grave, but their victory was in this life only. The devil has suffered complete defeat.[10]

On that Sunday in July, I had only the time to make out the general outline of what I have described. But it was enough to provide a profound sense of why the seven people sitting down in the visitors room below wished to emigrate from the Soviet Union.

That night I wrote the following to my parents: "The last few days and the coming few days I will remember as long as I live. There is a tragedy brewing in the American embassy." Indeed, there was, but no one dreamed the emigration ordeal would last five years.

GETTING THE STORY OUT

During the next month I spent nine full days translating materials the Vashchenkos brought with them to the embassy. It was too dangerous to take the Russian originals out of the embassy, nor would it have been wise to have had in my possession a copy of my translations. Fortunately, a member of the Roush Bible study had an apartment in the embassy compound that he could loan me during the day. At night, the forty-five minute trolleybus and subway ride back to the dorm where Jan and I lived was always a time for sober contemplation.

There could be no doubt that from the very beginning, the embassy was unhappy about the presence of the Siberian Seven in the embassy. They happened to arrive at a moment when the Carter administration was particularly reluctant to confront the Soviets on human rights, at least not in public. The SALT II Treaty was under consideration by the Senate, and graphic accounts of systematic violation of international human rights agreements by the Soviets were not deemed helpful in persuading uncertain senators to vote for a new treaty.

In addition, U.S. embassy facilities were cramped and inadequate, while the pressure on consular officials was relentless and draining. Moscow did not have the same draw for American diplomats as Paris or London, and living conditions for embassy officials were modest by Western standards. Consular officials had to deal almost daily with difficult cases, many of which they could simply not resolve (separated spouses, religious persecution, Jewish emigration).

Sometimes the irritation with being constantly put in awkward and near impossible situations produced a certain resentment of both the Soviet oppressors and the oppressed. And although the Siberian Seven case was highly unusual, the Americans were extremely concerned about setting a precedent that might invite others to storm the embassy gates. Had they made it absolutely clear to the public from the beginning that these folks had *not* intended to stay in the embassy, but had felt compelled to do so by Soviet violence at the gates, the Americans could have dealt with the precedent question.

The most important factor, however, was the decision of American officials to minimize as much as possible any publicity which the case might naturally generate.

What made all of this particularly unfortunate for the Seven was that their own past experiences with the Soviets left them with little doubt as to what awaited them just outside the embassy gates. In addition to the bitter memories of 1963, Peter Vashchenko remembered vividly the consequences of a short three-hour visit to the American embassy in 1968. Upon leaving the compound, he was immediately apprehended. Within a few hours he was in a psychiatric hospital, considered insane for wanting to leave the "workers' paradise" for the decadent West. Attempts to drug him were foiled by the feisty little Pentecostal, but he eventually found himself in a labor camp. All told, Peter had spent three-and-a-half years in labor camp. His wife had also spent two years in labor camp between 1968 and 1970, despite the fact that she had eleven children at that time (six under the age of ten).

We lived in daily fear that Ambassador Malcolm Toon would expel the Seven from their embassy sanctuary. So every hour possible was spent talking with the Siberians or pouring over the materials they had brought with them. Each day brought fresh revelations and the necessity of updating the written biographical material I regularly gave to the Moscow press corps and U.S. consular officials. I often was asked to interpret for the families and fill in background information for them when interviews were done.

In the early days and weeks of the emigration tug of war, the Roushes, myself, and the Protestant chaplain, Bill Villaume, were particularly concerned that the outside world learn who was sitting in the embassy waiting room. We were convinced that their ultimate fate with the Soviets, and very likely the continued de facto sanctuary with the Americans, depended on such publicity.

One day the Vice Consul called me into his office and said, "I want you to help me take the Seven to a part of the embassy where they can take showers." Thirty-four days had passed since their arrival, and they'd had no opportunity to clean themselves apart from what could be accomplished with a sink.

We went into the waiting room and announced that they were allowed to take showers. A stack of towels seemed to reinforce the point, but I immediately noticed several pairs of eyes asking, "Is this a trick, Kent? Have they convinced you that we must go?"

In order to get to the shower, it was necessary to walk down the same steps they had fled up thirty-four days before, cross through an archway, and then go through the courtyard to another wing of the building. In the archway, the Soviet militia were no more than a few feet away on our left. This was precisely the spot where the initial scuffle had taken place.

The tension mounted as we went down the stairs and approached the archway and I knew that their trust in me was on the line. Had I perhaps been talked into some plot to get them outside where either the Soviets or American marines could spirit them out of the embassy? As we passed through the archway, the Seven glanced furtively to their left and hurried in the opposite direction towards the courtyard. When nothing happened, the sigh of relief was unmistakable. At least the Americans intended to let them stay a bit longer. They grinned from ear to ear, and launched into their showers with enthusiasm. I thought they would never finish.

Western Church Silence

It was during these initial days that I learned a shocking piece of information: there was no well-established or organized Christian lobby in the West to speak up for their counterparts in the Soviet Union. In contrast to the Jews, who to their credit had established a solidarity of support in the United States among their own people, the press, and congress, the Christian lobby was virtually non-existent. Ecumenical church bodies (the World Council of Churches and the U.S. National Council of Churches), oldline Protestant denominations, and many Pentecostal and Evangelical groups were strangely silent about discrimination and persecution of believers in the Soviet Union.[11]

I was well aware that the Soviets likely knew by late July who was doing much of the translating and interpreting for the Seven. And yet, the press of time sometimes meant that it was necessary to take risks in arranging contacts that were almost certain to alert the Soviets to my activities. It became all the more critical to never have any notes or information in our university apartment or on our person. And, of course, we never talked about the Seven in our room. Long before the Seven had arrived in the embassy, we had learned from our Soviet friends that whenever you want to talk about something important you say, "let's take a walk." (The Soviet Union is one of the few places in the world that you can read Scripture aloud in the privacy of your room and witness to your faith at the same time.)

But now it was time to wind up our affairs in Moscow. Jan and I were scheduled to leave for Paris on August 19. The hardest task was saying "goodbye" to our friends. The night before we left we gathered together for a final dinner with some members of our Bible study and the Siberian Seven. The girls had become particularly fond of Janice, and I had become very attached to all of them, particularly Peter and Lida.

As we stood together and prayed, nobody knew what lay ahead. I knew that the worst I could expect was possible detention and questioning at the border. But for the Seven, it was an entirely different matter. I asked if they were sure they wanted me to do all I could to tell about their experiences.

"Surely you know that to tell the truth about your experiences makes you guilty of 'anti-Soviet slander.'" They assured me they wanted the West to know the truth, regardless of how it affected them.

I was having a hard time as it came time for our final embraces. After all, would we ever see them again? What was going to happen to them? Peter sensed my pain, came up to me, and put his arm around me. "Don't worry, Kent. We will be all right." Indeed, his faith had been tested more than mine, and he knew that the rock of their faith was sound.

The next day we left for Paris. Again a train ride would provide the occasion for reflections on what we had learned in the Soviet Union. Only this time there was even more to sort through than two months earlier when we had taken the midnight train from Leningrad to Moscow.

And what would we find at the end of this next train ride? One thing was certain: it would involve the fate of the Siberian Seven.

Notes

1. For basic factual information on the Siberian Seven, see John Pollock, *The Siberian Seven* (Waco, Texas: Word, 1979) and Timothy Chmykhalov, *The Last Christian: The Release of the Siberian Seven* (Grand Rapids, Michigan: Zondervan, 1986). Pollock's book deals primarily with the Vashchenko family. Chmykhalov's book deals with both his own family and the Seven's almost five years in the embassy.

2. See J.C. Pollock, *The Faith of the Russian Evangelicals* (New York: McGraw-Hill, 1964), 9-11, 172-86. Annette Roush had acquired a 1969 Zondervan paperback edition of this book, and it was reissued in 1972 as *Faith and Freedom in Russia*. The 1964 British edition was published by Hodder and Stoughton under the title *The Christians from Siberia*.

3. For the most recent account by John Pollock of the events of 1962 and 1963, see *The Siberian Seven*, 84-100.

4. See Pollock, *The Siberian Seven*, 65-83. For an early version of this and other stories related to the Siberian Seven, see "The Vashchenko Chronicle, An Attempt to Emigrate: 1962-78," *Religion in Communist Dominated Areas*, nos. 4-6 (1978), 84-88. I am the author, though at this time, because of the sensitive nature of the material, the information was published without any reference to the specific author.

5. Pollock, *The Siberian Seven*, 88.

6. Ibid., 95.

7. "Soviet Pentecostalists Dismayed," *Seattle Times*, February 5, 1983; "The 'Pents': Siberian Families Continue to Wait for Help in Moscow embassy," *Idaho Press-Tribune*, February 20, 1983.

8. Pollock, *The Siberian Seven*, 205.

9. Ibid., 209-10.

10. Ibid., 211.

11. This is a topic we will deal with in more detail in chapters 9 and 10. In 1978 I was just becoming aware of the consequences of such silence.

CHAPTER 2

THE BATTLE LINES
ARE DRAWN

I have often despised the commercialism of the West, but the flip side of it is an attention to consumers and freedom which is sorely absent in the Soviet Union. The colors, the advertisements, the activity of the western cities were a great contrast to where we had lived for the past seven months. And now we were in Paris, which is not known in the twentieth century for its religious faith. Nobody interferes with your church services, or what you teach your children religiously. It is hard to believe that where I had just come from believers are at the very least discriminated against and, if you are as stubborn as the Siberian Seven, persecuted.

There is frequently a casualness to Western religiosity which is quite offensive to those who have known what it means to suffer for one's religious faith. Tatiana Goricheva described what an emigrant from the Soviet Union can experience when confronted with the rather anemic faith of some Westerners:

> There are no beggar women in the churches here but people who are dressed well and tastefully. It seems even strange to me to see them in church. One soon notices that everyone's attitude is somehow not an attitude of prayer. The majority stand there absent-minded and indifferent, hands crossed on their chests. Only curious tourists stand around in Russian churches like that nowadays. Recently when I was talking here to Russian emigrants I told them sharply, "In our churches only KGB people stand like that."[1]

After settling into our apartment in Paris, I continued to translate the materials the Siberian Seven had brought to the embassy. Every week I would receive a new batch of materials from Moscow, through a contact at the American embassy in Paris, and I would send that week's translation to John

Pollock in Devon, England. As far as my own doctoral research in Paris, I mainly confined myself to making copies of hundreds of Russian source materials which were available to me there. The rest of my doctoral research was postponed; the present project was too urgent to delay.

The translation work was long and tedious. Learning to decipher seven different handwriting styles and the Siberian colloquialisms and prison jargon was a considerable challenge. But each day brought fascinating surprises as I sorted through what eventually amounted to about 1,500 pages of original Russian source materials. By the time several months of translation were completed, the final English text amounted to some 225,000 words, and we had one of the best documented family accounts of religious discrimination and persecution in the Soviet Union. Only a small part of this material made it into *The Siberian Seven.*

AN INHOSPITABLE HOST

While I was translating and making contacts with journalists, government officials, and church leaders in the West, the plight of the Siberian Seven was growing more grim in the American embassy. On Friday August 26, exactly one week after we had left Moscow, the American officials decided on a dramatic ruse to force the Siberian Seven to leave the safe confines of the embassy. A Marine guard entered and informed the Roushes, who were visiting the Seven, that he had been instructed to ask them to leave. Richard Combs, the acting political officer, and Cliff Gross, the consul, then arrived on the scene. Combs told the group calmly but firmly: "We received instructions from Washington about your case." He then began to read from a document.[2] The text included the following:

> Mr. and Mrs. Vashchenko and Mrs. Chmykhalov, your continued stay in the embassy with your children, rather than serving any useful purpose, appears to have had increasingly negative consequences for yourselves, your families and your fellow Pentecostalists throughout the Soviet Union. . . .

> Your continued stay in the embassy can serve no useful purpose; it can only be harmful. You will therefore leave without delay. I assure you that after your departure the Embassy will continue to do everything in its power to assist in your desire to emigrate to the United States. . . .

With that, Combs concluded, "That is the message from the Ambassador. Please gather your things and I will escort you to the gate."

Sixteen-year-old Timothy recalled his thoughts at this frightening point in his life:

> I could feel my heart begin to beat faster. My mouth was dry; I tried to speak but I could make no sound. Repeatedly we had been told by

the Soviet authorities, "The Americans don't want you." Now, it seemed, we were face to face with the facts. I knew what lay beyond the gates. The KGB would help us with transport and an escort. But where would that lead? I didn't look at anyone else. I felt my body begin to shake; I was very frightened. I never thought that the people with whom we had sought shelter would become the ones to hand us over to greater danger.[3]

When the Siberians failed to budge, the American officials withdrew. The whole episode turned out to be a bluff which only served to further erode the Seven's confidence in the embassy. In fact, there had been no authorization to expel them by force. Ambassador Toon was leaving for a month, and apparently this was an attempt to solve the "Siberian Seven problem" before he left town.

It had been a cruel hoax, but it had not worked. Two nights later, the Americans virtually admitted defeat when the Siberian Seven were moved to a ten-foot by sixteen-foot room in the basement. This was not just a recognition that they would not soon be leaving the embassy—it was also part of a new strategy to isolate and discourage the families. Too many people—embassy employees, embassy family members, and journalists—had easy access to the Seven when they were in the visitors area. Now they had been moved to a room well off the beaten track, next to a barber shop where a Soviet worked. The Marines referred to it as "the dungeon" because there was but one small window, and that looked out on the front sidewalk where Soviet militia regularly patrolled.

But the embassy was not content to just hope that fewer people would visit with the Seven. An order came down which prohibited communication with the Seven for all but those on a special access list. Their best friends, the Roushes, were not even on the initial access list. A number of embassy employees, while trying to stay within the bounds of stated and often unstated embassy guidelines, literally risked their careers doing what they could to provide the emotional support which the Siberian Christians needed.

It is quite true, as the embassy has always insisted, that the Vashchenkos and Chmykhalovs had access to a small refrigerator, stove, and shower facilities; that their food was provided for them; that physically they probably lived better than at home in Siberia. But the Seven would have gladly traded the refrigerator, stove, and shower for a strong sense that the Americans intended to support them actively and that they would not be thrown out of the embassy.

While embassy officials relentlessly pressed the Siberians to leave the embassy, assuring them that the Soviet authorities had promised that there would be no reprisals, fresh reports from Chernogorsk simply heightened their anxiety.

BAD NEWS FROM CHERNOGORSK

On September 15 the families received a phone call from their children two thousand miles away in Siberia. Word from Alexander (Sasha) Vashchenko, serving a term for refusal to be drafted into the military, was grim. A special commission from Moscow had arrived at the labor camp, and Alexander was summoned to speak with one of its members. When he refused to cooperate with the Soviet authorities, the official cursed him and shouted: "Do you want the same thing to be done to you that was done to your uncle in 1966?"[4]

Alexander understood the meaning of the threat. Twelve years earlier his Uncle Andrei, also serving time for conscientious objection, was deliberately left under a fallen log to die in minus forty-five degree (centigrade) weather. The authorities had claimed it was an "accident," but now this Moscow official was virtually admitting that Andrei had been murdered. However, Alexander was still unwilling to cooperate. "Do with me as you like, but reunite my family and let them go abroad."

The Moscow official responded: "That's not much of a sacrifice if you alone suffer for the whole family. It would be easier for us to collect all of you who are left [that is, not in the embassy], take you into the forest, and bury you under an old fallen tree."

The Moscow official alleged that Ambassador Toon had made the following comment regarding the families in the embassy: "Take your misfits away. I don't want them either." Alexander refused to believe his interrogator. Further abuse was hurled against his parents and sisters in the embassy for "pouring out filth" on the Soviet Union.

Based on this encounter, Alexander's message for his relatives in the embassy was: "Don't leave until the emigration question is resolved." The next scheduled contact with Alexander was not for six months. Would Andrei's fate at age twenty-three be Alexander's at nineteen? The Seven sent a letter to Ambassador Toon shortly after this phone conversation, detailing once again their desperate plight and requesting his help.

Despite the chilling news regarding Alexander, the embassy embarked on an even tougher policy toward the Pentecostals. The plans for John Pollock and me to collaborate on a book publicizing the story of the Siberian Seven did not sit well with the American staff. I had written to request permission for Pollock to visit the Seven. The official response in a letter of September 12 was as follows:

> The embassy would prefer not to have the Vashchenko Family interviewed by scholars. We believe that such interviews can only encourage the Vashchenkos to remain longer in the embassy, which would be counterproductive to both the fortunes of the Pentecostal movement and the Vashchenko Family.

Partly as a result of intervention by Paul Roush, permission was finally granted for at least some contact with Pollock. But under no conditions was the British author allowed to visit the families in their basement room. He would have to meet with them outside. It was a bitterly cold day, but for an hour-and-a-half John met with the families in the courtyard. The embassy refused his request for a second meeting with the families.

Ironically, while the American embassy in Moscow was pursuing its policy of trying to bottle up the story of the Siberian Seven, President Carter promised a continued vigilant and *public* denunciation of human rights violations. In a December 5, 1978 speech at a special White House ceremony, the president proclaimed:

> As long as I am president, the government of the United States will struggle for the enhancement of human rights. . . . From the prisons, the camps, the enforced exiles, we receive one message—speak up, persevere, let the voice of freedom be heard.[5]

But in Moscow there were no press conferences, there was no "speaking up." There was, however, a vigorous attempt to break the morale and the spirit of the Siberians so they would finally leave the embassy. Nobody seemed to be thinking much about what awaited the Seven outside the embassy gates.

THE QUEST FOR WESTERN SUPPORT

Since the earliest days of the Siberian Seven's stay in the embassy, Rev. Cecil Williamson, pastor of the Crescent Hill Presbyterian Church in Selma, Alabama, had tried to help. It was an invitation from him that the Vashchenkos had brought to the embassy on June 27, 1978. Eventually Williamson founded and became the president of the Society of Americans for Vashchenko Emigration (SAVE). The Soviet embassy in Washington, D.C., insisted that his invitations to the members of the Vashchenko family could not be processed for two reasons: only "close relatives" could invite people from the USSR to become permanent residents abroad, and the Seven were living illegally in the U.S. embassy in Moscow. In any event, they would have to go back to Chernogorsk before their case could be considered.

On the European front, there was encouraging support. In response to my letter to Hans Stuckelberger, president of Christian Solidarity International (CSI) in Zurich, Marianne Ridge of CSI called me. Rev. Stuckelberger was out of the country, but Marianne had been so excited about the documentation included in my letter that she had read them in one sitting, and then found it impossible to sleep.

During the next few weeks, Marianne activated the Christian Solidarity International network throughout Europe, and made countless contacts with European parliamentarians, government officials, and church leaders. Jan and

I travelled to Zurich and met with Rev. Stuckelberger and Marianne. On December 1, 1978, CSI released a press release in several European languages outlining the history of the Siberian Seven case and calling for concerted action. The European campaign was underway. During the following years CSI support was invaluable in putting pressure on the Soviets and the Americans from a variety of Western European countries.

On April 7, 1979 I went to Cambridge, England, to meet with well-known Russian dissident Vladimir Bukovsky.[6] I stayed the night and we discussed Christianity, the Soviet Union, and what could be done to help the Siberian Seven. Although not himself a believer, Bukovsky was extremely supportive and agreed to seek the intervention of Alexander Solzhenitsyn.

On June 4, 1979, the following letter from Bukovsky appeared in *Time* magazine:

> Your article on the two Russian families living in the U.S. embassy in Moscow (April 23) minimized one of the most disturbing aspects of the case: the shameful lack of support and even hostility exhibited by the American embassy. Though physically well cared for, they have been the victims of Ambassador Malcolm Toon's relentless efforts to isolate and discourage them. He has deprived them of letters of support. Embassy officials constantly urge them to leave, naively assuring these victims of years of Soviet internment that by so doing they will be better off. At the very least, should not the Soviets be required to honor past international agreements respecting emigration and human rights before we sign new ones with them? Let them demonstrate good faith and allow these Christians, and all others who wish it, to emigrate.

Members of the large Russian emigré community in Paris also became involved. My chief contact here was Kiril Elchaninov, a professor and Russian Orthodox activist involved in providing materials to Christians in the USSR. Kiril encouraged the Russian Orthodox community to write letters of encouragement to the Seven. He invited me to go into his little warehouse of books and together we picked out novels and religious literature to send back to the Seven in the embassy. His compassion for the Seven was moving. So much for the irreconcilable differences between the Russian Orthodox and the Pentecostals. Elchaninov's Christianity soared above such relatively insignificant differences.

THE RESTRAINED ECUMENICAL CHURCH

Elchaninov's response contrasted sharply with that of the World Council of Churches (WCC) and the National Council of Churches (NCC). The Rev. William Villaume, Protestant Chaplain at the Moscow embassy when the Seven arrived, was one of the first to seek the help of the ecumenical church bodies. On November 4, 1978, the Governing Board of the NCC sent a letter to President Carter on behalf of the Seven. The letter pledged an allocation of $2,000 to help maintain the Russian refugees in the embassy and requested that the president grant the Seven asylum.[7]

However, by March 1979 NCC officials decided that involvement on behalf of the Seven ought not to include "public activity." It was decided "to begin planning . . . efforts for the release of the Pentecostal refugees immediately," to research government and denomination attitudes towards the Seven as background for NCC involvement, and to avoid publicity. The reason was that the NCC was afraid that publicity about the case of the Seven would interfere with arms negotiations then underway with the Soviets.[8] It was this same attitude of the American government which, when pursued to its logical conclusion, resulted in an embassy policy designed to discourage the Seven from remaining within the safety of the U.S. compound.

Despite the decision to minimize public involvement, on May 10, 1979 the NCC passed the following resolution:

> The Governing Board . . . reaffirms its concern for the Soviet Christian refugees residing in the Moscow U.S. embassy; expresses its support for the on-going efforts by the officers and staff of the NCC . . . to effect their emigration and the emigration of their families; and requests the member churches to use their good offices on behalf of the refugees.

Observers close to the scene were skeptical that the resolution amounted to much. I confess a desire to give NCC officials the benefit of the doubt with regard to whether they, in fact, cared about the Siberian Seven. I think most of them really wanted to see them win their freedom. But it is fair to note that the NCC's involvement lacked any sense of passion and outrage. Just compare what the NCC has said and done with respect to the Vietnam War, apartheid in South Africa, and the arms race, with what they have done and said regarding the plight of believers in Communist countries. That gives a sense of what really is uppermost in the minds of the leadership. Furthermore, the judgment that public discussion of human rights violations is incompatible with progress in arms control deserves to be seriously challenged and debated.

There was similar lack of response by the WCC. In January 1979, the 140 members of the Central Committee of the World Council of Churches met in Kingston, Jamaica. They refused to put the question of the Siberian Seven on the agenda. However, Olga and Blahoslav Hruby, who edit *Religion in Communist Dominated Areas,* organized an appeal to Leonid Brezhnev which was signed by 28 participants in the WCC gathering. The cable called on the Soviet leader to allow the Seven to emigrate and thus give a "further evidence of détente." The fact that a minority within the WCC had to work independently to carry out what little action was taken is, unfortunately, typical for the

WCC when it comes to protesting religious repression in Communist countries.

EMBASSY POLICY HARDENS

Although the American government had decided to minimize publicity, the State Department did take some initiative to try and resolve the case. In the fall of 1978, Olin Robison, president of Middlebury College in Vermont, was sent to Moscow to see if he could quietly obtain exit visas. In September 1979, he finally got the Soviets to at least give verbal assurance that the families would not be prosecuted if they returned to Chernogorsk.

The other message the Soviets were sending at this time was less encouraging. Local Chernogorsk officials unleashed a propaganda campaign against the Seven under the headline: "Our Traitors are Coming Home." The Seven believed the newspaper account was a better reflection of the official attitude than a verbal promise from one Soviet official. They elected to remain in the embassy.[9]

One of the tactics used to discourage the Siberian Seven was to deprive them of mail from abroad which arrived through the Diplomatic Pouch. The pouch is the way Americans in Moscow communicate with friends and relatives at home, and it does not pass through the hands of the Soviets. In contrast, letters sent to the embassy via normal international mail are frequently intercepted and often not delivered by the Soviets. Ambassador Toon knew that refusal to allow the Siberian Seven to receive mail through the pouch would deprive them of virtually all written communication with the West. The excuse that the rules governing the pouch did not allow non-Americans access to it rang rather hollow since Soviet employees at the embassy routinely ordered Western consumer goods through the pouch.

Christian Solidarity International had encouraged a massive letter-writing campaign to Soviet and American officials, and recommended that letters of support be sent to the Seven through international mail. They calculated that even if many of these letters never reached the families, at least the Soviets would become aware of how many people in the West knew and cared about them. But CSI also sought to monitor how many letters were sent so that they could document whether the USSR was living up to its international agreements on the delivery of mail.

By mid-March 1979, CSI estimated that at least 15,000 letters had been sent to the Siberian Seven from Europeans via international post. Only a handful were delivered to the embassy. Armed with these statistics, CSI showed the American embassy copies of 1,300 letters sent to the Vashchenkos and Chmykhalovs. embassy officials confirmed that the originals had never been received, and Ambassador Toon "deplored" the Soviet confiscation.

In light of these serious Soviet violations of international mail agreements, CSI asked Toon to at least "show" the Siberian Seven the copies of the 1,300 letters. The ambassador refused. The Europeans were shocked and outraged by this apparently callous decision. But the explanation for his behavior was simple: if the Seven saw the letters, they might be encouraged to believe there was a strong Christian constituency supporting them in the West. And if they knew this, they might continue to resist U.S. efforts to get them to leave the embassy.

The ambassador also sought, at least on some occasions, to discourage U.S. senators who came to Moscow from meeting with the Seven. Senator Howard Baker and others were persuaded by Toon that a personal visit would both undermine the ambassador's ability to deal with the Soviets and make it less likely that the families would be able to leave the Soviet Union. The senators did not feel they should counter the ambassador's strong advice in this matter. The visit did not occur.

Amazingly, the embassy even interfered with the delivery of mail from two U.S. senators: Carl Levin of Michigan and Majority Leader Robert Byrd of West Virginia. On June 16, 1980, Senator Levin wrote a short letter to Maria Chmykhalov at the embassy, thanking her for knitting a sweater for the senator's wife. But what upset embassy officials was that it included the following statement: "I intend to introduce legislation on your behalf in the Senate in the near future. I hope that our legislation will be of some assistance to you but it will not be easy." The letter was not delivered. Instead an embassy official read parts of the letter to Maria but refused to leave it with the family on the grounds that it violated pouch regulations.

The embassy also sought to take action against those in its midst who were most closely tied with the Seven. That meant primarily my friend Lt. Col. Paul Roush and his wife Annette. Embassy officials were convinced the Roushes' continued presence at the compound undermined attempts to isolate the families from encouragement and support.

Ironically, the final incident which upset the ambassador was not related to the Siberian Seven but to one of the most famous Russian Orthodox priests of the time: Dmitry Dudko. Father Dudko had angered Soviet authorities because of his ability to attract young people to the Church.[10]

As pressure mounted on Father Dudko, concern for him increased both in the Soviet Union and the West. One of the last written communications Dudko had with friends in the West before his arrest in early January 1980 was arranged by Paul. It should be noted that, given the problems with international mail, it is not unusual for Americans in the Soviet Union to help Russian friends communicate with contacts in the West. But when the ambassador (now Thomas Watson) learned that Paul had passed Dudko's letter to the West, he was incensed and told Paul that he was going to request that the defense attaché at the embassy send Paul home from Moscow. Such can be the rewards of seeking to help Christians in distress when official U.S. policy at the moment doesn't encourage such support. The threat was not carried out. Paul left Moscow four months later when his tour of duty in the USSR ended.

THE STORY OF TWO AARONS

When Jan and I arrived in Paris in August 1978, we had been married just over six years. Within a few months I would complete my doctoral work, so we decided it was time to start our family. Our decision had nothing to do with the teasing and admonishments of our Russian friends in the embassy. Big families were considered a blessing from above to them, and the Seven thought it strange that we had waited so long to have children.

By the end of the year we learned that a July baby was on the way. We were warned to have blood tests each month to make sure Janice had not come in contact with toxoplasmosis—a disease which causes relatively minor headaches in an adult, but can produce blindness or severe mental retardation in an unborn child. The disease can be contracted quite easily in Europe, even from a piece of meat that is not sufficiently cooked. We were assured that if the test did show contact with the disease, there was medicine available which could effectively counter it. Janice dutifully tried to avoid red meat and took her monthly blood test.

In early May we were informed that Jan's blood test had been misread the two previous months. She had contracted the disease many weeks before. We immediately cut short our stay in Paris and returned to the United States.

On July 4, 1979, Christopher Aaron Hill was born at University Hospital in Seattle. He looked healthy and active, and the first cursory examination was positive. I left the hospital that evening as happy as I had ever been in my life. I jogged down to Puget Sound from our apartment, watched a beautiful sunset, and returned home to call relatives and friends.

One of the first things I did was cable the American embassy in Moscow. The Seven were extremely interested in this major event in our lives and were anxiously awaiting word on whether we had a boy or a girl. And we had a surprise for them! We had named our child after Aaron Vashchenko, the little boy Lida had adopted three years before and whose story had so gripped us in the early days of their stay in the embassy. We knew they would be pleased.

The next day was one of the darkest we have ever known. Further examinations revealed that Christopher Aaron was blind and had suffered extensive brain damage. We were stunned. I stayed with Janice and Christopher Aaron at the hospital, sleeping on a narrow cot the nurses set up for me. Soon more problems became apparent. He had trouble nursing, could not control his body temperature, did not open his eyes, and was losing muscle tone. We were taught how to feed Christopher by putting a very thin tube down his throat. We recognized that we probably faced the long-term prospect of caring for a severely handicapped child—a child we were becoming more and more attached to with each passing day.

After eighteen days Christopher Aaron slipped quietly away. During the final twenty-four hours his breathing had become irregular, and we were told that it was just a matter of time. We took him home, and I held him until he died. The emotions of such an experience are indescribable; nothing can ever be quite the same again.

As we buried Christopher in a cemetery overlooking Lake Washington, we sensed God's sustaining love and power. We had no doubt that Christopher Aaron was fine; it was we who were left with that aching loneliness that a family feels when a little one is snatched away. And then came a moment I particularly dreaded. Our friends in the embassy would have to be informed about what had happened to Christopher Aaron. For over a year they had sat in that often rather unfriendly embassy, knowing they were really not wanted by the Americans, knowing the Soviets detested them, and knowing that there was no end in sight to this awful dilemma. At times they must have felt that everything associated with them was tinged with tragedy. Now a little baby, named after one of their own lost children, had passed away as well. I knew it was inevitable that our pain would become their pain.

On Thursday, July 26, 1979, four days after Christopher Aaron died, Lida Vashchenko wrote us a moving letter of sympathy. To this day it remains one of our most treasured possessions:

Our Dear friends,

We have learned of the misfortune which has befallen you, and have been touched to the depths of our soul.

I know how terrible it is to lose one's first child!

And now you must experience this. How can I comfort you? Perhaps with that which also gave me comfort.

"Man born of woman is but of a few days," God said in His Word. And we know that all which is born must die. One day it will be our turn, even though it will be hard to be separated from our relatives and friends. Therefore, it is of course terrible to endure, but we will all experience the same.

I want to write for you a poem, which I composed in honor of Aaron. I want to give it to you, since now our two Aarons are with God united by a common acquaintance, though separated by a great distance. You labored for my Aaron, revealing Satan, who working through people killed him. But the same Satan has caused you grief, and therefore we must battle with great strength against him. The first battle must be conducted within, and this is much more difficult. It is easier to blame people and God for our misfortunes, and this does not help us, because God does not cause people sorrow.

To My Son

My first son, you are a beautiful thread
Which has crossed my earthly life.
The hands of the murderer did not quiver.
Without any guilt we were separated from each other.
　　You have gone away now and cannot come back.
　　And yet I remain among the living.
　　I know the cost of your loss
　　For it remains with me always.
Perhaps there will be other children.
I will also love them.
But these minutes, these sufferings
Will remain in my memory forever.
　　Oh mortal memory, you preserve so much
　　Innocently buried in the graves of people—
　　Christ and Christians who have lived
　　Who belong to centuries gone by.
There are many such; there is no human calculation
Who unto death loved their Christ
Though now concealed by earth and years
A young generation goes forth to meet them.
Goes to meet them though the world is indignant
That the flame of Christ grows and flowers.
And Satan in recent days doth snarl
But he is no match for the love of Christ.
　　Christ has defeated him long ago,
　　Right now he give us His victory!
　　And we are victorious and are rising with Him!
　　Although we are being buried deep in the earth.

How unsteady is life. I had wanted to congratulate you on your joyous day, and instead was forced to write for you the same poem that I wrote for my Aaron.

I give it to you. My loved ones do not know I composed it. I never showed it to anyone, but I GIVE it to you, because our sorrow is mutual.

I want God to comfort you and give you other children.

I want him to forgive you if there is any guilt before Him. May God bless you!

Lida

Though Lida wished to comfort us, there was fresh sorrow for her as well. After midnight she added a postscript:

We are looking at your photographs. We miss you very badly, and when this will end, God only knows. Today we received bad news from home. . . . Sasha [Alexander, in labor camp] was badly beaten. . . .

Indeed, for many months the Vashchenkos suffered over the fate of Alexander—their beloved Sasha. In Seattle we mourned the loss of our son— our beloved Christopher Aaron.

Lida's postscript was quite apt: "When this will end, God only knows." But this was a statement of faith, not despair.

Notes

1. Tatiana Goricheva, *Talking about God Is Dangerous: The Diary of a Russian Dissident* (New York: Crossroad, 1987), 96.

2. Letter from Annette Roush to Kent and Janice Hill, 9 September 1978.

3. Timothy Chmykhalov, *The Last Christian: The Release of the Siberian Seven* (Grand Rapids, Mich.: Zondervan, 1986), 84-85.

4. Facts related to the phone call of 15 September are from a letter written by the Siberian Seven to Ambassador Toon on 19 September 1978.

5. "Carter Reasserts Policy of Human Rights Support," *Denver Post,* 6 December 1978.

6. Bukovsky's book *To Build a Castle* is one of the finest works by a Soviet emigré describing what it is like to grow up in a totalitarian society and come to the realization that it is founded on a web of lies and deception.

7. In addition, the letter asked Carter to remember eleven other religious figures then in prison or labor camp (including Alexander Ginzburg, Viktoras Petkus, Georgi Vins and his son Peter, Anatoly Shcharansky, Vladimir Slepak, and Vasyl Romaniuk) if arrangements were made for an exchange for two Soviet diplomats arrested for spying while assigned to the United Nations.

8. Letter from John Collins, Director of the International Congregations and Lay Ministry (NCC Division of Overseas Ministries) to The Rev. William Villaume. In part the letter said: "It was agreed that *public activity* by the denominations in the immediate weeks ahead *could prove very unproductive.* Senator Scoop Jackson would use public concern for the Pentecostals to put an amendment to the SALT II Treaty to keep it from passing" (emphases mine).

9. Esther Fritz, "New Hope for the Siberian Seven," *Christian Century,* 5 November 1980, 1065-66.

10. See the beginning of chapter 8 for further information about Father Dudko.

CHAPTER 3

THE LONG BATTLE
FOR FREEDOM

*T*wo days before Lida wrote her letter of comfort to us, one of Moscow's
best correspondents, David Willis wrote a long article about the Seven in
the *Christian Science Monitor*. He correctly noted that soon after the Seven
arrived at the American compound, the embassy community divided into two
camps: "those who viewed the Vashchenkos as nuisances, religious fanatics
engaged in a hopeless venture, and others who admired their courage and
tenacity."[1]

Willis reported abuse the Seven had to face from the Soviets even while
in the relative safety of the American compound. At 2:00 one morning, the
Soviet militia ran their night sticks across the bars of their room making a
terrific racket. "Wake up you dog snouts . . . wake up and pray. Wait until we
get our hands on you." Such conduct by the guards was not uncommon.

The story also provided disturbing news about the relatives back in
Chernogorsk. Harassment of family members during 1979 was quite severe.
John, the young man who was dragged away from the embassy gates, had
turned eighteen and was thus liable to be sentenced to labor camp if he, like
Alexander, refused to serve in the military. John and three other Vashchenko
children traveled to Alexander's camp to see their brother. The visit was
denied, and instead the camp director, named Gutnik, took the four
Vashchenkos towards the isolation cells where Sasha had been confined for
fifteen days. His offense: he was caught sharing one page of the Bible with
fellow prisoners. While in the isolation cell, the prisoner gets only four
hundred grams of bread a day and one bowl of hot soup every two days.[2]

The labor camp director said to John: "Since you won't go in the army
this spring they will be bringing you here. After you have sat here for six
months, we will give you back dead to your parents."[3] Gutnik also added:
"Your Alexander cannot be reeducated; he is fit only for the pistol."[4]

For Alexander, things went from bad to worse. For trying to smuggle a letter to his family in the embassy, he was sentenced to an incredible six months in the isolation cell. (Two weeks is considered a severe sentence.) Fortunately, word reached the embassy and the United States. The Hrubys, of the Research Center for Religion and Human Rights in Closed Societies, started a letter-writing campaign to the chief Soviet prosecutor and to the head of Alexander's camp. Without explanation, Alexander was released in just under a month. The letter-writing campaign may well have saved Sasha's life.[5]

On October 24, 1979, the Vashchenkos talked by phone with their family in Chernogorsk. The KGB had instructed the supervisor of Jacob (17) and John (18) to change their assignments so that they would not be able to work the same shift and go home at the same time. John was assigned to a swing shift and it was now impossible to get home before 12:30 or 1:00 A.M. One night, John was attacked by three men who left him unconscious. He was taken to a hospital and treated for a brain concussion.

While concerns for the Siberian Seven's family in Chernogorsk mounted throughout 1979, so did the controversy surrounding the embassy's handling of the case. When Congressman Robert Dornan (California) returned to the United States in the fall of 1979, he reported having met with high-level Soviet authorities in the Kremlin. When he raised the question of the Vashchenko and Chmykhalov families, the Soviets responded that American authorities had yet to make "a formal written request" to the USSR for permission for the Seven to emigrate. Though U.S. officials had always reported that inquiries had been made to the Soviets regarding the Seven, the Kremlin's official stance was that they had little evidence that this was a high priority for the Americans.

A real thorn in the side of the American officials was Dan Fisher of the *Los Angeles Times*.[6] His articles were sometimes reprinted in the *International Herald Tribune,* available throughout Europe. Particularly embarrassing to the embassy was Fisher's December 28, 1979 report that five prominent Western Baptist leaders were refused permission to visit the Seven on December 19. Fisher reported that the embassy considered the refusal an unfortunate "misunderstanding" which was caused by a junior embassy official mistakenly barring the visit. Fisher noted that Englishman Michael Rowe, Keston College's authority on Soviet Pentecostals, was also refused a visit.

The *Los Angeles Times* went on to report that since Thomas J. Watson, Jr. had replaced Malcolm Toon in the fall, some policies affecting the Pentecostals had moderated somewhat. But on the two-year anniversary of the Siberian Seven's arrival at the embassy, Dan Fisher again embarrassed the embassy by revealing that contrary to earlier suggestions, the policy under Ambassador Watson was getting stricter. Evidence of this was a new regulation which required that an embassy employee be present during every non-embassy personnel visit to the Seven. An embassy official explained: "This policy is not meant to intimidate either interviewers or interviewees, and it applies to all visitors, not only to journalists."[7] Correspondents in Moscow were slow to grasp the subtleties of this remarkable new definition of "non-intimidation."

THE SILENCE OF WESTERN PENTECOSTAL LEADERS

Although the Siberian Seven were Pentecostal, the largest Pentecostal denomination in the United States, the Assemblies of God, was almost entirely silent and inactive during the entire Siberian Seven drama. There was great fear that public defense of these unregistered Pentecostals would endanger their relations with registered Pentecostals in the Soviet Union. This, of course, is precisely the result Soviet authorities had worked hard to achieve.

The seeds of the problem lie within the Soviet Union itself, in the division which has grown up between registered and unregistered believers. The registered believers, who have agreed to accept restrictions on the practice of their faith, have often refused to defend their unregistered counterparts. In fact, they have criticized them to Western leaders as extremists and lawbreakers.

The great tragedy of the conflict is that the Soviet Union has managed to drive a deadly spike into the heart of Christian unity. We must be careful not to charge that all who are members of the registered church have "compromised with Satan," just as we must not assert that all who are unregistered are "fanatics and chronic lawbreakers." There are those who have compromised too much, and others who have become religious fanatics. But for the majority, such labels are not accurate.

Why should Western Christian leaders and organizations get caught up in one side or the other of extremist polemics on these difficult issues? Why can't we maintain contact both with the registered churches while working for those persecuted in the unregistered world as well? But unfortunately, we have not been astute enough to counter the clever policies orchestrated in the Kremlin.

It should be noted that some individual congregations throughout the United States responded with sympathy and compassion when told of the plight of the Siberian Seven and other Soviet believers. The problem was that the official stances of denominations—from oldline Protestant to Baptist and Pentecostal—was often to rely almost exclusively on "quiet diplomacy," and even this appears to have been quite restrained.

CONGRESS GETS INVOLVED

On June 27, 1980, the second anniversary of the Seven's arrival at the embassy, Senators Levin, Boren, Hatfield, and DeConcini introduced legislation which proposed granting the Siberian Seven U.S. visas and "permanent resident" status. It was hoped that passage of the bill would constrain the U.S. Moscow embassy to be more supportive of the families. As Senator Levin observed in his speech when introducing the new legislation: "Granting them permanent resident status will help to alleviate one of the most unfortunate byproducts of the families' two years without status. The alienation they have experienced in the embassy has made them outcasts in the very place they seek refuge."[8]

The State Department vigorously opposed the bill, arguing that it would set a dangerous precedent. In fact, Levin had very carefully written the bill so that it could only be applied to the Siberian Seven. First, however, the bill had to pass through the Judiciary Committee, chaired by Senator Edward Kennedy. In spite of intense lobbying by those in support of the legislation, plus the fact that there were thirty senators sponsoring the bill (including six members of the Judiciary Committee), Kennedy was not responsive, and the bill never made it out of committee.

Meanwhile back in Moscow the embassy continued its policies of isolation. On July 10, 1980 Ambassador Watson sent a "Policy Statement on Pentecostalist Access" to all chiefs of sections. Though the ambassador noted that "no one who is familiar with the efforts of these families to practice their religion freely could fail to be moved by their plight," his one-page document of instructions to embassy personnel made it clear that being "moved by their plight" must not be translated into unrestricted contact or support.

Of course, this directive was not meant to "isolate" the families. Rather it was for their safety. Besides, even the Seven wouldn't want everyone to come and visit them. This is precisely the line two State Department officials took when meeting with two European representatives of Christian Solidarity International regarding the restrictive embassy policies towards the Seven.[9] None of these officials thought to ask the Seven what *they* wanted.

With the inauguration of President Reagan in January, 1981, the policies of the American embassy in Moscow towards the Seven changed for the better. Attempts to isolate and discourage the families were discontinued, and a more supportive and friendly atmosphere was created. There had always been American personnel and officials who cared deeply for the Seven, but now the embassy regulations and directives no longer interfered with the expression of that concern.

ENGLAND TAKES ON THE STRUGGLE

With all due respect to the many American Christians who sought to mobilize public opinion in this country, our British Christian friends had considerably more success than we had. Other European countries took note as well, and to some extent emulated the British example of active work for the embassy refugees. First, a letter-writing assault was made on the Soviet embassy in London. Church leaders were recruited and they secured seven thousand signatures on a twenty-two-foot-long banner that was sent to the Siberian Seven. Danny Smith, a key activist in the British Siberian Seven campaign, organized a rally in Trafalgar Square and an all-night prayer vigil outside the Soviet embassy. The British effort was a powerful force in the international pressure applied to the Soviet Union.

In 1981 another bill (S. 312) to grant the Siberian Seven "permanent resident" status was introduced. This time it was co-sponsored by sixty-five senators. I was asked to come to Washington to testify on behalf of the bill before the Immigration Subcommittee of the Judiciary Committee. In my November 19 comments I attempted to allay the fears of some that a dangerous precedent would be established if the bill were passed. The key factor here was that the Seven had not come to the embassy to demand asylum; they had come for a three-hour visit. It was violence by Soviet militia at the gates which had changed all that.

I also attempted to deal with the State Department contention that the Senate's action might frustrate their own work towards finding a solution.

> The time has come to take action—to grant the Siberian Seven some real guarantees to protect them from arbitrary changes in treatment within the embassy. It is no wonder the Soviets have done nothing. We cannot expect them to take this case seriously when we have not taken it seriously. The State Department fears offending the Soviets and thereby jeopardizing the case. But the evidence is conclusive that speaking out and taking firm action did not endanger Georgi Vins, Alexander Solzhenitsyn, and dozens of other Soviet dissidents. On the contrary, it was their only protection; it was, in fact, their ticket to freedom. S. 312 may very well be an important first step to freedom for the Siberian Seven. Let us not hesitate to take it.[10]

One of the critical turning points in the campaign to gain emigration for the Siberian Seven occurred in the fall of 1981. Lynn Buzzard, Executive Director of Christian Legal Society (Chicago), had become fascinated with the case and offered the assistance of his national association of Christian lawyers. On Thanksgiving weekend he went to Moscow to visit the families. By the time he returned, he was hopelessly entangled in the case. Indeed, contact with the Seven made it difficult to slip back into the normal routine of life so long as their increasingly desperate situation remained unresolved.

In November 1981 we also took our first formal steps towards forming an American Coalition to Free the Siberian Seven. The idea was to bring together a number of the main groups who had been working for some time on the case, and to press for the passage of S. 312.

During this time, a plan began to emerge for resolving the stalemate between the Soviets and the Siberian Seven. While in Moscow, Buzzard managed to get tentative agreement from the Seven to support the following proposal. The Seven would leave the embassy if: first, their family members at home in Chernogorsk, who had long ago applied for emigration with the authorities, were allowed to leave the Soviet Union, and second, assurance was provided by the Soviets that the Seven's applications would be approved, following the completion of the normal application procedures in Chernogorsk.

The Dark Hours before Dawn

It is only natural that being cooped up in the embassy for three-and-a-half years would take a toll on the Siberian Seven. Those who have known the Seven only from occasional news accounts or inspirational sermons have sometimes concluded that the Pentecostals were modern-day saints. They were not. They sometimes squabbled among themselves. The two families did not always get along with each other. Their often justified suspicion of American embassy officials sometimes made it impossible for them to see just how tough a spot the Americans were really in, or the degree to which they did try to help.

Uncertainty about their future, concern for their families back home in Siberia, the bitter/sweet relations with Americans in the embassy, and the cramped quarters of their existence within the U.S. compound (especially in the early years), all contributed to a certain irritability and despair. It was not that their faith in God wavered; it did not. But their optimism about a favorable outcome to the seemingly interminable ordeal did wane at times. One of the young Vashchenko women had confided to me in the embassy: "Here I am with no end in sight. I can't bear it. If I can't have a normal life, I'd sooner die."[11]

In late 1981, Andrei and Yelena Sakharov staged a highly publicized hunger strike which eventually resulted in the Soviets granting permission to their daughter-in-law to join her husband in the United States. Inspired by this example, two members of the Vashchenko family began contemplating a hunger strike to try and raise public consciousness about their case.

Many Western supporters of the Seven, including me, feared that this tactic would not be fruitful. For, as *Christianity Today* so accurately put it:

"Sakharov is a world-renowned physicist, while the Vashchenkos are obscure laborers from a remote Siberian village. . . ."[12] Furthermore, unlike world scientific, psychiatric, literary, and Jewish organizations, Christian denominations and ecumenical bodies could not be counted on to rally to their cause.

Friends in the West, a mission group based in the Pacific Northwest, asked me to make an urgent trip to the Soviet Union. The purpose was twofold. First, since I had spent time with the Seven early in their stay, I might be in a position to observe how the attitudes and mood of the Seven had changed over the past forty-two months. Second, I intended to urge Lida and Augustina not to embark on the hunger strike.

On Christmas Day, 1981, Lida commenced the strike. I arrived the next day. On the 28th, Augustina joined her daughter in the hunger strike. Between December 26 and January 2, I spent up to fourteen hours a day in tense, often emotional discussion with American officials and my Russian friends. I found the American embassy personnel in Moscow genuinely concerned about the families. There was particular worry about what might happen if the hunger strike became life-threatening. I supported the view of Ambassador Arthur Hartman and the number two man, Deputy Chief of Mission Warren Zimmerman, that the strike would only make their situation worse, that the Soviets would love to see them die within the confines of the American embassy.

Dr. John Schadler, the embassy doctor, and I talked numerous times. He made it clear that he would not allow the Siberians to die within the American compound. But if they did have to be hospitalized in a Soviet institution, what would happen then? No one knew for sure.

By the time I left Moscow on January 2, Lida's weight had already dropped from a thin 104 pounds, to an even thinner 98. The stouter Augustina had lost nine-and-a-half pounds, but her health was not good to begin with. When asked by the press upon my return how the families were doing, I replied: "They have reached the end of their rope. They are desperate now. I saw a marked deterioration emotionally in their ability to accurately perceive reality."[13]

On January 3, Lyuba Vashchenko wrote me a letter in English. (She was the member of the Seven who had tackled most seriously and with the greatest success the task of learning English.)

It is difficult to believe that your visit to Moscow is finished so quickly, Kent. We were waiting for you much longer than you were here. It is about 12 P.M. and Lida, Lilia and I are busy with the preparation of the envelope for you. . . .

What I can tell you about my mother and Lida? I thought that this morning they would not be able to get up from the beds. They are so weak today and I am not sure for how many days they will be able to walk by themselves. . . . Why your visit here was so short? What I shall do? If something terrible will happen to them soon I'll do the same. I am tired already to talk to the people. Sometimes they are (some of them) so naive. I understand that it is my role now to talk. But I do not want to do it any more. . . . I consider not only the Soviets guilty for the tragic case of my family members but the Americans as well. . . . I am writing this letter in English so that Janice could read it and it'll be less work for you to translate. I know the letter full of mistakes. Excuse me, please.

The first evidence that the hunger strike might indeed accomplish something occurred on January 8 when Ambassador Hartman held an embassy press conference. He attributed the hunger strike to growing frustration, which he contended that the embassy was helpless to control. On January 14, former President Jimmy Carter called and appealed, without success, to the two women to abandon their hunger strike.[14]

On Sunday January 24, 1982, the Vashchenko women intensified their hunger strike by refusing to drink any liquids. The embassy doctor said they could die within a week. On Tuesday, they were convinced to drink liquids again, but Lida's condition continued to deteriorate. The acting head of the American embassy, Warren Zimmerman, reported that the Soviets refused permission for an emergency medical evacuation of Lida out of the Soviet Union. The only alternative was to put Lida in a Soviet hospital.

Zimmerman commented that the U.S. government "can only deplore the harsh, restrictive emigration policies of the Soviet Union that have brought about today's sad events." He made it clear that Lida would be welcomed back in the embassy after she regained her health.[15]

At 2 A.M. Seattle time, January 30, Chief Consul Wayne Leininger called to inform me that they had just taken Lida to a Soviet hospital. When Dr. Schadler and an American consular official arrived at Botkin Hospital, the Soviets were given a letter from the American doctor which included the following statement. "In my examination of Miss Lydiia Vashchenko over the past several months, I have found no evidence of psychosis." The Americans were doing what they could to insure that Lida would not suffer the fate of many other Soviet religious and political dissidents: confinement to a psychiatric hospital.[16]

Botkin Hospital was the best hospital in Moscow, and the one used by foreign diplomats for medical emergencies. Lida did not resist going and was in good spirits, absolutely convinced that risking her life was the only way to achieve her family's emigration. Soviet hospital authorities allowed the Americans to sit in on the initial examination, promised that the officials could visit her, but made no guarantees on whether she would be allowed to return to the embassy.

NEGOTIATIONS: MOSCOW AND MADRID

Several days earlier Lynn Buzzard had suggested that we go back to Moscow as soon as possible to meet with Soviet and American officials to propose a way of resolving the Siberian Seven impasse. We left on January 31 for Moscow via Zurich, where we intended to meet with European supporters of the Seven. We would be in Moscow from February 2-9. On the way back we intended to visit the Madrid review meetings of the Conference on Security and Cooperation in Europe. The purpose of the Madrid conference was to monitor compliance with the Helsinki human rights accords.

We arrived in Zurich on Monday morning, February 1. Marianne Ridge of Christian Solidarity International informed us of recent parliamentary initiatives in Sweden, Holland, and Ireland, and brought us up to date on other European activities she was involved with or aware of. On Tuesday we flew on to Moscow.

On Wednesday we stopped by the embassy to meet with the Seven (now six) and discuss our schedule for the next few days with American officials. It was obvious that embassy personnel were much more supportive now than in the previous administration. We discussed the proposals we would be making to the Soviets.

At 4 P.M. we got the opportunity we had particularly anticipated: a visit to Lida in Botkin Hospital. A big grin flooded across her face when she saw us, and in a few moments I had my arms around her. I could feel her bones sticking through her hospital gown. She was very, very thin, but she looked peaceful and calm.

Lida informed us that she had been off the strike for a couple of days, and she was satisfied that she had made her point. She had received intravenous glucose; her EKG report was normal. Lida asked us to thank her friends in the West. She was convinced that their support had protected her. After forty-five minutes we left, immensely relieved and grateful.

The State Department and the American embassy helped set up meetings for us with key Soviet religious and government officials. On Thursday, we met with officials of the All-Union Council of Evangelical Christians-Baptists (AUCECB). This was my first direct contact with the rather Byzantine world of registered church leaders. There is often much more going on in the room than first meets the eye, or certainly the ear. For example, in such meetings there are often two categories of leaders present: those who say as little as possible, and the active propagandists who, without any apparent embarrassment, repeatedly state the official Kremlin position. In this case, we heard that the Vashchenkos and Chmykhalovs had been excommunicated by their churches, did not belong to any church at present, kept their kids out of the schools (no indication of why), were immoral, and had never been repressed.

We took issue with virtually every point and contended that millions of Christians in the West were measuring the Soviet Union and détente on the basis of whether the Soviets relented and allowed the Seven to emigrate. After more than an hour of discussion, it was proposed that we stand, join hands in a circle, and Lynn Buzzard led us in prayer.

Later that day we made our second visit to Lida at the hospital. Our forty minutes with her convinced us that she was in a considerably better frame of mind than her relatives in the embassy. The apparent reason for this was that she intended to go directly home from the hospital in order to see her younger brothers and sisters.

This turned out to be a modified version of what Buzzard and I had proposed—namely, that the Soviets be given an incentive to allow at least some to emigrate from Chernogorsk as a good faith gesture, after which the others would leave the embassy to pursue emigration through normal channels. Lida was going to give the Soviets a chance to consider her case from Chernogorsk, which is where they had always insisted the request had to come from. She was also going to test their earlier pledge not to prosecute anyone who had been in the embassy.

Friday was a full day. At 10 A.M. we went to the Moscow Russian Orthodox Patriarchate to meet with Metropolitan Filaret of Minsk. As we often did in these meetings, Buzzard spent the first fifteen minutes outlining our proposal for resolving the Siberian Seven case. The heart of the proposal was that emigration would be secured without the Soviets yielding on their central demand—that there would be no emigration directly from the embassy.

Metropolitan Filaret feigned to have no knowledge of the case until just two to three days before. (An embassy official assured us that that was simply not the case; Filaret had been asked about the case by Western religious leaders several times in recent years.) Filaret did criticize both the morality and the theology of the Russian families, though not as energetically as the registered Protestant leaders. As in the meeting with Protestant leaders, there was no admission of any serious problems for believers in the Soviet Union. (Ten years later, under *glasnost,* even Soviet journalists would describe a situation of religious repression and harassment markedly different from the rosy picture painted by these registered Protestants and Orthodox officials.)

We rushed immediately over to the Moscow College of Advocates for an 11:00 A.M. meeting with Konstantine Appraksin, the president of Moscow College and one of the most important legal authorities in the USSR. Lida had written a letter to Mr. Appraksin in which she requested that he come to the American embassy and advise the Seven on what their legal rights were under Soviet law. Lida also requested that Lynn and I witness this consultation. Appraksin rejected the request, saying he would not advise the Seven while they remained in the embassy. He contended that they had violated Soviet law by entering the embassy. He listened to our proposal, but made no suggestions of his own. Instead, he tried to direct us to the Ministry of Internal Affairs and to OVIR (the government agency which processes exit visas).

Next we went to the Council for Religious Affairs (CRA)—the Soviet government watchdog committee which seeks to regulate all religious activities in the Soviet Union. It did not comfort us when the Vice Chairman of the CRA, Vladimir Fitsev, tried to put us at ease by announcing: "I am an atheist. That means I am completely objective when it comes to religious matters." Fitsev was quite aggressive, at times seemed uninterested, and at one point insisted that the Siberian Seven case was not even in his area of authority. Then, strangely enough, he seemed to contradict himself when he promised: "I can absolutely guarantee that no harm will come to them if they leave the embassy."

Though the Siberians in the embassy were pleased, and even a little surprised, that we would press their case with Soviet religious and political authorities, they were concerned that the Soviets would find some way to trick us. Over the years, they had learned how naive foreigners often were. They needed reassurance that we understood the patterns of Soviet official rhetoric—the endless alternation between gross propaganda and apparent reasonableness. This discussion was important because ultimately, any risks in our plan were theirs, not ours.

My last visit to Lida took place on Monday. "Our story is going to have a happy ending," she beamed. She had entered the hospital weighing just eighty-five pounds; she was now up to ninety-two. It was clear that Lida believed that the hunger strike had broken some invisible obstacle to progress. She was now going home to see her family. She had renewed hopes that their almost twenty-year quest for emigration might finally be realized.

Now it was on to Madrid, where we arrived on Tuesday afternoon, February 9. There are few contrasts greater than that of trading in the dull grayness of the typical Moscow street for the color and activity of a Spanish city. The adjustment was not difficult.

Ambassador Max Kampelman, chairman of the American delegation, was supportive and encouraging. He told us about what the U.S. representatives in Madrid had been doing to try and raise the issue of the Seven.[17] He gave us some advice in preparation for our important meeting with the Deputy Chairman of the Soviet delegation, Sergei Kondrashev. Kampelman reminded us that Kondrashev was charming; he'd had much experience in dealing with foreigners. He was also the former head of the KGB's department of disinformation! Interesting qualifications for the number two representative of the Soviet Union at an international conference on compliance with the Helsinki accords.

Our meeting with Kondrashev gave us some important clues that the Soviets were ready to resolve the problem. For one thing, he met with us alone, which told us that he was among the Soviet inner sanctum of the more trusted. He gave the Soviet position, but not with embellishment and not without a sense that he had the authority to listen to what we had to say. In fact, he listened carefully to our proposal for resolving the case. For thirty-five minutes we discussed the matter and argued back and forth. But it was not the typical propaganda argument with no real give and take. This time there was a genuine exploration of possible solutions.

By the time I reached Seattle late on the evening of February 11, Lida had been discharged from Botkin Hospital. She was allowed to return to the American embassy to see her family. The next day she left the embassy and flew home to Siberia. She promptly applied to emigrate. Would the Soviets finally relent and send a good faith signal to the remaining six in the embassy? Lida's own emigration could be such a signal.

ON THE HOME FRONT

One month after the Siberian Six passed their four-year anniversary in the American embassy in Moscow, I was again in Washington, D.C. to testify on their behalf. Just a few weeks before, the Senate had approved the "permanent resident" status bill which had first been introduced in 1980. The House version was now being considered. However, I was in Washington to testify in favor of a congressional resolution which called on the President to utilize his contacts in the Soviet Union to press for full religious freedom. My comments were given before the Human Rights and International Organizations subcommittee of the House Committee on Foreign Affairs. I observed:

> For four long years they have languished in deep agony—insignificant pawns in a chess game between superpowers. For four long years supporters in the West have struggled in vain to find that right combination of factors which will win their emigration and that of their families in Siberia.[18]

I went on to note that though American authorities had been relatively unsupportive during the first two-and-a-half years, the past year and a half had seen a noticeable improvement in their treatment by American officials at the embassy. I lamented the failure of Western Christian leaders to exert leadership in the effort to find a solution to the protracted drama in Moscow. I noted the disturbing continuing signs of Soviet intransigence. I repeated once again the proposal that Lynn Buzzard and I had made in Moscow and Madrid to break the deadlock, and I urged acting "in some meaningful way" to press for a resolution of the case.

As 1982 drew to a close and the Siberians once again prepared to celebrate a lonely Christmas in the basement of the embassy, there was no sense that a solution was drawing near. On the contrary, there was often a feeling among supporters that we were just "going through the motions." We all hoped that little by little we were chipping at the edges of some edifice of unknown proportions and that one day it would crack.

One of the most important lessons I learned during the Siberian Seven years was the importance of persistence. I had a growing realization that sometimes one must be willing to fight in causes that may be "losing" causes. To be involved in a campaign where there is no certainty of victory means that sooner or later you will run up against the question: "Is this the best way I can expend my energies and resources?" Sometimes a prudent reallocation of resources is called for in order to apply one's influence in a worthy cause where one can do more good. But I have become convinced that there are times when we are called to campaigns which shall not prevail upon this earth, but they are God's will that we struggle in them anyway.

At this point, we had no idea what the outcome of this struggle would be, but we were determined to see it through to a conclusion.

FREEDOM FOR LIDA

At 5:00 A.M. April 6, 1983, I was awakened by a phone call from the embassy in Moscow. "Kent, I've got some news that I think will make your day," said the American official. "I've just put Lida on a plane to Vienna."

Thirteen months had passed since Lida had returned to Chernogorsk following her stay in Botkin Hospital. Finally, on March 23, 1983, she was summoned to the visa and emigration office (OVIR) and informed that permission had been granted to leave the Soviet Union. Until then, no one knew whether or when the Soviets intended to resolve this sticky international emigration impasse.

A week after the summons to the OVIR office Lida was given a choice of going to West Germany or to Israel. She chose Israel. A few days later she was on her way to Moscow to catch the plane to Vienna. Lida was accompanied to Moscow by her sister Vera and her brother John. Family members in the embassy were abuzz with anticipation. Augustina prepared pancakes in hopes that perhaps her three children would stop by the American compound before going to the airport. But Lida would have no communication with the embassy until she reached Vienna a few hours later.[19]

Meanwhile, back in Moscow, a momentous issue was under discussion. Should the remaining six in the embassy interpret the emigration of Lida as a sign that the Soviets would let them emigrate as well, once they had returned to Chernogorsk? Or was Lida's release simply a trick to get them to leave the embassy so they could be arrested?

On the same weekend that Lida arrived in Israel, John and Vera Vashchenko were back in Moscow and were allowed to enter the embassy to see their relatives. After much discussion, the Vashchenkos decided to leave. As Augustina put it, this is "the biggest risk of our lives."[20]

But the issue of leaving was even more agonizing for Maria and Timothy Chmykhalov. They were not as well known as the Vashchenkos. Though the book *The Siberian Seven* talked about some incidents from their past, for brevity's sake it focused on the Vashchenko chronicle of persecution. The Vashchenkos now had a relative in the West (Lida) who could invite her family members to join her, thus complying with a specific Soviet requirement. The Chmykhalovs had no relatives abroad. And finally, Timothy was afraid the Soviets might try to draft him into the military, which he knew would result in labor camp if he refused.

April 12, 1983, was an agonizing day for Timothy. His mother had decided to go with the Vashchenkos. Should he go with them?[21] The embassy was aware of his quandary and allowed him to phone me in Seattle. The call came through at about 3:00 A.M.[22] Timothy told me his dilemma, then said, "We don't have relatives abroad. The Soviets might treat us differently than the Vashchenkos. What do you think I should do, Kent?"

I had just a few seconds to collect my thoughts and give my opinion. It is one thing to speculate abstractly about what may or may not happen if a particular course of action is taken. It is quite another to be asked to make a judgment which, if you are wrong, may well endanger the person you are trying to help.

But in a sense this was not the first time I had faced such issues. Lynn Buzzard and I had talked for hours with the six in February, 1982, about conditions under which they might risk leaving the embassy. Our suggestion then was to make the precondition for their leaving the release of family members at home in Siberia.

This was a closer call. Only one person had been allowed to emigrate from the Vashchenko family, and none from the Chmykhalov family. Nevertheless, my recommendation was to go. I asserted that there was definite progress in the case, and that I did not think it would be possible to separate the fate of the Chmykhalov family from that of the Vashchenkos. The whole world knew about both families. The publicity, I contended, would provide them protection. We would vigorously continue our efforts to help him after he left, if he chose to do so.

Timothy said almost nothing. He mainly listened. When I concluded my recommendation, he simply said, "Goodbye." I hung up the receiver and felt physically ill. What if Timothy left the safety of the embassy and it turned out that my reading of the situation was incorrect? Who would pay the price? Certainly not me living in the safety of Seattle.

The next few hours were anxious ones as I awaited news on the events unfolding in Moscow. It was not easy to concentrate on teaching my classes that Tuesday. The picture on the front page of the *New York Times* the next day told the whole story.[23] On the left of the photo a Soviet militiaman watched an embassy van squeeze through the narrow gates of the American compound and pull out onto Tchaikovsky street. The van was not driven by a Soviet chauffeur, but by a consular officer. And on the passenger side sat Paul Roush. What was he doing in Moscow?

By a peculiar twist of fate (we Christians would call it providence), Paul just happened to be in Moscow on official business when the dramatic decision was made to leave the embassy. All had decided to leave, including Timothy, and Paul was to accompany them out of the embassy to the airport.

Before the six Russians left the embassy, they met with Ambassador Arthur Hartman and thanked him and the embassy staff for their help and protection over the past 260 weeks. Two embassy vans were then loaded up, plus a station wagon, and the procession headed south to Domededovo Airport—the one used for travel within the Soviet Union. A crowd of embassy employees huddled around to watch the six depart. Someone called out to Lyuba: ''We will probably meet again some day.'' Lyuba's response: ''Probably? We will definitely meet again.''[24]

A FIVE-YEAR ANNIVERSARY PRESENT

There were several false alarms on the imminent emigration of the rest of the Vashchenkos before the breakthrough finally came. But on Thursday, June 23, fifteen family members (including four of the Siberian Seven) boarded a train in Chernogorsk to begin their long three-and-a-half day journey to Moscow. By Saturday I was on my way to Vienna.

Although June 27th was the day the fifteen were expected to arrive in Vienna, everyone was nervous about whether that date would hold up. Even the most routine visa matters can involve unexpected delays, let alone a case that had caused as much international tension as this one had. We had all been extremely careful to avoid publicity of the possible emigration, not wanting in any way to tempt the Soviets to change their minds.

At 6:00 P.M. on the 26th in Vienna, I received a phone call from George Hein, the press coordinator at Seattle Pacific University. TASS had just announced that permission for emigration had been granted the Vashchenkos, and Reuters had already picked up the story. Finally the big day had arrived! The Soviets knew the significance of June 27th. It was almost as if the Vashchenkos had served their sentence, most of it in the basement of the American embassy, and now they could be released. Few would be tempted to pay that price for their freedom. And anyway, security was so much more strict at the embassy in 1983 than in 1978 that such incidents were not likely ever to be repeated.

At the airport in Vienna, several of us noted that there were people present dressed like security personnel or airport employees but who were obviously Russian. I overheard one of them say something in Russian. They were watching intently all that was taking place.

It was bedlam when the Vashchenkos landed. They were escorted to a private lounge where a photographer took their pictures for Israeli tourist visas. Lida read a statement to the press. The next morning, we were all on our way to Israel and the next few days were spent touring the Holy Land. (The Israeli government refused to allow the Vashchenkos to settle permanently in Israel. So at the end of July, they flew to Seattle and took up residence in the United States.)

The Vashchenko exit had taken place with the American officials being careful not to make any aggressive or negative statements about the Soviet Union. If one of the reasons for the Soviet presence in the Vienna airport was to see if the Americans sought to exploit the release for propaganda benefit, then surely they were relieved by what they saw. Perhaps this would encourage them to go ahead and let the Chmykhalovs go as well, and thus end the long deadlock. We would not need to wait long to see what the Soviets intended to do next.

FROM CHERNOGORSK TO ST. LOUIS

Exactly three weeks after the Vashchenkos had arrived in Vienna, friends and supporters watched as fifteen members of the Chmykhalov family formally ended the Siberian Seven case. Maria (almost sixty-one) and Petro Chmykhalov (fifty-seven) were accompanied by Maria's fifty-four-year-old sister Anna Makarenko, fours sons (including Timothy), one daughter, two daughters-in-law, and five grandchildren. Lida Vashchenko was on hand to greet them.

Once again the excitement was great as we watched the newly arrived emigrés step onto Austrian soil. The next day we were all on our way to St. Louis, minus Timothy and his new bride, Tatyana, who decided to spend five days sightseeing in Vienna.

One of the most moving scenes in the Siberian Seven drama was the arrival of the Chmykhalovs at Lambert Field in St. Louis. The plane arrived at 10:30 P.M., an hour and a half late. What a surprise it was to walk out into a packed waiting area of over three hundred people singing "Hallelujah! He's a Prayer-Answering God."[25] There were many tears and it was clear that these American Pentecostals were ready to take their Russian brothers and sisters into their hearts and lives.

HOW WAS THE EMIGRATION IMPASSE RESOLVED?

Once the Siberian Seven question was resolved, speculation began over who was responsible for their release. It was particularly ironic that the World Council of Churches immediately stepped forward to take credit. For five years they had assiduously avoided any serious mention of the problem, but on the very day the Vashchenkos arrived in Seattle, a Seattle newspaper carried a banner headline reporting the WCC's claim that it had played a major role in their release.[26]

That the WCC and other ecumenical groups raised the issue in private is undoubtedly true. But a more sober and convincing explanation for the release of the Seven is best found in looking at what had been going on quietly on the political front in both Washington and Madrid.

Although the Carter State Department had discouraged the families from staying in the embassy, Lida is convinced that it was a decision by President Carter which allowed them to stay in the embassy. Carter had dispatched a personal emissary to the Soviet Union in the late 1970s to work on the case, though the hoped-for resolution could not be obtained at that time.

The major breakthroughs came under President Reagan. There was a definite improvement in the attitude and policies of the Moscow embassy towards the families. Not long after Brezhnev's death, Reagan made a personal appeal in early December 1982 to the new Soviet leader Yury Andropov for permission for the Seven and their families to emigrate. Reagan hinted that progress on human rights questions would have an impact on the possibility of holding a summit.

Though Reagan, like Carter, was willing to work behind the scenes, there was greater public visibility to administration support for the case during the Reagan years. In fact, in early November 1982, when Secretary of State George Shultz and Vice President Bush were in Moscow to attend the funeral of Leonid Brezhnev, the Bushes and Mr. Shultz made a visit to the Seven. "We'll try to help you if we can," assured the Secretary of State. And the Vice President added: "Don't give up hope."[27]

Carter emissary Olin Robison, president of Middlebury, wrote an analysis of the releases for *Christian Science Monitor* under the title: "A Gentle Hurrah for Quiet Diplomacy." Robison complimented President Reagan "on the skill with which the process was handled: quiet, behind-the-scenes, effective."[28]

In fact, the release can best be attributed to a combination of both public protest and private diplomacy. The tough and serious private diplomacy would never have occurred had there not been public protest by members of Congress, American Christians and human rights activists, and their counterparts in Europe.

The final decisions to issue exit visas must be connected to the conclusion of the Conference on Security and Cooperation in Europe, and the de facto compromise between the Siberian Seven and the Soviet government, whereby steps of good faith were taken by both sides to allow the other side to save face and get something of what they wanted. A critical factor here was the great increase in publicity which surrounded Lida's hunger strike and hospitalization in early 1982. Her decision to return to Chernogorsk gave the

Kremlin authorities an opportunity to show their own willingness to begin to resolve the tense drama.

Isn't it strange that Christians so easily lapse into explanations that completely leave God out? For five years, concerned Christians throughout the world had prayed for the Siberian Seven. We ought not to forget that the final agreement to let the Seven go occurred during an unusually tense period in U.S./Soviet relations. Perhaps both sides were in the mood to put this matter behind them, but also perhaps God answered the prayers of millions who had prayed that freedom would come for the Seven and their families.

There is an important lesson to be learned from the Siberian Seven drama—the importance of selfless cooperation between Christians working for a common goal. Many individuals and organizations contributed in significant ways to advancing the campaign for the Siberian Seven. But those who accomplished the most were frequently those who were least concerned about whether or not their efforts were noticed by others.

I've never forgotten the saying which Paul Roush shared with me during a particularly frustrating time in the effort to bring Christian groups together for coordinated action. He said, "There is no end to the amount of good you can do if you don't care who gets the credit." I witnessed the truth of those words many times during the Siberian Seven campaign.

In the providence of God there is always an inscrutable combination of divine and human factors involved in whatever takes place. Neither ought to be ignored, and both clearly played a role in the solution of the Siberian Seven case.

The old adage to "work as if everything depends on you, and pray as if everything depends on God" is not bad advice.

Notes

1. David Willis, "Russian Christians: The Ambassador's Embarrassing Guests," *Christian Science Monitor,* 24 July 1979.

2. Ibid. A complete text of a March 1979 letter from the Vashchenkos describing the visit to Alexander's labor camp can be found in *Moody Monthly,* July-August 1979, 94-95.

3. Ibid.

4. Ibid., 94.

5. Kevin Lynch, "The Guests in the Basement" *National Review,* 21 March 1980, 356.

6. Dan Fisher, "Pentecostalists Caught Between 2 Superpowers," *Los Angeles Times,* 29 August 1979; "U.S. Denies Visit to Pentecostalists at Moscow Embassy," 28 December 1979; "7 in 2nd Year at U.S. Embassy," 27 June 1980.

7. Fisher, *Los Angeles Times,* 27 June 1980.

8. *Congressional Record,* vol. 126, no. 108, part II, 27 June 1980, 1.

9. Marianne Ridge of Christian Solidarity International in Zurich gave me a copy of the report on the meeting, which occurred on 26 September 1980 in Washington, D.C.

10. My complete remarks, answers to questions posed by Senator Simpson, as well as a reprint of my 18 September 1981 *Christianity Today* article, can be found in Relief of Seven Soviet Pentecostals Residing in the U.S. Embassy in Moscow, Hearing before the Subcommittee on

Immigration and Refugee Policy of the Committee on the Judiciary, U.S. Senate, Serial No. J-97-82, 19 November 1981, 136-46.

11. "Deadly Game in a U.S. Embassy: Soviet Pentecostalists Try to Win Freedom with a Hunger Strike," *Time,* 25 January 1982, 44.

12. Harry Genet, "Siberian 7: A Desperate Situation," *Christianity Today,* 5 February 1982, 76.

13. Suki Dardarian, "Seattleite Finds the 'Siberian 7' in Bad Shape," *Everett Herald* (Everett, Washington), 6 January 1982.

14. Genet, *Christianity Today,* 5 February 1982, 76, 81.

15. UPI wire story, 30 January 1982.

16. Steven R. Hurst, "Soviet Source Reports Pentecostalist's Fast Broken in Hospital," *Oregonian,* 31 January 1982.

17. For two specific examples of the U.S. raising the issue in public speeches at the Madrid review conference see R. Spencer Oliver (deputy chairman of U.S. delegation), "Statement on Principle VII," 5 December 1980; and Max Kampelman, "Statement," 28 July 1981.

18. "Religious Persecution as a Violation of Human Rights," Hearings and Markup before the Committee on Foreign Affairs and its Subcommittee on Human Rights and International Organizations (House of Representatives), conducted between 10 February and 14 December 1982, printed 1983, 306.

19. "Soviets Let One of Pentecostals Emigrate," *New York Times,* 7 April 1983.

20. Richard Owen, "Pentecostalists Leave Embassy Refuge," *The Times* (London), 13 April 1983.

21. Timothy Chmykhalov, *The Last Christian: The Release of the Siberian Seven* (Grand Rapids, Mich.: Zondervan, 1986), 160-64.

22. A newspaper account of the conversation can be found in "SPU Professor Lends a Hand," *Seattle Times,* 12 April 1983.

23. Serge Schmemann, "Pentecostals Leave U.S. Embassy in Moscow After 4 Years' Asylum," *New York Times,* 13 April 1983.

24. Schmemann, *New York Times.*

25. "16 Siberian Pentecostals End a Trip to Freedom," *New York Times,* 21 July 1983.

26. Carol M. Ostrom, "Council of Churches Claims Credit in Freeing Siberian 7," *Seattle Times,* 29 July 1983.

27. Chmykhalov, *The Last Christian,* 153-54.

28. Robison, *Christian Science Monitor,* 22 July 1983.

PART II

MARXISM
AND CHRISTIANITY:

The Historic Tension

CHAPTER 4

MARXISM
AND RELIGION

*T*here are moments in life when an uncanny sense of foreboding over-whelms the soul. It was at such a moment that Heinrich Marx penned the following lament in a letter to his son Karl, who was not yet twenty.

> I feel myself suddenly invaded by doubt and ask myself if your heart is equal to your intelligence and spiritual qualities, if it is open to the tender feelings which here on earth are so great a source of consolation for a sensitive soul: I wonder whether the peculiar demon, to which your heart is manifestly a prey, is the Spirit of God or that of Faust. I ask myself—and this is not the least of the other doubts that assail my heart—if you will ever know a simple happiness and family joys, and render happy those who surround you.[1]

The sad prediction of Heinrich Marx has a strangely haunting quality to it that can send chills up the spine of a late twentieth-century historian. Indeed, the simple joys of family life frequently eluded Karl Marx (born in 1818). He preferred to battle for humanity in the abstract rather than to provide for his family in the present. While Marx wrote tortuous tomes about the evils of capitalism, he found it necessary to depend on modest subsidies from his friend Friedrich Engels, who in turn obtained the money from an English division of his own father's capitalist textile enterprise.

Marx was obsessed by a vision of humanity freed from the evils of exploitation. Yet in this century some of history's greatest crimes against humanity have been committed in his name. By far more people have perished in the Gulag (network of labor camps) of the Soviet Union, the artificially-induced famines of the Ukraine, the "worker's paradise" of Communist China, and the "killing fields" of Cambodia than have died in all the concentration camps of Adolph Hitler. All of these victims have been sacrificed on the altar of the "future happiness of mankind."

In fact, the suffering and death inflicted by totalitarian regimes on their own citizens exceeds all the victims of this century's wars. Hitler exterminated approximately 11 million people in concentration camps; between 29 and 65 million Soviet citizens perished at the hands of Joseph Stalin. This does *not* include the Soviet Union's staggering World War II losses (perhaps as high as 20 million).[2]

What does all of this have to do with Karl Marx? Surely this is not what he intended. Indeed, I'm sure he did not. Nor do I think that Vladimir Lenin foresaw the millions who would perish in the Soviet Union at the hands of its own rulers during the quarter century following his own death.

THE KEY TO KARL MARX'S LEGACY

There is no more insidious nonsense than that which surrounds discussion of motives. So long as we intend "good" and are fighting "evil," then we are somehow immune from the hard and painful work of examining the consequences of our ideas and our actions. There is no surer recipe for disaster than this illogical and insensitive mindset. Compassion devoid of disciplined thought is a lethal weapon.

But we are just as inclined to another serious error: the temptation to succumb to "demonization." "Karl Marx was evil." "Lenin was evil." "Communists are evil." In fact, the problem is far more complex than these simple judgments reflect. Karl Marx, in fact, had neither horns nor tail.

When I taught the history of communism at Seattle Pacific University, I frequently startled my classes by having a Marxist come in to make the initial presentation of what Marxists believe. Like Marx, my apologist for Marxism did not have horns, though he did have a beard. The gentleman was a friend of mine and a former professor. He was soft-spoken, answered questions carefully, and threw not a single grenade during the entire two-hour session. He invariably condemned much that had been done in Marx's name, particularly under Stalin. But he also asserted the essential positions of classical Marxism: materialism, atheism, a basically positive view of human nature, and an anti-capitalist, pro-socialist economic analysis.

My students, usually Christians, were frequently surprised to hear someone actually assert and defend non-Christian beliefs about life. Somehow it had not seemed quite real when it was just their professor who contended that such views were held. The students were also pleasantly surprised by the warmth and approachability of the Marxist visitor.

Had Karl Marx made a surprise visit to our class, I think the reaction would have been much the same. He would have appeared more of an academic than a revolutionary. Most of what he wrote, after all, is not easy reading, and is hardly suitable for propaganda. True, Marx was obsessed with his cause, sometimes to the point of sacrificing his family, which he loved. But many Christian pastors have done the same thing, believing that Kingdom work was more important than family responsibilities.

Many mistakenly believe that Marx was simply a boring academician, an economist lost in analysis and not accessible to the average person. If this were true, Marxism would never have fired the imaginations of so many revolutionaries. In fact, the *Communist Manifesto* (1848) is not an economic primer but a moving plea for justice. Marx may have been wrong about many things, including the nature of man and the nature of ultimate reality, but there is sufficient power in certain key texts to move the heart.

Nor is it helpful or accurate to see Marx as some sort of alien Communist striking at the soul of Western man—the originator of the conflict between East and West. Karl Marx is the West. He was German and a full-fledged product of one major stream of Western thought.

Since the days of Greek philosopher Protagoras in the fifth century B.C., there have been those in the Western tradition who have insisted that "man is the measure of all things." The Hebrews, of course, date such an assertion to the very beginning of human history. The first human sin was to place the will of man above the will of God. Deliberate disobedience, not ignorance, has always been the core Christian understanding of human sinfulness.

The "man-centered" vs. "God-centered" debate has long roots in Western history. During the Renaissance (1300-1600) there was a heightened fascination with all things human. This was often not in conflict with orthodox Christian understandings of the dignity of the created human being. However, there were Renaissance themes which revived pagan materialism and "man as the measure of all things" thinking.

It was during the Enlightenment period, however, that in many ways the modern period as we now know it in the West was born. Particularly in its late eighteenth-century French form, certain Enlightenment thinkers rejected many orthodox Christian tenets, such as belief in God (or at least a personal God), the immortality of the soul, and the innate sinfulness of man. There was considerable skepticism about the institution of the Church and its clergy. These anti-clerical and anti-religious perspectives were far more likely to be encountered among the educated than among the masses.

These are the Western influences which shaped the thinking of Karl Marx. Marx's heritage was Jewish, though not strongly religious. His father had nominally converted to Christianity before Karl's birth; it was social standing, not conviction, that motivated the action.

Like the typical Enlightenment figure, Karl Marx had great faith in the power of reason and the perfectibility of human beings. He tended to locate evil in human institutions and particular economic arrangements rather than in the hearts and wills of human beings themselves. Though he was dismissive and scathing of the Socialist (particularly Christian) utopians of his day, many of Marx's own expectations for a rosy post-capitalist world were highly utopian. In this too he was unquestionably a child of nineteenth-century Western Europe, where hopes for the future knew almost no bounds.

Heinrich Marx, not a particularly religious man, was profoundly uneasy about something he sensed in his son: "I wonder whether the peculiar demon, to which your heart is manifestly a prey, is the Spirit of God or that of Faust?" In fact, from a religious perspective, Heinrich had arrived at the heart of the issue. Based in part on a sixteenth-century historical figure, Faust in legend form became symbolic for someone who was willing to trade his own soul for knowledge or power. There can be little question that Karl Marx's biography, from his earliest years, reveals an intense young man with a thoroughly secular humanist perspective. There was absolutely no place in the young Marx's thought for a transcendent God with any claim of sovereignty over human beings.

It is important to understand that Marx's ideas are thoroughly Western. From the same secular roots which produced Marxism, other secular fruit has grown in the West as well: an excessive individualism in some cases, lethargic cynicism and fatalism in others, and very frequently ethical relativism disguised as liberal pluralism. The point is not to assert that these are the only options for secular humanists, but rather to note that secular philosophies which rule out transcendent realities frequently fall prey to diverse and dangerous pitfalls. This is fully consistent with what orthodox Christianity has always insisted are the natural results from failing to come into proper relationship with the Creator.

The lesson for Western Christians is that however dangerous Marxism in power has been and can be, the same secular forces in somewhat different guises are capable of rotting the foundations of non-Marxist societies. We can collapse entirely by our own devices, or simply so dissipate our strength and character that we are unable or uwilling to resist an outside aggressor.

Marxism in the form of Communism in practice has indeed been a modern-day scourge. But many (though not all) of its roots are found in our own backyard.

KARL MARX ON RELIGION

Intense study of the writings and mystique of Karl Marx reveals that atheism was one of the key components of his thought.

Sergei Bulgakov, an early Russian Marxist who later converted to Christianity and became a Russian Orthodox priest, wrote a brilliant book on Marx in 1906. In it he argues convincingly that a major source of Marx's entire doctrine was his "militant atheism." Bulgakov insisted that there was "an inner bond between atheism and socialism in Marx" which was "usually either misunderstood or unnoticed."[3] Alexander Solzhenitsyn strongly echoed Bulgakov's central thesis in his 1973 letter to Soviet leaders: "Ferocious hostility to religion is Marxism's most persistent feature."[4]

It is revealing that Marx wrote his doctoral dissertation (completed in 1841) on the third-century B.C. Greek philosopher Epicurus. He quoted with approval the assertion of Epicurus: "Impiety does not consist in destroying the gods of the crowd but rather in ascribing to the gods the ideas of the crowd." He went on to insist: "Philosophy makes no secret of it. The proclamation of Prometheus: 'In one word—I hate all gods' is her own profession, her own slogan against all gods of heaven and earth who do not recognize man's self-consciousness as the highest divinity. There shall be none other beside it."[5]

Karl Marx was only twenty-three when he wrote the above lines. They amount to a virtual declaration of war against any notions of divine transcendence.

In 1844 Marx penned one of his best-known passages on the topic of religion.

> Man makes religion and religion does not make man. Religion is of itself the conscience of man, or when he has not yet found himself or when he has already lost himself . . . Religion is the sigh of the overwhelmed creature, the soul of a world without soul, the mind of a world without mind. It is the opium of the people. The destruction of religion, as an illusory good fortune of the people, is a requirement of its real good fortune. To demand the renouncement of his illusions in his situation, is to demand the renouncement of a situation which needs illusion. The critique of religion is therefore basically the critique of the valley of tears of which religion is the halo. . . .[6]

In other words, religion only exists because human beings seek compensation for that which they lack materially. The illusion of religion must be fought because it prevents human beings from seeing the true source of their unhappiness. If those material needs were met, then religion would simply disappear.

ARE MARXISM AND CHRISTIANITY RECONCILABLE?

On the basis of a serious study of Marx's specific views on religion, one must conclude that, in their core beliefs, Marxism and Christianity are irreconcilable. To some, such a statement indicates a kind of knee-jerk intolerance, an absence of ecumenism, and a hostility to pluralism. In fact, it is "none of the above." It is a straightforward, sober judgment based solely on an analysis of the respective classical positions of each. Any good scholar, whether a Marxist, a Christian, a Buddhist, an agnostic, an atheist, or a vegetarian graduate student, could come to precisely the same conclusion. It is only necessary that a scholar take seriously the basic tenets of the orthodox statements of each position and then apply faithfully the "law of non-contradiction" to decide whether those basic commitments are compatible with each other or not.

It is not a question of ideology, it is a question of logic. If one system believes in God, and the other considers belief in a transcendent being wishful thinking, then there is a disagreement. If one system asserts that human beings are inclined to evil and in need of God's divine help to overcome their inclinations, while the other system holds that human beings are basically good and capable of moving towards perfection in their own strength, then there is a basic disagreement. If one system views human beings as a complex mix of spiritual and material components, while the other sees only material and economic factors at work, then again you have a fundamental disagreement.

Does this mean that a Marxist and a Christian cannot dialogue together? Of course they can. There is nothing wrong with Marxist/Christian dialogue if what is meant by this is an honest and civil attempt to discover the common ground and differences which do, in fact, exist.

Does the fact that the two world views are in conflict regarding certain central affirmations mean that proponents of each cannot work together to advance world peace or deliver famine relief? Certainly there can be cooperative efforts towards these worthy ends. Unfortunately there has been a tendency in some religious circles where "dialogue" has been promoted to lose any meaningful sense of the distinctive identities of the parties involved.

I first became aware of this problem in 1982 when I was asked to debate my former Marxist professor on the question of whether Christianity and Marxism were compatible. We addressed a basically oldline Protestant and Catholic audience in Seattle. We made our initial presentations and came to precisely the same central conclusions. Despite the possibility, and desirability, of working together on certain critical issues, at the level of fundamental philosophical beliefs, classical Marxism and classical Christianity are seriously at odds.

My first reaction was that we had participated in a good exchange of views and that, in the words of the Catholic theologian John Courtney Murray, we had "achieved disagreement." A disagreement based on real differences properly understood is indeed something to celebrate. So often, there is only misunderstanding based on inaccurate perceptions of each other's positions. But as questions emerged from the audience, I realized that we had made many of our listeners rather uneasy. It was quite obvious that within the circles this audience moved there was an assumption that Christianity and Marxism could find some creative new synthesis.

Given the fundamental philosophical differences which divide the two world views, if there sometimes appears to be a synthesis it is invariably because one side or the other has abandoned certain tenets of its own core beliefs. A number of years back, the Mexican liberation theologian José Miranda wrote a book with the subtitle: "The Christian Humanism of Karl Marx." It should have come as no surprise that in the commentary, the author contended that Marx's atheism ought really not concern us that much since there was so much in the German philosopher that was "Christian."[7]

To suggest that Marx is really Christian because he shares with Christians a concern for humanity is like saying a scientist is really an infant because, like an infant, he needs to sleep and eat. There is an Alice in Wonderland flavor to the terms used here which, in the end, makes meaningful dialogue impossible.

The issue of whether atheism is essential to Marxism was discussed at some length in a fascinating series of articles published in a 1985 issue of the *Journal of Ecumenical Studies*.[8] Most of the authors agree with the view of Arthur F. McGovern that atheism does not necessarily have to be a part of Marxism. In McGovern's opinion:

> Marxism, moreover, is itself not a religion; it is not bound in faith to "what Marx said." If its fundamental value is human emancipation, and if Marxists were to judge (as I have) that religion can enhance rather than negate this emancipation, a conclusion could be reached that atheism is not essential to Marxism.[9]

To grasp the full meaning of this view, consider how it would sound if the subject were Christianity, rather than Marxism.

> Christianity, moreover, is itself not a religion; it is not bound in faith to "what Christ said." If its fundamental value is human emancipation, and if Christians were to judge (as I have) that Marxism can enhance rather than negate this emancipation, a conclusion could be reached that theism is not essential to Christianity.

In Christian terms, to depart from fidelity to the central tenets of the faith is heresy at best, and very likely apostasy. It is the same for the orthodox Marxist. A Marxist who says he now believes in God but remains a Marxist is talking nonsense. Even if we accepted the notion that Marxism in no way functions as a world religion (a view which would be strongly challenged by many serious scholars), simple respect for the integrity of a person's thought would require that we at least acknowledge when we reject self-described key elements of that thought. If a tree were to turn into a rock, it would make no sense to keep calling it a tree.

David McLellan, a non-Marxist, pays Karl Marx the ultimate intellectual compliment: he takes him seriously and at his word. "Marxism is a Christian heresy: it has *chosen* part of the Christian gospel relating to this worldly betterment of the human condition, but it has rejected the transcendental dimension. To ask Marxism to become theistic would be to rob it of its specificity."[10]

Also of some importance is the fact that most Marxists continue to accept Marx's view that atheism is essential to their world view. Paul Mojzes is correct when he observes: "in practice, there are many more Marxists who believe they must be militantly atheistic than those who believe that both the present and the future survival of theism are open questions."[11]

Sadly, there is frequently a euphoria in certain Christian circles over the possibility of a "new synthesis" emerging from dialogue with Marxists. The danger is that the "new synthesis" will be a product of Christians shedding their former convictions rather than Marxists abandoning theirs. The result can be a political radicalism with a religious veneer. It would be more honest to dispense with the veneer.

Whatever may be the present state of Western theoretical discussions about the relationship between religion and Marxism, in the Soviet Union Karl Marx's views on religion have played a key role in determining the relationship between Christians and the often militantly atheistic state.

THE VARIETIES OF THE MARXIST ATTACK ON RELIGION

One of the most serious errors in Western analysis of the impact of Marxism on religion is the assumption that Marxism always means an all-out attempt to destroy religion. In fact, the situation is far more complex, and the threat to religion frequently far more subtle.

We conjure up in our minds perhaps the worst days of the Stalin period, or modern-day Albania where all religion is outlawed, and visualize all-out war on believers. In fact, attempts to totally annihilate religion have been relatively rare in the history of Marxism.

More typically Marxist governments have had to settle for seeking to control or co-opt the churches rather than liquidate them. To be sure, this less obviously hostile approach is more the product of pragmatism than good will. Religion has simply been far too strong historically in Marxist countries for there to be any reasonable chance of wiping it out entirely, at least in the short run. It's true that atheist propaganda in virtually all Marxist states predicts that an inevitable scientific and political enlightenment of the people will result in the gradual disappearance of religion. But rushing the day along by direct physical attacks on the churches has not usually been considered prudent or possible.

Eastern Europe provides an excellent example of the wide variety of Church/State relationships in Communist nations. Poland, which is overwhelmingly Catholic, has considerable religious freedom. The Communist leaders in Poland do not exercise anywhere near the authority over the Catholic hierarchy that the Kremlin does over the Russian Orthodox Church in the Soviet Union. The Lutherans, and other religious groups in East Germany, are considerably more free than are Christians in the Soviet Union, Rumania, or Czechoslovakia. Hungary and Yugoslavia are also quite free.

It's a similar story in Latin America. Churches have traditionally had a rough time in Cuba. More recently, however, authorities seem to be following the Nicaraguan model, which deliberately seeks to cooperate with that part of the Church it considers "progressive." Many liberation theology advocates have heralded the Sandinista regime as a genuinely new phenomenon in the Third World—a creative synthesis of Christianity and Marxism.

To provide a broader context for evaluating the past, present, and future relationship between churches and the State in the Soviet Union, it is critical that we at least touch on the debate which is raging over the Sandinista experiment in Nicaragua. This is particularly appropriate since the Chairman of the Council for Religious Affairs in the Soviet Union, Konstantin Kharchev, has suggested that there may be something in common between the Soviet Union under Gorbachev and Sandinista Nicaragua. In an interview published in February 1988, Kharchev suggested that the Soviet Union's attitude towards believers reminded him of the Nicaraguan slogan, "There is no contradiction between religion and revolution."[12]

A full discussion of the Nicaraguan situation is beyond the scope of this book. But since the Marxist/Christian relationship there is proposed by some as the way to a less hostile attitude towards religion in other Marxist states, we must at least examine some of the main features of the argument.

NICARAGUA: A NEW MARXIST ATTITUDE TOWARDS RELIGION?[13]

The 1979 revolution which overthrew Somoza was the result of a broad coalition within Nicaragua. The Sandinistas, a self-described Marxist group, played a prominent role. But important roles were also played by many other groups which did not consider themselves Marxist. There was important support for the revolution from the Church and other religious elements in Nicaraguan society. It is crucial that we remember that many of those who are very critical of the present Sandinista government supported the revolution in 1979. This includes people like Miguel Cardinal Obando y Bravo and many others within the church world as well.

Critics of the Sandinistas correctly point out that Sandinista documents themselves indicate a classic Marxist "two-stage" revolutionary strategy is being employed by the present leaders. The first stage involves the necessity of a broad coalition taking power. The second centers on the Marxist-Leninist component of the coalition taking over all the key organs of control. The fact that the army in Nicaragua continues to be responsible to the Sandinista party, and not to the National Assembly, is a case in point. This has fueled much of the opposition to the present government. The claim that the opponents are simply old Somoza National Guard members is simply a smoke screen intended to hide the significant disillusionment of large sections of the earlier pro-revolution movement.

Sandinista actions which do not bode well for the future of independent religion in Nicaragua include: a plot in 1982 to discredit Monsignor Bismarck Carballo, one of Cardinal Obando's senior advisors and the head of Radio Catolica; a state-directed attempt to disrupt the Pope's 1983 visit to Managua; the banning or censoring of Radio Catolica, including the Cardinal's popular Sunday mass; the arrest and interrogation of independent evangelical leaders from CNPEN (National Council of Evangelical Pastors in Nicaragua) in 1985; the expulsion of prominent churchmen; the attempt to use government favors granted to CEPAD (Evangelical Committee for Aid and Development), a prominent evangelical association of pastors which cooperates closely with the government, to pressure more independent evangelicals to fall in step with the government; refusal to grant government registration (necessary to receive church funds from abroad) to independent groups such as CNPEN; the attempt to give a Sandinista slant to the curriculum of Catholic schools; and the general attempt to use the literacy program as a means of propagating Marxist, pro-Soviet/Cuban attitudes among the young.[14]

Nicaragua is not the Soviet Union; nor is it Cuba. But much of its support and its inspiration clearly comes from those parts of the world. The book kiosk in one of Managua's main tourist hotels, the Intercontinental, provides stark and unmistakable evidence of the orientation of the present regime. Works by Castro, Lenin, Marx, and Colonel Qaddafi are prominently displayed. In the *New York Times,* hardly a bastion of conservative thought or a supporter of the Contras, a 1986 editorial charged that "only the credulous can fail to see the long roots of the police state now emerging. . . . They are well down the totalitarian road traveled by Fidel Castro."[15]

What is the present religious involvement and commitment to the Sandinista government? Most of the top Sandinista leaders are devoted Marxist-Leninists and do not claim to be Christians, let alone liberation theologians. However, a 1980 official Sandinista communique noted that it had not been their experience that religion was an agent of alienation. Thus, in the opinion of liberation theologian Phillip Berryman, "they were rejecting Marx's own opinion that religion is inevitably an opiate."[16]

The Sandinistas, of course, welcome support from the "Popular Church," which, in fact, represents only a minority within either the Roman Catholic or Protestant church populations. However, one of the most prominent Sandinistas—Father Miguel d'Escoto, the Foreign Minister of Nicaragua—has very strong connections to the religious world, and has long been held up as a model of the positive role religion is playing in the new regime. What are the commitments of this Maryknoll priest? Is he an example of a liberation theologian who is Socialist, but not Marxist—of one who is independent and wishes to keep his distance from Soviet communism? Recent events are not reassuring.

In the spring of 1987, the Communist party of the USSR awarded Father d'Escoto its "Lenin Peace Prize." His acceptance comments are revealing.

> Am I worthy of such a high award? . . . This prize makes us Nicaraguans come into even closer contact with Lenin, that great personality of your state and of all mankind who is the passionate champion of peace. . . . I believe the Soviet Union is a great torch which emits hope for the preservation of peace on our planet. Always in the vanguard of the overall struggle for peace, the Soviet Union has become the personification of ethical and moral norms of international relations. I admire the revolutionary principles and consistency of the foreign policy of the Communist Party of the fraternal Soviet Union, which provides for deep thought for political and state figures and for philosophers in their struggle for the preservation of peace.[17]

Perhaps even more revealing than Father d'Escoto's remarks is the fact that there was no general outcry from the religious Left, or from the liberation theologians, suggesting that d'Escoto had too closely aligned himself with the Communist bloc. In fact, that there was not protest is not surprising. The numerous books written by liberation theologians focus almost exclusively on criticism of the West, not of the Marxist world.

Even if it were true that the Western democracies and their capitalist system were as bad as liberation theologians have argued, any objective comparison with the Marxist alternative would indicate that there is far more to fear from the part of the world which Father d'Escoto praised as "the personification of ethical and moral norms in international relations."

In seeking an explanation for the strong support of the Sandinista/Popular Church coalition from many religious activists in North America, it is important to understand that there is a tremendous desire within these circles to believe that somehow Nicaragua will not be like other Marxist governments. After all, one major difference between the Cuban Revolution and the Nicaraguan Revolution is the much more prominent role that the Church played in Nicaragua. Berryman asserts that the Nicaraguan experience has had a positive impact on Cuba, resulting in Castro becoming more tolerant towards religion.[18]

Unfortunately, there is considerable evidence that the Sandinista leadership is hostile to any religion which is not supportive of or subservient to the State. In this sense, the pattern points towards other Marxist regimes rather than away from them. For the time being, however, a measure of genuinely independent religious activity continues to exist, such as that reflected in large evangelical crusade meetings. Of course, a condition for permission to hold such crusades is that there be absolutely no mention of politics. If that restriction were imposed on the National Council of Churches in the United States or on various parachurch organizations on the Religious Right, there would be a justified outcry protesting government interference in religious affairs.

The debate over what, in fact, are the true intentions of the Sandinistas in Nicaragua will certainly continue. As time passes and the evidence continues to mount, we will be able to judge more clearly whether it is the Sandinistas' critics or their apologists who have understood them best.

CONCLUSION

Historically and across the globe, Marxism has dealt with religion in a variety of ways: from attempts to destroy it completely, to efforts to restrict, to a strategy of co-opting churches into the service of the State. Attempts to domesticate and control religion, though not as obviously hostile, represent one of the most insidious forms of government oppression.

As we consider the state of religious freedom in the Soviet Union, we must not forget that Marxism is quite capable of backing off its outward offensive against religion without abandoning its intention of controlling or manipulating it. It is possible that improvements in the situation of religious believers in the Soviet Union, or elsewhere in the world, may represent a genuine change of heart on the part of the Marxists. It is also possible that control of the Church is simply more subtle and less obvious than in the past.

It is imperative that neither alternative be ruled out in advance. Nor can the question be fully addressed without examining in some detail the unique history of Marxism on Russian soil.

Notes

1. Quoted by David McLellan, *Karl Marx: His Life and Thought* (London: Macmillan, 1973), 1. Biographical comments which follow on Marx are taken from McLellan's fine study.

2. Eugene H. Methvin, "20th Century Superkillers," *National Review,* 31 May 1985, 24.

3. Sergei Bulgakov, *Karl Marx as a Religious Type* (Belmont, Mass.: Nordland, 1979), 110, 62.

4. Alexander Solzhenitsyn, "Letter to the Soviet Leaders," *East and West* (New York: Harper and Row, 1980), 123.

5. Quoted in McLellan, *Karl Marx,* 37.

6. Karl Marx, *Contribution to the Critique of Philosophy of the Right by Hegel,* quoted in *Communism and Christianity in Theory and Practice: Doctrines/Facts/Conclusions* (United Kingdom: Aid to the Church in Need, 1978), 5.

7. José Miranda, *Marx Against the Marxists* (Maryknoll, N.Y.: Orbis Books, 1980). See my review essay in *Fides et Historia,* 14 (Fall-Winter 1981): 73-79.

8. *Journal of Ecumenical Studies,* 22 (Summer 1985), *Christian Marxist Encounter: Is Atheism Essential to Marxism?* ed. Paul Mojzes. There are twenty-two responses to the question, 435-593.

9. Arthur F. McGovern, "Atheism: Is It Essential to Marxism?" *Journal of Ecumenical Studies,* 497.

10. David McLellan, "Response to McGovern," *Journal of Ecumenical Studies,* 536.

11. Paul Mojzes, "Introduction," *Journal of Ecumenical Studies,* 439.

12. Quoted in William Teska, "How *Glasnost* Affects Religion," *Witness,* 6.

13. The following section is an edited version of a portion of my article entitled: "The Discipline of Discernment: Liberation Theology Reconsidered." To be published by the Graduate School of International Studies of the University of Miami, Florida, as part of a symposium of essays composed for a 22 March 1986 conference on "Religion and Revolution in Nicaragua."

14. For more detailed documentation of these matters, see Humberto Belli, *Breaking Faith: The Sandinista Revolution and Its Impact on Freedom and Christian Faith in Nicaragua* (Westchester, Ill.: The Puebla Institute, 1985); publications of the Puebla Institute, 910 17th Street, Suite 409, Washington, D.C. 20006; newsletters and publications of the Institute on Religion and Democracy, 729 15th St., N.W., Suite 900, Washington, D.C. 20005.

15. "The Sandinista Road to Stalinism," *New York Times,* 10 July 1986.

16. Phillip Berryman, *Liberation Theology* (New York: Pantheon Books, 1987), 147.

17. "D'Escoto Comes Clean," *Crisis,* January 1988, 2.

18. Berryman, *Liberation Theology*, 177.

CHAPTER 5

MARXISM
IN RUSSIA

R ussia and the Russian people can be characterized only by
contradictions. On the same grounds the Russian people may be
characterized as imperial-dogmatic and anarchic freedom-loving, as
a people inclined to nationalism and national conceit, and a people of
universal spirit, more than others capable of ecumenical views; cruel
and unusually humane; inclined to inflict suffering and illimitably
sympathetic. This contradiction is established by all Russian history
and by the eternal conflict of the instinct of imperial might with the
instinct of the people's love of freedom and justice.[1]

So wrote Nicolas Berdyaev, one of the most insightful Russian thinkers of the
twentieth century. And this reality has been recorded down through the
centuries innumerable times by visitors from the outside as well as by the
Russians themselves.

THE UNIQUELY RUSSIAN CONTEXT

The Eastern Slavs (Russians, Ukrainians, and Belorussians) defy catego-
rization. They are neither fully Western nor fully Eastern, but rather some
hybrid of the two. The old adage "scratch a Russian, find a Tartar" has a
strong basis in fact. Indeed, the very term *Tartar* reminds us of that period
from the thirteenth to the fifteenth century when Muscovite Russia was
controlled by Mongolian Tartars.

Both before and after the 1240 Mongol sack of Kiev, the capital of the
medieval Eastern Slavic state, Western influences were important. However,
Peter the Great's obsession with Westernization and modernization intensified
contacts with the West beginning in the late seventeenth century. There was
one problem, however. Russian tsars typically wanted the technological

knowledge that followed from developing relations with Westerners, but they sought to keep out Western political ideas which might undermine their authoritarian power. As a result, in the eighteenth century there developed a serious chasm between a small but growing intellectual elite, which was influenced by Western ideas, and the tsarist rulers who sought to prevent the spread of these often liberal or revolutionary ideas.

It is likely that the lack of access to real power tended to make more extreme the views held by Russian social critics of the nineteenth century. The small revolutionary elite, however, was not only alienated from the government, but also from the masses. In contrast to the bulk of the population who were quite conservative, supportive of the tsar, and traditionally religious, the revolutionary portion of the intelligentsia flirted with materialism and atheism.

Some say it is a product of the climate, others that it is just inherent in Russian nature; but whatever the cause, Russian history is filled with uncompromising believers. Nineteenth-century sons of priests became equally fervent in their revolutionary zeal for atheism. As Berdyaev has put it, "the typical Russian cannot go on doubting for very long, his inclination is to make a dogma for himself fairly quickly, and to surrender himself to that dogma whole-heartedly and entirely."[2] Furthermore, the Russian soul has long held an inclination towards messianism. After Constantinople fell to the Turks in 1492, the idea grew up in Russia that Moscow was the "Third Rome," the new center of world Christianity. Soviet communism has often represented a secular version of this historic national belief. And it is hard to miss a certain messianism in the way Alexander Solzhenitsyn dreams about a future world impact of a revitalized and free Russian Orthodoxy.

Christians in the West have come to identify atheism with evil. In the Russian context, however, there was a particularly strong moral dimension to the rejection of God. Western discussions of God have frequently focused on whether God exists. But the great Russian thinkers have often posed a far more interesting question: "What is the character of God?" Thus, theological debate often centered on why an allegedly all-powerful God would create a world in which there was so much innocent suffering. If the conclusion was that God, if he even existed, must somehow be responsible for evil, then the response might well be to reject God. This is what Ivan Karamazov did in Fedor Dostoevsky's *The Brothers Karamazov* (1879). (Literature or literary criticism, not systematic theological works, have usually served as the stage for discussion of Russia's most creative ideas.)

A major source of atheism and materialism for many Russian revolutionaries was the radical French Enlightenment. If a new intellectual trend or idea emerged in Europe one year, it was likely to turn up a few months later in Russia, often in a somewhat more extreme form. The point is clear. Long before the thought of Karl Marx reached Russia, a soil for it had developed which would both nourish it and Russify it. What Berdyaev called the "maximalist Russian temperament" would indeed put its unique stamp on Karl Marx's ideas.[3] Part of the Russian openness to Marxism in certain circles sprang from the fact that it was the latest idea to come from the "enlightened" political radicals of the West. And part of Russia's receptivity was due to a frustration with the forms of socialism (often utopian and peasant-oriented) which had failed to make much impact in Russia during the 1860s and 1870s.

The "father of Russian Marxism" is often considered to be George Plekhanov. As a Russian dissident exile in Zurich, he promoted Marxist thought among other exiles and among his friends in Russia. During the 1890s some of Russia's brightest young men became fervent converts to Marxism. Nicolas Berdyaev, Peter Struve, and Sergei Bulgakov were just a few of the most important. But the person who would emerge as the most tenacious and effective advocate of Marxism was Vladimir Lenin.[4]

A common myth of our day is that the Bolshevik Revolution of 1917, which brought proponents of Marxist communism to power, became virtually inevitable from the late nineteenth century on. Nothing could be further from the truth. In fact, there was an intense debate among the Russian intelligentsia in the early part of the twentieth century over the materialism and atheism which had come to characterize much of the revolutionary movement. One of the high points of the cultural and religious renaissance which followed was the publication in 1909 of *Signposts*—a collection of essays, mainly by former Marxists, denouncing the dangerous secular elements in the revolutionary movement. Berdyaev, one of these former Marxists, insisted that their commitment to political liberation was no less strong than in the past, but "political liberation is possible only in conjunction with, and on the basis of, a spiritual and cultural renaissance."[5] The contemporary debate over liberation theology could find a careful study of the controversy over *Signposts* a most worthwhile endeavor.

Not only did many of the finest intellectuals abandon Marxism, but Russian Marxism itself was riddled by internal divisions. In 1903, the (Marxist) Social Democratic Party split into two factions: Bolshevik and Menshevik. Lenin's faction, the Bolsheviks, insisted on a much smaller and more elite Party membership and pushed for an accelerated and pro-active involvement in bringing about the Revolution.

While the intelligentsia argued over the nature and course of the revolutionary events, there was slow and steady progress in Russia towards a constitutional monarchy. Serfdom, the Russian equivalent of slavery, had been abolished in the 1860s. A whole series of reforms were unleashed over the next few years which pushed Russia in a direction similar to that of its political neighbors in Western Europe. The tremendous pressures of World War I and the single-minded resolve of Vladimir Lenin were the key factors in the eventual victory of the Bolsheviks. Now, for the first time in world history, there would be an attempt to put Marxist ideas into practice.

LENIN AND RELIGION

The regime's new ruler left no doubt from his writings where he stood in relationship to religion. He stood firmly in the shadow of Karl Marx.

> Our program has been built up entirely on a scientific conception of the world, or more precisely on a materialistic conception. The explanation of our program therefore includes of necessity the explanation of true historic and economic origins of religious obscurantism. Our propaganda includes necessarily the propaganda of atheism.[6]

This statement by Lenin dates to 1905 and makes clear the "necessity" in Lenin's mind of aggressively pursuing antireligious and atheistic propaganda. Four years later, he wrote an essay dealing with the relationship of the workers' party to religion.

> Religion is the opium of the people; this sentence by Marx forms the cornerstone of all Marxist conception in matters of religion. Religions, modern churches, religious organizations of all kinds, Marxism considers them always as organs of bourgeois reaction.[7]

In the same pamphlet, Lenin provides a Russian spin to the famous Marxist phrase identifying religion with opium: "Religion is a kind of vodka by which the slaves of capital blacken their human figure and their aspirations for a more dignified human life."[8] It is not enough to have the proper attitude towards religion; it is necessary to combat it actively. "We must fight religion. This is the ABC of all Materialism and consequently of Marxism. . . . It is necessary to know how to fight religion. . . ."[9]

At first glance, it might seem that a Marxist-Christian dialogue session would last no longer with Lenin than with Marx. In the *ABC of Communism*, Lenin proclaimed: "Religion and Communism are incompatible in theory as well as in practice."[10] However, a more complete examination of his comments reveals that Lenin is sometimes willing to take a somewhat more moderate tact with religious believers. For example, regarding how the Party ought to respond to priests, Lenin gave the following advice in 1909:

> If a priest comes to us to dedicate himself to a common political work and if he fulfills his task conscientiously in the Party, without working against the program of the Party, we may admit him to our ranks, since the contradictions between the mind and bases of our program with the religious conviction of the priest could, under these conditions, convey the contradiction to him, in so far as it concerns him personally.[11]

But Lenin quickly added, should "this priest undertake within the Party, as the main and almost exclusive action, the active propaganda of religious conceptions, the Party should of necessity exclude him."[12] In other words, the priest may serve the Party so long as he does not act like a priest.

Lenin was an immensely flexible leader. Indeed, this was a critical key to his success. As he put it: "It is necessary to learn the art of accepting political compromises, schemes, zig-zags, maneuvers of conciliation and retreat, in short all the maneuvers necessary to accelerate the taking over of political power."[13] In 1905 in "Socialism and Religion," he was willing to go even further in this regard: "It is necessary that we are resolute in any sacrifice whatsoever, and even the need to practice everything possible: tricks, guiles, illegal methods; ready to suppress and conceal what is the truth; in short, it is in the interest of the struggle of the classes that we reduce our morals."[14]

It is a mistake to ignore or minimize what Lenin wrote to the Party faithful regarding religion and ethics. This is critical information, useful in interpreting historical events that follow. One measure of *glasnost* will have to be whether or not specific antireligious views of Marx and Lenin are categorically and publicly rejected. If such rejections are made, will these rejections find their way into the textbooks for their children? And if the rejections are made, will the future actions of the State be consistent with the publicly announced change of heart?

During Lenin's brief rule until his death in 1924, there was little opportunity to plan the final death of religion. The main focus had to be on defeating the counter-revolutionary Whites during the Civil War (1917-21) and hanging on to power during an incredibly destructive and anarchic period. Though there was considerable terror used by the Chekha (an early version of the KGB), it was simply not possible to force on the country the collectivism and complete communism which dedicated Marxists wanted.[15]

Lenin even found it necessary, beginning in 1921, to allow a limited return to capitalism (the New Economic Policy) in order to help the economy recover from the devastation caused by the Civil War and early crude attempts to institute radical communism. In the Communist dialectical understanding of the historical moment, this was the "one step back" in the overall pragmatic strategy of "two steps forward, one step back."

The Church suffered under Lenin, particularly the Russian Orthodox Church; but the worst days of persecution lay ahead, during the reign of Joseph Stalin.

STALIN AND RELIGION

The most important factor in Stalin's relationship to religion was not what he said, but what he did. To be sure, he affirmed the antireligious stances of Marx and Lenin. But more importantly, for a decade and a half he utilized every instrument of state power and terror at his disposal in a concerted effort to liquidate religion. Only during World War II, when he found it necessary to mobilize the moral authority which the church still had among the populous, did he back off from annihilation and settle for strict control. (The details of Stalin's persecution of the churches is discussed in the next two chapters.)

What was new about the Stalin era (1924-1953) was the inauguration of totalitarianism in 1928. Indeed, this was such a dramatic turning point in Soviet history that it could be labeled as a kind of "third revolution." (The first was in February 1917 when the tsarist regime abdicated and was replaced by the basically liberal Provisional government; the second was the Bolshevik Marxist coup of October 1917.) Stalin was not a great thinker, but he was a brilliant tactician. He outmaneuvered better known figures (such as Trotsky, Zinoviev, and Kamenev) through a masterful manipulation of Party appointments. He stands as a constant example of what can be achieved by the person who, for many years, is willing to exercise patience and discipline doing jobs that attract little attention and nobody wants.

By 1928 Stalin had consolidated his power base and was in a position to act. He ruthlessly eliminated virtually all opposition or potential opposition during the course of the next decade. Against the will of the peasant masses he brutally collectivized agriculture. In his quest for dramatic industrial growth, he allocated every available resource for heavy industry. There was virtually no consumer side of the economy. Millions perished during the Stalin era. The churches, its clergy, and its members all experienced tremendous suffering.

Religion has always been a particular target of totalitarian rulers. The reason is quite simple. A totalitarian dictator demands a citizen's absolute loyalty. Religion affirms a transcendent focus for human loyalty. Faithful believers of any religion are a constant and stubborn reminder to the totalitarian ruler that he does not enjoy absolute sovereignty. The fact that believers do not consider death the last reality means that even the ultimate power of the state, the power to take a citizen's life, is ineffective in forcing obedience.

Some of the most virulent antireligious propaganda was penned during the Stalin era. Anatoly Lunacharsky, the Commissar for Education, made the following comments in 1933 in the *New Anti-Religious Manual*: "We hate Christianity and the Christians. Even the best amongst them must be considered as our worst enemies. . . . Down with love of our neighbors. What we need is hatred. We must learn to hate: this is the way in which we will conquer the world."[16]

Totalitarianism invariably becomes a sort of bastardized religion, a religion shorn of any transcendent focus and scornful of the very notion that submission to sovereign authority might be unforced. Such secular religions in the twentieth century have proven themselves capable of oppression far greater and more widespread than that of even the most fanatical digressions of the world religions. The medieval Inquisition and Crusades surely are some of the low points in church history. Yet there was an internal moral equilibrium within the Church which was not snuffed out. Ultimately it managed to curb the abuses which occurred. It is precisely the absence of any vestige of a moral equilibrium or lodestar which typifies secular totalitarian regimes.

Though Stalin did find it necessary to back off his all-out crusade against religion during World War II, his successors continued to maintain a very antireligious orientation.

THE POST-STALIN ERA AND ATHEISM

Though there was a partial and temporary *glasnost* (they called it a "thaw" in the 1950s) under Nikita Khrushchev (1953-64), the strongly anti-religious Marxist views of the past were maintained. In fact, as will be clear in chapter 7, the period from 1959 to 1964 was one of particularly vicious persecution of the Church. So many churches were closed that even today under Mr. Gorbachev the number of churches open is considerably less than in 1953 when Stalin died.

Almost a century and a quarter after Marx penned much of his beliefs regarding religion, Khrushchev repeated basically the same points.

> Communist education supposes a conscience of prejudices and su-perstitions of religion, which still continue to prevent certain Soviet citizens from opening up entirely their creative forces. It requires a system maturely and harmoniously studied of scientific and atheistic education, affecting all the layers and all the groups of the population and impedes the spreading of religious conceptions, above all amongst children and young people.[17]

Key officials under Mr. Khrushchev were every bit as hostile to religion as their leader. Leonid Il'ichev, a prominent expert on ideology and member of the Communist Party Central Committee, was quoted in the January 17, 1964 issue of *Communist* as saying:

> It is true that communism and religion have nothing in common. Whatever the adornments of religion may be, they cannot change its nature. . . . Never has any religion been able and will never be able to preserve man from the yoke of exploiters and lead them to the triumph of the communist regime. Marxist atheism does not confine itself to the simple refutation of religion and its teaching, it sup-presses it.[18]

There has been a consistent attitude towards religion in the Kremlin from the time of Lenin right up to the 1980s.

As we will see later, there have been some remarkable shifts in official attitudes towards religion in the Soviet Union in recent years. But even well into the Gorbachev era, the admonition to the Party faithful stressed that they remain resolute in pursuing a vigorous atheist policy. Mr. Gorbachev, himself, in a November 26, 1986 speech in Soviet Central Asia (Tashkent) called for "a decisive and uncompromising struggle against manifestations of religion and strengthening of political work with the masses and of atheist propaganda."[19]

THE LESSON OF THE GRAND INQUISITOR

Why the persistent theme of atheism in classical and Soviet Marxism? Why the compulsion to attack religion, rather than simply be amused by those who childishly believe in illusions? After all, many would argue that that which is best in Marxism is its passionate attack on injustice. Laying aside, for a moment, the appalling record of what Marxism has produced in practice, the theory at least sounds laudable: end injustice, bring equality, and provide for the basic needs of the masses. So why all the fuss about atheism?

Is it perhaps because, despite Marx's claim of rooting his philosophy in materialism and humanitarianism, there were really other issues more fundamental to him? Was Heinrich Marx right when he feared that what drew his son was not the Spirit of God, but rather that of Faust—that is, of man in rebellion against his Maker? Berdyaev is convinced that "Communism in actual fact is the foe of every form of religion and especially of Christianity, not as a social system, but as itself a religion. It wants to be a religion itself, to take the place of Christianity."[20]

This is the critical issue. *Marxism is not simply socialism which happens to be atheist; it is atheism which happens to be socialist.* Christian socialism which is not compulsory may or may not work economically, but it does not represent a challenge to the theological tenets of the faith. In contrast, atheistic Marxism strikes at the very heart of religion because it places man, rather than God, at the center of the universe.

Many years before Marxism entered the Russian Empire and Bolshevism gained power, Dostoevsky explored the inevitable consequences of revolutionary ideas that were rooted in materialism and atheism.[21] He was convinced that terrible crimes would inevitably follow in the wake of such ideas and that they would be committed "for the sake of humanity." He recognized that the secular liturgy of social utopians would be draped in the verbiage of justice, peace, and equality.

In Dostoevsky's *The Brothers Karamazov*, religious skeptic Ivan tells his believer brother Alesha about a story he has written. The setting is sixteenth-century Seville, and Jesus Christ has returned to earth. He is immediately attacked by the Grand Inquisitor of the Church. Although the Grand Inquisitor is a Church authority figure, and the one with the particular responsibility of rooting out heresy, it is clear that in Dostoevsky's novel he voices the views of the new breed of all-powerful modern secular rulers. There is a religious veneer, but that is all it is.

The Grand Inquisitor ridicules Jesus for resisting the three temptations in the wilderness: resort to miracle, mystery, and authority. Sneering at Jesus, the Inquisitor chides:

> Did you forget that tranquility and even death is more precious to a human being than freedom of choice and the knowledge of good and evil? Nothing is more seductive for a human being than freedom of conscience, and yet there is also nothing more agonizing. Instead of providing once and for all a firm foundation for calming the human conscience, you chose all that is unusual, enigmatic, and vague. You chose everything that was beyond the strength of human beings, acting as if you did not love them at all. And you are the one who came to give your life for them! Instead of taking possession of human freedom, you increased it, and burdened the spiritual realm of human beings with freedom's torments forever.[22]

The Inquisitor informs Jesus: "we have corrected your work and have founded it upon *miracle, mystery and authority*. And people have rejoiced that they were anew led like sheep, and that the terrible gift that had brought them so much suffering, was, at last lifted from their hearts."[23]

Alesha breaks into Ivan's narration near the end of the story and a spirited exchange ensues. Alesha charges that this alleged Church authority has a terrible secret: "Your inquisitor does not believe in God, that's his big secret!" Ivan fires back: "What if it is so! At last you have guessed it."[24]

In the debate over bread or freedom, Dostoevsky concludes that the issue of atheism is somehow at the heart of the conflict. Why? Perhaps it is because the humanitarian quest sometimes is but a cloak for a fundamental rejection of God and His valuing of freedom. We make the world over in our own image, and that means a repudiation of the world created according to God's will. The issue is not whether it is appropriate to care for the poor. The issue is whether we have the right to deprive them of their freedom in order to force on them a particular secular definition of "the good."

It was not for thirty pieces of silver that Judas likely betrayed Jesus, but rather because Jesus did not turn out to be the political leader Judas craved. Jesus' words "My Kingdom is not of this world," infuriated Judas. It seemed like a pathetic cop-out. Today, too, we reject Jesus for the same reason, or what is worse, transform the Jesus of history into the very political zealot which Judas longed for, and which Jesus was not. As the Grand Inquisitor bragged to Jesus, "we shall tell them that we are obedient to you and rule in your name. We will deceive them again, for we will not let you come to us again."[25]

CONCLUSION

Perhaps Soviet Marxism can evolve towards Eurocommunism where Communist parties have seemingly adapted to existence within pluralist societies. They have been willing to promise Christian voters that their election will not endanger religious liberty. And there needs to be more study into whether atheism, at least militant atheism, can be logically removed from classical Marxism. If what remains is something radically different from what Marx, Lenin, and subsequent Soviet leaders have meant by the term, perhaps the term Marxism ought to be abandoned.

However, the discussion of Eurocommunism and Marxism in other parts of the world is beyond the scope of the present study. My objective has been to shed light on Marx's thought and the thought of those who have sought to follow him in the Soviet Union. The central theme of this chapter is that the Marxism of Karl Marx and his followers in the Soviet Union is intimately associated with an uncompromising stance on atheism. Nor is this just atheism in the abstract, but an active struggle against religion as a threat to the claims of totalitarian power.

If this thesis is correct, then we have an important explanation for why the Soviet State through the decades has so relentlessly pursued any manifestation of institutional or individual religious freedom. In this light, the words of St. Paul are particularly meaningful:

> For our struggle is not against flesh and blood, but against the rulers, against the authorities, against the powers of this dark world and against the spiritual forces of evil in the heavenly realms.[26]

The implications of this are sobering. Improvements for believers in the Gorbachev era can be real and encouraging. Yet they may not touch the core issues which have traditionally driven classical or Russian Marxism's profound hostility to religion. Apart from a fundamental departure from and rejection of central tenets or interpretations of Marxism, true religious freedom in the Soviet Union can never be more than an illusive reality.

In the providence of God, genuine change involving fundamental religious freedom is possible in the Soviet Union. But we do not hasten its coming by minimizing how radical the departure will have to be from past theory and practice.

Notes

1. Nicolas Berdyaev, *The Origin of Russian Communism* (Ann Arbor, Mich.: University of Michigan Press, 1960), 18.

2. Ibid., 47.

3. Ibid., 68.

4. For a brief history of Marxism in Russia to 1917, see Donald W. Treadgold, *The West in Russia and China*, vol. 1: *Russia, 1472-1917* (Cambridge: Cambridge University Press, 1973), 217-22.

5. Quoted in Treadgold, *The West in Russia and China*, 234. An excellent discussion of *Signposts* by Treadgold continues to 237.

6. *Communism and Christianity: Doctrines/Facts/Conclusions* (United Kingdom: Aid to the Church in Need, 1978), 5.

7. Ibid., 6.

8. Ibid.

9. Ibid.

10. Ibid., 7.

11. Ibid., 10.

12. Ibid.

13. Ibid.

14. Ibid., 11.

15. For further information on Soviet history, see Mikhail Heller and Aleksandr M. Nekrich, *Utopia in Power: The History of the Soviet Union from 1917 to the Present* (New York: Summit Books, 1986).

16. Quoted in *Communism and Christianity,* 11.

17. Ibid., 8.

18. Ibid.

19. Quoted in Oxana Antic, ''Religious Policy under Gorbachev,'' *RL Research,* 28 September 1987.

20. Berdyaev, 158.

21. Novels by Dostoevsky which explore such themes include: *The Possessed, The Brothers Karamazov, Notes from the Underground,* and *Crime and Punishment.*

22. F.M. Dostoevsky, *Brat'ia Karamazovy,* 2 vols. (Leningrad: Khudozhestvennaia Literatura, 1970), 1:298. Translation by Kent R. Hill.

23. Ibid., 301.

24. Ibid., 306.

25. Ibid., 297.

26. Ephesians 6:12 (New International Version).

PART III

CHURCH AND STATE IN THE SOVIET UNION:

1917 to 1985

CHAPTER 6

REVOLUTION
TO WORLD WAR II[1]

*I*t is estimated that during the first six years of Soviet rule, when Vladimir Lenin was still at the helm of state, twenty-eight Russian Orthodox bishops and more than twelve hundred priests perished at the hands of the Bolsheviks.[2] During the decades which followed, most of the fifty-four thousand Russian Orthodox churches which existed in 1914 were destroyed, shut down, or turned into warehouses, factories, or other "socially-useful" enterprises.[3] Of Stalin's millions of victims, many died specifically because of their religious convictions. Many other Christians simply were swallowed up by the indiscriminate terror and inhumane economic policies of the Stalin years.

A TALE OF PEOPLE, NOT NUMBERS

The problem with statistics is that they numb the brain without touching the heart. It is hard to feel any real sympathy with nameless numbers; but it is almost impossible not to be moved by the simple story of any one of the anonymous figures who make up the cold totals.

Take for example, Father Pavel. Before the October Revolution, Father Pavel was a typical priest in charge of a busy parish in what was then called St. Petersburg (Leningrad). He was married to a woman who was quite intelligent, though somewhat difficult to live with. His wife was swept into the whirlwind of the Revolution and became an atheist lecturer, though she remained married. With each passing day of the new regime, life got tougher for Father Pavel.

Finally, the awful moment came. Like many others Father Pavel found himself in prison, then in exile. But it was during his confinement that the most remarkable period of his ministry begin. Though he lived but three short years after his arrest, and despite being confined to the narrow limits of his cell and then to his sick bed in exile, he managed to inspire and help virtually all who came in contact with him. Hardened criminals became believers through his steadfast faith.

On the evening he died, half the collective farm turned out to pay their respects. His biographer later wrote the following epitaph in tribute to the meaning of this particular life, and to countless other similar lives, which have been lived faithfully for God amidst a sea of sorrow and persecution.

> So the story of the exiled pastor came to an end. . . . But though the storm blows over the new and old grave mounds, covering them with snow, though the snowstorm whirls over the distant cemetery, wrapping it in a mantle of white snow, though time goes by and the years disappear, though no one comes there any more and the small cross with its worn inscription falls off its base and collapses on to the ground . . . still the bird-cherry tree will go on arraying itself anew in its wedding colors every spring, and the path of remembrance, prayer and veneration, which leads to such graves, will never be overgrown. . . .[4]

Behind every number mentioned and church counted are tales like that of Father Pavel. Behind the statistics we find suffering, persecution, physical deprivation, separated families, and bereaved children. And we find those moments of truth when an individual must stand alone and make decisions of faith which will dramatically affect one's career, one's family, even one's very life. But most of all, the story behind the facts is one of hope and resilience—the victory of faith over cynicism, the triumph of those who believe in the one true God over those who have put their faith in false gods. Tertullian, the third-century theologian, was right when he reflected on two centuries of persecution by the Romans of the Christians: "The more you mow us down, the more we grow; the seed is the blood of Christians."[5]

CHURCH AND STATE IN RUSSIA BEFORE THE REVOLUTION

You can always tell you are dealing with historians because they never begin a story where you ask them to. They insist on starting someplace else, invariably much further back in time. Contrary to popular belief, this is not done to irritate the reader, but rather to make sense of the story. In this case, religion in the Soviet Union simply cannot be understood apart from an awareness of two things about pre-revolutionary Russia.

First, Russian culture is profoundly religious.[6] In 1988, the millennium of the coming of Byzantine Christianity (Eastern Orthodoxy) to the Slavs of Kievan Rus' was celebrated. The early medieval state was centered in Kiev, the capital of the Ukraine Soviet Republic today. Russian literature, architecture, music, and art are permeated with a sense of the importance of God, faith, and religious tradition. Even the religious skeptic, secular revolutionary, and cynic existed within a framework which would have been incomprehensible apart from a knowledge of religious language and symbols. Sons of priests, turned atheists, who were tried in the 1870s for acts of terrorism referred to the raised platform where they testified at their trials as "Golgotha."

Second, the relationship between the Russian Orthodox Church and the tsarist government during the two centuries prior to the Bolshevik Revolution had an important impact on the relationship which developed between the Communist rulers and the Russian Orthodox hierarchy. Peter the Great, tsar of Russia from 1689 to 1725, was the great Westernizer. He was also the tsar who virtually transformed the Russian Orthodox Church into a department of government. In 1721 he abolished the office of patriarch, the senior hierarch in the Russian Orthodox Church, and replaced it with the Holy Synod. The Synod had Church leaders, but the head of the Synod, the chief procurator, was not a Church leader. In fact, the procurator was often a military man and was considered "the eyes and ears" of the tsar.

It should also be noted that Peter the Great, himself, was not a religious man. In fact he despised the Church, for it was part of the old Russia he was striving to leave behind in his desperate attempt to catch up with the West. Unlike Peter, most other Russian tsars were religious.

The close ties which existed between the Russian Orthodox Church and the tsarist regime put the Church in a vulnerable position when the revolution came. Revolutionaries viewed the Russian Orthodox Church as a prop of the old regime, and it was always assumed that this was part of the established order that would need to be defeated. Indeed, after the Revolution many in the Church, and much of the hierarchy, were sympathetic with the cause of the Whites, the counterrevolutionary force which opposed the Reds (Communists). The Civil War lasted until 1921. It was in this atmosphere of Civil War that many in the Church died, though the Reds often did not stop to find out if the churchman or priest they killed was, in fact, an active opponent of the new leaders.

The subservience of the Russian Orthodox Church to the tsarist government not only put them into danger with the new government, but provided a historical precedent for the Communists not allowing the Church to exist independent from the State. Of course, there was one major difference. The new leaders were dogmatically and vocally opposed to the very idea of religion. Ultimately, they wanted to see religion disappear as a factor in national and social life. In stark contrast, the tsarist rulers, as a general rule, really did believe what the Church preached about ultimate reality and were shaped by convictions which the Church advanced. Thus, though the Church did not enjoy complete freedom under the tsars, neither was its continued existence in any jeopardy. In fact, the tsars supported and protected the Church in many ways.

Tragically, in the years preceding the Revolution and in the weeks immediately after the Revolution, the Russian Orthodox Church was taking major steps towards greater independence. A Church Council (*sobor*) had convened several weeks before the Bolsheviks took power. At the council they elected a patriarch for the first time in over two hundred years. Independence, however, was short-lived. The new rulers had no intention of tolerating an independent Russian Orthodox Church. The lack of any recent precedent for an Orthodox Church which was not, in some sense, under the thumb of the rulers made the Church even less capable of coping with hostile Bolshevik intentions.

Despite the subservient position of the Russian Orthodox Church under both tsars and commissars, the Church was immeasurably worse off under the new regime. It is regrettable if the Church is compelled in any sense to be a handmaiden for the politics of the State. But it is a much more fundamental indignity to not even be allowed the freedom to practice one's faith (choose one's own leaders, organize education for one's young, evangelize, control one's own affairs, and so on). And the latter is precisely what was imposed on the Russian Orthodox Church under the Communist rulers.

The Church in the hands of the Soviet authorities was very much like a mouse in the paws of a cat; there was little question what the cat ultimately intended to do with the mouse.

THE RUSSIAN ORTHODOX CHURCH: 1917-1923

Initially, however, the cat was in no position to destroy the mouse within its grasp. In fact, its own survival was too much at stake to have the luxury of making careful plans for the liquidation of the Church. That the Russian Orthodox Church had to be crippled, however, was obvious to Lenin and his comrades.

Tangible evidence of how the Church would fare with the new government was not long in coming. A bishop's report to the Church Council described what happened when the Red troops poured into the churches and the monasteries of the Kremlin in mid-November 1917: "During only a few hours of Red control of the Kremlin the churches have been desecrated and the icons shot at. . . ."[7] The Moscow Patriarchate made ten thousand copies of the report, most of which the Bolsheviks seized and destroyed.

One of the first major blows against the Church came with the November 1917 decree which nationalized all land. The Church had huge holdings which were affected by this decision.

The most important early Soviet document regarding religious matters was Lenin's historic "Decree on the Separation of the Church from the State." During the *glasnost* era, Soviet commentators have often mentioned this January 1918 decree in favorable terms and contrasted it with the "illegal and arbitrary'' treatment of believers by local authorities and Stalin's restrictive 1929 legislation on religious groups. According to Lenin's decree, henceforth "the Church is separate from the State," and "the school shall be separate from the Church." No longer was religious instruction to be allowed in public schools.

On the positive side, the decree declares that:

It is prohibited to enact on the territory of the Republic local laws or regulations which would put any restraint upon, or limit freedom of conscience. . . . Each citizen may confess any religion or no religion . . . . The mention in official papers of the religion of a citizen is not allowed. . . . The free performance of religious rites shall be granted so long as it does not disturb the public order. . . . Citizens may give and receive religious instruction privately.[8]

On the negative side, however, was the stipulation that "no ecclesiastical or religious association shall have the right to own property. Such associations shall not enjoy the right of legal entity." The decree also declared that "all property belonging to churches and religious associations existing in Russia shall become public property," although the authorities were given the right to let the churches use their buildings and religious objects free of charge.[9]

The separation of Church and State was reaffirmed in the July 1918 Soviet Constitution.

The fate of religious communities was directly in the hands of the new secular authorities. In the early period of the Revolution, the government confiscated six thousand churches and monastic buildings because they had historical or archaeological value to the State. In January 1918, a decree seized for the State all bank account holdings of all religious associations.[10]

The Orthodox Church did not think the new government would last long, and so issued its own defiant decrees made at the Church Council, which continued in session until September 1918. One of the clearest signs that the Church did not grasp the realities of the radically new situation was its December 1917 decree which declared that "the head of the Russian state, the ministers of religion and of education and their deputies must belong to the Orthodox Church."[11]

As it became more and more clear that the Bolsheviks were not going to go away, the patriarch began to seek ways to reduce the tension. By September 1919 the Orthodox leader approved disobedience to the civil authorities only if the government's orders were in direct violation of religious conscience. He even refused to send secret blessings to the White armies, though he also withheld blessings from the Red forces.

A government decree in June 1921 forbade any sermons that were not purely religious in subject matter. Other direct actions against the Church came in the spring of 1923. The closure of churches was legalized when the buildings were deemed useful to the State. Furthermore, a religious association could be dissolved on the basis of "political unreliability and anti-Sovietism."

Another tactic was to allow a local church to be used for religious purposes certain days of the week, but to allow dances and clubs to function in the church on the other days. When church members refused to hold services in the building because they considered it desecrated by this secular use, the church was officially closed down. The government excuse was that such closures were according to the wishes of the parishioners.[12]

At first the Soviets decided against arresting the patriarch; he, in fact, was under around-the-clock guard by unarmed, voluntary supporters. But the Bolsheviks did deprive him of his ration card for being a "bourgeois parasite."

By 1920, 673 out of 1,025 monasteries which had existed in 1914 had been dissolved by the authorities.[13] But one of the most vicious and dishonest moves against the Church was yet to occur—the confiscation of all Church resources under the cover of raising funds for starving citizens.

A terrible famine caused by droughts and the economic side effects of Civil War descended on the Soviet Union in the summer of 1921 and lasted a full year. The Orthodox Church immediately stepped in to help. Patriarch Tikhon launched a campaign to raise funds from every community within the Church to feed those with nothing to eat. But the ecclesiastical relief committee was ordered dissolved by the government, and all that it had collected was given to the state Famine Relief Committee. This is the first known example of Communist Russian rulers virtually outlawing independent church charity work.

One might think that the primary reason for the government's attack on independent famine relief was that the Church would be positively perceived by society. Actually, the main reason was the desire to strip the Church of virtually all its material possessions, and the famine provided the cover for these massive expropriations.

It was hard, however, for the government to find a publicly defensible way to carry out the attack on the Church's resources; after all, the Church was being extremely generous. In fact, in February 1922, the patriarch called on the parochial councils to donate all church items of value, *except* those used in administering the Sacraments. Nine days later, the government ordered *all* church valuables handed over to the Famine Relief Committee. The patriarch responded in a pastoral letter that sacramental valuables could not be surrendered.

Finally, the government had its long-awaited excuse. "The Church was selfishly refusing to help the starving!" A campaign of terror and forced confiscation of valuables was launched throughout the country.

Documentation of what the government intended to do is revealing. A reputable Russian emigre journal in Paris published the following document in 1970. It is dated February 22, 1922 and the author is Vladimir Lenin:

> We must confiscate in the shortest possible time as much as possible to create for ourselves a fund of several hundred million roubles. . . . With success we can do this only now . . . for no other opportunity but the current terrible famine will give us a mood . . . [with] the wide masses such as would provide us with their sympathies or at least neutrality . . . during the operation of confiscating the valuables. . . .
>
> Therefore . . . it is precisely now that we must wage a merciless battle against the reactionary clergy and suppress its resistance with such cruelty that it will remember it for several decades. . . .
>
> At the next party congress a secret session should be organized. . . . A secret decision of the congress should approve a mercilessly decisive confiscation of church valuables. The more members of the reactionary bourgeoisie we manage to shoot, the better. It is precisely now that we must give such a lesson to these characters that they would not dare to think of any resistance for at least the next few decades. . . . Lenin. (TOP SECRET. NO COPIES TO BE MADE.)[14]

Lenin's admonition—''the more members of the reactionary bourgeoisie we manage to shoot, the better''—was transformed into terrible reality. The Soviet press itself reported 1,414 incidents involving bloodshed as a result of the campaign to confiscate Church possessions.

In Petrograd (soon to be renamed Leningrad) Metropolitan Veniamin worked out a conciliatory way to avoid unnecessary bloodshed and confrontation. Believers were to be allowed to contribute from their own private resources amounts equivalent to the value of the sacramental items. At first it appeared this compromise was going to work, but finally the hardline opponents of the popular metropolitan prevailed. Veniamin and three others were executed in 1922. In all, between 1921 and 1923, 2,691 married priests, 3,447 nuns, and many laymen were killed in the government's confiscation of church valuables for ''famine relief.''[15]

EFFORTS TO DIVIDE AND SUBVERT: THE ''LIVING CHURCH''

Revolutionaries have long known that their most dangerous foe is not an intolerant, oppressive reactionary but a true reform-minded moderate. The assassin's knife rarely is thrust into the tyrant who by his very existence attracts converts to the revolutionary ranks; rather the assassin's deadly instrument seeks out that person whose conduct encourages the belief by the masses that slow, steady change is possible without resorting to the revolutionary agenda.

By the same token, an antireligious Marxist fears the popular priest, not the drunken one. As Lenin put it in a letter to Gorky in 1913, in the interests of compromising religion, Communists ought to tolerate "a priest who violates young girls," but not one who is well-educated and morally upright.[16]

In addition to attacking the most dynamic Church leaders, the Bolsheviks from the beginning sought out those in the Church who would likely be sympathetic to their aims, and did what they could to bring them to power within the ecclesiastical world.

It would be a mistake to consider the Marxist tactic of co-opting the Church a recent innovation. In fact, the early 1920s provide a fascinating case study of Soviet authorities seeking to advance the leftist wing of the Orthodox Church as the only legitimate authority.

The pro-government minority faction within the Orthodox Church was called the Renovationist movement, or the "Living Church." It was composed both of well-meaning religious Socialists and others who were power hungry and unscrupulous. At the end of April 1921, the Renovationists called a Church Council which passed resolutions supporting Soviet socialism. Lenin was praised as a fighter "for the great social truth." Patriarch Tikhon was not only stripped of his title but even deprived of his monastic status. Tikhon's earlier anathema of the Bolsheviks was revoked.

In early May 1922, these radical churchmen, with the obvious collusion of the authorities, attempted to take control of the Orthodox Church at the time Patriarch Tikhon was placed under house arrest. A few days later the plotters, led by Alexander Vedensky, appointed themselves the Supreme Church Administration. Throughout the ecclesiastical coup attempt, the rebels coordinated their work with the GPU, forerunner of the KGB.

But the attempted takeover did not succeed. The Council was obviously an illegitimate affair, with many staying away or not being allowed to attend or speak. The Soviets recognized that the plan to subvert the Church through the Renovationists had failed, so they shifted to a strategy of trying to control the official leadership.

By mid-1923 Tikhon was out of prison, rejecting the Renovationists' actions, but also expressing his own loyalty to the Soviet State. He apologized for his earlier involvement in politics and for his "anti-Soviet" orientation. The "Living Church" continued to exist for some time, but was never again a serious threat to the established religious hiearchy.

THE SHACKLES OF REGISTRATION

For many years Western Christians have been mystified by the divergent accounts of religion in the Soviet Union. Some reports sound reasonably positive. Though the situation is said not to be perfect, still the churches are open, packed, and there is apparently the freedom to conduct services as the members wish. Other accounts are much more negative: imprisonment, exile, church services broken up. What can account for such different perspectives?

In fact, there is considerable truth in both accounts, though not the full truth in either. The positive account describes the "for foreign visitor consumption" part of the registered church world. Even as a description of the registered Church it is woefully inadequate since it fails to note the serious discrimination which even registered believers face in Soviet society.

The negative account describes the persecution which has often been the fate of the unregistered believers, mainly Protestant. The registered believers have known discrimination, often quite severe, while the unregistered have frequently experienced outright persecution. The registered Christian is a "second-class citizen" at best, as Pope John Paul II has so accurately put it. The unregistered is a "third-class" citizen or an outcast.

But to get a full sense of the difference between the above-ground Church and the underground Church, it is necessary to understand how registration came into being and what it has meant to those compelled to submit to its severe limitations.

As early as 1922, Soviet rulers required religious societies to register with the local government. Thus, many years before the notorious 1929 religious sect laws, the pattern was established for using registration as a way of controlling and intimidating believers. Local authorities could set up all sorts of special criteria for registering, which, if accepted, would effectively harness a church's activities. If a church refused to register under those conditions, the magistrates would have a pretext for taking action against them.

Patriarch Tikhon's case illustrates the terrible dilemmas of that period. He showed both courage and accommodation as he tried to keep the Orthodox Church unified during difficult days. In February 1925, Tikhon applied for registration with the State authorities. Before the authorities responded, the patriarch died suddenly, probably at the hands of the secret police.[17] Metropolitan Peter became the acting head of the Church. He was informed that the conditions for registration included making statements the authorities required, excluding from official positions those bishops the government did not approve, and working with the government person in charge of religious affairs, who worked for the secret police.

Metropolitan Peter refused to register under these conditions, and by the end of 1925 he was imprisoned. Peter's replacement, Sergy, felt he had no choice but to seek registration, which he did in June 1926. It was Sergy's intention to bend but not break. He asserted in a letter to his clergy that the Church ought not to be involved in politics nor ought it "enter into any special involvement" to prove its loyalty.[18]

Soviet officials were not satisfied with the extent of Sergy's capitulation, and in December 1926 he too was arrested along with 117 bishops. This mass arrest and the subsequent compromise was an important turning point in Soviet Church history. Historian Matthew Spinka asserts that the secret police "succeeded in purging the Church of all who possessed moral courage to oppose the policies of the state. This . . . was the process of 'eradication of the best.' "[19]

Because Soviet authorities managed to place in leadership positions sufficiently docile Church hierarchs, the notion has grown up in the West that the Orthodox Church has never shown any courage or independence. This is simply not true. Consider the case of Metropolitan Kiril.

In the spring of 1927, while Sergy was still in jail, authorities tried to convince the man most likely to become the next patriarch, Kiril, to accept the conditions for registration. When one official tried to impress on the churchman the necessity of removing a bishop from his See, if the Soviets demanded it, Kiril responded, "If the bishop is guilty of an ecclesiastic offense, I shall do so. But otherwise I would call him and tell him: 'Brother, I've nothing against you, but the civil authorities want to retire you, and I am forced to do so.' "[20]

But the Communist bureaucrat was not satisfied. "No, you must pretend the initiative is yours, and find some accusation." Metropolitan Kiril would not budge. "You are not a cannon, and I am not a shell with which you want to destroy the Church from within." On the same day this confrontation occurred, Kiril was sent back into Arctic exile, where he died seventeen years later.

Shortly after the failure to compromise Kiril, the Soviets released Sergy from prison (March 1927). Sergy had been sufficiently broken to say much of what the Communists wanted. His "Declaration of Loyalty" (July 1927) caused a stir in the church world. Sergy asserted that he wanted the Soviet government to understand that it was possible to be both a serious Orthodox Christian and a loyal Soviet citizen. He told the emigre clergy that if they did not pledge their loyalty to the Soviet government, he would take them off the list of patriarchal clergy.

Though Sergy had been forced to compromise, he did not go nearly as far as the Soviets would have liked.[21] Still the July 1927 declaration had, as emigré historian Nikita Struve put it, "transformed the church into an active ally of the Soviet government." The majority of the clergy and their parishioners, however, understood that "this sin was necessary to save the church from destruction."[22]

An Orthodox underground or catacomb Church has existed since the early 1920s (two groups associated with this movement are the True Orthodox Christians and the True Orthodox Church). Its ranks swelled as a result of Metropolitan Sergy's declaration of loyalty to the Soviet government. Many rejoined the patriarchal Church when Patriarch Aleksy was elected in 1945, but many are still underground. Their numbers are difficult to determine since they utilize a cell-structure organization in which participants know only those in their own group.[23]

A TWENTIETH-CENTURY CLASSIC: THE SOLOVKY MEMORANDUM

At the time Metropolitan Sergy was deciding there was no way out for the Church short of major compromise, another powerful section of the Church was coming to a different conclusion. Two months before Sergy's July declaration, the bishops imprisoned at Solovky issued one of the most profound and moving Christian documents of the entire Soviet era.

Located in the frigid Arctic White Sea, the Solovky (Solovetsky) Islands were one of the initial outposts of the Soviet labor camp system.[24] A monastery was founded on the largest Solovky island in the fifteenth century. From 1718 to 1903 the tsars had used parts of the monastery as a prison, but the monastery itself continued to function until the October Revolution.

The origins of the Gulag archipelago—the phrase Alexander Solzhenitsyn used to describe the system of labor camps sprinkled across the Soviet map—are found on the Solovky Archipelago. The first batch of prisoners was brought here in the early 1920s, while Lenin was still in charge. The monks had already been forced to become collective farmers on the grounds, but now the old men were evicted. Within a few months, the agricultural productivity of the monks was a relic of the past.

The horrors which lay ahead for the involuntary twentieth-century inhabitants of the Solovky Islands were foretold two centuries earlier. According to the story, in 1712 a monk by the name of Job, during an all-night vigil, had a frightening visitation from Mary. "This hill from henceforth shall be called Golgotha, and on it shall be built a church and a monastery of the Crucifixion. And it will be whitened by the sufferings of countless millions."[25] Thus was born the Golgatha-Crucifixion Monastery on the island of Anzer. Piles of bearded corpses would indeed one day be stacked in the vestibule of the church, later to be taken out and rolled down Golgotha Hill.

An account of the terrors on Solovky Islands, told by one who miraculously managed to escape, was published in England in the late 1920s.[26] Embarrassed by the questions which the account raised, the esteemed Soviet author Maxim Gorky was sent to investigate in 1929. Despite the bravery of a boy who told Gorky the terrible truth about the abuse and murder of prisoners, Gorky came back and reported that the prisoners were well treated. The boy was taken out and shot shortly after Gorky left. On a single awful night in October 1929, exactly three hundred prisoners were executed, almost as many as the total number the tsars had incarcerated there during the centuries it was used as a prison.[27]

However, the Solovky camps produced not just death, but also an immortal statement on Church/State relations.

The Solovky memorandum brilliantly combines three separate themes. First, the bishops argue convincingly that the government had seriously undermined its own decree on the separation of Church and State. The State is systematically and aggressively intervening in the internal affairs of the Church by supporting one minority group (the Renovationists) while persecuting any who will not support it. Further, the State is not allowing the Church to provide religious education for its young people and is shutting down monasteries.

Second, the bishops display a keen sense of the philosophical differences between Christianity and Marxist communism:

> The Church recognizes spiritual principles of existence; communism rejects them. The Church believes in the living God, the Creator of the world, the leader of its life and destinies; communism denies his existence. . . . The Church preaches love and mercy; communism, *camaraderie* and merciless struggle. . . . The Church sees in religion a lifebearing force which . . . serves as the source for all greatness in man's creativity, as the basis of man's earthly happiness, sanity and welfare; communism sees religion as opium, drugging the people and relaxing their energies, as the source of their suffering and poverty. The Church wants to see religion flourish; communism wants its death. Such a deep contradiction in the very basis of their *Weltanschauungen* [worldviews] precludes any intrinsic approximation or reconciliation between the Church and state, as there cannot be any between affirmation and negation . . . *because the very soul of the Church, the condition of her existence and the sense of her being, is that which is categorically denied by communism.*[28](my emphasis)

This sober sense of reality about the differences between Christianity and classical Marxism has been sadly missing in many Western discussions in recent years.

Third, despite the deep philosophical differences, coexistence is possible under certain circumstances. These bishops were not reactionary, "fight to the death" anti-Communists. Their memorandum reminds us that Christians have managed to survive within such diverse political systems as the Ottoman Turkish Empire and democratic America, and they did so by "rendering unto Caesar that which is Caesar's, and unto God, that which is God's."

But coexistence can succeed, according to the bishops, only if there really is a separation of Church and State. If the Soviets only will respect Lenin's own decree on the separation of Church and State, coexistence can work. The Church is willing not to involve itself in the activities of the government and is willing for its members to discharge their civic duties. But the State must not interfere with the Church's internal spiritual affairs.

The bishops acknowledge that during the Civil War immediately following the Bolshevik seizure of power, the Church did oppose the political authorities. But this was to be expected, note the bishops, since criminals in the name of, but not necessarily with the authorization of, the new State were arbitrarily acting against the Church. That day is past, and order has returned. There is now no need to oppose the government.

The conclusion is straightforward and to the point. If the Soviet government agrees to coexistence based on true separation of Church and State, then the Church "will rejoice at the justice of those on whom such policies depend." If not, "she is ready to go on suffering, and will respond calmly, remembering that her power is not in the wholeness of her external administration, but in the unity of faith and love of her children; but most of all she lays her hopes upon the unconquerable power of her divine Founder."[29]

That the Solovky memorandum was composed by courageous Russian Orthodox bishops ought to temper the harsh judgments sometimes launched against the Orthodox Church. True, these bishops were barred from leadership in the Church, many paying the ultimate price for their courage. But within the Orthodox Church there have always been those who challenged the view that timid compromise is required for survival. Even now there is a bitter dispute between the official hierarchy and Orthodox dissidents.

Much of what followed this first decade of Soviet rule is simply a variation on the themes of this earliest period. It is significant that these themes were well established under Lenin and Stalin *before* the totalitarian period began at the end of the 1920s. But before we move on to the Stalin period, we need to discuss what was happening with the Protestants during this first decade of Soviet rule. There are some surprises here. For them in many ways this was the best decade of the Soviet era. However, first we must consider the roots of Protestantism in Russia.

PROTESTANTS IN TSARIST RUSSIA

This was a time of horrible persecutions. Exiles, arrests, fines, and beatings of believers rained down abundantly upon the audacious followers of the Gospel. Under continual fear of being caught by the police, the brothers nevertheless did not cease their meetings, holding them in basements, across the Dnieper, in the woods, in the cemetery, in ravines, and in the apartments of the more well-to-do brothers.[30]

A firsthand description of evangelical persecution under the Communists? No, the account is what happened to the late nineteenth-century Protestant *Stundists* by the order of tsarist officials and Orthodox hierarchs.

Not all Protestants were treated this badly by the government and church officials of their day. But many were, and many more were discriminated against. The hierarchy of the Russian Orthodox Church did not look kindly on religious competition.

The new Soviet authorities considered the Russian Orthodox Church their chief religious rival, and they concentrated on breaking the backbone of the Orthodox Church, not on interfering with the activities of the Protestants. There was even a sense that to the extent the evangelicals picked up strength, the Orthodox Church would be weakened. The amazing numerical growth the Protestants experienced confirms historian Walter Sawatsky's judgment that the 1920s were a kind of "golden age" for the evangelicals.[31]

But who were these Protestants, and how did they enter the Russian Empire in the first place? From the time of Ivan the Great in the sixteenth century, there had been at least some Lutheran German immigrant churches in Russia. More Germans, including Lutherans and Mennonites, were brought to Russia through the influence of Peter the Great (1682-1725) and through Catherine the Great (1762-96) and her son Alexander (1801-25). These rulers were more interested in the immigrants' technical expertise than their theology.

By 1914 there were approximately two million German farmers in Russia. Of the half million Mennonites in the world at the beginning of World War I, an estimated 20 percent lived in the Russian Empire.[32] The Russian capital of St. Petersburg had the highest concentration of Protestants of any major Russian city—about one hundred thousand Protestants or 10 percent of the population. To protect the Russian population from the influence of these Protestants, the government forbade any of the Protestant services to be held in Russian. Though Protestant influence was largely confined to the foreign communities in the Russian Empire, their presence helped prepare the way for the subsequent growth of Protestantism among the Russians themselves.

An example of this spreading influence is the rise of *Stundism,* which originated with German Pietists and Mennonites in the Ukraine. The religious vitality of the *Stundists* was attractive to many Russians and Ukrainians, and it spread rapidly in the first half of the nineteenth century. The Orthodox Church often reacted with great resentment and intolerance, and *Stundists* discovered within Orthodox ranks were often expelled. Eventually the *Stundists* joined with the Baptists, whose roots can be traced to German Baptists who were in Russia by the second half of the nineteenth century.

Non-Orthodox Christians in the Russian Empire, particularly native Russians or Ukrainians, experienced much discrimination and persecution during the tsarist period. There were only occasional moments of toleration. For this vibrant Christian minority, the arrival of the Bolsheviks spelled greater freedom than any they had known under the tsars. In time, their lot would become virtually identical to or worse than that of their Orthodox brothers and sisters, but this was not the case during the first decade.

THE EVANGELICAL "GOLDEN AGE": 1917-1929

The Communist rulers' decision to leave the evangelicals alone was a serious miscalculation. The authorities not only failed to understand that the growth of the evangelicals would not necessarily undermine the Orthodox Church, they seriously underestimated how much growth would occur.

The Orthodox Church itself grew despite the persecution of the 1920s. Even a Soviet source recognized that "at least since 1923 there was felt a rise in religiosity across the whole country." Another Soviet source noted that in the first ten months of 1925, the increase in a number of religious communities was pronounced.[33]

But it was the growth of the evangelicals that forced the Communists to sit up and take notice. The evangelical Church grew from 107,000 in 1905 to 350,000 by 1921 and to 500,000 by 1929. These figures do not even include the Pentecostals, who by 1928 had grown to over 17,000.[34]

An interesting sidelight to the explosion of evangelical growth is the conversions which occurred during World War I in German prisoner-of-war camps. Through the mission society *Licht im Osten,* Russian New Testaments were distributed among Russian POWs on German soil. As a result, about two thousand soldiers brought back evangelical convictions to their native soil. I had an opportunity to witness the consequences of this firsthand when Peter Vashchenko, the leader of the Siberian Seven, told me his father had been converted in a World War I German POW camp.

There was no perceptible Pentecostal movement in the Soviet Union before the 1920s. The first Pentecostal missionary to the Soviet Union was Ivan Voronaev, a Russian Baptist preacher who had fled tsarist persecution and then converted to Pentecostal beliefs in New York City. He established a Russian Pentecostal congregation in New York, and then felt the call of God to be a missionary to his native land.[35]

The Voronaevs arrived in Odessa in 1921 in the midst of the terrible famine. Dead bodies were strewn throughout the streets awaiting the burial crews to cart them away. The missionary work went extremely well. By 1928 there were 350 Pentecostal churches with a membership of over seventeen thousand in the Odessa region and in Ukraine.

Pacifism was common among Russian Baptists and evangelical Christians, and at first the new Soviet government accommodated these believers. In 1919 the government permitted exemptions from military service for reasons of conscience, and more than forty thousand were eventually given permission not to serve.[36]

However, by the early 1920s it was clear that the "Golden Age" would have a few clouds. The Communist authorities became increasingly intolerant toward pacifists, and by the late 1920s, the pacifist exemption became a dead

letter. In 1926 both evangelical unions were compelled to condemn pacifism.[37] Under the intensifying pressure and the threat of prison, most evangelical groups abandoned or compromised their views on nonviolence over
the next several decades.

Between 1929 and 1935, the number of evangelicals declined dramatically (by about 50 percent) providing stark evidence of a sharp change in
Soviet policy. The evangelical upsurge had deeply disturbed the Party leaders.
Hopes that religion would quietly die out were proving unfounded. "Active"
opposition to evangelicals became the order of the day.

An important part of the spread of evangelical ideas was the printing of
religious literature and Bibles. But the printing of Bibles ended in 1927, and
twenty-nine years would pass before they were printed again on Soviet soil.[38]

THE NIGHTMARE YEARS: 1929-1939

Totalitarianism came to the Soviet Union at the end of the 1920s.
Following Lenin's death in 1924, Stalin cleverly eliminated virtually all of his
major rivals. He was now ready to force on the country an accelerated
industrialization plan aimed at making sure the Soviet Union would catch up
with the more advanced West. Furthermore, he intended to collectivize agriculture by force and to terrorize the population into absolute submission to the
State. The State was identified entirely with the will of Stalin, who spoke with
unquestioned authority for the Communist party. By the time the terror ended,
millions were dead.

The realization of a totalitarian vision requires the liquidation of independent or rival sources of authority. Thus, any religious group is in great danger
when a ruler begins to act with totalitarian intent.

One of Stalin's first acts of aggression against the Church was the April
1929 law dealing with religious cults. The alleged purpose of the law was to
provide the rules under which communities of twenty or more could become
legally recognized by the State. In fact, the law "served as the pretext for
closing most of the churches, arresting the ministers, and bringing evangelical
church life to a standstill."[39] According to the law: minors could not go to
church; special meetings could not be arranged for young people, children,
and women; church libraries were not permitted; individual churches were not
even allowed to give material assistance to their own.

The damage done to the Church between 1929 and 1943 was staggering.
An estimated 42,000 priests lost their lives between 1918 and 1940; most of
those perished in the 1930s. If a priest was lucky enough to beat the mortality
rates in Stalin's prisons (80-90 percent did not come out),[40] he had virtually
no chance of ever being a priest again. Massive church closings occurred. By
1933, 500 of Moscow's 600 churches had been closed. By 1941, 98 out of
every 100 Orthodox Churches was closed down.[41]

Orthodox and Protestant alike now felt the hard boot of the atheist State. Typical is the experience of the Pentecostal leader Ivan Voronaev. After enjoying dramatic growth in the 1920s and even publishing eight issues in 1928 of a Pentecostal periodical called *Evangelist,* his world came crashing down. After midnight one night in 1929 or 1930, Stalin's secret police barged in, searched his house, and took Ivan away. Voronaev was accused of being a spy for imperialist America, and the fact that he had received some financial support from the Assemblies of God and the Russian and East European Mission was used as evidence against him.

In 1933, Ivan's wife, Katherine, followed her husband into the camps of Siberia. Her release from the Gulag would have to wait for twenty-four years, until after the death of Stalin in 1953. Ivan never did come home. He was last seen in 1937. His life ended when he was placed in a cell with vicious dogs. He lies in an unknown Siberian grave.[42]

A woman who emigrated many years ago from the Soviet Union told me an incident from her childhood. Around 1939, when she was about ten years old, she overheard three construction workers at a building site in Kiev talking intently about theology. Though they were whispering, she soon won their confidence. They then proceeded to tell her about God and the Church. As it turned out all three had recently emerged from labor camps. Their last request to her has remained firmly embedded in her memory for fifty years. "Please, don't tell anyone what we talked to you about, or we will surely be sent back to the camps!" Tens of thousands of such stories haunt the Gulag.

AT WHAT PRICE SURVIVAL? THE TRAGEDY OF SERGY

The unsavory relationship between the acting patriarch of the Orthodox Church, Metropolitan Sergy, and the totalitarian rulers was becoming an even greater cause for bitterness. Though many have had nothing but contempt for Sergy, his plight was more tragic than treacherous. It is true that he deliberately lied to the world about the status of the Russian Orthodox Church. He told foreign correspondents in 1930 that there was no persecution of religion in the Soviet Union, and he repeated the assertion in his book *The Truth about Religion in Russia,* published during the war. (The book had little distribution in the USSR; it was intended for foreign consumption.)[43]

But Sergy had convinced himself that the survival of the Church depended on such lies. He told a priest who challenged his false statement that the authorities had written the statement for him. In addition, the authorities kept him under arrest for a week while threatening to arrest every remaining bishop and destroy the main church administration if he did not sign the document. Sergy felt he had no choice but to sign.[44]

One of Sergy's close associates offered the following explanation for the hierarchy's behavior:

The feasibility of putting the brakes on the destruction of the Church undertaken by the Bolsheviks was always the main concern of the patriarchate . . . we [were like] chickens in a shed, from which the cook snatches out her victim in turn. . . . For the sake of the Church we reconciled ourselves to our humiliating position, believing in her certain victory and trying somehow to preserve her for better times, for the downfall of Bolshevism.[45]

Sergy was gambling that his capitulation would purchase the survival of the Church. As the years passed, however, and the Church's survival was more and more in doubt, even Sergy realized that the painful concessions he had made had not pacified Stalin. Sergy lamented to a Russian priest in May 1941, "Formerly they used to strangle us, but at least they fulfilled their promises. Now they continue to strangle us, but they no longer fulfill the promises they give while strangling us."[46] It is bad enough to be slowly suffocated; it is worse when many of the faithful believe you have betrayed them as well.

We should not be too quick to judge those who have faced choices most of us will never have to make. But we also ought to be aware of the radically different response others have made to the Communist authorities. The Solovky bishops offered coexistence with the authorities, but not at the price of the betrayal of their most fundamental beliefs. Sergy was obsessed with maintaining the skeleton of the church, the administrative structure. But what is that worth if the living flesh of the body—the priests and the people—lose respect for the structure? The Solovky bishops had a different conception of the essence of the Church. If the State will not accept honorable coexistence, said the bishops, then the Church is ready to go on suffering.

Alexander Solzhenitsyn's advice to all who must deal with those who would shackle and enslave is: *"Never believe them, never fear them, never ask them for anything."* The courageous Russian Orthodox poet Irina Ratushinkaya, released on the eve of the Reagan/Gorbachev summit in October 1986, credits the survival of her spirit in labor camp to following Solzhenitsyn's advice.[47]

Notes

1. Much of the basic factual information on the Russian Orthodox Church in this and the next two chapters is taken from: Dmitry Pospielovsky, *The Russian Church under the Soviet Regime: 1917-1982*, 2 vols. (Crestwood, N.Y.: St. Vladimir's Seminary Press, 1984) and Jane Ellis, *The Russian Orthodox Church: A Contemporary History* (Bloomington: Indiana University Press, 1986). For information on the evangelicals I have relied on Hans Brandenburg, *The Meek and the Mighty* (London: Mowbrays, 1974) and Walter Sawatsky, *Soviet Evangelicals Since World War II* (Scottdale, Penn.: Herald Press, 1981). Particularly recommended to the reader as good, relatively short introductions to religion in the Soviet Union are the following: Trevor Beeson, *Discretion*

and Valour: Religious Conditions in Russia and Eastern Europe (London: Collins, Fount Paperback, 1982); Gerald Buss, *The Bear's Hug: Christian Belief and the Soviet State, 1917-86* (Grand Rapids, Mich.: Wm. B. Eerdmans Publishing Co., 1987); and the first 106 pages of Philip Walters, ed., *World Christianity: Eastern Europe* (Monrovia, Calif.: Missions Advanced Research and Communication Center, 1988).

2. Beeson, *Discretion and Valour*, 37. Beeson's statistics are based on an emigré church source who maintained close contacts with the Soviet Union during the years immediately following the Revolution.

3. Ellis, *Russian Orthodox Church*, 14. It is interesting that the Soviet journal *Nash Sovremenik* (Our Contemporary), in its December 1988 issue, printed a letter from a Vl. Soloukhin with the same information that Ellis reports on church closings.

4. *The Unknown Homeland*, quoted in Michael Bourdeaux, *Risen Indeed: Lessons in Faith from the USSR* (Crestwood, N.Y.: St. Vladimir's Seminary Press, 1983), 15-17. *The Unknown Homeland* was first published in English in 1978; the author is anonymous.

5. Quoted in Bourdeaux, *Risen Indeed*, 13.

6. For the sake of brevity and illustration, I will often talk of "Russian" matters. The Soviet Union, however, is made up of many nationalities (Ukrainian, Armenian, and Georgian, for example) which have religious traditions as old as or older than the traditions of the Russians. But since the Russians are the dominant group in both the modern pre-revolutionary Russian Empire and in the Soviet Union, frequently the focus will be on them.

7. Pospielovsky, *Russian Church*, 1:37.

8. Quoted in Beeson, *Discretion and Valor*, 34-35.

9. Ibid., 35.

10. Pospielovsky, *Russian Church*, 1:31-32.

11. Quoted in ibid., 1:37.

12. Ibid., 1:32.

13. Buss, *Bear's Hug*, 22.

14. Quoted in Pospielovsky, *Russian Church*, 1:94-95. Western historians have debated whether Stalin was an aberration in Soviet history, someone who radically departed from the course set by Marx and Lenin. Even if one concedes that Stalin was mentally unbalanced, a strong case can be made that there is far more continuity between the early Bolsheviks and Stalin than is often recognized. This is the thesis of Alexander Solzhenitsyn, and Lenin's comments in 1922 provide powerful evidence in support of that interpretation.

15. Ibid., 1:97-99. St. Petersburg had been renamed Petrograd during World War I.

16. Ibid., 1:53.

17. Ibid., 1:63.

18. Quoted in ibid., 1:106.

19. Quoted in ibid., 1:107.

20. Quoted in ibid., 1:106.

21. Ibid., 1:109-10.

22. Quoted in Mikhail Heller and Aleksandr Nekrich, *Utopia in Power: The History of the Soviet Union From 1917 to the Present*, (New York: Summit Books, 1986), 176.

23. Walters, *World Christianity*, 53.

24. Aleksandr I. Solzhenitsyn, *Gulag Archipelago Two: The Destructive Labor Camps, the Soul and Barbed Wire* (New York: Harper and Row, 1975), 25-70. Also see Vera Tolz, "Soviet Film Describes Birth of Gulag System," *Report on the USSR*, Radio Free Europe/Radio Liberty 1 (21 April 1989): 9-13. Tolz discusses a fascinating new Soviet film titled *Vlast' Solovetskaia* (Solovetsky Power), which is based largely on Solzhenitsyn's research.

25. Quoted in Solzhenitsyn, *Gulag Archipelago*, 52.

26. S. A. Malsagoff, *An Island Hell*. Reported by Solzhenitsyn, *Gulag Archipelago*, 59.

27. Tolz, "Soviet Film," 12.

28. Quoted in Pospielovsky, *Russian Church*, 1:144-45.

29. Quoted in ibid., 1:146.

30. Quoted in Sawatsky, *Soviet Evangelicals*, 35.

31. Ibid., 28.

32. Brandenburg, *The Meek and the Mighty*, 19-22.

33. Reported in Pospielovsky, *Russian Church*, 1:100.

34. Sawatsky, *Soviet Evangelicals*, 27, 39, 43.

35. Steve Durasoff, *Pentecost Behind the Iron Curtain* (Plainfield, N.J.: Logos International, 1972), 17-18.

36. Sawatsky, *Soviet Evangelicals*, 32, 115-16.

37. Ibid., 117.

38. Sawatsky, *Soviet Evangelicals*, 40.

39. Ibid., 46.

40. Pospielovsky, *Russian Church*, 1:177.

41. Ibid., 1:173-75. The statistic of 98 percent church closures is based on a comparison of the Russian Orthodox Church's report of 54,147 churches in 1914 (Ellis, p. 14) with Pospielovsky's evidence of no more than 1,200 Orthodox churches left open in 1941, not counting the newly annexed territories (Pospielovsky, p. 1:173-74).

42. Durasoff, *Pentecost Behind the Iron Curtain*, 20-22; Gordon William Carlson, "Russian Protestants and American Evangelicals Since the Death of Stalin: Patterns of Interaction and Response," (Ph.D. diss., University of Minnesota, 1986), 286. In 1960, at the age of seventy-three, Katherine Voronaev managed to emigrate to the United States where she spent the last five years of her life with her children and grandchildren. The account of Voronaev's death was told to me by Boris Perchatkin, a Pentecostal from Siberia who emigrated to the United States in July 1988. The account is based on reports of those who were in labor camp with Voronaev.

43. Pospielovsky, *Russian Church*, 1:187, 197.

44. Ibid., 1:166-67.

45. Quoted in ibid., 1:187-88.

46. Quoted in ibid., 1:191.

47. Irina Ratushinskaya, "En Route to the Gulag," *Commentary,* (September 1988):36. The selection from Ratushinskaya is taken from her book *Grey Is the Color of Hope* (New York: Knopf, 1988).

CHAPTER 7

WORLD WAR II
THROUGH KHRUSHCHEV

S talin must bear at least partial responsibility for the twenty million Soviet citizens who died in World War II. Stalin's purges were so sweeping that he wiped out most of his senior officer corps. In addition, he badly misread Hitler's intentions. When Hitler invaded in 1939, the USSR was not prepared for the onslaught. As terrible as the war was for the Soviet Union, it did compel Stalin to seek help from the very institution he intended to liquidate—the Church.

THE MERCIES OF WAR: THE CHURCH REVIVES

Ironically, the Soviet Union's own aggressive behavior provided the first reason to moderate the attack on the Church. As the Soviet army took over the Baltic states, western Ukraine, western Belorussia, Moldavia, and sections of eastern Finland, it acquired large Orthodox populations.[1]

Official Soviet statistics for 1941 report over forty-two hundred Orthodox Churches in the USSR, of which over three thousand were in the areas the Soviet Union took over in 1939 and 1940. Being in no position to attack these local churches, prudence demanded tolerance for the time being, and this had a positive effect on the Orthodox Church in the rest of the USSR.[2] There was a noticeable decline in Soviet antireligious propaganda when the war started.

Metropolitan Sergy sensed a golden opportunity for the Church to exert moral leadership and perhaps to gain some much-needed breathing room. On the very day the Nazis began their offensive against the Soviet Union, June 22, 1941, Sergy issued a patriotic appeal to the nation and the Church to defend their homeland. But Stalin was uncertain of Sergy's loyalty and forcibly had him put on a train for Ulianovsk, 450 miles east of Moscow. Not until the Germans were retreating in the summer of 1943 did Stalin allow

Sergy to return to Moscow. Stalin utilized another metropolitan, Nikolai, to do some of his dirty work in 1942.

In November 1942, Metropolitan Nikolai participated in the Soviet commission investigating ''German Crimes on the Occupied Territory.'' The Poles were pressing for information on what had happened to 15,000 Polish officers who disappeared in 1940. Nikolai dutifully signed his name to a document that blamed the Nazis for the murders of thousands of Polish officers. The bodies of more than 4,200 Polish officers were later discovered by the Nazis in the Katyn forest near Smolensk, when they occupied the area in 1941.[3]

During the period of *glasnost,* the Polish government published a 1945 Red Cross report which places the time of death for the 4,200-plus Polish officers as the spring of 1940, when the territory was still occupied by the Soviets. The officers were executed by bullets to the back of the head.[4] Sadly, once again the Russian Orthodox Church hierarchy had been used by the Communists to lie about what they were doing. The graves of the other ten thousand Polish officers have never been located.

Conditions improved for the Church during the war. On Easter night 1942 the authorities granted permission to hold candlelight processions. Sergy telegrammed Stalin in January 1943 requesting permission to collect funds for the national defense. Stalin agreed. Thus the Church was allowed to violate the legal prohibitions against charity by collecting money in its own name and depositing them in its own bank account to help the war effort. By October 1944, 150 million roubles had been collected.[5]

The big breakthrough for the Church occurred on September 4, 1943, when Stalin met with Sergy and three other metropolitans in his Kremlin office. That something was radically different was obvious when Sergy arrived from Ulianovsk the day before the meeting. Instead of being taken to his unpretentious wooden house, a government car took him to the luxurious home of the former German Ambassador.[6]

Stalin had decided to make a shift from a policy of virtual annihilation of the Church to that of co-optation. He found he desperately needed the Church's help because of the war. As a result of the meeting, which lasted from shortly after 9 P.M. until 3 A.M., Stalin agreed to open many churches and seminaries, and a Church Council was to be held to elect a patriarch (since one had not been formally elected since Tikhon's death in 1926). Four days later a council of nineteen bishops elected Sergy as patriarch. Although exact information is not available, Stalin may have eventually allowed as many as half the number of prerevolutionary Orthodox churches to reopen.[7]

The new relationship between Church and State was regulated by the Council for Russian Orthodox Church Affairs, created in 1943. In July 1944 a similar body—the Council for the Affairs of Religious Cults—was created to deal with the Protestants. These councils were combined in 1965 to form the Council for Religious Affairs, which continues to exist today.

Just eight months after his historic meeting with Stalin, Sergy died and was replaced by Aleksy, who served as patriarch until his death in 1971.

One final development deserves to be noted. During World War II a policy emerged whereby one person among the senior Orthodox hierarchy was assigned by the Kremlin the task of maintaining the "foreign policy" portfolio of the Church. This was the person with whom the authorities maintained closest contact, in whom they had the greatest trust, and who would invariably parrot the Kremlin foreign policy line abroad or with foreign visitors.

During the last years of Sergy's life, Metropolitan Nikolai carried out this function in part. But under Patriarch Aleksy, the division of labor became more pronounced. Not surprisingly, it was Nikolai who became the head of the Department of External Ecclesiastical Relations. An example of how the Soviets intended to use their patriarchal foreign policy contact emerged in late May 1945. Patriarch Aleksy traveled to the Middle East with Nikolai "to impress the noncommunist world that the Russian Church was a genuine and 'free' institution, i.e., that the Soviet state had changed for the better and that all anticommunist propaganda in this respect was grossly exaggerated."[8]

In the fall of 1944, the All-Union Council of Evangelical Christians-Baptists (AUCECB) was formed.[9] Though the results of the unity congress pleased the Evangelical Christians and Baptists who participated, the Soviet State was also certain that it had something to gain. The State, therefore, had provided the transportation to bring the forty-five delegates to the meeting, and then had taken care of all food and housing costs.

Like the Orthodox, the Protestants who cooperated with the authorities felt obliged to do homage to Stalin. The unity congress dutifully sent a telegram to Stalin thanking him for taking care of the needs of Christians.[10]

In August 1945 the Pentecostals were forced to join the AUCECB and to agree that no tongue-speaking would occur at their general meetings. In short, they had to give up their main theological distinctive. Though many of them would soon leave the AUCECB, in 1945 an estimated four hundred congregations of Pentecostals with a total membership of twenty-five thousand joined the newly formed union.

CHURCH AND STATE: 1945-1959

By 1947 any hopes that the hiatus in state-sponsored antireligious propaganda might continue permanently were dashed. The Communist youth paper *Komsomol Pravda* declared it was impossible to be both a Komsomol member and a believer. The main teacher's newspaper attacked the notion that there could be a nonreligious education, insisting that education had to be vigorously antireligious.[11]

After the war, a more sinister use of the Orthodox Church was hatched in the Kremlin. The Church would be used in the front lines of a "peace offensive" aimed at the West. Moscow's chief concern was the substantial lead the United States had in military power, especially in nuclear weapons.

Few pages in the history of the Church's subservience to the Soviet authorities can compare with the role the Orthodox Church played in the peace initiatives. At the first USSR Conference for Peace held in August 1949, Metropolitan Nikolai called the United States "the rabid fornicatress of resurrected Babylon . . . [who] is trying to seduce the people of the world while pushing them toward war."[12] The wartime alliance between the United States and the Soviet Union was obviously breaking up.

Subtlety was not one of Nikolai's virtues as he trumpeted in the name of the Russian Orthodox Church the crude propaganda of the puppetmaster. During the Korean War, for example, he made the following observations:

No sooner had they begun their criminal aggression than the American neo-fascists began the planned, cannibalistic extermination of the "inferior" Korean race.

[They perform] executions without trial . . . held in secret . . . they cut off ears, noses, and breasts, gouge out eyes, break arms and legs, crucify patriots, bury women and infants alive . . . they scalp Korean patriots for "souvenirs."

The American criminals first of all slaughtered political prisoners (from 200,000 to 400,000 people), forcing them to dig their own graves beforehand. . . .

Under the pretext of affording them medical aid, American scientists and doctors experiment on the prisoners with the latest vaccines and chemical preparations. Every night executions take place. . . . First on the list are the intelligentsia of Korea: doctors, teachers, engineers, technicians, agronomists. . . .[13]

It's as if Nikolai anticipated Solzhenitsyn's revelations about Stalin or the bloody atrocities of the Khmer Rouge in Cambodia, then substituted the United States for the true perpetrators of the crimes.

The Russian Orthodox Church had only the highest praise for the Soviet Union's own leaders. On Stalin's seventieth birthday, December 21, 1949, Patriarch Aleksy had the following to say about one of the greatest mass murderers of all time:

Stalin is the first amongst the fighters for peace among all the nations of the world . . . he is our leader, whose charming personality disarms any who have met him by his kindness and attentiveness to everybody's needs . . . by the power and wisdom of his speech.[14]

People who made much milder statements about Stalin are now, during the *glasnost* era, routinely pilloried in the Soviet press.

If only the first impulse that grips us when confronted with apparently black and white judgments were correct. Alas, reality is often more complicated and more tragic. Even Nikolai, the crude propagandist for Stalin, had another side. William Fletcher's book on Nikolai, published in 1968, reveals that Russian believers were fond of his moving sermons and considered his propagandist work a necessary evil. In contrast to the 1920s and early 1930s, when parishioners rebuked clerics for simply praying for the Soviet rulers, the parishioners were now silent. As Pospielovsky puts it, "The lie has become an accepted part of life!"[15]

To be sure, many Russian Orthodox faithful disagreed that the lies were justified. To lie and practice religious piety simultaneously requires strenuous mental and spiritual gymnastics, though it is far less rare than we might like to admit. However, it is not easy to maintain a sense of right and wrong in the process.

Strong statements of support for the Communist government were not confined to the Orthodox Church. Registered leaders of the All-Union Council of Evangelical Christians-Baptists (AUCECB) cooperated as well. In 1947, Jacob Zhidkov, one of the main leaders of the Baptists, wrote in their official journal, *Fraternal Messenger*: "God not only established but also strengthened the Soviet state. As a result the Soviet land became the chief of all freedom-loving peoples in its unceasing struggle for peace, for social and political justice."[16]

That same year Zhidkov lied about the state of religious freedom in the Soviet Union: "Evangelical Christians-Baptists have full freedom, not only for their divine services but also to conduct the necessary activities embracing all aspects of our religious life."[17] In recent years Jacob's son Michael has continued in his father's footsteps by asserting that foreign reports which question the religious freedom of the Soviet Union are false.[18]

Soviet writers under *glasnost* now acknowledge that not only was the notion of religious freedom inaccurate, but the very legislation on religious cults that the AUCECB had to agree to abide by bound the Church hand and foot.[19]

The evangelicals experienced a revival in the months following the end of World War II, but within a couple of years the horizon clouded with an impending new Stalin crackdown on religion. Stalin's last five years were difficult ones for evangelicals. Between 1948 and 1953 there were almost no contacts with foreigners, and unregistered believers often received twenty-five-year sentences for allegedly violating Article 58 of the criminal code—"anti-soviet" slander.

Though we associate the post-Stalin period with a bit of a thaw, it did not start immediately. The months following Stalin's death in March 1953 were filled with a renewed assault against religion. In August 1954 a new periodical was announced, *Science and Religion,* which was to lead the offensive against religious belief. Plans for the journal were later temporarily shelved, and Khrushchev signed a Central Committee resolution criticizing administrative interference in the affairs of religious groups. Also, Khrushchev reduced some of the twenty-five-year sentences to eight.[20] The new journal would have to await publication until 1959, the beginning of the Khrushchev attack on the Church.

By the mid-1950s the evangelicals were still growing at an impressive rate, even if the statistics given by the registered leaders are somewhat high. Jacob Zhidkov claimed for the AUCECB 12,000 baptisms and a total of 512,000 members (5,400 congregations) for the year 1954.[21]

Zhidkov would often contrast the religious freedom available to the evangelicals under the Communists with that which had been available under the tsars. Walter Sawatsky's response to this assertion is judicious: ''It would be more accurate to say they had enough freedom to continue to exist, yet enough difficulties to ensure that the emerging church was a church of the highly committed only.''[22]

Many who have been upset that the plight of unregistered Christians gets far too little attention by Western Christians have implied that only the unregistered have suffered. It is more a question of degree. True, the underground Baptist or Pentecostal has frequently endured harsh persecution: labor camp sentences, fines, stays in psychiatric hospitals, services forcibly broken up. But the registered have made sacrifices just to belong publicly to a registered church. To be identified even with a legal religious association means certain discrimination at work (there will be few, if any, promotions) and in the schools (universities will likely be closed to believers). The standard of living that a registered believer can provide his wife and children will probably be considerably less than what he might be able to give them were he not associated with the Church. Registered Christian parents know it will not be easy for their children in public schools, which are openly antagonistic to religious belief.

How many Western Christians would pay the price registered believers routinely face, let alone the often much greater price the catacomb Christians must pay?

KHRUSHCHEV'S ASSAULT ON THE CHURCH: 1959-1964

The Soviet state is by nature irritable. Any foreign body sets up in it an intolerable itch which sooner or later must be relieved by a violent scratch.[23]

So suggested Harry Willetts in explaining why Soviet policy so often has reverted to oppression. By any standards, what happened in the Soviet Union between 1959 and 1964 was a "violent scratch." Over half of the evangelical churches were closed. Of the 20,000 to 25,000 Orthodox Churches functioning on the eve of the crackdown, less than 8,000 were still open in 1965. Most have remained closed even during the period of Gorbachev's *glasnost.* Of ninety Orthodox monasteries functioning around 1955, only seventeen or eighteen were left by 1965.[24]

The Soviets used a variety of excuses for closing down the churches. In western Ukraine, church reopenings that had occurred under the Nazis were declared illegal. Churches were declared historical monuments, too close to a school, a hindrance to traffic, or in need of repair. (However, permission to repair the churches was routinely denied.)[25]

Many are shocked to learn that in the 1960s, well after the Stalin horrors had supposedly passed, a new wave of violent suppression occurred. A decision was made at the highest levels, and the assault on believers in the press and the schools followed soon after. The legal code was changed to make it even easier to incriminate believers. This campaign was well organized and directed from Moscow. The person behind it was Nikita Khrushchev, reputed to be liberal by Soviet standards and the man who had delivered a secret speech at the XX Party Congress in 1956 denouncing some of Stalin's actions.

The attack on the Church went well beyond an intensification of atheist propaganda; it included a physically violent campaign against the Church and its members. Some children were forcibly taken from their parents because a religious upbringing was allegedly causing them psychological damage. That mothers and fathers might be "deprived of parental rights," as the Soviet legal papers put it, is not surprising when Khrushchev's top ideologue in the antireligious campaign was saying as late as January 1964:

> The facts show that it is the family which is the main center of maintaining the religious spirit. . . . We cannot accept that blind and ignorant people raise their children in their own image and deform them. . . .

> We cannot and we shall not remain indifferent to the fate of children on whom their parents—fanatical believers—in reality commit an act of spiritual violence. We are not indifferent to the fact that, in the Soviet society, a family is a cell of communist education or a refuge of backward conceptions.[26]

While church meetings were brutally broken up, Orthodox monasteries were also targeted for violent "administrative" measures. Pilgrims on the way to the Pochaev monastery in Ukraine were attacked en masse by the police. Women in the group were raped. One young woman, who had taken her vows of chastity and often attended services at the monastery, was dragged from her home by the police, raped, then dragged up to her own attic and thrown out the window. She died a few hours later. Several monks were forcibly committed to a mental hospital, and one died two months later. Another monk died during interrogation. His body, returned to his parents, exhibited signs of severe torture.[27]

In the western Siberian town of Kalunda, Nikolai Khmara, a recent convert from a life of drunkenness, was arrested and sentenced to prison for his activities in an unregistered congregation. Since becoming a Christian, Nikolai had become a fine family man and a strong member of the church. Just two weeks after his trial, his family was informed that he had died in prison. Though they were told not to, the Kalunda Christians opened Nikolai's coffin and discovered his badly mutilated body. His tongue had been torn out, as had his fingernails and toenails; his body was covered with burns. Fellow prisoners later reported that his tormentors had finally ripped out his tongue because he would not stop talking about Christ.[28]

The authorities subjected believers to vicious attacks in the press as well. In one 1960 example of slander, monks were charged with raping female pilgrims, and mass secret abortions were allegedly performed in monasteries to hide the illicit sexual liaisons of the nuns and monks.[29]

The leaders of the Orthodox Church showed more courage in dealing with the vigorous assault on religion than did the leaders of AUCECB. Patriarch Aleksy wrote several letters to Khrushchev protesting the persecutions and requesting a personal audience with him. He did not get a response. But what showed particular courage was Aleksy's public pronouncement in February 1960 at a Conference of the Soviet Public for Disarmament. After listing all the wonderful things the Church had given to Russia, the patriarch stated:

> Yet, despite all this, Christ's Church, whose very aim is human well-being, is suffering insults and attacks from humans. . . . Jesus Christ himself predicted indestructibility of the Church when he said: "The gates of hell will not overcome the *Church*."[30]

The patriarch's uncharacteristic and unexpected comments unleashed a barrage of verbal attacks. "You want to assure us that the whole Russian culture has been created by the Church . . . this is not true!" shouted a member of the audience.

The great irony is that it was Metropolitan Nikolai, the sycophant to the Kremlin on foreign policy, who had written the patriarch's speech. Pospielovsky believes this is probably the reason Nikolai was forced to retire as head of the Church's Department of External Ecclesiastical Relations. Also a factor in his falling out with the Soviet overlords was a collection of his unpublished sermons which responded strongly to atheist attacks on religion.[31] Such is the mystery of life that within the same breast can beat both the heart of a coward and of a man of courage.

By the end of 1960, Patriarch Aleksy had no more energy to resist, and he quietly submitted to what was expected of him. In July 1961 he helped force on the Church changes in its statutes which stripped the individual priest of administrative authority over his parish. Local power was now in the hands of an executive committee of three from the parish community. The Soviets had insisted on this, certain that it would make it easier to have their way with the churches. They were right. Fortunately, religious *perestroika* in the Gorbachev era is allowing the restoration of local administrative authority to the individual priest.

Schism among the Evangelicals

The conduct of the AUCECB during the Khrushchev era was anything but courageous. The leadership was so timid and capitulatory that a major split occurred within its ranks—a split which survives to this day.

To avoid confrontation with the secular authorities, the AUCECB revised their church statutes to bring them into conformity with the 1929 law on religious cults. In the summer of 1960 the senior Protestant leaders sent these revised statutes and a "Letter of Instruction" to their senior presbyters. The letter does not reflect evangelical convictions. It forbids children to attend church services and makes reference to "unhealthy missionary tendencies." One wonders what had happened to Christ's commandment "to go into all the world and make disciples," for registered AUCECB leaders assert: "*the chief goal of religious services at the present time is not the attraction of new members but satisfaction of the spiritual needs of believers.*" [my emphasis]

The decidedly unevangelical AUCECB letter also observes:

> In the past, due to insufficient knowledge of Soviet legislation on cults, certain of our congregations have violated it. There have been occasions of baptizing persons younger than 18 years, giving material aid from the congregation's treasury, holding biblical and other meetings of a specialist character, permitting declarations of poetry, there were excursions for believing youth, financial accounts for mutual aid were created, meetings for preachers and for training choir leaders were held. . . . All this must now be eliminated in our congregations and our activities must be conducted in agreement with existing legislation.[32]

Tens of thousands of registered Protestants felt betrayed by their leaders.

Within a year, the rebellion among the membership resulted in a delegation delivering a letter condemning both the new church statutes and the "Letter of Instruction." The protesters called themselves the Initiative Group (*Initsiativniki*). They called on the AUCECB leaders to repent and summon a congress to elect new leaders and write new church statutes. The Baptist leaders responded that they could never get Soviet permission to hold a new congress.

Within two weeks, the Initiative Group wrote all AUCECB congregations describing what had happened and calling on all to rededicate themselves to Christian holiness. Sawatsky estimates that at this point about half of the AUCECB supported the Initiative Group.

During the early 1960s believers found themselves restricted not only by the very limiting 1929 rules but also by secret guidelines never made public. The councils (there were still two until the end of 1965) that controlled the Orthodox and the Protestants would give church leaders verbal instructions which were often not part of any written, formally-declared government policy.

Those who protested were frequently arrested. The early leader of the Initiative Group, A. F. Prokofiev, was taken into custody in May 1962 and given a five-year sentence plus five years in exile. Boris Zdorovets was also incarcerated, leaving Gennadi Kriuchkov and Georgi Vins as the main leaders of the reformers.

In 1963 the AUCECB managed to gain permission from the Soviets to hold a conference, which once convened became a congress. The 1960 church statutes were rejected and declared but a ''proposal.'' However, by this time the schism had gone too far to bring back many who were still furious with the leaders' earlier actions. The bitterness spawned by this schism continues to the present, even among groups outside the Soviet Union.

The Soviets' decision to back off from the harshest demands of 1960 may have been motivated by a desire to avert the AUCECB losing most of its membership. Soviet authorities have always feared the underground churches because they have no agreements with them which can restrict believer activities. Better to make a few concessions from time to time to those who will register than risk losing any hold over them. The Initiative Group's adamant refusal to be cowed by the authorities, either Soviet or ecclesiastical, may have provided the incentive for the Communist rulers to ease up on the registered groups.

The Initiative Group was amazingly bold. When they could not make satisfactory progress with the AUCECB, they appealed directly to the Soviet authorities for clarification of the laws which governed believers. Chairman Puzin of the Council for the Affairs of Religious Cults talked to them but did not mention the secret 1962 revisions to the 1929 religious sect laws. It was later discovered that in June 1964, Puzin reported to a government group that investigations had confirmed the allegations of the Initiative Group that local officials had dealt improperly with believers.

In September 1965 the Initiative Group transformed itself into a new and independent organization called the Council of Churches of the Evangelical Christians-Baptists (CCECB). It still exists today.

With the removal of Khrushchev in October 1964 and the sacking of his chief antireligious ideologue, hopes ran high that conditions would improve for believers.

AN APPRAISAL OF THE KHRUSHCHEV PERSECUTION

Two factors may help explain why Khrushchev launched his antireligious offensive. First, the post-Stalin Communist leaders' objections to Stalin's tyranny did not include disagreement with his fundamental hostility to religion. These leaders recognized the great dangers in a "cult of personality," not the least being the threat to their own lives. But Stalin's shortcomings did not alter their own fidelity to classical Marxist notions on religion.

Second, Soviet leaders had to face a reality that Karl Marx never did— they had to contend with religious belief which refused to wither away. We don't know what Marx would have done under such circumstances. Would he have revised his views of human nature, given the evidence that there was something to religious consciousness besides unmet economic needs? We don't know, of course. But we do know that Marxist states have often succumbed to the temptation to force the decline of religion when it refuses to disappear on its own.

At the end of the Khrushchev era the upper echelons of the Party conducted an evaluation of the antireligious campaign. "Their general conclusion," according to Pospielovsky, "was that it had not paid off."[33] The Church had survived, though much of it had been driven underground—a situation potentially more dangerous to the regime than if the Church were above ground and on a leash.

Soviet self-criticism of past religious practices did not begin with Gorbachev. The Central Committee of the Communist party released a declaration in November 1964 titled "On Errors Committed in the Conduct of Atheist Propaganda." This document followed a pattern seen in the 1920s, 1930, and 1954—after every major period of antireligious activity by the State, official condemnations of "excesses" were lodged. The 1964 declaration insists there ought not to be administrative interference in the life of the Church.

In August 1965, the chairman of the Council for Affairs of Religious Cults acknowledged:

> The grossest and most widespread administrative measures that have been taken against believers are the closure of prayer houses, refusal to register religious communities . . . breaking up prayer meetings of believers forcibly with police and auxiliary police, arbitrary searches of believers' homes and prayer houses, confiscation of religious literature, illegal arrests of believers. . . .[34]

This frank admission is almost as strong as what is being said during the *glasnost* period. But the level of contrition was not matched by actions. Most of the churches closed under Khrushchev remain closed under his successors. The laws written to imprison and intimidate believers were not only left on the books but often utilized. And though there was less physical violence against believers, hostility continued in countless ways throughout the next two decades.

One important difference between the 1965 admission of past wrong-doing and the admission at the end of the 1980s is that the latter has been made public. Millions of people, not only in the Soviet Union but also in the West, have read the *glasnost*-era confessions of past misconduct.

SOVIET CHURCHMEN AND THE TRUTH ABOUT PERSECUTION

At the very time Soviet persecution was at its height, registered Church leaders, both Protestant and Orthodox, were telling the World Council of Churches and other international Church bodies that there were no serious problems with religious freedom in the Soviet Union. Many in the West were impressed with the liberality of the Soviet decision to allow the Russian Orthodox Church (1961) and the AUCECB (1962) to join the World Council of Churches and attend international ecumenical or denominational meetings.[35] They were inclined to accept the Soviet Churchmen's assurances about religious freedom.

One of the strongest statements denouncing this misinformation was made by Georgi Vins on Capitol Hill. In his June 1979 testimony before the Commission on Security and Cooperation in Europe, Vins, a leader of the Baptist group which broke away from the official Church union during the Khrushchev persecution, protested:

> The All-Union Council [of Evangelical Christians-Baptists], that is, the leadership, is a body linked in the closest possible way with the state authorities, including the KGB. Its prescribed role is to act as a screen for religious freedom in the USSR. Representatives of the All-Union Council travel widely throughout the whole world proclaiming the imaginary religious freedom in the USSR. They perform the same role inside the country when they receive foreign religious organizations and maintain correspondence with them.

Vins manifests no interest in possible explanations for the registered leaders' conduct. By omission, he even denies them the cover of good intentions. Such strong feelings reflect the bitter knowledge that even while he testified, many of his fellow unregistered Baptists were sitting in prisons while the registered Baptist leaders continued to assure foreigners that there is religious freedom.

Although it is important to understand why Vins and other unregistered Baptists are so angry with the registered Church leaders, it is also essential to understand better who these registered leaders are. In Sawatsky's view,

In general these were men whose actions and statements on behalf of the Soviet state caused suspicion yet whose spiritual and pastoral qualities are equally striking. These contradictory qualities remind one of Metropolitan Nikolai and his successor Metropolitan Nikodim.[36]

All three of the major AUCECB leaders in 1960 had experienced prison or exile under Stalin. Alexander Karev, the much-loved general secretary of the AUCECB, had spent eight years in exile. Ilia Ivanov, who replaced Zhidkov as president of the AUCECB in 1960, displayed considerable timidity toward the State during his fourteen years in that office. Sawatsky suggests some factors that may have contributed to Ivanov's unusually docile relationship with the State:

> Perhaps he had experienced especially severe prison conditions, perhaps he was especially susceptible to pain, perhaps the authorities were able to blackmail him, or perhaps he truly felt that Romans 13 demanded full submission to state authorities. That must remain speculation, but what is more apparent is that as a church leader he was one of the first to tremble before the authorities.[37]

Jacob Zhidkov is the most fascinating of the three AUCECB leaders. Between 1938 and 1942 he was either in prison or in exile. In 1955 he became one of the vice-presidents of the Baptist World Alliance. Though he faithfully stayed to the script dictated by the Soviet authorities when meeting with foreigners, he felt remorse over his role in the events of 1960 when the AUCECB caved in to pressure from the government. In 1966, Zhidkov left his sick bed long enough to attend the registered Protestant union congress. He told the delegates that he had begged God to be allowed to live long enough to plead with members of the congress to forgive him for the part he played in issuing the 1960 Church statutes and the accompanying "Letter of Instructions." He died three weeks later.[38]

But questions of motives aside, the central point in Vins's 1979 testimony is beyond doubt: the Kremlin has perceived the registered Church leaders, both Orthodox and Protestant, as a primary means of misinforming the West about the true state of churches in the Soviet Union.

Even during this early period of officially-allowed contacts with Western co-religionists, the traffic back and forth was considerable. At the AUCECB Congress in 1963, registered evangelical leaders reported that between 1957 and 1963 nearly five thousand foreign guests were entertained in Moscow.[39] These guests were told that religious freedom is not a serious problem and those in prison are there for breaking laws, not for their religious convictions. (No mention was made that the laws themselves conflict with religious convictions.)

The first half of the 1960s witnessed a masterful coup in Soviet disinformation. The Soviet authorities managed simultaneously to crack down on religion at home and to score public relations points abroad for their religious tolerance in letting registered Soviet leaders travel abroad.

The Orthodox pointman for Soviet propaganda about religion during the Khrushchev campaign was Nikodim.[40] He was just thirty-one when he became the head of the Department of External Ecclesiastical Relations in 1960, following Nikolai's demise in the wake of his mild protest at the Kremlin. Nikodim later became bishop, archbishop, and finally the Metropolitan of Leningrad. Though Nikodim articulated the Party line on foreign policy and "religious freedom," he must be seen as a complex figure. He had become a Christian as a teenager and had grown up amidst the stark realities of a society dominated by an antireligious government.

Whatever the justification (or lack of it) for the disinformation Nikodim spread at international Church meetings, the naivete and gullibility of his Western listeners is even more disconcerting. Pospielovsky once asked Nikodim about the false statements that he and other Russian bishops made in public; Nikodim replied with a "sad smile":

> It is you in the West who react so readily to untrue statements. . . .
> The Soviet public has got used to them. . . . I am not saying that this
> is good or bad, I am merely stating the fact that what shocks you here
> does not evoke a similar response in our country.[41]

There are two problems with a lie. The first is in telling it; the second is in believing it when we ought to know better. In the case of Soviet religious propaganda, the telling has frequently been the product of considerable outside pressure; the believing has all too often been the result of ignorance and laziness.

Notes

1. Although chronologically the histories of the Baltic peoples and western Ukraine have been inextricably mixed with the Soviet Union since the war, discussion of the Baltic denominations, as well as the Ukrainian Catholic and Orthodox Churches, will be deferred until the next chapter.

2. Dmitry Pospielovsky, *The Russian Church Under the Soviet Regime: 1917-1982*, 2 vols. (Crestwood, N.Y.: St. Vladimir's Press, 1984), 1:193-94.

3. For a good summary of the controversy of the Katyn massacre, see Mikhail Heller and Aleksandr Nekrich, *Utopia in Power: The History of the Soviet Union from 1917 to the Present,*(New York: Summit Books, 1986), 403-7; for Metropolitan Nikolai's involvement in the Soviet cover-up, see Pospielovsky, *Russian Church*, 1:197.

4. Jackson Diehl, "Exhuming a Massacre," *Washington Post,* 17 February 1989.

5. Pospielovsky, *Russian Church*, 1:200.

6. Ibid., 1:201.

7. Gerald Buss, *The Bear's Hug: Christian Belief and the Soviet State, 1917-86* (Grand Rapids, Mich.: Wm. B. Eerdmans Publishing Co., 1987), 36.

8. Pospielovsky, *Russian Church*, 1:219.

9. Most basic factual material related to Soviet evangelicals since 1944, unless otherwise indicated, is taken from Walter Sawatsky's excellent and detailed study. Walter Sawatsky, *Soviet Evangelicals Since World War II* 114 (Scottdale, Penn.: Herald Press, 1981).

10. Ibid., 85.

11. Pospielovsky, *Russian Church*, 1:316.

12. Quoted in ibid., 2:313.

13. Quoted in ibid.

14. Quoted in Buss, *Bear's Hug*, 35-36.

15. Pospielovsky, *Russian Church*, 1:318.

16. Quoted in Sawatsky, *Soviet Evangelicals*, 105.

17. Quoted in ibid.

18. Ibid., 107.

19. See chapter 13, "Religion in the Public Square," particularly the discussion of the interview with Kharchev in the December 1988 issue of *Ogonek*.

20. Sawatsky, *Soviet Evangelicals*, 63-65.

21. Ibid., 67.

22. Ibid., 71.

23. Harry Willetts, quoted in ibid., 132.

24. Pospielovsky, *Russian Church*, 2:343, 349; Sawatsky, *Soviet Evangelicals*, 131-32.

25. Sawatsky, *Soviet Evangelicals*, 138.

26. N. Il'ichev, quoted in *Communism and Christianity in Theory and Practice: Doctrines/Facts/Conclusions* (United Kingdom: Aid to the Church in Need, 1978), 12.

27. Pospielovsky, *Russian Church*, 2:345.

28. Sawatsky, *Soviet Evangelicals*, 143. For a full account of these events, see Anita and Peter Deyneka, Jr., *A Song in Siberia* (Elgin, Ill.: David C. Cook, 1977).

29. Pospielovsky, *Russian Church*, 2:345.

30. Quoted in ibid., 1:335.

31. Ibid., 2:335.

32. Quoted in Sawatsky, *Soviet Evangelicals*, 115 139.

33. Pospielovsky, *Russian Church*, 2:358.

34. Quoted in Sawatsky, *Soviet Evangelicals*, 131.

35. Also allowed to join the World Council of Churches in 1962 from the Soviet Union were the Armenian Orthodox Church, the Georgian Orthodox Church, and the Evangelical Lutherans of Latvia and Estonia. All the Soviet delegates have consistently voted together to block any serious criticism of the Soviet Union or her religious policies.

36. Sawatsky, *Soviet Evangelicals*, 180.

37. Ibid., 181.

38. Ibid., 200.

39. Ibid., 205.

40. For more information on Nikodim, see Pospielovsky, *Russian Church*, 2:359-63.

41. Quoted in ibid., 2:361.

CHAPTER 8

BREZHNEV
TO GORBACHEV

No story better epitomizes the hopes, dilemmas, and tragedies of the Christian Church in a hostile atheist sea than that of Father Dmitry Dudko. Anyone harboring illusions that persecution was confined to Lenin or to Stalin or to Khrushchev will discover in Dudko's wrenching biography evidence that persecution has lasted right into the 1980s, to the very threshold of Gorbachev's rise to power. Nor did Dudko's international reputation save him from the humiliating and degrading treatment he was to receive at the hands of the State. The fate of the thousands unknown to the West has often been much worse.

THE TRAGEDY OF FATHER DUDKO

Father Dudko was in his late thirties when he was ordained a priest in 1960.[1] He had already endured more than eight-and-a-half years in labor camp under Stalin for having had in his possession religious poetry. He began to attract attention in the early 1960s because of his unusually warm and effective ministry at the Church of St. Nicholas in Moscow. Natalia Solzhenitsyn described why people from all over Moscow came to his services and sought contact with him:

> After every encounter with him you are left with the feeling: how deep and joyful is his faith! He is a man of surprising integrity and simplicity, and his preaching finds a direct and accurate path to a person's heart.[2]

It was inevitable that such a successful pastor would disturb the Communist authorities. In September 1972 Dudko was told that he was going to be stripped of his parish. In untypical fashion, the next Sunday he informed his congregation of his impending dismissal, asked for their help, and even expressed the likelihood that there were people present (informers) to disturb the internal affairs of the church. The authorities delayed following through on their threat.

Father Dudko is best known for the remarkable discussion sessions he held at his church beginning in December 1973. They were typically held after the Saturday evening service. His purpose was to give people an opportunity to ask questions about theology, the Church, and faith. Questions were written out, and the questioners were not required to sign their names.

The response to these sessions was electric. Raised in an atheist society, with little religious literature available, people were starved to hear what a man of God had to say about the atheist notions with which they were constantly deluged. Dudko became a highly skilled and effective apologist of Christian truths to both religious and secular attenders of his discussions. Youth in particular were drawn to the dynamic priest. By early 1974, his conversations were known throughout Moscow and beyond.[3]

But a better way to gain insight into how his activities were perceived by the authorities is to read "The Furov Report." This paper was prepared for the Communist Party Central Committee in 1975 by V. Furov, a deputy chairman of the Council for Religious Affairs (CRA).[4] The document reached the West in the late 1970s and confirmed in graphic detail the concerted efforts by the CRA to control and co-opt the Russian Orthodox Church. One of the most revealing and sinister sections of the Furov report is a lengthy passage about Dudko.

Dudko is identified as one of those clergy who have "been imprisoned for various crimes. They concealed their hostility toward the Soviet government and now they exploit religious organizations in order to incite distrust and antagonism toward atheists and toward our socialist government."[5] He is specifically charged in the report with making appeals "for a struggle against godlessness which he identified with the Soviet government." All of these allegations relate to the pre-1956 period, before he was released from prison.

And what is his crime in the more recent period? According to Furov, "he continued to write libelous materials and preach slanderous sermons, train young people in dangerous ideology, and collect and disseminate *samizdat* and other literature from abroad."[6]

Dudko, the report contends, has been warned about his "antisocial activity" and his ideological work with young people; but he has refused to change his behavior. As evidence against the priest, the report quotes from his April 20, 1974 sermon.

> Atheists are taking advantage of our fear of suffering. They oppress our spirit, our free thoughts and feelings. They abuse us. We must overcome our fear of suffering and then we shall be truly free, vital, active, and invincible. . . .

We must become Christian brethren to students expelled for their religious belief from colleges. We must become brethren in Christ to those who lost their jobs and are oppressed by scores of persecutors. . . . Now is the time when encouragement is needed. One must cry out loud about the danger. People are perishing.

. . . We must fear godlessness as the most dreaded plague. . . . I think that whoever tears man away from his faith, from his belief in God is committing sin. We must remember that to believe is to struggle. Christians cannot, and must not, stand on the sidelines when everything around is perishing.[7]

It is revealing that the passages quoted by the Council for Religious Affairs do not refer to political matters but to Dudko's undermining of atheism. In subsequent public accusations against Dudko, the authorities take issue with his "political" views and his connections with the West, not his religious views. In fact, it is clear that the Soviet definition of "political" includes expressing religious views that oppose atheism.

The CRA reports that with the cooperation of Patriarch Pimen, Father Dudko was transferred to the Moscow suburbs. Further, Dudko signed a pledge to avoid sermon topics which might be interpreted as political.[8] Furov is particularly irritated that a report about the sermon quoted above appeared in a Russian newspaper in the United States.

The discussion of Dudko ends with the following assurances to the Communist Party Central Committee: "Thus, with the assistance of the loyal hierarchy in the church it was possible to dismiss Dudko from the staff of Moscow clergy. In his new post he has not expressed thus far his anti-Soviet views."[9]

In fact, the patriarch had been enlisted by the authorities in May 1974 to prohibit Dudko from preaching at the church in Moscow. In September he was transferred to the village of Kobanovo, fifty miles out of Moscow. However, Father Dudko continued to attract more and more people to the Church. A decision was made to deal with Dudko more forcibly. In March 1975 he was involved in a serious and suspicious accident, which left him with two broken legs. The militia refused to go to the scene of the accident, and no charges were filed.

In April 1977, the authorities launched their next missile at the pesky priest—two issues of the nationally prominent journal *Literary Gazette* contained attacks not only on Dudko, but on three other prominent Orthodox figures: Gleb Yakunin, Lev Regelson, and Alexander Ogorodnikov. On April 27, the four gathered at Dudko's Moscow apartment to protest to the Western press that the allegations of "anti-Soviet" slander were absolutely false.

At the end of the year the Church hierarchy once again responded to an order from the CRA and dismissed Dudko from his parish. His congregation protested vigorously, but to no avail. His new parish, in Grebnevo, was a full two hours from Moscow.

By this time the outside world had become aware of the actions taken against Father Dudko. To their credit, the World Council of Churches raised questions with the authorities›about him.[10]

Next the authorities sought to frighten Dudko by going after one of his three children. Mikhail, just seventeen years old, was subjected in December 1977 to an involuntary psychiatric examination, a frequent precursor of compulsory incarceration in a psychiatric hospital. Mikhail was not imprisoned, nor did his father cease his infectious Christian apologetics. In November of 1978, Dudko began printing a parish newsletter called *In the Light of the Transfiguration*. It focused on religious topics but also reported on the authorities' harassment of church members.

Just five months after the Siberian Seven drama got underway in June 1978, the Soviet authorities initiated their next offensive against Father Dudko. The militia invaded the building next to his church, where he occasionally spent the night, threatened to shoot everyone, and dragged out one of Dudko's followers. The young man, dressed only in his underwear, was pistol whipped in the snow. The militia took him in but refused to treat his injuries.

The young people, however, continued to make the lengthy journey to Grebnevo to hear the engaging priest. Finally, the authorities decided to take Dudko into custody. There seemed no other way to stop his ministry; nothing frightens the authorities more than churchmen capable of conveying to young people an attractive view of religion. Father Dudko's direct, open style was quietly and calmly destroying the stereotypes of atheist propaganda about what it means to be a believer.

On January 15, 1980 twelve KGB officers arrived at 8 A.M. to take him into custody. Within a few hours he was in the dreaded Lefortovo prison in Moscow. Though many both in the Soviet Union and abroad were quick to protest the imprisonment of this gentle priest, his own church hierarchy was not among them. Archbishop Pitirim of the Moscow Patriarchate could not avoid fielding questions in Stockholm about the imprisoned priest. Pitirim, however, recalled that he had been in seminary in 1945 with Dudko, whom he remembered as a "nervous and unbalanced person."[11] Metropolitan Alexy of Tallinn, while traveling in Austria, said the patriarch was unaware of the reasons for the arrest but could not take any stance on the basis of Western speculations. He went on to note: "In the Soviet Union, citizens are never arrested for their religious or ideological convictions."[12]

No one knows exactly what happened between that January morning when Dudko was arrested and June 5 when he signed a recantation for his "anti-Soviet" activities. We do know that his public confession disappointed and divided his followers and left Dudko disoriented and lonely. One of the spiritual heroes of the late Soviet period had apparently been broken by his interrogators.

Dudko's confession was orchestrated by Soviet authorities to get the maximum domestic and foreign coverage. The full text was published in *Izvestiia* on June 21, 1980, the day after the television recantation was seen by millions of Soviets. Dudko asserted that he was "arrested not for believing in God but for crime." His confession focused on his alleged role in bringing Church and State into conflict in the Soviet Union, and his part in providing information to the West which discredited his country. "I renounce what I have done, and I regard my so called struggle with godlessness as a struggle with Soviet power."[13]

The day after his televised confession, Dudko was released from custody and allowed to return home. Over the next few months he wrote and said many things which indicated that he was in a state of considerable anguish. On July 27 he wrote the following in a letter to his "Spiritual Children."

> I cannot forgive myself for my weakness, and my heart is torn asunder seeing your confusion and hearing garbled interpretations. I shudder at the thought of how I must appear to everyone, into what temptation I have led people, how I have disheartened those whom I had previously heartened. I prostrate myself before you and beg for your forgiveness.[14]

He also expressed surprise that people did not read between the lines of his confession. Dudko was unable to grasp fully the message his signed statement had conveyed. Six years before he had said in a sermon:

> The atheists have capitalized upon our fear of suffering and are now suppressing our spirit, they are suppressing free thinking and feelings, and they are scolding us. We must surmount this fear of suffering. . . .

But now he had told the world that this courageous message was "anti-Soviet" and criminal behavior.

Dudko's confession compelled many not only to speculate about what had happened to him, but to wonder if the same thing could happen to them. Some sought to guard in advance against being compromised in the future. Irina Zalesskaia wrote: "If I should make a similar 'confession' or renounce my views, I ask that this be considered the result of physical or psychological torture."[15]

A number of factors may have played a role in Dudko's transformation and his inability to come to grips with it afterward. First, the cumulative impact of years of fear may have taken their toll. Even if concern for himself had not become dominant, concern for his family or his spiritual followers may have driven him to recant. One observer, aware of the strain Dudko experienced in conducting his popular discussions, said at the time:

I can't understand how he continues. He is quite different from Solzhenitsyn. I have spoken to them both. Solzhenitsyn simply was afraid of nothing and nobody, but this man is afraid all the time. Yet he carries on.[16]

In fact, he was not able to carry on indefinitely.

A second factor may have been the impact of the months of isolation following his arrest. A third factor is closely related—his subsequent comments reveal that he felt he had developed a special relationship with his chief interrogator. Recent studies of hostages confirm that many do begin to identify with their captors as a defense mechanism and can therefore justify doing what they are told to do.

Dudko has sought to characterize what he did as an example of extreme humility. It is unclear if this or something less noble (though entirely human and understandable) was behind his actions. None of us can presume to stand in judgment. We would do well to remember what Dudko said six years before his own confession when asked why he defended the Church when the patriarch was always groveling before the authorities in abject cowardice. Dudko, perhaps already understanding his own limitations, fired back:

Who has fewer civil rights than the Patriarch? They say he's surrounded by thousands of informers. He so much as sighs and it's heard in every government department. Everything he does against his conscience he does under pressure and, of course, out of weakness, like any man. But you don't want to be compassionate. You sit in the judge's seat and pronounce sentence.[17]

It is a shame that more people did not know of a letter Dudko wrote to a friend abroad just two-and-a-half weeks before his arrest: "If anything happens to me, let this be my word from captivity. I ask you to pray."[18] Unfortunately, his last word from captivity said a good deal more. But it is up to us to remember that letter, and also to remember the full life of Father Dmitry Dudko.

I have given considerable space to one man's drama in hopes that we can better grasp what it has meant to serve God in this Communist country. That a gifted man, perhaps the most skilled communicator of Christian truths to the secular Soviet world of our day, could be reduced to denouncing his nonpolitical religious activities as crimes is itself a crime against the human spirit. It is a crime that has been committed repeatedly in every decade of Communist rule in this troubled land.

In 1981 the criminal charges against Dudko were formally dropped due to his age and his "repentance." But for many others the charges were not dropped. During most of the seventies the number of known Christian prisoners averaged about one hundred. But the wave of arrests in the late seventies and early eighties swelled the number to at least three hundred, about the average during the Khrushchev assault on religion in the first half of the sixties.[19]

EVANGELICALS IN THE POST-KHRUSHCHEV ERA

The period from 1964 to 1985 is more difficult to define than previous periods in Soviet history. The concerted attack on the Church ended, though as we have just seen, numerous incidents of violence against individual believers continued. It was as if both Church and State settled into a long holding pattern characterized by continued persecution of the unregistered believers and continued discrimination and harassment of the registered.

Though weakened by the schism of the early sixties, by 1966 the All-Union Council of Evangelical Christians-Baptists (AUCECB) was regaining some of its members. In 1966 the AUCECB had about 250,000 members, and by 1980 it had grown to about 350,000. At its apex in 1966 the rival Council of Churches of Evangelical Christians-Baptists (CCECB) had approximately 155,000 members; by 1980 it was down to 100,000.[20]

Much of the strength of the evangelical movement is based in Ukraine. In fact, approximately half of the AUCECB membership is found there. Many of the unregistered Baptists and Pentecostals who served time in labor camps during this period were from Ukraine.

In 1966 sixteen thousand Mennonites joined the AUCECB. The decision to join was more the product of a few Mennonite leaders than a decision by local congregations. Many of the theological distinctives, such as pacifism and not taking oaths, were no longer prevalent in the Mennonite communities, which made it more palatable to join.

However, a few months after the Mennonite group joined, one Mennonite congregation managed to register separately with the Soviet authorities. Similar independent registrations have occurred on a number of occasions in the two decades preceding Gorbachev; Pentecostals, Mennonites, Seventh Day Adventists, Baptists, and others have established official relations with the government on their own, rather than through the AUCECB. So in effect, in relationship to the State, there are now three groups of evangelicals in the USSR: those registered through the AUCECB, those registered independently, and those not registered at all.

In 1971 the CCECB began to publish an underground journal. Continual warfare was waged through the years between authorities trying to locate the underground printing operations and stubborn believers who sought to elude them. Far more has been smuggled in than produced locally, but the underground Baptists even managed to print some Bibles in 1978.

The price of being a part of the underground Christian world is high. Baptist leader Georgi Vins spent three years in prison between 1966 and 1969, was in hiding from 1970 until his arrest in March 1974, served five more years in prison, and was finally deported with other dissidents in April 1979 in an exchange for Soviet spies held in the West. Even into the Gorbachev era, unregistered Baptist leaders remain in hiding.

In 1988, an unregistered Baptist from Kiev helped explain to me the difference between those who join the registered churches and those who do not. He told me about an acquaintance of his who had recently become a believer. "I will have to go to the registered church for a while," this new convert said, "because for a few months it will be all I can handle to accept the suffering which will come from being associated with them. Perhaps when my faith is stronger, and I can endure more, I will come and join your unregistered fellowship."

One of the saddest dimensions to the life of the Soviet Baptists and Pentecostals, especially since 1960, has been the animosity between registered and unregistered groups. At a 1969 AUCECB Congress the CCECB was criticized for reporting in the West that "the condition of the church is worsening." It was partly a game of semantics. The real issue was not whether Church/State relations had worsened or improved but over more basic issues such as whether the AUCECB communicated accurately with the West about the plight of believers in the USSR.

At one of its most extreme moments, the CCECB declared in a 1970 document sent to churches belonging to the AUCECB: "Your salvation is in danger, if you continue to fellowship with AUCECB workers. . . . You cannot be in union with the AUCECB and in union with God at the same time."[21]

There has also been the war of Scripture verses. The registered accuse the unregistered of disobeying Romans 13:2 ("He who rebels against the authorities is rebelling against what God has instituted"). The unregistered fire back with Acts 5:29 ("We must obey God rather than men!"). In either case, the accusation is accompanied by the stated or implied judgment that the other side is in conflict with God himself.

It is easy for observers to suggest as a third solution Jesus' words, "Give to Caesar what is Caesar's, and to God what is God's." But this solves little, since this is precisely what the debate is all about: "What is Caesar's and what is God's?"

As difficult as the dilemma is, a fateful divide is crossed when Christians can no longer disagree without threatening damnation to those who see things differently. All of us face this temptation at one time or another. In the pressure cooker atmosphere of the Soviet Union, it is easy to succumb.

The authorities of course are delighted. Division is precisely what they want to foster, and their policies have done a good job cultivating it. Incidentally, the divisions are not just between the registered and the unregistered, but *within* both groups as well. In the mid-seventies there were major splits within the CCECB. There is also friction between the unregistered Baptists and the unregistered Pentecostals. One would think that the pressure of a common outside foe would force these groups onto common ground, but it has not always worked that way.

Two other factors contribute to the division and suspicion within the Christian community. The first is the impact of prison and persecution. Though the grace of God can temper the impact, we all bear the scars of our experiences. Soviet believers bear the scars of their terrible suffering. Second, living in a totalitarian State breeds distrust and suspicion even among family members, friends, and fellow Christians. Westerners in contact with Russian emigres are often surprised that a simple misunderstanding or failure to communicate can result in an exceedingly harsh judgment on one's motives or character.

This tendency toward divisiveness regrettably has expressed itself also in divisions between emigres in the West working on behalf of believers in Communist countries.

THE RUSSIAN ORTHODOX CHURCH IN THE POST-KHRUSHCHEV ERA

By far the largest group of Christians in the Soviet Union are the Orthodox—at least fifty million. In 1984, the chairman of the Council for Religious Affairs gave an inflated figure of eighty-five hundred Orthodox churches.[22] (Through an unfortunate error, a recent National Council of Churches publication quoted a figure of twenty thousand Russian Orthodox churches.[23])

Information in the Gorbachev era has been generally more reliable. It reveals some remarkable continuing declines in the number of registered churches over the past twenty-five years. The source of the new information is none other than Konstantin Kharchev, who in 1985 became chairman of the Council for Religious Affairs. In the November 1987 issue of *Religion and Science,* Kharchev reveals that the number of registered Orthodox churches dropped from 11,742 in 1961 to 6,794 in 1986—a decline of 42 percent! The 1986 figure under Gorbachev shows 729 *fewer* churches than existed in 1966 after the Khrushchev antireligious campaign had ended and Brezhnev was beginning his long tenure as Party leader. The statistics also indicate declines in the number of Catholic and Evangelical-Christian Baptist churches. The totals for all religious communities, including Muslim, show a decline of 19 percent (2,471 fewer churches, synagogues, or mosques) between the early Brezhnev era and the early Gorbachev era.[24]

At the beginning of the seventies, Soviet sociologists began to note an alarming trend: the Russian Orthodox Church was attracting more and more young Soviets with a higher education.[25] Furthermore, partly through the efforts of Metropolitan Nikodim, a higher percentage of well-educated young men were being allowed to attend the seminaries. Nikodim also managed to arrange for some seminarians to study abroad. These changes were worrisome to the authorities because they might set the stage for even more defections from the secular intelligentsia in the future.

The Orthodox Church has borne witness to these encouraging signs of life. One of the most moving testimonies was given in the London Orthodox Cathedral in 1980 by Father Vitaly Borovoi, the head Soviet patriarchal representative in Geneva to the World Council of Churches, and since the early eighties a deputy chairman of the Department of External Ecclesiastical Relations.[26]

There is a significance to his comments that goes beyond the inspiring news of the growth of religious vitality in the USSR. Borovoi, it must be remembered, like so many before and after him, has asserted repeatedly that the Soviet government has not and does not intervene in the affairs of the Church. And yet in this sermon, his obvious enthusiasm for the renewed religious interest spills over into an acknowledgment of problems in the past for believers. There is also a recognition that the Church has often failed.

A new movement has begun among the educated youth, the coming of the young generation into Church, a generation which has been brought up in atheistic homes as convinced unbelievers. [This generation] gained its conversion to Christ on its own, by way of the most profound reflections and inner trials.

This is not to our credit. . . . It is to the credit of our believing people; and the glory and thanks be to God, who spreads his mission through the Holy spirit among these people who are far away from the Church and, it seems, for whom there is no road to lead them there. And yet they come to the Church by many different ways. . . . This often results in the break-up of families, educational and professional sacrifices, or even in the need to part with a loved one: a bride or a fiancée. . . .

And we have now hundreds and thousands of such concrete living examples. . . . This is what is new in our Church; it can be slowed down, of course . . . but no one in this world has the power to totally stop it. This movement has begun and it will be accelerating, for behind it is the charisma and power of our Lord Jesus Christ, who has seen the confession of faith by his people; who has put his people to the test in humiliation, difficulties, in such conditions that for a while it appeared that just a little more and the end would come.

The Lord has tested [the faith] . . . of our Russian people. . . . Yes, historically the Russian Church . . . has sinned a lot. But the Lord sees how she has been passing through the crucible of tests; he sees that in these sixty years we have had thousands of times more saints than during the rest of the history of the Russian Church, that today living saints walk the face of the earth in Russia. . . . Thus the Lord has seen the faith of his people and now tells it: "Your sins are forgiven, get up and walk!" And the Russian Church rises and goes in the glory of God to preach Christ to the whole world.[27]

Russian reality is unsettling to us. Is it possible that despite the enmity between the confrontational Russian Orthodox dissidents and the meek, submissive hierarchy, a strong common bond of faith unites them? We ought to take Father Borovoi at his word when he says it "is not to our credit" that the educated youth are turning to Christ, that "the Russian Church has sinned." Indeed, this is a poignant confession.

In addition, in the 1970s the number of priests being ordained in the USSR was on the rise, though the numbers were pathetically small compared to the number of Orthodox believers. In 1981 the income tax rate for a priest was reduced from 81 percent to 69 percent! (Yakunin reports that the tax rate for the patriarch, the permanent members of the Synod, and the officials of the Department of External Ecclesiastical Relations is 13 percent, the same rate as for a normal Soviet citizen.)[28]

Patriarch Aleksy died in April 1970 at the age of ninety-two. During his last five years as patriarch he had become increasingly inactive and ineffective. About a year later, Pimen was elected to succeed Aleksy. Alexander Solzhenitsyn's open "Lenten Letter" to Pimen in 1972 was one of the strongest critiques leveled at the Orthodox hierarchy since the time of Khrushchev. Solzhenitsyn upbraided the patriarch for not looking after children's religious education and for letting the Church be "ruled dictatorially by atheists—a sight never before seen in two millennia!" He ridiculed the hierarchy's willingness to condemn evil in Africa or Asia while remaining silent about problems at home. He directly challenged the hierarchs' longstanding reason for capitulating to the authorities:

> By what reasoning is it possible to convince oneself that the planned *destruction* of the spirit and body of the church under the guidance of atheists is the best way of *preserving* it? Preserving it *for whom?* Certainly not for Christ. Preserving it *by what means? By falsehood?* But after the falsehood by whose hands are the holy sacraments to be celebrated.[29]

Solzhenitsyn contrasted the present cowardice of the Orthodox Church with the courage shown by the Christians in the early Roman Empire, when things were no easier. Solzhenitsyn's advice can be summed up by his famous admonition: "Live not by lies!" He believes strongly that the moral corruption in Soviet society caused by widespread lying and deceit will be reversed only when each individual determines to live by the truth. It is particularly disgraceful that in the matter of lying, the Church is one of the chief sinners.

The patriarchal entourage had an opportunity to respond to Solzhenitsyn's "Lenten Letter" at a press conference in Athens in October 1972. The newly-appointed head of the Department of External Ecclesiastical Relations acknowledged, without emotion, the reception of the letter. But he asserted that it contained "many inaccuracies" which demonstrated Solzhenitsyn's "insufficient acquaintance with the spiritual work of the Russian Church."[30]

While the Orthodox hierarchy has adamantly rejected the critiques of Solzhenitsyn and others, Dmitry Pospielovsky speculates that "deep down in their hearts many a Russian cleric undoubtedly admires the actions of those heroic individuals who dare to stand up almost singlehandedly against the might of the police in defense of civic and religious rights."[31]

THE FUROV REPORT: STATE MANIPULATION OF THE CHURCH

I referred earlier to "The Furov Report" and the account it gave of the troublesome priest Dmitry Dudko. The report contains much additional information which reflects how successfully atheist authorities feel they have muzzled the Church.

Furov evaluates the church leadership, dividing the bishops into three groups. The first are those who are entirely loyal to the State and "who foster the same spirit in their parish clergy and believers. . . ." They strictly follow the religious sect laws and "are not personally involved in spreading Orthodoxy among our population." This group properly understands that "our government is not interested in expanding the role of religion and church in our society."[32]

Bishops in the second group are loyal to the State and comply with religious sect laws. But they "are trying to activate the clergy and the church body . . . are trying to expand the role of the church in the private, family and social life . . . [and] are recruiting for priesthood young zealots of Orthodox piety."[33] These bishops go along with the authorities when they must, but steadfastly pursue the traditional mission of the Church.

The third group attempts to evade the laws governing religion.

Furov describes how the CRA gives meticulous attention to transfers and other personnel matters within the Church. He says that ideologically the clergy "always held and always will hold positions alien to Marxism" and reports that "individual priests in some of their statements demonstrate a certain dichotomy in their views on social processes." However, this does not disturb Furov at all. He thinks it works to the government's advantage, because "obvious contradictions in the hierarchs' words and approaches to social, and thus also to political problems are extremely puzzling and very confusing for the believers."[34]

Furov stresses the importance of having the appropriate clergy available to meet with foreign guests:

We have increasingly more demands for clergymen who may be

trusted in contacts with foreigners because foreign tourism is esca-
lating and because foreigners are especially interested in the situation
of religion and the church in the USSR. It should be noted that in
most cases the clergymen deserve our confidence.[35]

The report provides examples of how the CRA has successfully motivated bishops to discipline priests not in compliance with the religious laws.
Furov claims that the patriotic speeches of hierarchs are the result of "systematic work in educating the clergy" by the Council for Religious Affairs. And
yet Pimen is criticized for one of his speeches abroad in which he faults
"strong tendencies" of some churches to focus the ecumenical movement on
"social problems."[36]

Furov reports with pride that there is a serious shortage of priests and that
applicants to the seminaries are carefully monitored.[37]

OTHER RELIGIOUS GROUPS IN THE POST-KHRUSHCHEV ERA

It is the curse of every relatively small nation or religious group to be
either skipped or briefly discussed in general histories. The big neighbors
always get the attention. Unfortunately, this book is little different.

By necessity my main focus has been the evangelicals and the Orthodox
Church. However, these two groups do not represent the totality of Christen-
dom in the Soviet Union. There are numerous minority groups that have
experienced much of the same suffering. Our discussion of Church and State
in the Soviet Union would not be complete without at least briefly recounting
the history and fate of some of these other groups.

Divisions within the *Seventh Day Adventist* world are similar to those
between the registered and the unregistered Baptists and Pentecostals. The
underground Adventists, the True and Free, have survived despite cruel
persecution. Their early leaders died in labor camps in the thirties and forties,
but they found a strong new leader in 1954 when Vladimir Shelkov took
control. An illegal printing press ("True Witness") managed to produce 110
samizdat works. The underground Adventists cooperated with Russian Orthodox and other religious dissidents, and like them paid a similar high price. The
True and Free produced an eight-hundred-page collection of materials documenting religious persecution, which they sent to the Madrid conference
reviewing compliance with the Helsinki accords.[38]

In March 1979 Shelkov was arrested and sentenced to five years in a
strict-regime labor camp despite his advanced age (he was eighty-four). He
died in the camps on January 27, 1980.

The main body of registered Adventists grew throughout the seventies.
Their leader is M.P. Kulakov, a former labor camp prisoner under Stalin. They
have managed to maintain good relations with the authorities and are allowed

to have contacts with Adventists abroad, to send students to foreign countries to study theology, and to do some publishing.[39]

The *Jehovah's Witnesses* have been one of the most persecuted religious groups in Soviet history. When the Soviets annexed the Baltic region, they acquired this group and began deporting them to other areas in the USSR, which contributed to a spread of their ideas. They combine a fervent enthusiasm to propagate their views, a stubborn refusal to compromise with the authorities, and a willingness to endure great suffering at the hands of their enemies. Their refusal to serve in the military has meant almost certain imprisonment for the young men in their communities.[40]

Many will be surprised to learn that the largest illegal religious group in the Soviet Union is the *Ukrainian Catholic Church,* also known as the Uniate, Eastern Rite Catholic, and Greek Catholic Church. There are approximately four million Ukrainian Catholics.[41]

The present plight of the Ukrainian Catholics cannot be understood apart from a brief glance into their history. In 1596, when Ukraine was part of the Polish-Lithuanian Commonwealth, an agreement was signed between the Vatican and the Orthodox Metropolitan of Kiev. According to this Union of Brest, the Orthodox Ukrainians under the control of the Catholic Commonwealth would accept papal authority but retain their Byzantine (Orthodox) rites and customs. (Thus, for example, they were allowed to have married clergy, in contrast to the Roman Catholic practice.)

Though many Orthodox originally opposed the Union of Brest, in time most came to accept it. When the Soviets gained control over this region after World War II, Stalin decided to absorb by force the Ukrainian Catholics into the Russian Orthodox Church. He emphatically did not want a large religious group in Ukraine with primary loyalties to the Pope. Furthermore, a separate Ukrainian Catholic Church represented a focal point of national resistance to Soviet sovereignty. Like the Baltic peoples, Ukrainians have plenty of reason to dislike the Soviets for their oppressive postwar policies. Between 1946 and 1950, over three hundred thousand Ukrainians were deported, exiled, or arrested.[42] Since 1946 the Ukrainian Catholics have not enjoyed legal status.

Attempts to destroy the Ukrainian Catholic Church have not succeeded. The underground church has maintained contacts with the Vatican, and the Ukrainian church leader, Cardinal Lubachivsky, lives in Rome. There are between eight hundred and one thousand priests in the illegal church, a number of underground seminaries and monasteries, and since 1984, a secretly published *samizdat* periodical—*Chronicle of the Catholic Church in Ukraine.* In the Baltic states (Latvia, Lithuania, and Estonia), which were independent between the wars, the question of religious freedom must be addressed in a highly-charged nationalist atmosphere. Imagine a situation where twenty million Americans were deported by an alien power within a decade and you will have some sense of the Soviet impact on the Baltic states between 1940 and 1950.[43] There is tremendous bitterness toward the USSR even before the issue of religion freedom comes up.

Catholics in other parts of the Soviet Union suffered right along with other religious denominations during the early decades of Communist rule. Within a few days of the Soviet occupation of Lithuania and Latvia in 1940, the antireligious attitudes of the invader became obvious. By the time those Catholic deportees fortunate enough to survive came home in 1953, half the churches and all the monasteries and convents were shut down. Only two seminaries were left.[44]

The Khrushchev persecution was a unionwide phenomenon, and Lithuania and the other Baltic states were not spared. The Lithuanian Catholics have been unusually tenacious, and since 1972 have published *The Chronicle of the Catholic Church in Lithuania*. It consistently provides reliable information on religious persecution in Lithuania.

In 1978 a "Catholic Committee for the Defense of Believers' Rights" was established and sought to cooperate with an ecumenical counterpart established in Moscow a couple of years before. The Catholic Committee's two principal founders, Father Alfonsas Svarinskas and Father Sigitas Tamkevicius were both sentenced to five years labor camp and five years exile in 1983. Both have been released under Gorbachev.

In 1917 the biggest denomination in both Estonia and Latvia was Lutheran, but the situation has radically changed since 1940. Most of the Lutheran leaders were either deported or emigrated westward during World War II.[45] Estonia has a relatively small number of Methodists and a variety of other churches.

Despite the little attention given the smaller or non-Russian Christian groups, their religious traditions are rich. The Armenian Orthodox and the Georgian Orthodox traditions are several centuries older than the late tenth-century Byzantine variety which grew up in Kiev.[46]

The Georgian Orthodox Church is one of the world's oldest national churches, dating to at least the fourth century. It has fared much like the rest of the Christian Church during the Soviet period: considerable destruction in the 1920s, severe persecution in the 1930s, and relaxation of tensions when it received independence from the Russian Orthodox Church in 1943. There was much corruption in the 1970s (in government as well as the Church), but since about 1977 there has been reform. The Church claims approximately three million members.

The Armenian Orthodox Church dates to the year 301. It too has suffered much persecution in the past, and the majority of its churches remain closed. However, in recent years there has been more religious freedom here than in most other parts of the Soviet Union. There are about three million Orthodox in Armenia and another million and a half elsewhere in the USSR.

As we conclude our brief survey of religion since the Bolshevik Revolution, it is appropriate to examine the life of one more man. Since the mid-1960s, Gleb Yakunin has been at the center of the Soviet human rights movement and the quest for religious freedom.[47] In many ways, his struggle symbolizes the issues that are finally being addressed, at least partially, during the Gorbachev era.

THE COURAGEOUS QUEST OF GLEB YAKUNIN

Though Yakunin's family was religious, by 1949, at age fifteen, he had abandoned his childhood faith. In the providence of God, however, Yakunin came face to face with one of the spiritual giants of Orthodoxy in the mid-Soviet period—Father Alexander Men. Yakunin had gone to Irkutsk, Siberia, to study at a forestry institute. But because of Father Men, the whole direction of Yakunin's life changed, and he resolutely turned towards the priesthood.[48]

According to Dmitry Pospielovsky, Father Men was "one of the most outstanding, intellectually brilliant and prolific priests of the . . . Moscow Patriarchal Church, who had been baptized and spiritually educated by catacomb priests in the vicinity of Moscow in the 1940s."[49] The catacomb priests often provided religious education for children when it was not available, because of State interference, through the official Church.

With difficulty Yakunin managed to get accepted into a seminary, and in 1962 he was ordained at the height of the Khrushchev antireligious crusade. One of the first crises the young priest faced was how he should respond to the mass closures of churches and monasteries, and the shameful silence of his own Church authorities to this State-initiated oppression.

By late 1965, Yakunin had made his decision; he felt he must speak out against his Church's silence and the State's attack. Together with a fellow priest, Nikolai Eshliman, open letters were sent to Patriarch Aleksy and the Soviet government. To the patriarch, the priests made a plea: "The suffering church turns to you with hope." But the patriarch responded by stripping them both of their office; they still were considered priests, but they had no parish in which to serve.[50]

The bold action by the brave priests was noted abroad and was immensely inspiring to fellow Christians in the Soviet Union. As Solzhenitsyn later wrote:

> I had been delighted to read the protest written by two priests, Eshliman and Yakunin, a courageous, pure and honest voice in defense of a church which of old had lacked and lacks now both the skill and the will to defend itself. I read, and was envious. Why had I not done something like this myself, why was I so unenterprising? . . . I must do something similar![51]

Indeed, Solzhenitsyn would one day do something similar—his "Lenten Letter" to the patriarch in 1972.

For several years Yakunin was forced to go from job to job, unable to fulfill the divine vocation to which he had been called and ordained. Beginning about 1974, however, he once more was involved in a series of highly publicized letters to the Church, the government, and those abroad.

Yakunin was never narrowly concerned with religious freedom for just his Orthodox community. As early as June 1975 he was part of an impressive coalition of religious groups which appealed to the Soviet government. In that first major ecumenical protest, participants included representatives of the unregistered Pentecostals (including one of the Vashchenkos related to the Siberian Seven group), the unregistered Baptists, the Church of Christ, the Church of Faithful and Free Adventists, the Lithuanian Catholic Church, and the Russian Orthodox Church. The 1975 appeal began: "We, representatives of different Christian confessions, are meeting—for the first time, it seems, in the history of our country—in order to express to you [the Presidium of the Supreme Council of the USSR] our views concerning the religious situation in our State."[52] Their carefully documented charge was that the situation was worsening for believers in the USSR.

Yakunin's best-known appeal during these years was coauthored with Lev Regelson and was directed in November 1975 to the World Council of Churches Assembly then meeting in Nairobi. This letter to the WCC described the serious persecution of the Church in the Soviet Union. It noted with regret that the WCC had been almost totally silent about religious persecution in the Soviet Union, China, and Albania. The Russian priests appealed to the WCC for help.

The founding of the "Christian Committee for Defense of the Rights of Religious Believers" gave a more permanent form to ecumenical work for religious freedom in the Soviet Union.[53] And the catalyst for its founding was Gleb Yakunin.

The purpose of the Christian Committee was to document and publicize violations of religious freedom in the USSR. The documents of this courageous group repeatedly reached the West and provided accurate and invaluable information. In its first three years the Christian Committee managed to send 417 documents to the West totaling 1,302 pages. Michael Bourdeaux sums up the significance of this work:

> By any criterion, but most especially in Soviet conditions, this must rank as one of the outstanding ecumenical initiatives of this century. The network of contacts necessary to do this under the eyes of the secret police can only be guessed at; Soviet church history of the twentieth century was suddenly being brought to the attention of the world. Not one single fact in any of these 417 documents has so far been shown to be false and their tone is objective.[54]

It is a tragedy that more Western Churchmen did not supplement their meager knowledge about religion in the Soviet Union (often provided by Soviet Churchmen guilty of equivocation) with this impressive material provided at such personal cost.

The Soviet authorities, however, knew what was at stake. Both the information pipeline to the West and the possibility of further expansion of the religious human rights movement had to be forcibly halted. Yakunin and his cohorts would have to be dealt with. On November 1, 1979, just a few weeks before Father Dudko was taken into custody, Gleb Yakunin was arrested. Alexander Ogorodnikov, another well-known Orthodox dissident, had already been in prison for a year. Vladimir Poresh had been arrested in August. And Yakunin's good friend Lev Regelson would be in prison by the end of the year.

Unlike Father Dudko, Yakunin refused to cooperate with the authorities and was sentenced to five years in a strict-regime labor camp and five years in exile for "anti-Soviet propaganda." Apart from one appeal to the World Council of Churches Assembly in Vancouver in 1983, the Christian Committee was silenced by the wave of arrests.

Conclusion

On the eve of Mikhail Gorbachev's rise to power in 1985, the conflict and tension between Church and State were still very noticeable. Although battered and bloodied, the Christian faith in a variety of denominational forms had survived concerted efforts to weaken or destroy it.

Two different conceptions of the role of religion in society continued to be at odds. There was the Marxist view that religion was a kind of opium, a foreign substance that caused great harm in the society. And there was the Christian notion that religion was essential to society's very survival. As Gleb Yakunin put it: "Religion is like salt which protects humanity from decomposition and disintegration. Any attempt to banish it from social life invariably leads to a degradation of society."[55]

That is the essence of the debate: Is religion a society's opium or its salt? And can a society that has viewed religion as an opium for seven decades begin to view it as salt, or at least as an element that poses no threat?

Notes

1. Basic facts on Dudko are taken from Jane Ellis's excellent account, *The Russian Orthodox Church: A Contemporary History* (Bloomington: Indiana University Press, 1986), 309-15, 406-13, 422-27, 430-39.

2. Quoted in ibid., 310.

3. The text of eleven of Father Dudko's famous discussions are available in an English paperback translation and are highly recommended to the reader. Father Dmitrii Dudko, *Our Hope* (Crestwood, N. Y.: St. Vladimir's Press, 1977).

4. See Ellis, *Russian Orthodox Church*, 8-9, 455-56. Since there is a reference in the Furov report to a 1975 article, I have used 1975 rather than Ellis's 1974 as the probable date of the document. An English translation of the Furov document can be found in *Religion and Communist Dominated Areas (RCDA)* 19, nos. 9-11 (1980):148-61; *RCDA* 20, nos. 1-3 (1981):4- 13, 19.

5. Quoted in RCDA 20, nos. 1-3 (1981):10.

6. Quoted in ibid., 11.

7. Quoted in ibid.

8. Ibid.

9. Ibid.

10. Ellis, *Russian Orthodox Church*, 410.

11. Quoted in ibid., 427.

12. Quoted in ibid., 426.

13. Quoted in ibid., 430-31.

14. Quoted in ibid., 434.

15. Quoted in ibid., 433.

16. Quoted in ibid., 315.

17. Quoted in ibid., 313.

18. Quoted in ibid., 423.

19. Ibid., 419.

20. Walter Sawatsky, *Soviet Evangelicals Since World War II* (Scottdale, Penn.: Herald Press, 1981), 211, 442, 468.

21. Quoted in ibid., 351.

22. Ellis, *Russian Orthodox Church*, 16.

23. The National Council of Churches millennium commemoration materials contained a serious error on the number of Russian Orthodox churches. J. Martin Bailey, in *One Thousand Years: Stories from the History of Christianity in the USSR, 988-1988* (New York: Friendship Press, 1987), asserts on p. 5 that there are twenty thousand Russian Orthodox parishes. This is almost triple the amount that even the Soviets quote. Evidently the problem originates with the 1982 World Council of Churches *Handbook of Member Churches*, which inaccurately gives the twenty thousand figure. It is hard to know just how the mistake was first made, but for years the Soviets have given an exaggerated figure of twenty thousand for the total number of registered religious communities (see *Keston News Service*, no. 289, 3 December 1987, 22). The last time, according to Soviet statistics, there were as many as twenty thousand total registered communities was in the early 1960s, and the last time there was anywhere close to twenty thousand open Orthodox communities would have been in the early 1950s. Perhaps the WCC took an already exaggerated total figure and by mistake applied it just to the Russian Orthodox Church. The 1987 NCC book then repeated the earlier WCC error. I am grateful to Catherine P. Henry, a member of the National Capitol Presbytery Education Subcommittee for the Study of the Millennium, who was able to discover the probable source of the mistake.

24. *Keston News Service*, no. 289, 3 December 1987, 22.

25. For a good summary of these encouraging signs of growth among the secular intelligentsia, see Dmitry Pospielovsky, *The Russian Church Under the Soviet Regime: 1917-1982*, 2 vols. (Crestwood, N. Y.: St. Vladimir's Seminary Press, 1984), 2:454-60. Tatiana Goricheva, a 1980 emigre from the Soviet Union, is a good example of one of these bright young converts. See Tatiana Goricheva, *Talking About God Is Dangerous: The Diary of a Russian Dissident* (New York: Crossroad, 1987).

26. Pospielovsky, *Russian Church*, 2:458; Ellis, *Russian Orthodox Church*, 250.

27. Quoted in Pospielovsky, *Russian Church*, 2:458- 59.

28. Ibid., 2:431.

29. Quoted in Ellis, *Russian Orthodox Church*, 304. Her fine discussion of the "Lenten Letter" debate occurs on pages 304-9.

30. Quoted in Pospielovsky, *Russian Church*, 1:445.

31. Ibid., 2:446.

32. *RCDA* 19, nos. 9-11 (1980):150.

33. Ibid.

34. Ibid., 152.

35. *RCDA* 20, nos. 1-3 (1981):7.

36. *RCDA* 19, nos. 9-11 (1980):151-53.

37. *RCDA* 20, nos. 1-3 (1981):4-5.

38. Philip Walters, ed., *World Christianity: Eastern Europe* (Monrovia, Calif.: MARC, 1988), 81.

39. Ibid., 82.

40. Ibid., 92-93.

41. The information on the Ukrainian Catholics is taken primarily from Walters, *World Christianity*, 59-65. Also see, Pospielovsky, *Russian Church*, 2:306-09.

42. Mikhail Heller and Aleksandr Nekrich, *Utopia in Power: The History of the Soviet Union from 1917 to the Present* (New York: Summit Books, 1986), 456.

43. *These Names Accuse: Nominal List of Latvians Deported to Soviet Union* (Stockholm: Latvian National Foundation, 1982), vi.

44. Walters, *World Christianity*, 54-55.

45. Ibid., 85.

46. See ibid., 49-52, 89-93.

47. The best and most detailed account of Russian Orthodox dissent in the Soviet Union is contained in Part 2 of Ellis, *Russian Orthodox Church*, 292-454. Unless otherwise noted, information on Yakunin is taken from Ellis, pages 292-94, 352-68, and elsewhere as indicated in her index. For an excellent general treatment of the religious liberty movement in the Soviet Union (the Baptists, Pentecostals, True and Free Seventh-Day Adventists, and the Russian Orthodox Church), see Ludmilla Alexeyeva's fine book *Soviet Dissent* (Middletown, Conn: Wesleyan University Press, 1987), 201-64.

48. Michael Bourdeaux, *Risen Indeed: Lessons in Faith from the USSR* (Crestwood, N.Y.: St. Vladimir's Seminary Press, 1983), 19.

49. Pospielovsky, *Russian Church*, 1:179.

50. Ellis, *Russian Orthodox Church*, 292-93.

51. Quoted in ibid., 294.

52. For a copy of the 20 June 1976 appeal, see *Communism and Christianity* (Britain: Aid to the Church in Need, 1978), 101-12.

53. See Alexeyeva, *Soviet Dissent*, 255-59.

54. Michael Bourdeaux, "The Russian Church, Religious Liberty and the World Council of Churches," *Religion in Communist Lands* 13 (Spring 1985):15.

55. Yakunin's comment was made on 30 May 1988 in Moscow at a special reception hosted by the American Ambassador to the USSR. Warren Zimmermann, chairman of the United States delegation to the Vienna Commission for Security and Cooperation in Europe, quoted Yakunin in his 10 June 1988 speech on religious freedom to a plenary session of the CSCE meetings in Vienna.

PART IV

WESTERN RESPONSES TO CHRISTIANS IN THE USSR

GLASNOST IS A
TWO-WAY STREET

Y our Christian preachers return home from the USSR with a host
of pleasant memories: you are inspired by the simple beauty of
our churches and the numbers of people filling them. This picture
lingers in your memory, evoking the best and warmest emotions. But
you must understand that what you have seen is the sum total of what
is permitted to us. In all other aspects of our lives—family, social,
political and cultural—we are not allowed to be Christians . . .
abstain from helping the persecutors to hammer yet another nail into
the crucified body of our Lord Jesus Christ, which you do every time
one of you makes confident assertions that there is no persecution of
believers in the USSR. (Appeal to Western Christians from Russian
Orthodox Christians, 1986.)[1]

* * * *

Rumors of these [Soviet] infringements have reached western Christians in an exaggerated and sometimes distorted form, provoking
inappropriate reactions which complicate the resolution of internal
church problems. (Erich Weingartner, World Council of Churches
official, 1983.)[2]

* * * *

. . . a Christian in our country cannot freely follow his doctrine
without risk of being subject to proceedings for breaking the law.
Bible study circles are banned, yet the Gospels instruct us to "follow
the Scriptures"; works of charity and benevolence are banned, yet
the Gospels say: "Love thy neighbor as thyself," and a Christian
should show that love not in words, but in energetic social action;
any form of religious education of children or adults is banned, but

Jesus Christ said: "Go ye into all the world, and preach the Gospel to every creature . . . ." (Soviet journalist, December 1988.)[3]

* * * *

In this encouraging time of change and openness, it would be a great shame if only the Soviet Union committed itself to confronting what it calls its "blank spots"—the skeletons in its historical closet.

Glasnost ought to be a two-way street. Just as the Soviets are acknowledging at least some of the improper and even reprehensible treatment they have inflicted on believers over the past seventy years, so too we in the West ought to confess our own frequent failures to respond with wisdom and courage to the sufferings of fellow Christians in the USSR. The Western Church must examine what it has *not* said as well as what it *has* said about the situation of believers in the Soviet Union.

Any serious study of the accounts given by Soviet church leaders concerning religious freedom in their nation will reveal statements riddled with inaccuracies.[4] It is certain that registered church leaders would not have been able to travel abroad or enjoy regular contact with Western visitors had they frankly described State-imposed limitations on the practice of religious faith. It is equally obvious that the majority of these leaders have felt it necessary to play this unhappy role in order to keep their churches open.

It is silly and unfair to charge, as some on the Right have charged for years, that these church leaders are nothing but KGB agents. Certainly some who host Westerners in the Soviet Union and a few among the delegations which travel to the West give their primary loyalty to the Soviet State and not to the Church; but they are in the minority. Those who fit such descriptions will most likely be found in church departments devoted to international affairs.

There are few signs that Western church leaders—whether ecumenical, oldline Protestant, or evangelical—realize or are willing to acknowledge the degree to which they have been effectively (and often unwittingly) manipulated by Kremlin strategists. On the contrary, there are distressing signs that some circles consider the present Soviet *glasnost* a vindication of past silence (often misdescribed as "silent diplomacy") on religious freedom issues. Consider the words of Dr. Arie Brouwer, the general secretary of the National Council of Churches, to Mikhail Gorbachev at a December 8, 1987, gathering at the Soviet Embassy in Washington, D.C.

... as you know, one of the sources of fear of the Soviet Union is on the religious Right in this country. And I want you to know, I want to testify here, that the relationship of more than thirty years' standing between the National Council of Churches and the churches in the Soviet Union has done a great deal to alleviate some of that concern and express appreciation to you for your policies of *glasnost* and *perestroika* which have *helped to improve our reputation, because people have begun to believe that what we've been saying for many years may be true.* Thank you. [my emphasis][5]

Unfortunately, the National Council of Churches, the World Council of Churches, many oldline Protestant church leaders, and many evangelical leaders often *said* there was considerably more religious freedom in the Soviet Union than there was in fact. It is concerning this that we need Western *glasnost*.

A second example of how far we have to go in the West is what happened in the spring of 1988 at the United Methodist General Conference.[6] An amendment proposed in the Church and Society Committee to a resolution on the Soviet Union would have extended to the USSR congratulations on the millennium of Christianity, complimented Gorbachev for his pledge to support greater toleration for religion in the Soviet Union, and called on the General Secretary to expand religious freedom even further. Only the greetings survived the committee; anything which might have been considered critical was excised. The reasons given for the gutting of the amendment are a microcosm of the attitudes which have dominated influential Western church circles for much of the last two decades.

The tone of the amendment was considered "imperialistic" and "preachy," and its eleven detailed points (the call for unlimited importation of Bibles, the release of all remaining prisoners of conscience, ending restrictions on seminary enrollment, etc.) were judged unhelpful in promoting "delicate negotiations."

The amendment stated, "While no society is free of church/state conflict, we observe that democratic systems of governance best protect religious freedom." Opponents objected to "code" words and "statements which would play into the hands of those who have too narrow a definition of democracy." An observer of the committee was heard to comment: "Our task is to move the General Conference [of the Methodist Church] as far to the Right as Gorbachev."[7]

This extraordinary reluctance to defend democracy and human rights for fear that they reflect a Western bias harmful to good relations between nations and churches stands in stark contrast to what prominent Soviets themselves have called for during the era of *glasnost*.

What is remarkable about the present era is that it is precisely the agenda of the much-maligned dissidents which has been so influential. The dissidents, and now some Kremlin reformers, do not consider talk of democracy and human rights to be Western "code" words offensive to Soviet sensibilities. They consider democracy a practical necessity for reform and human rights, the property of the entire human family and not just its Western branch.

In 1970, Andrei Sakharov, Roy Medvedev, and Valery Turchin wrote Brezhnev and warned that if fundamental economic and political reforms did not take place, the USSR would become a "second-rate provincial power." They called for democratization, amnesty of political prisoners, an end to the jamming of foreign radio broadcasts, and open discussion of societal problems. Many years before the Gorbachev reassessment of Stalin, dissident historian Roy Medvedev told much of the truth about the dictator in his *Let History Judge*.[8]

It is the program of the dissidents, and not that of Western church leaders who repeatedly tempered calls for justice and religious freedom, which is getting a hearing in the Soviet Union during *glasnost*. As a commentator in *New Republic* recently put it:

> Under Gorbachev, liberal-minded Party members who read dissident works with sympathy in the 1970s have become influential policy makers, editors and writers. They have adapted dissident ideas to current political reality.[9]

We owe tribute to those men and women who suffered in labor camps and exile for proclaiming what is now said openly in Soviet newspapers—*not* to those who viewed those dissidents as obstacles to world peace.

Discussion of the Western Church's record on religious oppression in the Soviet Union is volatile and controversial. Coming to grips with the problem requires that we face squarely our own failings. We dare not sidestep the hard questions about our pre-Gorbachev era record. We cannot hope to do better in the future unless we learn from the mistakes of our past.

Sadly, when this question is raised, it is typically besieged by a whole set of false dilemmas and bogus issues. These must be addressed at the outset.

What the Debate Is NOT About

First, *this is NOT a debate about the intentions of Western church leaders.* There can be little doubt that the vast majority of church leaders want very much to do what is right. The debate is about the wisdom of their methods of relating to and working for Christians in the USSR.

Second, *this is NOT a debate over the merits of "quiet diplomacy."* It is true that "quiet diplomacy" is frequently an effective way to bring about a desired result. But there is a serious question about whether it is either wise or necessary for churches to rely almost exclusively on "quiet diplomacy."

Furthermore, those who have suffered most at the hands of the Soviets have insisted repeatedly that it was precisely public pressure from the West which protected them and eased their lot. Our Jewish friends learned this lesson long ago, but we in the Christian world have been slow to grasp it. What has always been needed is a prudent combination of private intervention and public pressure; to rely exclusively on either tactic is a prescription for failure.

Western church leaders frequently insist that "in private" they have pushed the Soviets on religious freedom issues. No doubt they have. But given the often inaccurate and misleading character of official Western church public comments on religion in the USSR, it is difficult to place great confidence in either the quality or the fervency of these private protestations.

Another point related to the question of "quiet diplomacy" is whether we have practiced it faithfully. In other words, the difficulty often has not been in keeping silent about persecution or discrimination, but in publicly *denying* their existence.

Third, *this is NOT a debate over whether we ought to have contact with Soviet registered churches.* We must—in fact, such contacts ought to be expanded. But we can do a better job of making sure that the contacts do not put us in a straitjacket where we cannot speak out or energetically press for religious liberty for *both* the registered and unregistered.

Fourth, *this is NOT a debate about whether the Church should abandon its concern for peace.* Among oldline Protestants, there has been a strong tendency to connect speaking candidly about problems in the Soviet Union with Cold War politics. This "anti-anti-communism" has come to function much like an ideology, and it is in part based on the false notion that a strong public commitment to human rights is incompatible with progress on arms control. It also reflects a belief that being actively opposed to communism is more dangerous than communism itself.

CONCLUSION

The next two chapters will consider how Western Christians and church organizations have responded to Soviet disinformation distributed in the West through registered church leaders. Leaders from the oldline Protestant world usually focus on political and peace concerns, with a tendency to highlight problems found in regimes of the Right rather than of the Left. For evangelicals the major issue is fear that the registered church will be hurt and opportunities to spread the gospel diminished if strong stances are taken.

In both cases, their public statements reflect considerable ignorance (if they truly believe what they say). To put it another way: Either their statements are sincere, but based on misinformation; or they are not completely candid, and thus contribute significantly to others being misinformed.

The next chapters will also touch on more balanced Western responses: Catholic, some parachurch mission societies, and a number of outstanding research centers. At times, individuals and groups within oldline and evangelical organizations responded with more skill and effectiveness than did the larger organizations to which they belonged.

There is no attempt here to cover all of the existing Western/Soviet Christian contacts. Many denominations and groups are not discussed. Rather,

I have chosen some of the most important and controversial of the contacts in order to raise the critical issues.[10]

The point of these chapters is not to throw stones or to dredge up an unpleasant past. The Soviets need to discuss what really happened under Stalin so they can build into their system safeguards which can avoid figures like him in the future. And Westerners need to discuss their responses so that they, too, can avoid repeating the errors of the past.

Notes

1. Quoted in *Keston News Service*, no. 257, 21 August 1986, 2-3.

2. Erich Weingartner, *Human Rights on the Ecumenical Agenda*, WCC Commission of the Churches on International Affairs, Background Information pamphlet prepared for delegates to the Sixth General Assembly of the World Council of Churches (July 1983, Vancouver). Weingartner has served the WCC as the Executive Director of the Commission of the Churches on International Affairs. Quoted in Michael Bourdeaux, "The Russian Church, Religious Liberty and the World Council of Churches," *Religion in Communist Lands* 13, no. 1 (Spring 1985):24.

3. Alexander Nezhnyi, conversation with Konstantin Kharchev, *Ogonek*, no. 50, December 1988, 4-5. As quoted in Foreign Broadcast Information Service, SOV-89-006, 10 January 1989, 5.

4. Chapters 6-8 detail the Church/State relationship which has created this sad state of affairs.

5. Quoted in *Religion and Democracy*, Institute on Religion and Democracy, June 1988, 4.

6. See Diane L. Knippers, "Is the United Methodist Church Poised for Reform?" *Religion and Democracy*, Institute on Religion and Democracy, July 1988, 3-4.

7. Quoted in ibid.

8. Stuart Anderson, "Gorbie's Choice," *New Republic*, 17 April 1989, 11.

9. Ibid.

10. Mark Elliott, "A Typology of Western-Soviet Christian Contacts," (Unpublished manuscript, Institute for the Study of Christianity and Marxism, Wheaton College, Wheaton, Ill., 1988), is highly recommended. Elliott is the director of the Institute for the Study of Christianity and Marxism. Published materials by Elliott which include sections of the unpublished manuscript are: "How the Churches Have Seen Their Roles in the USSR," *Pulse* (Evangelical Missions Information Service, Wheaton, Ill.), no. 22, 9 January 1987, 2-5; "Parachurch Groups Take Different Routes to USSR," *Pulse*, no. 22, 23 January 1987, 2-5; "Eastern Europe: Responding to Crisis in the Household of Faith," *Eternity*, July-August 1986, 24-29.

CHAPTER 9

PLAYING BY
SOMEONE ELSE'S RULES:

Ecumenical Church Bodies and Christians
in the USSR

*I*s it true that Western church leaders have often either remained silent or
seriously exaggerated the amount of religious freedom in the Soviet Union?

An examination of the historical record is the best way to answer that
question. And now, of course, what has been said and done by the ecumenical
bodies can be measured both by the best Western scholarship on religion in
the Soviet Union and by what the Soviets themselves are revealing under
glasnost.

I. THE WORLD COUNCIL OF CHURCHES

The World Council of Churches (WCC), formed in 1948 and now
including more than three hundred member churches, is the largest non-
Catholic Christian organization in the world. From its earliest days, even those
firmly committed to promoting ecumenism and Christian unity had expressed
concern about the possibility of its becoming heavily politicized. Sadly, many
of those fears have been realized.

J.A. Emerson Vermaat, one of the foremost historians of the WCC, opens
his latest book with the following observation: "Churches today sometimes
resemble political institutions more than religious ones."[1] As the Dutch
scholar's work goes on to document, his comment especially fits ecumenical
bodies such as the World Council of Churches and the U.S. National Council
of Churches.

It is not difficult to identify the basic political orientation of these bodies.
"The WCC has gained a reputation," Vermaat says, "for being pro-leftist
and anti-Western."[2] This, in part, explains the remarkable silence and inac-
tivity of the WCC with respect to religious repression in the USSR. But it is
important to recognize that nothing in the late 1950s and early 1960s

precluded the movement from evolving in a more balanced and thoughtful direction.

Soviet Churches Join the WCC: A Mixed Blessing

The dilemmas facing the WCC were considerably complicated by events in the early 1960s. The Russian Orthodox Church formally joined the organization in late 1961, at the very inception of Nikita Khrushchev's vicious antireligious crusade.[3] Ironically, while many in the West hailed the expanded ecumenical breadth of the WCC as a sign of greater liberality in the Soviet Union, the Church suffered its worst persecution since Stalin. In 1962, the All-Union Council of Evangelical Christians-Baptists and several other Soviet churches were admitted to WCC membership. By 1966, Eastern bloc members had risen to about ten.[4] These delegates usually voted as a bloc.

The tragedy of the next three decades was the unwillingness, or at least inability, of the WCC to include delegates from the Eastern Communist bloc in its numbers while at the same time remaining an effective advocate for religious freedom in those countries. That the Kremlin managed to handcuff the largest Protestant organization in the world is one of its greatest foreign policy achievements since World War II.

But in 1961 almost no one in the West had any knowledge of official Soviet persecution. This was before desperate appeals for help began to leak out of the Soviet Union. Michael Bourdeaux was a firsthand observer of the WCC in these years, and he has noted that the "the leaders of the WCC were people of outstanding ability and complete integrity."[5] Nor did anyone realize the degree to which Soviet representatives would push a political agenda—an agenda indistinguishable from that of the Kremlin.

In thirty years the WCC has produced only one serious work on the situation of believers in the USSR. It came out in 1959, two years before the Russian Orthodox Church joined the WCC, and was entitled *Current Developments in the Eastern European Churches*. It was careful in its language, understandable considering the possible addition of East European members to the WCC. But it reflected solid scholarship and pointed out disturbing signs on the horizon relative to religious repression. By 1962, it was discontinued.

The election of Dr. Eugene Carson Blake, an American Presbyterian, to the position of General Secretary may have been a critical turning point for the WCC. Blake had edged out Patrick Rodger, the future Bishop of Oxford and a man unusually knowledgeable about the Soviet Union. Henceforth, expertise on the Soviet Union was not to be a forte of WCC leadership.

Drift to the Left

It is a mistake to attribute the WCC's well left-of-center politics simply to the presence of official Soviet church representatives in the organization. In fact, as Bourdeaux has observed, often the "Soviet delegates were able to sit back and simply watch the Assembly's work engaged upon a whole series of measures which were in line with Soviet foreign policy."[6]

The drift toward the Left is clearly evident in WCC decisions taken at its Fourth General Assembly (Uppsala, Sweden), in July 1968. Third World issues were treated in ways reflecting a leftward orientation, and only the United States was requested to restrain its military involvement in Vietnam. As Canon Bernard Pawley put it in London's *Church Times,* "the old dark shadow of appeasement fell over the Assembly—there will have been joy in the Kremlin that night."[7]

Yet the WCC was still willing to address a few issues dealing with problems on the Left. WCC leadership condemned the 1968 Soviet invasion of Czechoslovakia, and a few weeks before Alexander Solzhenitsyn was deported in early 1974, the WCC issued a statement in his defense. In 1974 it even defended the unregistered Baptist leader Georgi Vins who had just been imprisoned for a second time. But these were exceptions to a general trend which opposed forceful involvement in human rights issues in Communist countries.

THE POLITICS OF PEACE: THE WPC AND CPC

Perhaps no single issue has raised more doubts about the wisdom of the ecumenical and oldline church world than its often imprudent involvement in efforts to advance world peace. One frequent allegation is that Western church activists have wittingly or unwittingly been the pawns of Soviet disinformation campaigns.

However, one of the Soviet Union's first efforts did not meet with much success. Founded in 1949, the World Peace Conference was "an organization controlled and sponsored by the Soviet government." Walter Sawatsky notes that its initial propaganda "was so transparently pro-Soviet that Western churches and Western public opinion rejected the statements with incredulity."[8] During the Gorbachev era, even a member of the Presidium of the Soviet Peace Committee has moved to set the record straight: "The WPC ended up as a continuation and reflection of the Soviet Union's foreign policy."[9]

The Prague-based Christian Peace Conference (CPC) was founded in 1958 by the Czech theologian Josef Hromadka. For the first ten years of its existence, many Western church leaders sympathized with efforts by the CPC to increase dialogue between Christians in the West and in the East. Though controlled by pro-Soviet forces, the CPC had some Eastern and Western voices who sought independence.[10]

Hromadka's views had nearly always corresponded with those of the USSR. But in 1968, when Soviet tanks rumbled into his own country, Hromadka resigned his CPC presidency when the organization declined to protest the invasion. With Russians and Hungarians at the helm, the CPC lost considerable Western support. The CPC, like the World Peace Conference, consistently took a pro-Soviet foreign policy stance. Much of the funding for both came from the Soviet Peace Fund, funneled through the Russian Orthodox Church.

According to CIA testimony to the House Permanent Select Committee on Intelligence in 1982:

> On peace and disarmament issues, the Soviet-controlled World Peace Council (WPC) has long played the vanguard role in promoting the pro-Soviet campaigns; but it has relied heavily on a major sister front, the Christian Peace Conference (CPC), which has given unqualified support to all WPC programs. *The CPC has been, and remains, a classic example of Soviet exploitation of religious groups to further Soviet foreign policy.* (my emphasis)[11]

Any who doubt that the WPC, and to a somewhat lesser extent the CPC, consistently supports the Soviet foreign policy line need not rely on the testimony of the CIA, but may simply examine the positions taken by these organizations over the last several decades. Neither could be accused of balance when it comes to the conflict between the West and the Soviet Union.

The WCC is not a Communist front. Nevertheless, as Vermaat points out, "During the period of 1975-86 the WCC did not distance itself too much from known Soviet front groups."[12] Indeed, important figures in the primary worldwide socialist organization, Socialist International, sometimes showed more caution than the WCC in attending events orchestrated by the Communists.[13] It was not so much the direct influence of the fronts that impacted the WCC, as individuals in key staff positions involved in some way with one of the groups in question.[14]

Although we can debate the judgments of independent Western religious activists who frequently disagree with their own government's military policies, it is indisputable that their counterparts in the Soviet bloc do not enjoy similar independence. Yet in our ecumenical church bodies, a kind of unholy alliance has been formed based on an asymmetrical union between East bloc government-controlled organizations and independent Western groups.

Hans Hebly has summarized the comments of Bishop Krushche, former head of the Federation of Evangelical Churches in East Germany, on this point:

> The churches can only serve peace if they do not simply serve their own national interests and behave as megaphones for the foreign policy of their own government. If they only play the role of megaphones, they lose their function as peacemakers. Churches which do

not ask critical questions about the policy of their own government, but declare this policy exclusively as peace policy, are not the salt of the earth; they are the marmalade of their state.[15]

True independence does not rule out agreeing with your government if you truly believe that its actions promote peace. But it also allows you to be critical when circumstances so require. Soviet church leaders do not have such independence.

THE POLITICAL BIAS OF THE WCC

An examination of the pronouncements and activities of the WCC is the best way to determine its political preferences. Vermaat concludes that particularly between 1975 and 1986:

The WCC's statements on international affairs . . . coincided with Soviet views and positions. . . . In addition, the Russian Orthodox Church often played a decisive role in preventing the WCC from making statements which strongly deviated from the Soviet line.[16]

Political bias was expressed as much by what was not said as by what was. Hans Hebly has spent many years examining WCC policies, and he makes the following observation.

The WCC does speak critically about the Western world and about Western social and political problems, but it does not speak in the same way about the socialist world: or, more precisely, does not speak about it at all.[17]

Hebly argues that a credible ecumenism would have to keep its distance from both capitalism and socialism. That the WCC has clearly not done this has allowed it to be used by political propagandists.

The Western world is the object of severe moral criticism by the churches, and there are many good reasons for that. But the silence of the WCC about the socialist world is interpreted as its moral justification by the propagandists of socialism or in any case is used as such.[18]

The WCC approach has often not been "moral equivalence"—the fashionable and morally evasive tendency to put a curse on the houses of both capitalism and socialism. In fact, the WCC's criticism has been so one-sided as to suggest a bias toward socialism. Moral equivalence would be an improvement, though still far removed from a sober judgment about twentieth-century realities. This bias in favor of the Left, especially when the empirical evidence suggests that the world's poor have done much better in free-market oriented societies, undermines the council's credibility.

There is an integral connection between the political orientation of the WCC, its Soviet church representatives, and the positions it has taken relative to religion in the Soviet Union.

GLEB YAKUNIN AND THE WCC

Massive evidence of government manipulation of the registered churches should have informed Western church leaders that Soviet WCC delegates were in no position to provide independent church perspectives—especially when it came to discussing foreign policy positions and the status of religious freedom in the USSR.

In the 1970s the WCC began to receive many letters from ordinary Christians in the USSR, particularly Orthodox believers, describing serious problems. Ignoring the fact that these notes arrived at the WCC headquarters in Geneva as "open letters," Russian Orthodox Church representatives successfully argued the letters ought not be widely circulated. Often they didn't even reach Central Committee members.[19] Thus, even within the WCC, there was a major effort to bottle up stories of persecution.

In 1972, WCC General Secretary Carson Blake acknowledged that Christians were persecuted in the USSR, but he argued that public protests were ineffective and might well hurt the WCC Soviet member churches. He contended that "our expression of critical concern becomes cheap and can only be understood in the countries concerned as anti-Communist, i.e. political declarations."[20]

What has particularly paralyzed the WCC is a policy requiring prior consultation with the member churches of any country in which questions are raised. Ninan Koshy, Director of the Commission of the Churches on International Affairs, explained at a press conference in 1981: "Appeals from groups or individuals for World Council of Churches' intervention cannot be acted on by the Assembly without the support of delegates of member churches. . . ."[21]

Since the consulted Baptist and Orthodox leaders are only free to give the Kremlin's position on "alleged" persecution, and since the WCC refuses to act on independent information, the result has frequently been silence. As Michael Bourdeaux has put it:

> . . . the Soviet representatives could now *de facto* exercise a veto over any WCC activities in defense of human rights in the Eastern bloc, to be circumvented only when some event of special magnitude made it impossible for the WCC staff to do any other than react—such as over Czechoslovakia and Solzhenitsyn.[22]

Since silence has often been justified as a more "effective" way to help the oppressed, it is worth getting the opinion of those with the most at stake. In 1975, at the Nairobi General Assembly, the World Council of Churches had a splendid opportunity to do just that. Though the WCC assembly organizers had scheduled no discussion on the problems of Soviet believers, on the third day of the gathering the Kenyan newspaper *Target,* serving temporarily as an assembly news source, printed a letter from two Soviet Christians: Father Gleb Yakunin and Lev Regelson (a lay physicist). One of their central points was: "the matter of religious persecution has failed to take its due place— although it ought to become the central theme of Christian ecumenism." Among other things, the Russians charged that the WCC had been silent "when the Russian Orthodox Church was half destroyed" in the 1960s.[23]

Yakunin and Regelson made specific recommendations on how to rectify the problems of the WCC. Among their most important recommendations:

1. The WCC ought to found a multi-lingual, mass circulation bulletin to distribute accurate information.
2. Call for worldwide prayer by churches.
3. PUBLICIZE THE PERSECUTION because the Soviets are "extraordinarily concerned about their international reputation."
4. Defend those in prison and mental institutions.
5. Defend the right of emigration.
6. Organize help to deal with the extreme shortage of religious literature.[24]

Soviet church representatives immediately attacked the credibility of the authors, but many delegates urged the WCC to act. Finally, two days before the end of the assembly, a Swiss delegate proposed an addition to a report on disarmament and the Helsinki Agreements. The addition included the following: "The WCC is concerned about restrictions to religious liberty, particularly in the USSR." For the first and only time in WCC history, such a resolution was voted on and passed.

After a break, however, the session chairman declared the motion out of order because the committee which had submitted the original report had not considered the question of religious persecution. The matter was referred to the resolutions committee. A heated debate occurred over the next few hours before the entire body formally took up the matter again. The assembly finally formally requested:

> the General Secretary to see to it that the question of religious liberty be the subject of intense consultation with the member churches of the signatory states of the Helsinki Agreement and the first report [on the consultation] be presented at the next Central Committee meeting of August 1976.[25]

Though there was no mention here of the Soviet Union, Yakunin and Regelson interpreted the WCC action as giving a positive sign. In March 1976 they communicated that belief to Philip Potter, the new general secretary. The two Russians warned the WCC that the Council for Religious Affairs of the Soviet government had already sent out orders to their church representatives "to undermine any possible attempt by the WCC to adopt a resolution of protest against the limitation on believers' rights in the USSR."[26]

Unfortunately, Yakunin's warning had no effect. Soviet delegates blocked any strong statement by the WCC, and no meaningful changes were made in the way the WCC handled religious oppression in the USSR. Soviet church representatives succeeded in their cover-up efforts despite the prior warning to WCC officials about the problem.

Members of the WCC hierarchy held a meeting in March 1976 with three major research institutes who study religion in the Soviet Union: Keston College (England), *Glaube in der 2 Welt* (Zurich), and the Inter-Academical Institute for Missiological and Ecumenical Research (Utrecht). So as not to offend Soviet churchmen, the meeting took place secretly at a hotel near the train station in Geneva.[27]

During the next several months, these three research institutes prepared a one-hundred-page briefing book for the WCC hierarchy and Central Committee titled *Religious Liberty in the Soviet Union: WCC and USSR.* The WCC also had at its disposal the excellent study by Trevor Beeson on religion in Eastern Europe and the Soviet Union, *Discretion and Valour.* This was a project of the British Council of Churches which, in contrast to the U.S. National Council of Churches, has been more involved in supporting research and distributing information on the situation of believers in the USSR.

Four months later, in July 1976, the WCC held five days of private consultations on the plight of Soviet believers. No minutes of the meeting were ever made public. But it was learned that views of the Soviet churchmen were presented in person, while no one formally represented the issues raised by Yakunin and Regelson. The main Soviet spokesman at the meeting, Alexei Buevsky, argued that in the future the WCC ought not to cooperate with the three research institutes or other such groups. No formal action was taken, but the Soviet position prevailed thereafter—much as it had, in fact, previously.

The next month General Secretary Potter simply reported to the Central Committee that the consultation confirmed the previous WCC work in this area and with the United Nations. Potter then immediately changed the topic to condemn the rich nations of the world for their treatment of the poor.

On November 1, 1979, Yakunin was arrested; his friend Regelson was taken into custody on Christmas day. Regelson was pressured into renouncing his activities, but Yakunin would not yield. Eventually he received a five-year prison sentence, to be followed by five years in exile. Yakunin's trial on the charge of "anti-Soviet agitation and propaganda" included the accusation that he had sullied the reputation of the Russian Church by writing the 1975 letter to the WCC.[28]

And how did the WCC respond to this? A telex to Keston College from the WCC Director of International Affairs summed it up succinctly: "Presently no immediate action contemplated." Later the WCC did raise the matter privately with the Moscow Patriarchate—hardly a likely source of support for Yakunin. About a year later a letter was made public from the acting general secretary of the WCC to a Russian metropolitan, but WCC member churches were never provided any details about the case, or even asked to support Yakunin in prayer.[29] Yakunin was on his own.

More clues to the WCC perspective on religious liberty and human rights in the Soviet Union can be found in an information pamphlet prepared for the Sixth General Assembly of the WCC, held in July 1983. Though *Human Rights on the Ecumenical Agenda* asserts that "the views expressed do not necessarily reflect positions taken by the WCC," it was released by the WCC's Commission of the Churches on International Affairs (CCIA), and was written by Erich Weingartner, a senior official in the CCIA. In fact, the views are consistent with official WCC actions and attitudes.

Referring to the Yakunin/Regelson letter of 1975, Weingartner comments that "rumors" of Soviet "infringements have reached Western Christians in an exaggerated and sometimes distorted form. . . ."[30] He notes that Russian Church leaders claimed many of those in trouble had only themselves to blame because they broke the law. Such unsubstantiated statements go beyond abandoning dissidents to the mercies of the State; they actually provide the Soviet authorities with foreign "testimony" against accused believers.

Weingartner asserts that the Nairobi debate on religious freedom in the USSR supplanted "far more urgent human rights problems" elsewhere in the world. Several times he contends that those who bring up issues involving religious liberty in Eastern Europe are motivated by political goals and are contributing to the Cold War. He argues that "collective rights take priority over those of the individual, that social, economic, and cultural rights are the foundation of real freedom of the person. . . ."[31]

More than a decade before Mikhail Gorbachev would acknowledge how seriously Soviet society had failed to meet many basic human needs, this WCC executive confidently asserted that "communism has guaranteed employment, food, shelter, education, medical care and social security. . . ."[32] Many of Weingartner's remarks are indistinguishable from those a Brezhnev functionary might have made in the pre-Gorbachev era. Such figures are ridiculed in the Soviet press today.

DEACON RUSAK AND THE WCC

The organizers of the Vancouver General Assembly in 1983 distributed no documents on religious persecution from either inside or outside the Soviet Union. Dr. David Russell, a British Baptist leader, did make one strong statement, but it caused no major discussion. The Archbishop of Canterbury tried to help by sharing a communication he had received from Deacon Rusak of the Russian Orthodox Church. In both a press conference and a BBC radio broadcast, he reported that Rusak was being persecuted for writing a history of the Russian Orthodox Church.

Deacon Rusak's "open letter" to the delegates was nothing if not direct:

The aim of the Soviet authorities in using the church is purely propagandistic. It helps increase the political dividends reaped by the authorities on the international scene and rationalizes the continued existence of the church in a socialist state, as the interchurch and international activity of our church's representatives is directed first and foremost, to serve the interests of the secular (i.e., Soviet-atheist) regime to the detriment of the interests of the church and all the faithful.[33]

Russian Orthodox Church representatives were ready with a response. Their spokesman charged that Rusak could not be taken seriously, since he had been kicked in the head by a horse as a child. If this were true, it was not at all clear how he managed to get accepted into seminary and rise to the editorial staff of the *Journal of the Moscow Patriarchate*. But in any case, the assembly took no action.[34]

In April 1986, Rusak was arrested and received a combined labor camp/exile sentence of twelve years.[35] The WCC stood passively on the sidelines.

It wasn't just the WCC's silence on religious oppression in the Soviet Union which angered many participants and observers at the 1983 General Assembly. The WCC also refused to condemn the USSR for invading Afghanistan. For some, this was the last straw. The Right Rev. Arne Rudvin, a bishop from Pakistan, lamented:

I have great difficulty in respecting the World Council of Churches. It seems to me that it has fully compromised with the Russian Church and that it is bending over backwards not to offend the Russians.

Imagine a World Council of Churches being similarly pressured by the so-called German Christians in the late thirties and the Second World War so that it could not condemn Hitler's actions in Europe. That would be a parallel to what the WCC has done in Vancouver. It has now been shown that the WCC is not truly representing the Church of Christ, but is a political body. I cannot have any respect for its attitude.[36]

"Appeasement"—that's the term Michael Bourdeaux uses to describe the policy of the WCC from 1968 through 1984 relative to the Soviet Union. "It is not too much to say," he concludes, "that the Geneva policy has misled the worldwide membership of the WCC on the real situation of Soviet believers."[37]

CURRENT THINKING IN THE WCC

Late in 1988, the Commission of the Churches on International Affairs published a booklet which reveals some of the WCC's latest thinking on recent changes in the Soviet Union. The author, Ninan Koshy, is the director of the CCIA and a longtime specialist for the WCC in the field of international relations.[38]

Much of the material presented is a straightforward and accurate recounting of current affairs in the USSR. Following in the *glasnost* footsteps of the Soviets themselves, mention is made of the serious abridgements of religious freedom which have been a major part of Soviet history. The difficulties of 1941-59 are underestimated, though the main problems of the Khrushchev antireligious campaign (1959-64) are noted.[39]

It is troubling, however, when a statement such as the following is still made:

> The expectation that religion will weaken and eventually even disappear under socialism has proved to be incorrect. On the contrary in many socialist societies including the Soviet Union the church has considerably grown and is still growing.[40]

Yes, the Church has survived. No, it certainly has not "considerably grown." The great majority of Orthodox churches closed during the Soviet period remain closed. How can a senior WCC official apparently be unaware of this indisputable fact?

Two aspects of Koshy's analysis are particularly revealing. First, in the discussion of *perestroika* there is no serious treatment of the deeper questions raised by the present economic and societal crisis of the Soviet Union. There is no addressing of the issue of whether or not the present economic malaise can be attributed to fundamental failure of Marxist socialism. Soviet economists are asking these tough questions. Why isn't the WCC's top international affairs leadership? Is it because their affection for socialism interferes with a deeper analysis of the Soviet experience?

Second, there is a reassertion of traditional WCC themes, namely the possibility and value of Christian/Marxist cooperation.

> To [a] large number of Christians in all parts of the world, the social and political message of Marxism has been a challenge and even inspiration. Many have sought to reconcile their Christian faith with the vision of society offered by socialism. This has led to new and significant theological insights especially when affirming the Christian gospel's preferential option for the poor. It has also led to active collaboration between Christians and Marxists in liberation movements, in struggles for peace and justice in revolutionary situations

and in building socialism together. Neither the Marxist state nor the church can afford to ignore these developments.[41]

At the very moment when the failures of Marxist socialism are being frankly discussed (admittedly, not as much in the Kremlin as elsewhere in Soviet society), a WCC leader is praising the "social and political message of Marxism."

There may be "new thinking" in Moscow, but there does not appear to be in Geneva.

II. THE NATIONAL COUNCIL OF CHURCHES

[The] communistic social system, grounded on avowed atheism, is an unprecedented threat, especially since it claims to serve ethical purposes such as justice.[42]

* * * *

The Communist Party of the Soviet Union with all its national branches is dedicated to world conquest often camouflaged under the banner of peace. Moreover, Communism comes preaching brotherhood but practicing a new type of imperialism growing out of the dream of world revolution, an imperialism that not only resorts to military conquest but is not satisfied until it imposes its absolute control over the minds and hearts of men. It is in effect a Soviet colonialism.[43]

* * * *

The exploitation and manipulation of anti-Soviet sentiments by political factions and special interests has been one of the most perverse aspects of the Cold War for four decades.[44]

* * * *

The United States' tendency to distort reality in its description of the Soviet Union hurts the U.S. more than it does the Soviet Union . . . . The Christian community bears the major responsibility for breaking down the dividing wall of hostility between the United States and the Soviet Union, for creating a new dynamic, a new relationship between our two peoples.[45]

Which of these views originated with the Religious Right, and which with the U.S. National Council of Churches?

The answer is not as easy as it looks. Actually, all four quotations come from the NCC. The first is an official Governing Board policy statement of May 1951, while the second citation comes from the 1962 edition of *A Christian's Handbook on Communism*—a product of the NCC's Division of Foreign Missions.

The last two quotations come from *Together on the Way*, a 1984 booklet produced by the NCC's U.S.-USSR Church Relations Committee. The latter views are no longer mainstream, either within the NCC constituent churches or within American society as a whole. The rather sharp difference of perspective between the 1960s and the 1980s goes a long way towards explaining how the transformation occurred from "mainline" to "oldline"—or, as some have quipped, "sideline."

LEFT TURN AND DECLINE

Paralleling an abandonment of a distinctively spiritual mission in favor of a role resembling that of political action lobbying groups, the American member churches of both the NCC and WCC have experienced a sharp and steady membership decline for two decades. The five largest Protestant denominations which make up the NCC (and form a support base for the WCC as well) closed down an equivalent of one seven-hundred-member congregation every day for fifteen years during the 1970s and into the 1980s.[46]

It is very important we understand clearly that the NCC's leftward-leaning political reputation is a product of the last half of its existence, not the first. For the better part of two decades following its founding in 1950, the NCC was clear in its opposition to communism. But since the late 1960s, there has been a clear shift among many of its leaders and staff from "anti-communism" to "anti-anti-communism." This ought not to be confused with being "pro-Communist," although there is obviously much sympathy for the ideal of socialism. What it really means is that these leaders have come to fear strong criticism of or actions against Communist states more than they fear communism itself.

Three principal factors have contributed to this remarkable break with the past: (1) the disillusionment with America caused by the Vietnam War, (2) a growing concern about the possibility of nuclear war, (3) a hope that Christian-Marxist dialogue might produce a creative new ideological synthesis and thereby contribute to the prospects of peace. This is not the place to discuss arguments regarding these three points, but whatever their merits (or lack thereof), they helped shape a dramatic new perspective within the ruling ranks and bureaucracy of the NCC.

That the NCC's foreign policy judgments have focused far more on the problems of authoritarian right-wing regimes than on the problems of socialist or Communist regimes is beyond question. That is not a moral or ideological judgment, but rather a simple statement of fact. What one thinks about that orientation is where a value judgment must be made.

From 1981 to 1987, Roy Beck, then a correspondent for the *United Methodist Reporter*, had a front-row seat to evaluate the commitments of his own denomination and the National Council of Churches. In response to strong criticisms of the NCC in 1983 by CBS's "Sixty Minutes," an article in

Reader's Digest, and the Institute on Religion and Democracy, he conducted his own investigation into the politics of the NCC.

Using as his criteria the NCC's own 1963 human rights policy statement, Beck, a Democrat, discovered that over the previous five years (1978-83), 80 percent of all press releases and resolutions issued by the NCC critiqued regimes on the Right. But the bias is even more skewed than the statistics themselves indicate. Resolutions dealing with leftist governments were frequently just that, simple resolutions; statements critiquing the Right were often backed by campaigns involving significant expenditures of time and financial resources.[47]

The debate is not over whether it is appropriate to critique authoritarian regimes of the Right; it *is* appropriate. The question is why one should ignore the crimes of another (and frequently much more brutal in terms of the number of victims) part of the political spectrum.

THE PEACE AGENDA

Like the WCC, the NCC has been deeply involved in the politics of peace. In 1965 a United States Committee for the Christian Peace Conference was established. Because of disagreements spawned by the Soviet invasion of Czechoslovakia in 1968 and the CPC's failure to address it responsibly, the American group reorganized itself as Christians Associated for Relationships with Eastern Europe (CAREE).[48] From 1968 to the present, CAREE has maintained a certain public distance from the CPC, although as one of their informational brochures from the early 1980s put it, CAREE "continues to relate" to the CPC. A critic of CAREE, Joshua Muravchik, explained in 1984:

> CAREE labors to maintain a hair's breadth of distance between itself and the CPC, stressing that it is not a mere national chapter of the CPC like those that exist in Eastern Europe. But this is a distinction without much difference. CAREE sends delegations to CPC assemblies. It is described in CPC publications as the CPC's US affiliate. It makes annual contributions, equivalent to dues, to the CPC. It nominates its members to serve on the CPC's governing bodies, and at least some of these, like other CPC officers, use free tickets supplied by Aeroflot, the Soviet airline, to attend CPC meetings.[49]

Historically there has been a strong tie between CAREE and the National Council of Churches. Professor Bruce Rigdon, one of the NCC's leading authorities on the Soviet Union, was a former chairman of CAREE, as was former United Methodist bishop and NCC president James Armstrong. These people are not pro-Communist, but their understanding of how best to work for peace has aligned them closely with groups such as the CPC whose agenda often parallels that of the Kremlin.

In 1987, the more radical wing of CAREE broke off and established the North American Christian Peace Conference—a full-fledged chapter member of the CPC. The more moderate part of CAREE has refused to join the chapter, but is committed to maintaining its contacts with the CPC in Prague.

Under the editorship of Paul Mojzes, CAREE's publication *Occasional Papers on Religion in Eastern Europe (OPREE)* has made available views which are considerably broader than the ones which have traditionally dominated the CPC. There have been some excellent recent issues in particular which have explored the debate over the condition of the Church in the Soviet Union under *glasnost*.

Articles in OPREE itself have highlighted the one-sided character of the CPC. For example, Paul Stefanik noted the irony at a 1978 international Christian Peace Conference of official greetings being given to the conference by representatives of Kosygin, Castro, Honecker, and Arafat. That the conference had a heightened "leftist-orientation" could not be in doubt, according to Stefanik.[50]

The Lutheran observer's assessment could hardly have been more critical.

> "The depressing restraints of reality and reason" were simply not reflected in the [CPC] Assembly's rhetoric. Its recommendations were largely without merit; its convictions lacked credibility. "The ideologically-inspired misinformation" that was so much in evidence affected the judgment of both the speakers and the listeners.[51]

Surprisingly, Stefanik still believes the CPC has a redeeming feature, and this may provide a key to understanding the thinking of some church activists who continue to affiliate with such controversial Soviet-influenced organizations.

> . . . the CPC pronouncements *are,* at least, "*instrumental,*" assuring the continued existence of the organized church and enabling it to fulfill its "*fundamental*" mission of worship and witness—and the "extravagant" and "unreasonable" protestations may be discounted as merely "*incidental.*"[52]

In other words, mouthing the leftist and unreasonable party line is the price of keeping the churches open in Eastern Europe. For many other Western participants, however, the politics of Moscow may really be more convincing than those of their own Western governments. Perhaps during the *glasnost* era those who have not agreed with the politics of the CPC can branch out to establish contacts with those Eastern-bloc Christians whose politics are much more independent from the ruling parties.

TENTATIVE SUPPORT OF BELIEVERS IN THE USSR

Tangible evidence that the NCC's attitude towards the Soviet Union really did shift during the last twenty years is found in the history of *Religion in Communist Dominated Areas* (RCDA). It was founded by the NCC in 1962 as an information service of the Department of International Affairs. Its initial editors, Paul Anderson and Blahoslav Hruby, were extremely knowledgeable on the topic. Anderson was the NCC's foremost expert on Russian Christians, and Hruby was a Czech emigre with much firsthand experience. For ten years this was the only major English periodical dedicated to the study of religion under communism. (Keston College's *Religion in Communist Lands* did not begin until 1972.)

But in 1972 the NCC withdrew its support of RCDA, claiming inadequate funds. Paul Anderson retired, and Hruby was constrained to carry on the work independently. The real cause for the cutoff of NCC support was not lack of funds, but lack of commitment to the cause. The council was swayed by critics who argued that affiliation with a publication that documented religious repression would harm East/West relations and undermine Christian-Marxist dialogue. This interpretation of what was required to support detente won out.[53]

During the past twenty years the NCC has from time to time been more willing than the WCC to issue public statements critical of the Soviet Union or in defense of believers. In 1968 the NCC reported in a "Resolution on Religious Intolerance in the USSR" that it felt "compelled to raise its voice against the persecution of dissenting Baptists in the USSR" (February 22). The resolution specifically mentioned two hundred Baptist dissidents imprisoned in 1966 and 1967, and noted that their children had sometimes been inhumanely treated. In that same year it strongly criticized the invasion of Czechoslovakia.

It is true, however, that a tendency toward moral equivalency analysis was beginning to creep into NCC statements. Thus, on January 23, 1969, while another resolution noted the continued oppression in Czechoslovakia, it added that the United States, too, "has been guilty of oppression."

Resolutions on the problems of believers in the Soviet Union appeared in 1972, 1973, and 1975.[54] On November 11, 1977, the Governing Board requested all "religious communities in the U.S.A. to pray and act for the confessing Church, for all prisoners of conscience in the USSR and other countries under Soviet domination. . . . " A resolution in defense of the Siberian Seven was passed on May 10, 1979, and on November 10, a resolution called the arrest of Gleb Yakunin "a distressing encroachment on the discussion and exercise of human rights. . . ." An appeal was sent to Brezhnev in 1981 seeking amnesty for prisoners of conscience.

THE 1980s: ONE-SIDED DOCUMENTARY AND RED CARPET TOURS

Though the NCC has a better track record than does the WCC in publicly protesting religious freedom violations in the USSR, two events in the 1980s made it quite clear that the NCC was not willing to act as forthrightly as the situation warranted.

First was the controversial 1983 two-hour television documentary which the NCC produced in cooperation with NBC. The program eventually aired twice, and was called ''The Church of the Russians.'' Bruce Rigdon, a professor from McCormick Seminary in Chicago, was mainly responsible for the enterprise.

The production did demonstrate the continued existence, beauty, and vitality of the Russian Orthodox Church. But viewers were only given details about the registered church, and even here they were treated to a one-sided presentation which left much unsaid. What was said was sometimes flatly false. For example, a Russian Orthodox official went unchallenged when he stated the following about Church/State relations in the Soviet Union:

> Our discussions are absolutely free. There is no control over us . . . not in the preparation of our work, nor in our work, nor in conversation. Such control cannot exist because the sphere of our work is clearly religious. It is quite apart from government concerns.
>
> They [the Soviet authorities] are not interested in our activities or how our decisions are made.[55]

This is simply propaganda, and no legitimate ''quiet diplomacy'' would allow it to pass as truth.

Also in the NBC program, Rigdon asserted that ''perhaps the very existence of the Council for Religious Affairs is an example of cooperation'' between Church and State.[56] This is a bit like suggesting that cats ''cooperate'' with mice.

The NCC/NBC collaborative effort attracted considerable criticism. Particularly because of the protests of Peter Reddaway, an authority on human rights in the Soviet Union, NBC eventually aired a one-hour discussion on July 15, 1984, dealing with the earlier broadcast.[57]

A second example of soft-pedaling the problems of believers in the Soviet Union was the controversial June, 1984, NCC-sponsored trip to the Soviet Union. A delegation of 266 participants was the largest American church group ever to visit the Soviet Union. The NCC described the tour as a ''peace invasion,'' but an editorial in the *Wall Street Journal* (June 27, 1984) described the pilgrimage as an example of ''rose-colored diplomacy.''[58]

In few areas have Western church groups shown themselves to be more vulnerable than in the sphere of Soviet-hosted visits or tours to the USSR.

Since the 1930s "political pilgrims" have gone to the USSR, been shown a limited portion of Soviet reality, and have returned home to pass on views about the Soviet Union which owe more to Soviet propaganda than to sober analysis.[59]

A long history of elaborately staged tours for foreigners in Russia dates back at least to Catherine the Great at the end of the eighteenth century. All governments can be expected to put their best foot forward when serving as tour guides for guests, but in 1787 one of Catherine's senior advisors outdid himself. Potemkin constructed Hollywood-style facades of model peasant villages in the newly acquired territories of southern Russia and the Caucasus to impress Emperor Joseph of Austria.[60]

Although there have been examples of healthy Soviet security personnel donning prison uniforms to impress political guests with how well Soviet prisoners are cared for, "Potemkin villages" are not the main way foreigners are misled. The usual method is for Soviet authorities to control the itinerary. The most effective propaganda is not in telling outright lies, but rather in showing part of the truth as if it were the whole truth.

What can Western church visitors expect to hear from their Soviet guides? The three previous historical chapters provide the answer. Officially approved Soviet religious leaders have consistently distorted and falsified the situation of believers in the USSR. At best, they have remained silent.

If there is any doubt about this, simply compare the statements being made under *glasnost* by Soviet correspondents and Council for Religious Affairs officials with those made in 1983 by Russian Orthodox and Baptist registered leaders.[61] *I'm Free to Believe* was published by Novosti Press Agency in English two years before Gorbachev came to power. Archbishop Pitirim, in charge of publishing for the Russian Orthodox Church, responds in the book to Western charges of discrimination against believers in the USSR.

> I think such material is spread by those who are constantly seeking ways of increasing confrontation between countries. The Soviet Constitution guarantees freedom of conscience to citizens of the country. Soviet people may profess any religion they wish or not profess any at all. The faithful make full use of this right. Moreover, Soviet legislation has special provisions protecting believers from any encroachments.[62]

Alexei Bychkov, the prominent Baptist leader, was just as categorical. He insisted that Soviet Baptists "profess their faith in absolute freedom." Compliant Jewish leaders have argued the same. Adolph Shayevich, the rabbi of the Moscow Choral Synagogue, wrote, "in all sincerity I can say that I have never experienced any pressure on myself from the state nor have I felt any discrimination."[63] Interestingly, Western Jewish leaders have been far more skeptical of such blanket assurances than their Christian counterparts.

But is it really true that tour participants swallow inaccurate portrayals of the Soviet reality? Helen Hamilton, one of the NCC 1984 trip leaders, appeared on the "Phil Donahue" show after her return from the Soviet Union. She commented that though the Bolsheviks sought to eliminate religion, "sixty years later, the church has grown. It's continuing to grow."[64] The statement is utter nonsense. If she had said that the Church had survived and its faith is alive and strong, that would have been true. Or she could even have reported that there had been a recent increase in interest in religion in the Soviet Union. But to say that the Church has grown since the Bolshevik Revolution is to ignore the facts.

Even if one accepts an optimistic estimate of the number of Russian Orthodox believers today (60 million), that would be just over half of the number in 1914, and the population today is much greater. According to Soviet statistics in early 1989, there exist about seventy-five hundred Russian Orthodox Churches, compared with approximately seven or eight times that many in 1914. In Moscow in the early 1980s, less than fifty Russian Orthodox Churches were left out of more than five hundred functioning Orthodox churches in 1914—when the population was only a quarter of today's.[65]

By any objective measure, the strength of the Russian Orthodox Church is much less today than before the Communists took power. In addition, there are literally millions of Soviet citizens, educated in an aggressively anti-religious environment, who have never been exposed to what Christianity really teaches.

The briefing materials prepared for those 266 NCC delegates indicated a predisposition *not* to encounter any unpleasant surprises. Ms. Hamilton sought to assure her fellow travelers that, on the basis of her past trips to the USSR, "while we heard of past persecution, it seems that the relationship between the church and the government is stable now."[66] The delegation apparently saw what Ms. Hamilton had prepared it to see, because at the press conference upon its return the group testified that the situation was improving with the Church.[67]

How wrong they were. We now know from Soviet statistics released under *glasnost* that the number of Orthodox churches steadily declined from the 1960s right through until 1986. And Michael Bourdeaux, when asked in an interview within a few months of the NCC trip to characterize the situation of believers in the Soviet Union in recent months, responded: "Unquestionably it has gotten significantly worse over the last five years."[68]

Another essay in the 1984 NCC briefing packet was written by a leader of the United Presbyterian Women. She passed on as satisfactory an explanation she had received at the Soviet Peace Council: the reason there were Christians in prison was not because they were Christian, but because they had broken the law. After all, she said, there are Christians in American jails, too.[69]

That someone with little knowledge of the Soviet Union might find convincing such an explanation is perhaps understandable; that the NCC would publish such a flawed observation in a guide for people visiting the Soviet Union is inexcusable. What is missing, of course, is a simple explanation that the Soviet laws being violated are those which prevent free exercise of religious belief—holding religious meetings, printing religious literature not controlled by the State, evangelism outside of the registered church structure, or organizing religious instruction for children. Such activities have been completely illegal unless the religious communities allow themselves to be significantly regulated in carrying out their religious activities.

It should not comes as any surprise that the NCC trip did not encounter any significant problems of religious repression. Organizers had urged participants to "overcome their stereotypes about Marxists and Communists." Briefing materials noted the need to combat "the exploitation and manipulation of anti-Soviet sentiments by political factions" in America.[70] This was a trip designed to promote "peace," not a serious encounter with the problems of believers.

When two women at the Moscow Baptist Church sought, at considerable risk, to communicate a different scenario than that presented in the "red carpet" tour, they irritated, rather than impressed, U.S. tour organizers. One of the small signs unfurled from the balcony said: "Pray for the persecuted church." Tour participants later reported that one of the NCC tour leaders tried to dissuade delegates from talking to one of the women outside afterwards, because to do so would be impolite to the Soviet hosts.[71]

Comments from tour organizers about the potential of the U.S./USSR church contacts to enhance world peace raise serious questions about the reliability and sobriety of the NCC analysis of the Soviet Union. The press release from the group following the trip included the following: "Rigdon said the 'degree of internal freedom' the [Soviet] churches have to continue their peacemaking work is 'enormously important' to Americans." Another key delegation leader, Rev. Robert White, was quoted in the *New York Tribune* as saying that Soviet churchmen have "influence in the government because they represent 60 million people." He also stated that the Soviet leaders were "expressing their own passion for peace, not someone else's party line."[72]

There is no convincing evidence to support Rigdon's assertion of "internal freedom" of the Russian church to work for peace in any way other than that which parrots the official line of the Kremlin. There is scant, if any, evidence that the Church has been able to influence the State. There is massive evidence that the Church cannot even influence its own affairs at key points, let alone those of the government.

In the final analysis, the 1984 NCC "peace offensive" to the Soviet

Union contributed as much to misunderstanding as to understanding. Mark Elliott has concluded:

> Statements emanating from tour leaders and subsequently from NCC materials highlighting the trip would not allow one to receive an accurate impression of the reality of Soviet church life. In this instance NCC spokespersons, press releases, and published tour accounts downplayed difficulties faced by believers and accepted without qualification claims of improvements voiced by government or state-sanctioned church sources.[73]

On a number of occasions in private, and occasionally in public, NCC personnel are more forthright about problems of believers in the USSR. The problem is that these periodic acknowledgments of difficulties are, for the general public, swamped by messages which communicate something very different.

PROSPECTS FOR MORE RESPONSIBLE POLICIES IN THE NCC

There are signs of some improvement in the way the NCC treats the topic of religion in the USSR. Consider the following 1987 statement from an NCC study booklet honoring the millennium—the one-thousand-year anniversary of the official coming of Christianity to Kievan Rus'.[74]

> Today, religious life in the Soviet Union continues to be restricted to worship. Believers are not legally permitted to engage in charitable activities, set up study groups or lectures, create youth groups or other organizations, publish parochial or diocesan newsletters. Thus most of the expressions of religious life which North American Christians consider intrinsic to their religious witness—as indeed, Soviet Christians also do—are outlawed in the USSR.[75]

The authors of this statement are a rather unlikely pair—Professor Bruce Rigdon and Father Leonid Kishkovsky. The former has been associated for many years with avoiding such statements. The latter is a remarkable priest of the Orthodox Church in America and the president-elect of the National Council of Churches, scheduled to assume his duties in 1990.

For many years Kishkovsky has walked a tightrope between his involvement on the Board of Directors of the organization which publishes *Religion in Communist Dominated Areas* (the group the NCC cut from its budget in 1972) and his ecumenical responsibilities for the Orthodox Church in America to the NCC. In a speech on January 26, 1989, he called on the NCC to rebuild a good relationship with the Research Center for Religion and Human Rights in Closed Societies, which publishes RCDA.[76]

The Rigdon/Kishkovsky statement appears in a foreword to a book by J. Martin Bailey, one of the leaders of the 1984 NCC trip to the USSR. The foreword frankly acknowledges that "Christian witness in the Soviet Union has . . . brought hundreds of men and women to trial, imprisonment and exile," and it goes on to note that "a North American visitor to the USSR is not likely to meet these Christians or their families."[77]

Despite its many positive points, the foreword does repeat one old and not very convincing argument. The reader is told that a major reason for the preparation of the mission study is to provide "a much-needed corrective and challenge" to the notion held by some in the West that all Soviet citizens are members of the Communist party and atheists. To be sure, there undoubtedly are some in the West who believe such nonsense, but not nearly as many as the NCC seems to imagine. Responsible critics of the NCC and WCC have long been aware of the tenacity and vibrancy of religious faith in the Soviet Union. The complaint of these commentators has been that the plight of believers in the USSR has consistently been much worse than that acknowledged by the ecumenical church world.

There are many positive features to the basic Bailey text, the study guide, and other NCC-produced materials related to the millennium. American Christians can learn a great deal about the history, theology, liturgy, music, art, and customs of Russian Orthodoxy. The bibliographies include many of the top scholars on the topic of religion in the Soviet Union.

But serious problems of balance remain. The basic NCC text focuses on the biographies of seven prominent figures from the Russian Church, two of whom are from the Soviet period. Though there is some fine praise of Yakunin in the foreword, he is not one of the two Soviets singled out for special biographical treatment. The two who are selected are predictably from the registered church world—Metropolitan Nikodim (who died in the early 1980s) and Alexei Bychkov—and both have often done what was required of them by Kremlin officials. At least the text acknowledges that controversy has followed in the wake of some of what they have said.

Occasionally, serious factual errors appear in the text. The number of churches closed by Stalin during the 1920s and 1930s is significantly underestimated. Bailey puts the number at twelve thousand, whereas it was much, much higher. Also the author puts the number of Russian Orthodox parishes at twenty thousand, nearly three times the number which both Soviet and Western sources usually cited at the time.[78]

The NCC preference for the registered perspective over the non-registered emerges again in the discussion of smuggling Bibles into the Soviet Union. Bailey noted that Baptist leader Bychkov favors receiving Bibles only "through legal channels" and quotes him as saying that the Bible smugglers "mainly create noise."[79] The statement is simply false. Millions more Bibles reached the Soviet Union in the pre-Gorbachev era "unofficially" than through the occasional concessions which registered leaders managed, with great difficulty (though much fanfare), to wring from Soviet authorities.

What is currently being said by the Kremlin (and finally more openly by the NCC) during *glasnost*—namely, that there really have been serious problems for religious believers in the Soviet Union—has been said for many years by others who have tried to get the NCC to speak out more forthrightly on these issues.

Some will conclude that the greater frankness of the NCC in dealing with the problems of believers in the USSR simply parallels the Kremlin's own willingness to be more open. Such an explanation, however, tells only part of the story. A few officials within the NCC are pushing for a more balanced and responsible advocacy for believers, both registered and unregistered, in the Soviet Union.

As president of the NCC, Leonid Kishkovsky will not have nearly the power or authority which is vested in the general secretary. Nonetheless, he represents an important possibility of helping the NCC move back toward the center, toward the more balanced and responsible policies of earlier times. He has the intelligence, compassion, and commitment to the ecumenical movement and to believers in the USSR to enable him to carry on the fine tradition which Paul Anderson represented before his retirement in 1972. In recent years Kishkovsky has experienced visa problems at the hands of the Soviets, a sign in his case that the Soviets understand the independence of his witness.

Kishkovsky is not alone at the NCC in representing the potential of a more balanced approached toward believers in the Soviet Union. Deacon Michael Roshak, like Kishkovsky an Orthodox believer, has been the Director of the NCC Europe/USSR office since 1986. He is a young man who clearly understands the full picture of religion in the USSR. In 1986, 1987, and 1988, Roshak led NCC tours into the Soviet Union, and he has helped in orientations which can last up to four days before the tours begin.

To the extent that Father Kishkovsky and Deacon Roshak are involved in giving briefings, arranging for knowledgeable persons to give briefings, or leading NCC delegations into the Soviet Union, the NCC can begin to recover some of the credibility and respect it lost in recent years. It is noteworthy that the most hopeful signs in the present NCC come from two Orthodox officials, although it is not clear how much support they have or how long they will be in key positions. In the spring of 1989, Roshak's position was already less than full time, and with all the NCC staff cutbacks in process his continued presence is not at all certain.

Ultimately, the development of a more prudent NCC policy toward Soviet believers and the restoration of the NCC's reputation will require a sharp break with the sort of comments made in 1984 by the leaders of the NCC tour to the USSR. There are signs of hope, but it is much too early to judge whether and to what degree that hope will be realized.

Some in the NCC are open to reconsidering the consequences of past practices; unfortunately, not many of them are in senior leadership positions.

The big question is whether the more moderate voices will be heard, and whether the constituent memberships will be assertive enough to express their wishes. Rigdon has left McCormick Seminary and is now a pastor in the Detroit area. As of March 1989, he is still involved in the planning of trips to the Soviet Union. Time alone will reveal if his perspectives and approaches are different from those which characterized his involvement in the controversial events of 1983 and 1984.

If the Soviets retreat from *glasnost,* will the NCC also revert to earlier patterns, reluctant to defend forcefully those most in need of its support?

There is at least the potential of a move back toward a more effective and balanced National Council of Churches. Such a shift is unlikely, however, unless apathetic and timid constituencies become concerned enough to make their opinions known.

Those who believe most in the ideal of the ecumenical movement would very much like to see its potential realized by combining with evangelical and Catholic communities to create an effective and wiser Christian support base for believers in distress everywhere in the world—including the Soviet Union.

Notes

1. J. A. Emerson Vermaat, *The World Council of Churches and Politics: 1975-1986* (New York: Freedom House, 1989), 1. For further information on the WCC, see Ernest W. Lefever, *Amsterdam to Nairobi: The World Council of Churches and the Third World* and *Nairobi to Vancouver: The World Council of Churches and the World, 1975-87* (Washington, D.C.: Ethics and Public Policy Center, 1979, 1987).

2. Vermaat, *World Council of Churches*, 5.

3. Basic information in this chapter on the World Council of Churches and its relationship to its member churches from the Soviet bloc, unless otherwise indicated, is taken from Michael Bourdeaux, "The Russian Church, Religious Liberty and the World Council of Churches,"*Religion in Communist Lands*, vol. 13 (Spring 1985), 4-27.

4. The Orthodox Churches of Rumania, Bulgaria, and Poland joined the WCC in 1961, the same year the Russian Orthodox Church did. In 1962, the Soviet Union gained several new memberships in the WCC: the All-Union Council of Evangelical Christians-Baptists, the Georgian Orthodox Church, and the Evangelical Lutherans of Latvia and Estonia. The Serbian Orthodox Church (Yugoslavia) joined in 1965 and the Czechoslovakian Orthodox Church in 1966. Harold E. Fey, ed. *A History of the Ecumenical Movement* (Geneva: World Council of Churches, 1970), vol. 2, *The Ecumenical Advance: 1948-1968,* 15, 304-5; Walter Sawatsky, *Soviet Evangelicals Since World War II* (Scottdale, Penn.: Herald Press, 1981), 368.

5. Bourdeaux, "Russian Church," 7.

6. Ibid., 8.

7. Quoted in ibid.

8. Sawatsky, *Soviet Evangelicals*, 122-23.

9. The comment is from Tair Tairov, and it was published in the Soviet newspaper *Tribune.* Quoted in "World Peace Council in Crisis," *News Weekly,* 19 October 1988, 4.

10. On the history of the CPC, see Trevor Beeson, *Discretion and Valour,* 2nd ed. (London: Collins, 1982), 393-96. Paul Mojzes, a longtime observer of the CPC, argues that unlike the WPC,

which was controlled by the Soviets from the beginning, the CPC's initial foundation was a product of a desire for genuine dialogue between West German and Czech theologians. Telephone interview with author, 20 April 1989.

11. *Soviet Active Measures*, hearings before the Permanent Select Committee on Intelligence, House of Representatives, 13-14 July 1982, 67.

12. Vermaat, *World Council of Churches*, 7.

13. In 1984 there was an "International Conference on Nicaragua and for Peace in Central America" convened in Lisbon, sponsored by the World Peace Conference and the WCC's Commission of the Churches on International Affairs (CCIA). Mario Soares, Prime Minister of Portugal, convinced his friends in the Socialist International not to send important delegates, since the Lisbon meeting was, in his view, a Communist-inspired event. (Ibid.)

14. Ibid., 6-7.

15. Hans Hebly, " 'The Captive Churches' and the Ecumenical Movement," Briefing Paper of the Institute on Religion and Democracy, Washington, D.C., January 1984, 2-3.

16. Vermaat, *World Council of Churches*, 7.

17. Hans Hebly, *Eastbound Ecumenism: A Collection of Essays on the World Council of Churches and Eastern Europe* (Lanham, Md.: University Press of America, 1986), 91.

18. Ibid., 93.

19. Bourdeaux, "Russian Church," 9.

20. Quoted in Vermaat, *World Council of Churches*, 11.

21. Ibid., 23.

22. Bourdeaux, "Russian Church," 10.

23. Quoted in Vermaat, *World Council of Churches*, 9.

24. Bourdeaux, "Russian Church," 11.

25. Quoted in ibid., 13.

26. Quoted in ibid., 14.

27. Ibid., 16.

28. Vermaat, *World Council of Churches*, 20.

29. Ibid.

30. Quoted in Bourdeaux, "Russian Church," 24.

31. Quoted in ibid., 22, 24.

32. Quoted in ibid., 23.

33. Quoted in Vermaat, *World Council of Churches*, 23.

34. Bourdeaux, "Russian Church," 24-25.

35. Lisa Gibney, "Religious Liberty Alert," *Religion and Democracy*, Institute on Religion and Democracy, August 1988. In 1987, a three-volume edition in Russian of Rusak's history of the Russian Orthodox Church (*Witness of the Prosecution*) was published by the Holy Trinity Monastery (Jordanville, N. Y.). In 1989, Deacon Rusak was allowed to emigrate to the West with his wife. On May 3 at a Capitol Hill reception when I told Rusak about my research on Western church responses to believers in the USSR, he grabbed my arm and with great intensity said, "This is just what we need!"

36. Quoted in Vermaat, *World Council of Churches*, 49.

37. Bourdeaux, "Russian Church," 26.

38. Ninan Koshy, *Perestroika: Some Preliminary Comments* (Geneva: WCC Commission of the Church on International Affairs, 1988). CCIA Background Information Series, 1988/No. 1.

39. Ibid., 18-19.

40. Ibid., 22-23.

41. Ibid., 23.

42. "The National Council of Churches Views Its Task in Christian Life and Work," policy statement, 16 May 1951. I am grateful to K. L. Billingsley for sharing with me the four quotations which open this section. His forthcoming book on the National Council of Churches will be published by the Ethics and Public Policy Center, Washington, D.C.

43. *A Christian's Handbook on Communism*, National Council of Churches' Committee on World Literacy and Christian Literature, Division of Foreign missions, 1962, 45.

44. Alan Geyer, in *Together on the Way* (New York: US-USSR Church Relations Committee, National Council of Churches, 1984), 5.

45. Robert F. Smylie, "What About the Russians?" in *Together on the Way*, 14.

46. William H. Willimon and Robert L. Wilson, *Rekindling the Flame* (Nashville: Abingdon Press, 1987), 12-15.

47. Roy Howard Beck, *On This Ice* (Wilmore, Ky.: Bristol Books, 1988), 185-86.

48. Information on the Christian Peace Conference and Christians Associated for Relationships with Eastern Europe, unless otherwise indicated, is taken from CAREE informational brochures or publications, and minutes of several annual meetings.

49. Joshua Muravchik, "The National Council of Churches and the U.S.S.R.," *This World* (Fall 1984):48.

50. Paul Stefanik, "The Christian Peace Conference—Propaganda? . . . or Prophecy?" *Occasional Papers on Religion in Eastern Europe*, vol. 5, no. 3 (May 1985), 51.

51. Ibid., 55.

52. Ibid., 56.

53. For Hruby's discussion of why the NCC decided to cease its support of RCDA, see *Religion in Communist Dominated Areas*, vol. 11, nos. 1-3 (1972), 2-3.

54. See "Violation of Religious Freedom and Human Rights," 14 February 1972; "The Violation of Human Rights in Chile and the USSR," 14 October 1973; and, "Resolution on Secret Trials in the Soviet Union," 10-12 October 1975. Noted in Billingsley's manuscript on the NCC.

55. Quoted in Muravchik, "National Council of Churches," 51.

56. Quoted in ibid.

57. Readers can obtain a transcript of the 1984 program by sending $2 to Journal Graphics, 2 John Street, New York, NY 10038. The transcript of the original NBC production can also be obtained for $2 from the John T. Conner Center for US/USSR Reconciliation, 320 North Street, West Lafayette, IN 47906. For this and other bibliographic information related to the NBC/NCC program see Mark Elliott, "A Typology of Western-Soviet Christian Contacts," (Unpublished manuscript, Institute for the Study of Christianity and Marxism, Wheaton College, Wheaton, Ill., 1988), n. 20, 44-45.

58. Quoted in Elliott, "Western-Soviet Contacts," 16.

59. A good introduction to this phenomenon can be found by reading Paul Hollander, *Political Pilgrims: Travels of Western Intellectuals to the Soviet Union, China, and Cuba, 1928-1978* (New York: Oxford University Press, 1981). A new edition is scheduled for publication in 1989 by University Press of America.

60. See Michael T. Florinsky, *Russia: A History and an Interpretation* (New York: Macmillan Company, 1968), 1:529.

61. See chapter 13 for details about what the Soviets themselves are now saying about past and present state restrictions on religion.

62. Quoted in Muravchik, "National Council of Churches," 39.

63. Quoted in ibid.

64. Quoted in ibid., 50.

65. Marshall Winokur, "Book Reviews," *St. Vladimir's Theological Quarterly*, vol. 26, no. 1 (1982), 58.

66. Quoted in Muravchik, "National Council of Churches," 47.

67. Ibid., 50.

68. Quoted in ibid., 50-51.

69. Ibid., 47.

70. Quoted in ibid., 32.

71. Ibid., 31.

72. Quoted in ibid., 45, 49.

73. Elliott, "Western-Soviet Contacts," 16.

74. Sections of the following analysis are taken from Kent R. Hill, "Glasnost in the NCC?" *Religion and Democracy*, Institute on Religion and Democracy, June 1988, 1-4, 6.

75. Bruce Rigdon and Leonid Kishkovsky, foreword to J. Martin Bailey, *One Thousand Years: Stories from the History of Christianity in the USSR, 988-1988* (New York: Friendship Press, 1987), vi.

76. Walter Skold, "NCC Official Seeks Tie with Group Monitoring Communist Countries," *Religious News Service*, 31 January 1989, 9.

77. Rigdon and Kishkovsky, foreword, vii.

78. Bailey, *One Thousand Years*, 5, 46. See note 23 in chapter 8, which provides further information on the probable origin of the NCC error on the number of functioning Russian Orthodox churches.

79. Ibid., 60.

CHAPTER 10

A MIXED RECORD:

Evangelicals, Lutherans, Catholics, and Parachurch Groups

*E*cumenical church leaders are not the only ones who have often failed to defend Christians in the USSR; influential parts of the evangelical world are just as guilty. Evangelicals have been just as vulnerable to disinformation and to misunderstanding about what would and would not help Christians in the Soviet Union as have their more liberal church counterparts.

To be sure, as in the ecumenical and oldline church world, some good did come from many of the contacts with Soviet believers. This chapter, however, is an analysis of why evangelicals fell so far short of what they were capable.

On other fronts, the record is spotty. The Lutheran response fits very much the pattern of the ecumenical and evangelical church world. In general, Roman Catholics have been more supportive of their co-religionists than have Protestants. The largest relief agency dealing with the Soviet Union is a West German-based Catholic organization (Aid to the Church in Need), and the 1988 statement by the U.S. Catholic Council of Bishops on religious freedom and the situation of believers in the USSR is excellent. The record of parachurch mission societies is generally much better than that of the organized church, though there are some major exceptions. And one of the bright spots in this whole area is the work of several fine research organizations.

BILLY GRAHAM IN MOSCOW: A CASE STUDY

A careful examination of the controversial visit of Billy Graham to Moscow is useful for purposes of illustration. There are two reasons for this. First, Graham is one of the most influential church leaders of the twentieth century. The mistakes made by Dr. Graham are compelling evidence not only that all of us are fallible, but that the Soviets have proven particularly adept at manipulating some of our best leaders.

Second, the fact that this experience occurred to an evangelical should warn us that it is not just the ecumenical or oldline church world which needs to reconsider its views on dealing with believers in the USSR.

Long before Graham arrived in Moscow in May 1982, the possibility of his appearance there touched off considerable debate and protest. Graham was invited to give an address to the "World Conference of Religious Workers for Saving the Sacred Gift of Life from Nuclear Catastrophe." The conference was hosted by the Russian Orthodox Church, but the Prague-based Christian Peace Conference (CPC) planned much of it.[1]

The invitation to speak at the conference seemed to offer, from Graham's perspective, the possibility of making progress towards fulfilling a lifelong dream: preaching the gospel to large audiences in the Soviet Union. The Soviets clearly were aware of Graham's hopes in this regard, and agreed to allow him to speak outside the conference as well.

Many in the West urged Graham not to accept. As *Christianity Today* put it the month before the conference, "the clear risk was that he would be perceived as lending his fame and stature to what is essentially a propaganda exercise."[2]

But Graham decided to accept anyway, noting, "I feel it is a God-given opportunity for me to proclaim the gospel of Jesus Christ in a country where I have not had this privilege before."[3]

While Graham visited Moscow, seven Russian Pentecostals seeking emigration neared their fourth anniversary inside the American embassy. It seems clear the American evangelist was very nervous about meeting with the Siberian Seven; at least that is what the stringent "no-publicity" conditions for his visit conveyed to the refugees. But he did meet them, and his visit ended up being one of the least comforting encounters the Seven had during their five years in the embassy.

Particularly revealing was an exchange between Dr. Graham and twenty-year-old Timothy Chmykhalov. When the young man asked the evangelist if he would help the Seven, Graham replied that he would "pray" for them. He did note that he had talked with Soviet officials about their case, and he "hoped" they would resolve it. Then he added something which particularly troubled the Seven: "I came to preach, not to get involved with any political issues." The Seven were deeply hurt because they did not consider themselves political dissidents at all. Their problem was that the Soviets had for several decades systematically deprived them and millions of others of the right to practice their faith without government intervention or restriction.[4]

How had the question of religious freedom been swallowed up by "politics"? Graham seems to have accepted the Soviet definition of politics—a definition which includes almost everything in life, except one narrow part of religious activity (liturgical worship in a registered and restricted church). By expanding the definition of politics, the Soviets are able to claim that religious freedom is not abridged, only the freedom to break Soviet laws. Thus, the Siberian Seven are transformed into lawbreakers and ought therefore to be avoided by religious leaders from the West. This linguistic sleight of hand has proven to be a highly effective method of dealing with foreign religious leaders anxious not to offend their Soviet hosts.

Had Graham elected to remain completely silent while in Moscow on all matters related to the condition of religion in the country, he would have fared better. What got him into trouble was what he said, not just what he didn't say.

Newsweek quoted Graham as remarking, it is "a wonderful thing that in a country that officially professes atheism, so many churches are open."[5] No mention was made that six of every seven churches existing in 1917 had been closed by the authorities. As *Time* put it: "Graham seemed oblivious to the precarious role of religion in a country that endorses scientific atheism and outlaws public evangelism."[6]

The day after Graham's hour-and-fifteen-minute meeting with the Siberian Seven, the evangelist was asked, "Have you personally witnessed any religious persecution while you have been here?" Graham's response: "I have seen no religious persecution during my stay in Russia."[7]

It should be noted that Graham later expressed great regret that he did not mention the Siberian Seven when asked whether he had witnessed religious persecution. He also explained:

> I am an evangelist—not an expert in church-state relations in the Soviet Union. I regret that some of the statements I made regarding my visit to the Soviet Union were misconstrued and misinterpreted by the media. I care deeply about the plight and suffering of believers everywhere in the world where religious freedoms are restricted, including the Soviet Union. I sincerely regret any public statements which I made that might seem to indicate otherwise.[8]

It is interesting to contrast Graham's Moscow comments in 1982 with his response to the same issue following his first trip to the Soviet Union in 1959. Graham observed then that it is quite evident that to be

> an open Christian is costly in Russia. To be a member of a Church is a great privilege and responsibility. The cost has been carefully calculated over many months or years. It's not just meeting a board of deacons or elders, signing a decision card, or walking forward, or even being baptized—it is the rearrangement of one's whole way of life.[9]

This is hardly the statement of a Cold War McCarthyite who needed to become more sophisticated in his understanding of the Soviet Union. Rather, it is an accurate and sensitive recognition of the price one must pay to be a Christian in that country.

Graham's public relations people later contended that Graham had been misquoted in the West, and this undoubtedly happened in some of the literally hundreds of stories written about his controversial comments. Much of the time, however, Graham was *not* misquoted.

Even Graham's own May 19, 1982, press release from the "Crusade Information Service" contains quotes which confirm that he became the mouthpiece for inaccurate information. Though he acknowledged much more fully in the press release than he did while in the USSR that religion is restricted in the Soviet Union, he also made the following comment:

> In the Soviet Union there are an estimated 20,000 places of worship of various religions open and each year hundreds of permits are granted for new churches.[10]

The statement is inaccurate and very misleading. It is virtually identical to what the Soviets had been telling visiting Western religious leaders for years. Why did Graham repeat this view of religion in the USSR rather than that of the main Western research centers?

What *was* the true situation in 1982 when Graham visited Moscow? The Soviets themselves have provided the answer. The successor to the man in Moscow who orchestrated Graham's itinerary is Konstantin Kharchev, the chairman of the Council for Religious Affairs. In November 1988 he released statistics on the number of religious organizations in the Soviet Union over the last twenty-five years. For 1981, they show 15,687 religious organizations. But what is far more important is which way the statistics were heading. Not only were hundreds of new churches *not* being registered each year as Graham claimed, but during the two decades prior to his trip, the number of registrations had actually *dropped* by about seven thousand. And the numbers continued to drop until 1986.[11]

While Western leaders frequently make incorrect statements, they also make statements which lend themselves to misinterpretation. The Soviets commonly use such quotations to deny the extent to which religious freedom is abridged in the USSR.

But the best way to get a sense of how this is so is to quote the Soviets themselves. On Radio Moscow on August 4, 1982, commentator Boris Bolitsky responded to an inquiry about Pentecostals from a listener "clearly written under the influence of propaganda issuing from anti-Soviet centers in the West."

> I could cite no end of evidence, Mr. Molden, on the extent of religious freedom that exists in this country, but since this evidence coming from me and from Radio Moscow might seem suspect to you, for that very reason I will instead quote the testimony of unimpeachable witnesses. The latest of these has been the American evangelist, Dr. Billy Graham, whom no one in his right mind would

suspect of sympathizing with the Soviet system. Now at the conclusion of his visit to the Soviet Union earlier this summer, Billy Graham said he had found more religious freedom in the Soviet Union than in Britain, with its established Church of England. Here are Billy Graham's exact words: "I think there is a lot more freedom here than the impression that has been given in the States, because there are hundreds or even thousands of churches open. In Great Britain they have a state church, in other countries you have state churches, here the church is not a state church, it's a free church."[12]

Some disclaimers or partial apologies by Graham claim that his words were misconstrued, but the sad reality is that his original comments had much greater publicity than any explanations given since. In addition, Dr. Graham has often seemed more defensive than apologetic for his 1982 comments. He does not appear to grasp the degree to which he is responsible for his words and actions while in the Soviet Union.

Damage was extensive in the Soviet Union. As Lyuba Vashchenko, one of the Siberian Seven, put it:

The Soviet press went all-out to build up the significance of Billy Graham's visit. They use it as evidence that there is religious freedom. It is still hard for me to understand why we had to close the curtain during his visit [to the embassy].[13]

Nor was it just the Siberian Seven who were upset with Graham's conduct. According to Michael Bourdeaux in a letter to *Christianity Today*:

The Soviet press has begun to build up Graham as the man who dared to tell the American public the truth [that there is] no religious persecution in the Soviet Union.

The views of ordinary believers—that is, those not represented at the peace conference or hand-picked to hear the sermon in the Moscow Baptist Church—have also begun to filter through. A recent visitor, who is one of the world's best informed commentators on Soviet religious life, did not find a single believer who was not numbed and shocked by Graham's apparent lack of sensitivity to the persecuted.

The attempt by defenders of Graham's conduct to reduce the whole affair to one of misrepresentation by the Western press is unworthy. The views of Russian Christians being received here at Keston College have not been filtered through a single Western correspondent. What the suffering church waited to hear in vain was one unequivocal sentence of support.[14]

Indeed, while Graham preached in Moscow Baptist Church, dozens of his fellow Baptists languished in labor camps and prison.

Alexander Solzhenitsyn charged that Graham's remarks gave:

public support to Communist lies by his deplorable statement that he had not noticed the persecution of religion in the USSR. Before the multitude of those who have perished and who are oppressed today, may God be his judge.[15]

What particularly frustrated me about this whole episode was that several weeks before Graham's trip to Moscow, Lynn Buzzard, then the head of Christian Legal Society, and I had a two-and-a-half-hour session in New York City with two of Graham's top advisors. We discussed in detail the difference between the discrimination suffered by registered believers and the persecution directed at the unregistered. We were assured the advisors comprehended these distinctions and that Graham would get a full report.

Toward the end of our meeting I stressed one major point: If Dr. Graham did not feel it appropriate to raise publicly the issue of the Siberian Seven, it was imperative that he at least not do what many Western religious leaders had done in the past—namely, say things which gave the appearance of much greater religious freedom than there was in fact.

Graham's most inexplicable comment, in light of his own literature's insistence that "he had been thoroughly briefed on practically everything he was to encounter,"[16] was this: "There is a lot more freedom here than has been given the impression in the States, because there are hundreds, thousands, of churches open."[17] Unfortunately, the statement implies Graham was surprised by the open, crowded churches and the fervency of the faith. The most basic materials available in the West on religion in the Soviet Union could have prepared him for this. It is what is *behind* the open, crowded churches, what is *not* visible on red carpet trips, which cries out for Western attention. To whatever extent Graham was aware of this side of Soviet life, his public comments did not reflect it.

Dr. Graham's motives in going to Moscow were noble: He wanted to assert the importance of Christians being involved in the quest for world peace and he wanted to try to create a favorable climate for arranging future evangelism opportunities. It takes more than good intentions, however, to advance these causes. And in this case, Dr. Graham's visit set back accurate understanding by millions in the West on the situation of believers in the USSR. Those who knew the situation well were angered; many, who knew it less well, were confused. Many in the Soviet Union, particularly among those who have suffered the most for their faith, felt betrayed. And the Soviets were delighted.

CAUTIOUS BAPTISTS AND INTEMPERATE CRITICS

Russian delegates were present at the founding of the Baptist World Alliance (BWA) in 1905. They also attended BWA congresses in 1911, 1923, and 1928. Then came Joseph Stalin, and contacts with Western Baptists disappeared for a quarter of a century. Only after Stalin's death in 1953 was it possible to again consider formal contact with Western Baptists. In 1958 Russian Baptists joined the European Baptist Federation (EBF). In 1975 Alexei Bychkov, a leader in the registered Soviet Baptist community, became the first East European churchman ever to head the EBF.[18]

Much like their Russian Orthodox colleagues, official Russian Baptist leaders seriously misrepresented Soviet reality to Western visitors. In June 1954, F. Townley Lord, president of the BWA, and two other senior Baptist leaders visited the Soviet Union. Upon returning they reported: "Our Russian brethren assured us that there is now complete freedom of worship in the Soviet territories and that all religious communities enjoy equal rights and opportunities. . . ."[19]

The next year Russian delegates attended the BWA Congress in London. Jacob Zhidkov, president of the All-Union Council of Evangelical Christians-Baptists, stated:

> All our churches enjoy full freedom for preaching the gospel, and
> bringing up and educating new members. This liberty, this freedom,
> is guaranteed by the main laws of the country, and in conducting
> services we do not encounter any obstacles.[20]

He then argued against the Cold War and nuclear armaments. Zhidkov performed admirably the two tasks assigned to him by Communist authorities: he passed on disinformation to Western Christians about the state of religion in the Soviet Union, and he supported the Kremlin line on foreign policy matters. The pattern was repeated often by registered leaders during the next three decades. In addition, Zhidkov was elected one of nine vice presidents of the BWA.

The Soviets must have been pleased by Western response to the attendance of Russian delegates at the London congress. William Lipphard, editor of the Baptist journal *Missions* was almost beside himself with excitement.

> So the Russians came to London and received a tremendous ovation.
> . . . the world was given a demonstration that it is possible, it is
> pleasant, it is mutually helpful, it is reciprocally inspiring to have
> fraternal relations with the Russians. At least it was proved con-
> clusively that peaceful coexistence is preferable to the coextermina-
> tion that would result from another world war. Temporarily, let us
> hope permanently, the voices in the United States that have been
> preaching ill will against Russia, have been silenced.[21]

A few such quotations should cure any who think political naivete is the monopoly of any particular part of the theological spectrum. There were, of course, those who found statements such as Mr. Lipphard's unacceptable and silly. Just two short years after Lipphard's comments, a far more sober article appeared in *Missions*. John Slemp had visited the Soviet Union and was struck by both the antireligious character of the government and the fervency of the faith. He concluded that Russian faith "may be crucified and buried, but surely on the third day it will rise again."[22]

An extreme reaction from the Right popped up at the 1959 BWA Congress in the person of the Rev. Carl McIntire, founder of the International Council of Christian Churches (ICCC). The ICCC was founded in 1948 as a response to the World Council of Churches, and by 1959 it purported to represent sixty-four Protestant denominations in sixty different countries.[23] McIntire flooded the conference with leaflets claiming that the Russian Baptists were nothing more than Soviet agents. This less-than-subtle approach prompted a parallel response by a BWA spokesperson: "Every Garden of Eden has its Satan and the happy Christian fellowship was clouded by the appearance in Rio of Carl McIntire before the opening of the Congress...."[24]

In 1972 McIntire became furious with President Nixon for visiting Moscow Baptist Church on a trip to the Soviet Union. He demanded that the president apologize for lending credence to a church which McIntire insisted was completely controlled by the KGB.[25] McIntire and his adherents on the far Right seem to have no sense of the degree to which genuine spirituality has managed to survive even under highly compromised circumstances. Hundreds of travel reports written by visitors to the Soviet Union over the past several decades, regardless of religious affiliation, confirm one fact: the quality and depth of worship in "registered" Protestant services is inspiring.

The KGB is capable of manipulating disinformation about the amount of religious freedom in the USSR; it is emphatically not capable of staging such displays of religious emotion day in and day out over many years. This is one of the puzzles of the Soviet church, and until we in the West come to grips with it, we will not be able to respond as effectively and sensitively as we ought.

The extent to which the extreme Right and the extreme Left resemble each other is striking. Both frequently have a legitimate concern but lack perspective and balance in pursuing it. In the process, they discredit themselves and set back whatever worthwhile goals they may pursue.

McIntire's shrill attack on Russian registered churchmen and their role in the World Council of Churches, the National Council of Churches, and the Baptist World Alliance, springs in part from his hatred of the ecumenical movement, which he considers heretical.[26] Thus, to the extent McIntire's efforts are aimed at destroying rather than improving the ecumenical movement, his assertions—even the true ones—often fall on deaf ears.

One lesson in all of this is that legitimate concerns, regardless of the religious or political spectrum from which they come, will be undermined by intemperate, hateful, and extreme rhetoric.

By failing to distinguish between real communist agents and men pressured into misrepresenting the facts in order to keep the church doors open, McIntire slandered the Russian delegates to the congress. This is no way to encourage the BWA or Russian Baptist delegates to address more prudently the difficult dilemmas which they face. Legitimate disagreements do exist on how best to respond to the presence of Soviet approved religious leaders in international ecumenical and denominational bodies.

Unfortunately, two of the largest mission groups seeking to help Christians in the USSR and Eastern Europe—Richard Wurmbrand's Jesus to the Communist World and Joe Bass's Underground Evangelism—were sometimes guilty of mudslinging worse than any by Carl McIntire. Wurmbrand and Bass regard the registered churches as nothing more than pawns of the State, devoid of real spirituality, and they have sometimes sensationalized the plight of the unregistered. There are plenty of real horror stories that can be told, but on some occasions the accuracy of reports from these groups has been challenged. To make matters worse, the two groups were involved in the late seventies in suits and countersuits against each other.[27]

It is beyond the scope of this study to examine this matter in detail, and undoubtedly many good people in both organizations have been hurt by the rhetorical and moral excesses of their leaders. Unfortunately, the scandals not only damaged the credibility of the groups involved, but for a time hurt the work of quality parachurch mission groups struggling to raise funds for their own work. The vast majority of mission groups have a fine record. Groups like Slavic Gospel Association and Brother Andrew's Open Doors do particularly splendid work, and deserve generous support from the Christian community.

We who are irritated and angered by the far Right and the far Left often make a serious mistake in responding to them. We refuse to acknowledge where they are correct for fear that we will seem to support them or be identified with them. This is quite natural, but it is neither honest nor helpful.

Refusing to view all Russian churchmen as Soviet agents should not blind us to the overwhelming evidence that the Kremlin often *does* use Soviet church leaders for propagandistic purposes. The issue is this: How can we develop a relationship with these leaders which aids the registered churches and which at the same time provides aid and comfort to Christians not favored by the government? We must prevent the Western church from becoming an extension of the disinformation network. It can be done, but it requires a level of prudence and wisdom which our church bodies have often not demonstrated.

In 1983, Dr. Edwin Tuller, General Secretary of the American Baptist Convention, exchanged letters with Carl McIntire regarding the propriety of Russian Baptists visiting the American Baptist Churches' headquarters in Valley Forge, Pennsylvania. Tuller responded well to McIntire's concerns.

> We are all aware that they must say and do certain things in order to get out of the country, and when they get back, to continue their work for Christ. They know that we know these things. When we hear them speak about "peace" many times at points where the subject is not germane to the rest of what is being said, it is perfectly clear that this is one of the prices that they must pay. . . . They know we understand this. After it is said and they have discharged their required obligation we get down to discussing the things that concerns us as Christians and church people.[28]

It would be quite comforting if most Western church leaders displayed the understanding Dr. Tuller shows here. Whenever church officials, however, repeat Russian testimony as fact, or transmit it with no explanation to millions of trusting parishioners, there is legitimate fear that truth has been lost or sacrificed somewhere along the way.

Compelling evidence suggests that the presence of registered Baptists from the Soviet Union in the Baptist World Alliance and in the European Baptist Federation has had much the same impact on these bodies that the presence of Soviet registered delegates have had on the World Council of Churches. Namely, all of these religious organizations became much more quiet about problems within the USSR.

Both the BWA and the EBF tended to side with registered Baptists in their dispute with the unregistered splinter group (the Initiative group; *Initsiativniki*) during the antireligious campaign of Khrushchev and its aftermath in the 1960s. According to Walter Sawatsky, an authority on Soviet evangelicals, "the early failure to hear and understand the *Initsiativniki* appeal damaged the reputation of the BWA."[29]

It was not primarily through the BWA that word reached the larger Christian community about the suffering of Soviet Baptists during the 1960s. Rather, it was through a 1968 book by Michael Bourdeaux.[30] Only then did the BWA begin to acknowledge the schism, "taking great care in its official utterances," in the words of William Fletcher, "to give all due consideration to the evaluations made by the non-schismatic, state-sanctioned Russian Baptist organization which was a member of the BWA."[31]

In 1970, William Tolbert, president of the BWA from 1965 to 1970, visited the USSR and in published comments said:

> I would . . . like to remind this group of Baptists [the unregistered or reform Baptists] that to go along this road is wrong. Indeed it is wrong to ignore the laws of the country or to permit disobedience, and also to treat the authorities with disrespect.[32]

The comments caused considerable embarrassment among other Western Baptist leaders, particularly since Tolbert had evidently not been properly briefed about the Baptist split before going to the Soviet Union.

In effect, the BWA, by its silence and often open support for the registered Baptists, declined to defend forcefully the group which refused to go along with strident new antireligious regulations imposed by the Soviet authorities. Sawatsky concluded:

> The overwhelming documentation that was accumulating clearly pointed to systematic violation of religious liberty. The Baptist World Alliance, which prided itself on being a spokesman for religious liberty, found itself muzzled in this case.[33]

In 1971 Andrew MacRae, president of the EBF, visited the USSR. He was impressed that no one censored his sermons and appears to have believed virtually everything he was told. He returned to the West and published observations that failed to reflect accurately the dispute between the registered and the unregistered Baptists. Six years later, he did nearly the same thing. Clearly frustrated, Sawatsky laments: "One would expect a Western Baptist leader in such a critical situation to exert a bit more effort to discover the facts or else to keep silent."[34]

Since 1975, however, Sawatsky believes there has been more willingness to intervene on behalf of imprisoned Baptists.[35] The preferred method is behind the scenes, with Baptist leaders often writing or speaking with Soviet officials. Both the BWA and the WCC requested permission from the Soviets to attend the mid-1970s trial of Georgi Vins, a prominent leader of the unregistered Baptists, but were refused.[36]

In 1989 General Secretary Denton Lotz connected the release of Vins in 1979 to intervention on his behalf by the BWA.[37] Indeed, upon Vins' release, then BWA General Secretary Robert Denny gave the following warm tribute to the unregistered leader: "The Christian world has come to know the name of our distinguished brother in Christ, Georgi Vins. His story of faith and courage and witness has been told across the world."[38] He also reported that BWA and the EBF had "repeatedly" intervened on behalf of Vins and other prisoners with the Soviet authorities.[39]

The dilemmas faced by the BWA and other Baptist organizations in dealing with the Soviets are well illustrated by what happened in 1980 at the BWA Congress in Toronto. Vins attended the congress as a delegate from the United States. Alexei Bychkov, a Soviet Baptist leader, protested Vins' registration. No action was taken to strip Vins of the right to participate, and it was clear the BWA was trying to retain relations with both groups.[40]

During the 1980s the relationship between the BWA and Vins and his organization (which supported unregistered Soviet Baptists) became increasingly strained. Although the BWA expresses concern for the unregistered, its primary focus is on registered Baptists.

In 1987 the American Baptist Church published a little booklet titled *Baptist Witness in the USSR*.[41] It was compiled by Denton Lotz, who the following year was named general secretary of the BWA. The work provides an excellent opportunity to observe how the complex Soviet Baptist situation is communicated to Baptists in the United States.

The book strongly emphasizes the perspective of the registered Soviet Baptists. Greetings are extended by the president of the All-Union Council of Evangelical Christians-Baptists, and three of the seven chapters are written by registered Soviet Baptist leaders. None are written by anyone in the unregistered church.

Nevertheless, there is a chapter on "Religious Freedom in the USSR" written by Gerhard Class, a German Baptist leader and then general secretary of the BWA. The reader is informed of restrictions placed on the practice of religious faith and about differences between registered and unregistered believers. To partly explain the differences in religious liberty between the Communist and the Western worlds, the reader is reminded that

> There is a different understanding of freedom in the socialist countries . . . and the capitalist world . . . . Where in the West the absolute freedom of the individual is supreme, Socialist countries are concerned about the freedom of the whole society.[42]

This is disconcerting since this is precisely the argument the Soviets use to justify their refusal to honor human rights commitments. The statement by Class is also inaccurate. Nowhere in the West is "absolute freedom of the individual supreme." Such libertarianism exists in theory only, not in the Western democracies as they have evolved. Furthermore, it is not clear why concern for "the freedom of the whole society" would justify interfering with a religious community's right to organize religious instruction for its children.

Class warns the reader that "no one has the right to judge and condemn other people. We just have to respect the decision Christians in the socialist countries will make. . . ." It becomes obvious the author does not quite achieve balance, however, when he adds that in not judging we must bear in mind that:

> Whoever cooperates with the state is not naturally a betrayer or a KGB agent;
>
> Whoever opposes the state constitution and bylaws is not automatically a martyr and a true witness for Christ.[43]

Is there an attempt here to protect the registered Baptists from negative charges, and to deprive the unregistered of positive praise?

Still, a Western reader studying this booklet has at least some sense that the religious situation in the Soviet Union is not completely free. It is a credit to the book's compiler that the chapter on religious freedom is not omitted.

Denton Lotz reports that BWA officials meet with both registered and unregistered Baptists when they travel to the USSR. The BWA has even brought the rival groups together for meetings to promote reconciliation, although the BWA leadership quite clearly identifies more with the registered than the unregistered. The BWA has worked closely with the registered Soviet Baptists to help them acquire religious literature and set up theological training (abroad, through correspondence, and hopefully, soon through Soviet Baptist seminaries). Hard feelings have developed between the BWA and Georgi Vins. There is also considerable concern on the part of current BWA leadership that much public discussion of "religious persecution" in the Soviet Union is motivated by political "anticommunism" and an unjustifiable "wrapping oneself in the flag."[44]

On October 3, 1988, the Baptist Joint Committee on Public Affairs (which represents a number of Baptist denominations in the U.S.) issued a strong statement calling on Mr. Gorbachev to expand significantly religious freedom in the Soviet Union. It urged him to provide legal safeguards for increased freedoms, allow alternative service for pacifists, register promptly those congregations seeking registration, and permit theological education and the religious education of children. The statement also called on Baptists to open their arms to support believers from the Soviet Union who choose to emigrate.

THE TIMIDITY OF THE PENTECOSTALS

Robert Makish, an American Pentecostal pastor, in 1967 helped initiate formal fraternal ties between Soviet registered Pentecostals and their U.S. Assemblies of God counterparts. Three years later Soviet churchmen for the first time attended a World Congress of Pentecostals. Soviet delegations to Pentecostal events come from the All-Union Council of Evangelical Christians-Baptists. Some of the registered Soviet Pentecostals are members, but the delegations have not been led by a Pentecostal.[45]

Assemblies of God Pentecostals have strongly supported the registered position. In a 1974 visit to the Soviet Union, Thomas Zimmerman, head of the American Assemblies of God and president of a world body of Pentecostals, sought to convince Soviet Pentecostals to register. In 1977 a Soviet religious publication quoted Percy Brewster, a British Pentecostal and leader in the international Pentecostal community, as saying:

> Regardless of where we live, we must be obedient to the laws of our own country. The church should be registered. In England registration is obligatory. I cannot marry a couple unless I am registered.[46]

Sawatsky's response is direct and to the point:

> The statement sounded perfectly natural when applied to the British context which he knew. It was apparent that both he and his colleague Zimmerman before him were uninformed about the restrictive meaning of registration in the Soviet Union.[47]

If they did understand the restrictions, these men apparently were unwilling to support believers whose Christian consciences refused to subordinate their religious faith to the government.

Typical of this refusal on the part of Western Pentecostal groups to express solidarity with Pentecostals in the Soviet Union was what happened (or rather, didn't happen) at the 12th World Pentecostal Conference in Vancouver, Canada, September 25-30, 1979.[48]

While delegates from sixty-eight countries met, and the conference was drawing between ten thousand and fifteen thousand people a day, forty Soviet Pentecostals were in labor camp, thirty thousand were seeking emigration to the West, and seven were clinging to a *de facto* asylum in the U.S. embassy in Moscow. Yet the conference planning committee refused to put these compelling issues on the agenda.

The explanation sometimes given for not discussing these matters is that the World Pentecostal Conference is a loosely organized fellowship, not a legislative body. But the real explanation is to be found elsewhere. After all, a simple expression of concern and a call for prayer would be matters of fellowship, not legislation.

The seeds of the problem must be sought within the Soviet Union itself, in the division which has grown up between registered and unregistered believers. The registered believers have often refused to defend their unregistered counterparts. In fact, they have criticized them to Western leaders as extremists and lawbreakers.

More than eight hundred Soviet Pentecostals sent an appeal to the Vancouver conference on behalf of thirty thousand other Pentecostals who wanted to emigrate. The signatories included some of the main unregistered Pentecostal leaders in the Soviet Union: Nikolai Goretoi, Vasily Gorelkin, and Boris Perchatkin. It is important for Westerners to get a sense of their concerns:

> We have taken up the sign of EXODUS from this country of demonic hypocrisy, where the authorities and the government not only fail to defend justice but they themselves are the evildoers. There are still many skeptics in the countries of the West doubting this fact, and among them, to our greatest sorrow, are believers and even leaders of churches, who not only do not believe the facts about our unusually wretched conditions, but even dare accuse us for our complaining. They have become extremely friendly with the leadership of the All-Union Council of Evangelical Christians-Baptists and the Moscow Patriarchate and are acting against our purposes. . . . They betrayed us because they are afraid. . . . Many of our brethren perished in prisons because of their betrayal and denunciations, and now when they were given a special mission to visit your churches, they are alleging that as before, even now these believers who are in

prison are not suffering for their faith but for the violation of the Soviet law on religious cults, as if it were not the same thing. . . .

They [Western church leaders preaching in the USSR] told us that we are like native flowers that should grow here and not be transplanted, i.e., not to change our domicile. In their sermons they never mentioned the fact that we are not permitted to grow here but are being torn out with our roots. . . . Perplexed, we asked: "Why such hypocritical sermons?" In reply we heard that if they would say anything else, the Soviet government would not admit them to the USSR again, which means that in order to visit this country, they are ready to subject themselves to this humiliation and instead of helping us, they are helping the enemies of Christ make our shackles even heavier and fan the flames of this dreadful GULAG . . . .[49]

The language is tough, the emotions are raw, and it is not surprising that Western Pentecostal leaders would bristle at such an appeal. After all, if the appeal is even half correct, Western leaders would have much to repent of regarding past policies toward Soviet Pentecostals.

For the six days the Vancouver conference was in session, Arkady Polishchuk and about twenty others sought to gain the attention of organizers with a peaceful fast and demonstration outside the coliseum where the conference was taking place. Polishchuk's own background is fascinating. A former member of the Communist party and correspondent for *Pravda,* he later became a Pentecostal and was expelled from the Soviet Union in 1977 for helping Christian dissidents.[50]

A spokesperson for the conference explained that a statement by Polishchuk was not read because his credibility was in question and because delegates were present from East European countries.[51]

The Siberian Seven sent a special appeal to the delegates of the Vancouver conference, which Polishchuk distributed along with the appeal from the eight hundred. The Seven's call for help concluded with the following:

Soviet authorities do not want to allow those Christians to come to you [who want to emigrate], because they would tell you the truth about the situation of believers in Communist countries. Therefore, many of you believe and think that Christians here are really free, but that is very far from the way things are. Of course, it is possible to make a compromise with Satan, which some people have done, but those who do not want to compromise are deprived of contact with their fellow Christians, families and children, and they themselves are languishing somewhere in psychiatric hospitals or prisons, while their children are being re-educated in the spirit of atheism. Such persons wait for the time when someone will remember them and they will be freed. It frequently happens that they die in loneliness, not in the presence of their loved ones and friends. There are such people in all the denominations—Catholics, Baptists, Adventists, Pentecostals, Russian Orthodox, and many, many others.

It is for them we intercede with you![52]

But the leadership of the Vancouver World Conference refused to say a word in defense or support of their Soviet counterparts. There was no room on the agenda for persecuted Soviet Pentecostals.

The great tragedy of the conflict between the registered and the unregistered is that the Soviet Union has managed to drive a deadly spike into the heart of Christian unity. We must be careful not to charge that all who are members of the registered church have "compromised with Satan," just as we must not assert that all who are unregistered are "fanatics and chronic lawbreakers." That there are those who have compromised too much, and others who have become religious fanatics, is certainly true. But for the majority, such labels are inaccurate.

Many Pentecostals have been involved in praying for and aiding fellow believers in the Soviet Union. But they have tended to come from local churches, some of the smaller denominations, parachurch organizations, and certain Pentecostal Eastern Europe mission organizations.

The Assemblies of God, the Pentecostals' largest denomination, and various international Pentecostal fellowships have almost totally ignored the plight of fellow believers in the Soviet Union. As late as 1989, senior officials of the Assembly showed real nervousness about appearing to encourage emigration from the Soviet Union. Though modest sums have been allocated to help in refugee resettlement, they do not wish to encourage emigration.

A key factor in this hesitancy to respond is the fear that speaking out or attempting more direct dealings with the large unregistered Pentecostal community may jeopardize contacts with registered Pentecostals in the Soviet Union. (Ironically, the group with whom Assembly officials have the most contact represents a tiny minority of the total Soviet Pentecostal population.)[53]

Soviet threats of severed contacts have not worked with Jews, the world psychiatric association, or the international scientific community; but they have repeatedly worked with a wide variety of Western Christian groups.

Though leading Pentecostals have often been inactive or uninvolved, at least they have not usually made public statements which exaggerate the amount of existing religious freedom in the USSR.

LUTHERAN SILENCE

Idealizing unrecognized religious groups in the Soviet Union would be unjust to the many faithful Christians who want to practice their belief within the laws of the State. (Paul Hansen, Lutheran World Federation, 1977)[54]

After the Baptists, the Lutherans are the second largest Protestant group in the Soviet Union. There are about 600,000 Lutherans in the Estonian and Latvian Baltic Republics, and another half million in Central Asia and Siberia.[55]

In 1963 Soviet authorities permitted the Lutherans to join the Lutheran World Federation (LWF). Under the direction of Dr. Paul Hansen, European Secretary for the LWF Department of Church Cooperation, the Lutherans have been even more committed to working through "quiet diplomacy" than the Baptist World Alliance. In 1978 Hansen explained the LWF position:

> We do not believe that it would help anyone for the LWF to make the kind of publicity about these problems which is typical for the East Missions, and we certainly don't want our efforts to be associated with activities which could be regarded as having some political motivation.[56]

In 1984 Hungarian Bishop Zoltan Kaldy was elected president of the Lutheran World Federation. For two decades Kaldy has been a supporter of "diakonia theology," which advocates church service to socialism. His strong preference for the Eastern bloc is clear from his 1975 TV comment: "It is unthinkable to me that anyone would oppose socialism."[57]

As with other denominations, a variety of Lutheran perspectives compete with that of the international leadership. One of the most vociferous opponents of the policies of the LWF is Richard Wurmbrand, the former Romanian Lutheran pastor and founder of Jesus to the Communist World. In addition, many Lutheran churches support *Misjon Bak Jernteppet* (Mission Behind the Iron Curtain), a Norwegian mission group which helps smuggle religious literature into the Soviet Union when official channels are blocked.[58]

THE U.S. CATHOLIC BISHOPS ON RELIGION IN THE USSR

In November 1988, the U.S. bishops approved a fine analysis of the situation in both Eastern Europe and the USSR.[59] Echoing the perspective of their 1980 pastoral letter on Marxist communism, the bishops note the strong connection between Communist movements and vigorous antireligious actions and attitudes. The statement summarizes the long history of religious repression in the Soviet Union and specifies the legal parameters by which even the registered church is constrained. The bishops do not mince words: "The Catholic Church in the Soviet Union has been repressed systematically under communist rule."[60] The plight of the largest unregistered religious group in the Soviet Union—the Ukrainian Catholics—is protested. In addition, the bishops provide a detailed list of the specific changes needed under *glasnost* for religious liberty to be realized.[61]

PARACHURCH MISSION GROUPS

While large official church organizations, both ecumenical and denominational, have been reluctant to speak out on behalf of Christians in the USSR,
parachurch mission groups have frequently taken on this task with considerable vigor. They have particularly focused their attention on helping unregistered believers through public advocacy and by providing unofficial material
support, especially in the form of smuggled religious literature.

Dr. Mark Elliott has documented the existence of well over two hundred
mission groups who seek to help Christians in Eastern Europe and the
USSR.[62] According to Elliott, "the eight largest missions annually allocate
one to fourteen million dollars each for Soviet-bloc efforts."[63] Approximately
60 percent of these missions have headquarters in the United States, with most
of the rest based in Europe. The largest by far is Aid to the Church in Need—a
Catholic charity with its home base in Konigstein, West Germany. The next
three in size are: Inter-Aid Inc. (Joe Bass's group, a division of which is
Underground Evangelism, Camarillo, California); Jesus to the Communist
World (Wurmbrand's group, Middlebury, Indiana); and Slavic Gospel Association (Wheaton, Illinois). Then come *Licht Im Osten* (Light in the East;
Korntal, West Germany), *Misjon Bak Jernteppet* (Mission Behind the Iron
Curtain; Oslo, Norway), Brother Andrew's Open Doors (Ermelo, Holland),
and *Slaviska Missionen* (Bromma, Sweden).[64]

With the exception of Aid to the Church in Need and Lithuanian Catholic
Religious Aid, most of the mission groups are Protestant, and many of the
largest ones were founded by persons with Soviet and East European ethnic
roots. Victor Potapov (Washington, D.C.) heads the Committee for the Defense of Persecuted Orthodox Christians, and there are Orthodox support
groups in Western Europe as well.

These mission groups tend to be conservative in theology and strongly
support evangelism. Pentecostals are well represented, though not in the
majority. The groups founded by charismatics or Pentecostals are not exclusively Pentecostal in their focus.

Some European-based groups receive significant denominational support,
but the U.S.-based organizations rely mainly on the contributions of individual churches and members. Oldline denominations tend not to support these
groups out of distaste for their theological and political conservatism and a
concern to maintain their own perceived delicate relations with registered
Soviet church leaders.[65]

Radio broadcasts provide another major point of contact between Western and Soviet Christians. The thirteen largest international Christian radio
stations broadcasting to the USSR transmitted a total 364 hours per week,
according to Elliott's calculations in early 1988. Eighty percent of the pro-

gramming is in Russian.[66] According to David Barrett's *World Christian Encyclopedia,* there may be close to forty thousand radio fellowships in the USSR—groups dependent upon shortwave radio broadcasts.[67]

Elliott lists three principal differences between the contacts of Soviet believers with oldline/ecumenical bodies and those that exist with parachurch missions groups. First, the oldline tends to be more liberal in both its politics and its theology. Second, the oldline "churches are haunted by the specter of a world enchained by missiles; the missions are haunted by the specter of a world in chains." And third, oldline/ecumenical bodies favor "quiet diplomacy," while many of the mission groups believe public advocacy is more effective.[68]

RESEARCH CENTERS

One key way Western Christians can help Christians in the Soviet Union is by providing accurate information on Soviet conditions. Very little was done in a formal, organized manner to study religion in the Soviet Union before the 1960s and 1970s.[69]

Italian scholars Giovanni Codevilla and Pietro Modesto in 1960 established *Russia Cristiana*—a research center devoted to studying the conditions of Soviet believers (especially Roman Catholics). It also collects materials on Soviet atheism and produces a journal (*Rivista del Centro studi Russia Cristiana*).

The most important research center to emerge in the English-speaking world is Keston College in England. It is not a college in the American sense, but rather a research institute. Keston was founded in 1969 by Anglican priest Michael Bourdeaux, and has approximately two dozen on staff, including specialists on Eastern Europe and the Soviet Union. Two of its most important publications are *Religion in Communist Lands* (quarterly) and *Keston News Service* (KNS, bi-weekly).

The Research Center for Religion and Human Rights in Closed Societies (New York City) was founded in 1962. It publishes the very informative *Religion in Communist Dominated Areas.*[70]

The equivalent to Keston in the German-speaking world is *Glaube in der 2 Welt* (Faith in the Second World), based in Zurich and under the leadership of the Swiss pastor Eugene Voss. It was founded in 1972.

One of the most important new research centers is the Institute for the Study of Christianity and Marxism on the campus of Wheaton College. Dr. Mark Elliott, formerly a professor at Asbury College, has been the director since the Institute's founding in 1986.

A wide variety of Christian mission groups have their own links to the Soviet Union but also rely heavily on the research of groups like Keston College, which they pass on to their constituencies.[71]

CONCLUSION

The great paradox of religion in the Soviet Union—understood by neither the Right, which often sees only KGB agents in the registered churches, nor the Left, which frequently imagines more freedom than actually exists—is that a genuine spirituality exists within a deeply compromised and registered religious establishment. It also exists within the unregistered communities and in dissident Russian Orthodox circles. This is one of the great puzzles of the Soviet Church.

Until we come to terms with this reality, the Western Christian community will fail to realize its full potential in relating to and helping the Christian communities of the Soviet Union.

Notes

1. Harry Genet, "Graham Will Preach in Moscow," *Christianity Today*, 9 April 1982, 44. See chapter 9 for further information on the Christian Peace Conference.

2. Ibid.

3. Quoted in ibid.

4. Timothy Chmykhalov, *The Last Christian* (Grand Rapids, Mich.: Zondervan Publishing House, 1986), 149.

5. "Billy Renders Unto Caesar," *Newsweek*, 24 May 1982, 89.

6. "Questionable Mission to Moscow," *Time*, 24 May 1982, 60.

7. "Graham in Moscow: What Did He Really Say?" *Christianity Today*, 18 June 1982, 12.

8. Quoted in *Christianity Today*, 18 June 1982, 12.

9. Quoted in Gordon William Carlson, "Russian Protestants and American Evangelicals Since the Death of Stalin: Patterns of Interaction and Response" (Ph.D. diss., University of Minnesota, 1986), 221.

10. "Press Release by Dr. Billy Graham," New York, Crusade Information Service, 19 May 1982, 3.

11. Interview with Konstantin Kharchev, "The Guarantee of Freedom," *Science and Religion* (*Nauka i religiia*), no. 11 (November 1987), 23.

12. "Vantage Point," broadcast by Radio Moscow, 4 August 1982. A slightly abridged version can be found in Chmykhalov, *Last Christian*, 150.

13. Quoted in Allan C. Brownfeld, "Pentecostalists Show Courage in Face of Religious Persecution and World's Indifference," *Human Events*, 6 November 1982, 12.

14. Letter to the editor by Michael Bourdeaux, *Christianity Today*, 3 September 1982, 8.

15. "Solzhenitsyn Roasts Graham on View of Soviets," *Seattle Times*, 11 May 1983.

16. Bob Terrell, *Billy Graham in the Soviet Union* (Minneapolis: Billy Graham Evangelical Association, 1985), 9.

17. Quoted in "Graham May Brief Reagan on Moscow Visit," AP story, *Seattle Times*, 13 May 1982. In September 1984, while on a trip to Moscow, Graham declared that he still held to the view that there is more religious freedom in the USSR "than the average American has been led to believe" ("Dr. Graham, in USSR, Says Path to Peace Is Knowing God," *Christian Science Monitor*, 11 September 1984).

18. Mark Elliott, "A Typology of Western-Soviet Christian Contacts," (Unpublished manuscript, Institute for the Study of Christianity and Marxism, Wheaton College, Wheaton, Ill., 1988), 7-8. Also see Walter Sawatsky, *Soviet Evangelicals Since World War II* (Scottdale, Penn.: Herald Press, 1981), 373-78.

19. Quoted in Carlson, "Russian Protestants," 182.

20. Quoted in ibid., 188.

21. Quoted in ibid., 190.

22. Quoted in ibid., 209-10.

23. *Josef L. Hromadka: No. 1 Protestant Defender of Communism* (Collingswood, N.J.: 20th Century Reformation Hour, 1959), 70. Since 1953 McIntire has propagated his views in the *Christian Beacon.*

24. John Bradbury, quoted in Carlson, "Russian Protestants," 226.

25. Carlson, "Russian Protestants," 430-433.

26. Ibid., 288.

27. See "West Coast Bible Smugglers: Less Cloak and More Dagger," *Christianity Today*, 2 March 1979, 50-52. Also see, Sawatsky, *Soviet Evangelicals*, 407-10.

28. Quoted in Carlson, "Russian Protestants," 251.

29. Sawatsky, *Soviet Evangelicals*, 375.

30. Michael Bourdeaux, *Religious Ferment in Russia: Protestant Opposition to Soviet Religious Policy* (London: Macmillan, 1968).

31. Noted in Elliott, "Western-Soviet Contacts," 8.

32. Quoted in Sawatsky, *Soviet Evangelicals*, 377.

33. Ibid.

34. Ibid.

35. Ibid.

36. Carlson, "Russian Protestants," 483.

37. Interview with Denton Lotz (BWA General Secretary) and Archie Goldie (Director of Baptist World Aid), Baptist World Alliance headquarters, McLean, Va., 21 March 1989.

38. Quoted in Carlson, "Russian Protestants," 21.

39. Ibid., 516.

40. Ibid., 530.

41. Denton Lotz, comp., *Baptist Witness in the USSR* (Valley Forge, Penn.: American Baptist Churches, 1987).

42. Gerhard Class, "Religious Freedom in the USSR," in *Baptist Witness*, 44.

43. Ibid., 47.

44. Interview with Lotz and Goldie.

45. Sawatsky, *Soviet Evangelicals*, 382.

46. Quoted in ibid.

47. Ibid.

48. Miguel Moya, "Pentecostals Turn Down Friend of Soviet Dissidents," *The Vancouver Sun*, 1 October 1979.

49. Quoted from the appeal distributed outside the Pacific Coliseum in Vancouver, Canada, where the Pentecostal international meeting was taking place.

50. Moya, "Pentecostals Turn Down Friend."

51. Ibid.

52. Copy of letter distributed at the Vancouver Conference.

53. Boris Perchatkin, 1988 Soviet Pentecostal emigre, conversations between August 1988 and April 1989; phone interview with Michael Rowe, Keston College, 19 April 1989.

54. Quoted by J. A. Emerson Vermaat, *The World Council of Churches and Politics: 1975-1986* (New York: Freedom House, 1989), 18. Subsequent information in this section on the Lutherans is based on Elliott, "Western-Soviet Contacts," 9-11.

55. Philip Walters, ed., *World Christianity: Eastern Europe* (Monrovia, Calif.: Missions Advanced Research and Communication Center, 1988), 86.

56. Quoted in Elliott, "Western-Soviet Contacts," 10.

57. Trevor Beeson, *Discretion and Valour: Religious Conditions in Russia and Eastern Europe*, rev. ed. (London: Collins, Fount Paperback, 1982), 279.

58. Elliott, "Western-Soviet Contacts," 10-11.

59. "Statement on Religious Freedom in Eastern Europe and the Soviet Union," *Origins: NC Documentary Service*, 8 December 1988, 417-21.

60. Ibid., 419.

61. Ibid., 420-21.

62. Elliott, "Western-Soviet Contacts," 33.

63. Ibid., 3.

64. Ibid., 34-35. The organizations run by Bass and Wurmbrand were initially hurt financially by their conflicts with each other. Recent information on them is not at my disposal. In contrast, under the capable leadership of Peter and Anita Deyneka, Slavic Gospel Association has steadily been gaining support. Their 1988 budget was 6.2 million dollars.

65. See ibid., 35-36.

66. Ibid., 38-39. Also see chapter 11, "The Information Monolith: Chipping at the Edges," for further information on broadcasting into the Soviet Union.

67. Ibid., 40.

68. Ibid., 41.

69. Information in this section is based on ibid., 28-33.

70. See chapter 9 for more information on the history of the Research Center for Religious and Human Rights in Closed Societies.

71. The appendices contain detailed information about how to get in contact with the main research groups and mission organizations.

THE GORBACHEV ERA AND BEYOND

GLASNOST AND PERESTROIKA:

Gorbachev's Perspective

*A*ccording to Mikhail Gorbachev, *perestroika* (restructuring) is "a policy of accelerating the country's social and economic progress and renewing all spheres of life."[1] Throughout his book, *Perestroika,* which he was asked to write by an American publisher, Gorbachev insists that though economic renewal is a key ingredient in *perestroika,* the ultimate purpose is "a thorough renewal of every aspect of Soviet life."[2]

Perestroika is required, asserts Gorbachev, because beginning in the late 1970s the Soviet economy began to stagnate. "Economic failures became more frequent," and "a gradual erosion of the ideological and moral values of our people began."[3]

This unhappy state of affairs, according to the Soviet leader, is emphatically *not* because socialism has failed, as some in the West believe. Rather it has occurred because the potential of socialism has not been realized. The solution, therefore, is to return to the legacy of Vladimir Lenin.[4]

The general secretary dates the general shift of policy to April 1985, just a month after his own election by the Central Committee to the top position in the Communist party. He believes that the Central Committee's adoption in June 1987 of "Fundamentals of Radical Restructuring of Economic Management" may be the most important economic reform in the Soviet Union since 1921, when Lenin launched his New Economic Policy.[5]

Historians have widely interpreted Lenin's 1920s plan as a concession towards capitalism in order to allow the economy to recover from the Civil War. Like Lenin, however, Gorbachev has repeatedly assured faithful Communists that his actions are not to be interpreted in any way as a retreat from socialist ideals or goals.

In addition to returning to Lenin, Gorbachev emphasizes two other ways of furthering *perestroika*: *glasnost* (openness) and democratization. The former is directly related to the mobilization of the "human factor," which is not possible apart from a new openness or *glasnost*. As Gorbachev puts it,

> unless we activate the human factor, that is, unless we take into consideration the diverse interests of people, work collectives, public bodies, and various social groups, unless we rely on them, and draw them into active, constructive endeavor, it will be impossible for us to accomplish any of the tasks set, or to change the situation in the country.[6]

There is an assumption that the success of *perestroika* is directly tied to the individual and whether his noneconomic needs are met. In Gorbachev's words,

> our main job is to lift the individual spiritually, respecting his inner world and giving him moral strength. . . . An individual must know and feel that his contribution is needed, and his dignity is not being infringed upon, that he is being treated with trust and respect.[7]

Gorbachev contends that many of the Soviet Union's problems exist because democratic processes were not allowed to develop. This must not be allowed to continue. "*We need broad democratization of all aspects of society.*" That democratization is also the main guarantee that the current processes are irreversible.[8]

* * * *

What has changed, and what has not, since Gorbachev became the leader of the Soviet Union? Have *glasnost* and *perestroika* made any significant impact on Soviet society and the Church? The chapters that follow will help answer these questions and look at prospects for the future. Finally, some recommendations will be made for how Western Christians ought to respond to the unique opportunities the present historical moment provides.

Notes

1. Mikhail Gorbachev, *Perestroika: New Thinking for Our Country and the World*, updated ed. (New York: Harper and Row, 1988), xii.
2. Ibid., 21.
3. Ibid., 5, 7.
4. Ibid., xii-xiii, 22-23.
5. Ibid., 19.
6. Ibid., 15.
7. Ibid., 16.
8. Ibid., 18.

CHAPTER 11

THE INFORMATION MONOLITH:

Chipping at the Edges

E xactly one hundred years before Nikita Khrushchev launched his vicious attack on the churches in 1959, England's John Stuart Mill penned one of the most remarkable essays on freedom ever written. *On Liberty* sought to protect the unbeliever from unwarranted public censorship of his ideas when Christians held the reigns of power. Mill went so far as to assert that "if all mankind minus one, were of one opinion, and only one person were of the contrary opinion, mankind would be no more justified in silencing that one person, than he, if he had the power, would be justified in silencing mankind."[1]

Mill's thesis is that truth is strengthened by the competition of ideas. Even false, or partially false, ideas help determine the contours of true ones. Furthermore, the best way to defeat false and dangerous ideas is in the marketplace of ideas, not with the censor's scissors.

Modern totalitarian states have muffled the public expressions not only of solitary individuals but of tens of millions of people.

Before we consider in detail some of the recent signs of liberalization in the Soviet Union, we must first examine the historical nature of the problem.

IDEAS AND INFORMATION:
TRADITIONALLY A SOVIET STATE MONOPOLY

An American and a Soviet were arguing one day about the relative freedoms of their respective countries. "My country is so free," bragged the American, "that I can stand in front of the White House and criticize the president of the United States as much as I want— even have my protest aired on national TV—and nothing will happen to me."

"That's not such a big deal," responded the Soviet. "I can stand in
front of the Kremlin and say anything I want about the president of
the United States, too, and nothing will happen to me either."

This bit of Russian humor points to the sobering reality that, since 1917,
Soviet control of its people has been based on two things: physical coercion
and the control of information. Too little attention has been paid to the latter in
our studies of the Soviet Union.

This is only natural. After all, the Soviet Union's terrorization of millions
of its citizens produced a wave of graphic stories of suffering, death, and
human courage. We know something of the awesome power the USSR has
employed to insure the obedience or at least passivity of its people. We are
much less aware of how crucial the control of information is for manipulating
the minds of the population.

In 1978 a good Soviet friend and I were on an excursion from Moscow to
Peredelkino—the literary colony where Boris Pasternak had lived and was
buried. We managed to find Pasternak's dacha and had looked out the very
window he had gazed through when he wrote the beautiful scenes of *Dr.
Zhivago*.

Now we were in the cemetery. Snow was on Pasternak's grave, as were
some bread crumbs. "What are the bread crumbs for?" I queried, thinking it a
strange place to leave food for the birds.

"It's food for the dead. Old women leave it," he responded.

Certain he was joking, I tried again. "Oh come on, what is it really for?"

My friend looked me square in the face and said in all seriousness: "It's a
Russian Orthodox belief that you can feed the dead by leaving bread crumbs
on the grave."

We argued for several minutes. I contended that this was not a basic
doctrine of the faith, while he countered that it was part of the Orthodox creed.

My friend was an intelligent graduate student. He was favorably inclined
toward religion, though not himself a believer, and he was aware that his own
government often did not tell the truth. Yet because he had never encountered
any information to the contrary and was basically ignorant about Christian
history and theology, he had accepted without thinking some crude propaganda about the Russian Orthodox faith. In fact, placing bread crumbs on the
grave is an old Russian custom—originally food given for the poor, later just
left for the birds. But it was for the living, not the dead.

Soviet schools have typically displayed on their walls antireligious
posters which depict believers as superstitious and ignorant. From the earliest
grades reason and religion are presented as at odds. A well-known poster
pictures a Soviet cosmonaut in space, hand to forehead scanning the limitless
horizon, with the caption: "No God!" Of course, in the Soviet schools and

media no alternative perspectives have been provided. No Christians permitted to give their views on whether science and the Bible are really at war with each other. No priest or pastor to present his version of what the church believes about God and the world.

Article 52 of the Soviet Constitution, which guarantees the right of religious worship, makes crystal clear the State's exclusive access to the public through the media on matters of religion. Antireligious propaganda is specifically guaranteed, with no similar right provided for believers. Scientific Marxism risks no argument about its "reasonable and empirically grounded" worldview.

A typical tack taken against troublesome local believers—such as those who refuse to agree to the restrictive state regulations governing the Church—is to vilify them in print. Their patriotism, intelligence, and morality have been pilloried for decades. They have often been accused of conspiring with foreign intelligence networks. Those who were publicly defamed have had no legal right to respond or defend themselves in print to the millions of readers exposed to the State-sponsored attacks.

There can be no question about it: the control of the press is a powerful and deadly weapon in the hands of an antireligious government.

A bright young man repeating as truth some nonsense about what Christians believe is most likely to happen in an environment where it is difficult to get alternative points of view. Publications in the Soviet Union are run by the same management, and diversity or disagreement has traditionally been taboo. At least this was overwhelmingly the case before the emergence of *glasnost*.

It is difficult for Westerners to appreciate the impact of propaganda. To be sure, we have some sense from our own experience that the key to advertising is repetition in a controlled environment, and we recognize that this is a form of propaganda. However, governmental consumer checks rule out the grosser forms of lying by those who would sell us their products.

In a pluralistic society, however, the primary check comes not from a government watchdog agency but from the opportunity consumers have to choose between products. Competition between producers tends to raise the standards of what the consumer is able to buy.

It works the same in the world of information. If anything, the Western information consumer is overwhelmed by a glut of viewpoints. He can buy literature or listen to programming which reflects virtually every point on the political spectrum. The overall impact is that lies or half-truths are more easily ferreted out by a serious reader in a pluralistic news environment than in an environment where diverse points of view are suppressed or controlled.

Every government seeks to present its actions in the best possible light. But it does not follow that every government is equally involved in propaganda. Propaganda and having a point of view are not synonymous. Government persons with strong convictions may willingly submit a disputed matter to full public scrutiny in the firm belief that when alternative views are heard, their own views will fare well with an objective outside observer.

In contrast, an ideologue or a propagandist will deliberately manipulate a situation in such a way that there will not be a full or fair discussion of the issue. An occasion when alternative points of view are not available is deliberately exploited in order to deceive and distort.

For many decades the Soviet Union has coveted its control of information. It has properly understood that a free and independent press and an uncontrolled literary culture represent a threat to its monopoly of information and perspective.

In the late 1970s I had an opportunity to hear a Communist viewpoint on these matters firsthand. A Party member from Moscow State University asked me to give my frank reactions to living in the Soviet Union. "What have you been most struck by while working here these past five months?"

I thought for a moment and then replied, "The control of information. I am surprised by the extent to which Soviet citizens are not allowed to read other points of view. In the university where I am a graduate student in the United States, I can go to my library and read *Pravda, Izvestiia,* and virtually any book or periodical the Soviet Union publishes, but your citizens do not have the right to read *Time,* the *Washington Post,* or the *New York Times.* Nor do your students know the most basic, indisputable facts about the Stalin era."

The eyes of the Communist party member flashed, and he declared with unusual frankness: "What's the point of reopening old debates? Besides if we gave people a choice, they would want to return to capitalism. And as for Stalin, there is no point in dredging up all that old history. The people are children, and we must control what information they have."

That comment was made seven years before Gorbachev came to power, and it reflects well the Party's traditional attitude toward the control of information. Nor is it a view that has been finally and unquestionably defeated in the Soviet Union today. It is, however, being seriously challenged by some at the highest levels of government and Party.

STOPPING THE JAMMING

As significant as are the changes in the way religion is treated in Soviet literature and the press is what people are allowed to hear about it from outside sources.

The *New York Times* reports that before the Soviets stopped jamming, they were estimated to be spending more than a billion dollars a year to block foreign radio transmissions into their country.[2] The USSR has probably spent far more on jamming Western programming than the West has spent on producing and transmitting it. Despite the Soviet's best efforts, however, considerable Western programming has reached Soviet shortwave radios.

According to Dr. Mark Elliott (as noted in the previous chapter), in early 1988 over 360 hours a week of religious broadcasting was being transmitted into the Soviet Union. Since jamming was frequently sporadic and aimed primarily at the Western government-sponsored broadcasts, much religious broadcasting got through, particularly when it confined itself to nonpolitical religious subject matter.[3]

A more modest thirteen-plus hours a week is provided for Christian programming by five government-funded stations: the British Broadcasting Corporation (BBC), Deutsche Welle, Radio Liberty, Radio Free Europe, and Voice of America. Much of the government-funded broadcasting is aimed at the Orthodox, while most of the private programming is Protestant in character. Radio Vatican seeks to meet the needs of Catholics.[4]

As late as 1987, a detailed article giving the standard denunciation of Western broadcasting appeared in the Soviet serial *Questions of Scientific Atheism*. The programming was described as politically reactionary and anti-Soviet and a tool of carefully coordinated religious propaganda which, in addition to talking about God, criticized the lack of spirituality in Soviet society.[5]

In January 1988 the Soviets ceased jamming the BBC. In May of that year they stopped interfering with Voice of America, and in late November the last jammed foreign broadcast, Radio Liberty, was allowed to transmit freely. Radio Liberty is funded by the U.S. government and broadcasts into the Soviet Union in twelve languages to an estimated sixteen million listeners.[6] It was praised even in Moscow newspapers for having better coverage of the December 1988 Armenian earthquake than did their own media.[7]

The timing of the decision to cease jamming was not accidental. Moscow was actively seeking Western support for its bid to host an international human rights conference in 1991. By the end of 1988, it had won support from its fellow members of the Commission for Security and Cooperation in Europe who were meeting in Vienna when the jamming stopped.

The decision to cease jamming is a tangible sign that *glasnost* is not just window dressing. It will not only make it easier for Soviet citizens to gain information on both internal and external matters, thus forcing the Soviet press to be more responsible, but it will provide new opportunities for religious programming to reach the ears of believers and nonbelievers alike. This is a significant step toward religious freedom.

THE RECOVERY OF THE PAST

Memory is returning to us. It is returning in the form of books that previously went unpublished. . . .[8]

These words appeared in August 1988 in the introduction to a Soviet edition of the *Memoirs* of Nadezhda Mandelstam, which recounts the suffering and confusion of the 1930s. Similar firsthand accounts told previously often led to fresh encounters with the Gulag.

For many years Boris Pasternak's *Dr. Zhivago* has circulated in the Soviet underground. Not considered nearly as dangerous as Solzhenitsyn's works, *Dr. Zhivago* nevertheless was unsettling to the authorities because its depiction of the early months and years of the Revolution raised questions about whether or not the lofty ideals of the revolutionaries were swept aside early on by narrowness and cruelty.

In 1958 the important Soviet journal *Novyi Mir* (New World) refused to publish *Dr. Zhivago*. The editors later explained to the author their reasons for rejecting his work:

> The spirit of your novel is the spirit of rejection of the Socialist Revolution. . . . The author's views on the past . . . can be summed up as meaning that the October Revolution was a mistake, that participation in it for that part of the intelligentsia who supported it was an irreparable calamity, and that everything that took place after it was an evil. . . . We cannot even consider the publication of your novel. . . .[9]

Thirty years later, *Novyi Mir* published *Dr. Zhivago*. Another taboo topic for the Soviet Union has been why committed Communists have sometimes abandoned their Communist convictions. Thus, Arthur Koestler's *Darkness at Noon* (1941) was not published in Russian and was forbidden reading material. In this fascinating novel, the English writer speculates on why completely loyal Bolsheviks confessed in the 1930s to crimes they never committed. Koestler argues that blind, indiscriminate loyalty to Communist ideology warped the minds and judgment of true Bolshevik believers. Furthermore their willingness to lie constantly for the ''good of the Party'' eventually robbed them of their ability to distinguish between truth and falsehood.

In July 1988, the literary magazine *Neva* began publishing *Darkness at Noon*. The Soviet introduction does not agree with Koestler's rejection of communism, but it argues that Koestler's decision was understandable and Soviet readers should be acquainted with the book.[10]

The Soviet Union has made a habit of condemning its own creative citizens, even those who have gained the most prestigious literary honor the world has to offer. Pasternak could not leave the Soviet Union in 1958 to receive the Nobel Prize for fear that Khrushchev would not let him back into the country. Solzhenitsyn's Nobel Prize of 1970 was followed four years later by his expulsion from the Soviet Union.

In 1963 a Leningrad newspaper carried a major attack on a poet in his early twenties. ''It's time to stop coddling this literary parasite. There is no place in Leningrad for the likes of Brodsky. . . .'' The next year, Joseph Brodsky was arrested for ''parasitism'' and sent to labor camp. Following his emigration in 1972, Brodsky was awarded the Nobel Prize in 1987 for his poetry.[11]

But during *glasnost,* Brodsky and other formerly forbidden writers are being perceived differently. In 1989 two *Izvestiia* correspondents filed a story on Brodsky which noted that articles about his unfair trial were being planned. They wrote:

> If we really want to move forward, not just in word but in deed, don't we have to evaluate ourselves? When should we do it, if not today? And not merely for self-purification or repentance (we have the knack of repenting and then sinning all over again), but so that in the future it will be impossible, or at least more difficult, to decide someone's fate so drastically.[12]

Brodsky was just one of Khrushchev's victims. There were millions more under Stalin. Does *glasnost* extend to a discussion of their fates?

Exorcising a Demon: Facing the Truth about Stalin

Some events in life sear themselves into our memories. For one man those memories involve reliving numerous truck rides several miles out of town to the top of a hill. "We'd shout, 'Come on out! Line up!' They get out, and in front of them there's a pit dug for them. They'd get out and start huddling closer together, and we'd immediately open fire."[13]

The words are those of one of Stalin's executioners from Omsk, and they were recorded in a late 1988 issue of the Soviet journal *Moscow News.* In 1937 and 1938 alone, according to Solzhenitsyn, 1.7 million may have been executed. Even more died in labor camps, and millions more perished in the mass terror against the peasantry between 1930 and 1934.[14] Hitler has been the embodiment of evil for most people, yet Joseph Stalin was responsible for the death of far more of his own citizens than was Hitler.

In a 1989 article in the Soviet periodical *Arguments and Facts,* dissident Soviet historian Roy Medvedev estimates that Stalin was responsible for about twenty million deaths in labor camps, executions, forced collectivization, and deliberately induced famines. Soviet Poet Andrei Voznesensky told an audience that Stalin was responsible for the deaths of over thirty million people. About the same time TASS reported that a mass grave had been discovered in Siberia. Fifty people had been shot in the head near one of Stalin's camps. In March 1988 TASS confirmed that a mass grave discovered near Kiev last year was the product of the terror of the 1930s.[15] Historians have been aware of these facts for several decades, but it is unusual for them to be discussed in such detail in the Soviet press.

The Soviets are even showing some openness to publishing the views of the most prominent Western experts on the Stalin period. In early 1989 an interview with Robert Conquest, author of *The Great Terror* and *Harvest of*

Sorrow, appeared in *Moscow News.* The introductory comments noted that shortly after *The Great Terror* was published in the West in 1968, it reached the Soviet Union through *samizdat* and was immediately recognized by the Soviet intelligentsia as "one of the most important Western research works on Soviet history."[16]

It is ironic that Conquest has been praised in the Soviet press in recent months for scholarly work that earned him only disdain from Western religious and political leftists and peace activists. For two decades they have belittled his research and accused his work of fueling the Cold War.

Many facets of the Stalin years are being rewritten. A Soviet historian revealed in the large-circulation *Literary Gazette* that Trotsky, Stalin's main Marxist rival, was murdered on Stalin's order in Mexico in 1940. Historian Dmitry Volkogonov, who is writing an official Soviet biography of Stalin, has said that Stalin's nonaggression pact with Hitler in 1939 was "a great political mistake."[17] In addition, positive articles are appearing in the Soviet press about one of Stalin's chief rivals in the late twenties and thirties, Nikolai Bukharin, who was executed by Stalin in 1938.

Anatoli Rybakov's *Children of the Arbat,* denied publication for over two decades, was finally released officially to the Soviet public in 1987. Set in the 1930s, this fictional account of the Stalin period is highly critical of the man who ruled the Soviet Union during much of its early history. Though the book contains no new revelations for the informed Western reader, and the literary quality is only mediocre, it is significant for the Soviet public that it was published at all.[18] The demand for the book far exceeds its availability.

The dismantling of Stalin is also occurring through the powerful medium of the stage. In February 1989 Muscovites were treated to the opening of a new play (*The Hard Route*) based on the memoirs of Eugenia Ginzburg. The audience responded with a fifteen-minute standing ovation at the end of the premiere of the bitterly anti-Stalinist play.[19]

The new openness toward Stalin began sometime around the spring of 1987. Within a few months two of the most *glasnost*-oriented Soviet periodicals, *Ogonek* and *Moscow News,* along with prominent cultural figures and some dissidents, founded the Memorial Society to help the Soviet populace come to grips with a past the textbooks and authorities have pretended never happened. In June 1988 Gorbachev expressed his support for the idea of a memorial in honor of Stalin's victims.[20]

For nine extraordinary days in November 1988, more than thirty-five thousand Soviet citizens filed silently through an exhibit in Moscow devoted to Stalin's repressions. They stood and gazed, some with tears in their eyes, at a bulletin board which gave information on the disappearances and deaths of loved ones—a few of the countless millions driven into the infamous prison camps dotting the Soviet landscape. By the time the exhibition closed, more than 50,000 roubles ($80,000) had been deposited in a wheelbarrow for the construction of a research complex and a permanent memorial dedicated to the victims of Stalin's crimes.[21]

The authorities have mixed reactions to the Memorial Society. Though official policy is *glasnost* and reform, the preference is for Gorbachev and the Politburo to lead the way. The authorities get nervous when the openness wells up from the people.

The Memorial Society held a Congress in Moscow in January 1989. Andrei Sakharov reported that Central Committee officials warned the organizers not to hold the meeting, but they went ahead anyway. Over 700 delegates from 108 cities gathered and voted to become an official organization with the legal right to publish a newspaper and put up candidates for the Soviet legislature. They passed a resolution calling for the rehabilitation of all political prisoners during and after Stalin. They also called for the publication and rehabilitation of Alexander Solzhenitsyn's works. The total raised for the memorial by the end of January stood at over 500,000 roubles ($800,000).[22]

Perhaps the most dramatic sign of *glasnost* in the Soviet Union is the plan to publish Solzhenitsyn's *Gulag Archipelago,* his monumental study of Stalin's labor camps. This is particularly unusual in that the authorities have considered no author more subversive in past decades than Solzhenitsyn.[23]

What has particularly disturbed the Soviets is not that Solzhenitsyn has provided voluminous documentation of Stalin's crimes, but that he has laid them at Lenin's doorstep. Lenin and Marx have almost always been preserved from official criticism in the Soviet Union. Even when Khrushchev and Gorbachev have attacked the excesses of Stalin, they have been careful to insist that Stalin departed from the Leninist path.

In contrast, Solzhenitsyn asserts that the seeds of Stalin's excesses are to be found in Lenin's conception of a narrow Party. He also believes that a departure from religion, from God, is bound to lead a country into great crimes. The dogmatic atheist Marx, according to Solzhenitsyn, cannot escape responsibility for what has happened in the Soviet Union.

In the summer of 1988, Sergei Zalygin, editor of *Novyi Mir,* was ready to publish *Cancer Ward* and *The First Circle,* but Solzhenitsyn balked. The feisty author, who has lived in Vermont since his exile in 1974, insisted that *Gulag* be published first. As late as November 1988, prospects for publishing Solzhenitsyn's most controversial works were very much in doubt. At a meeting of senior editors, the Party chief of ideology, Vadim Medvedev, declared his opposition to the publication of *Gulag* and *Lenin in Zurich.* He charged that the negative treatment of Lenin and the October Revolution would "undermine the foundations on which today's life rests."[24]

Not long before Medvedev's comments, a small newspaper in Ukraine published Solzhenitsyn's 1974 essay "Live Not by Lies." Shortly after that, two Baltic newspapers reprinted the article, and then in February 1989 it appeared in a Moscow periodical. The editor of the Moscow paper describes

Solzhenitsyn as "the greatest Russian writer of today" and insists that it makes no sense to ban any of his works.[25]

The editor of *Novyi Mir* is certain that Gorbachev and others in the Politburo favor publishing *Gulag*. Solzhenitsyn has given the journal permission to devote three issues to publishing portions of his lengthy study of the labor camps. Once these issues are out, a one-volume collection of his writings (including *Cancer Ward*) is scheduled for publication by a Soviet publishing house.

It is hard to overestimate the historical and political significance of the publication of *Gulag* in the Soviet Union. If this does indeed occur, then *glasnost* has reached a depth few could have anticipated. Whether or not the many important works of Solzhenitsyn (including *The Red Wheel*, an historical cycle of novels spanning the period from World War I into the Soviet period) are published in the coming months will provide a meaningful indicator of the strength of *glasnost*.

The information monolith which has for so long held the Soviet Union in its granitelike grip is gradually being chipped away. But to allow the publication of Solzhenitsyn's works amounts to blows struck at the monolith's very foundation. Will the Soviets really allow this to occur? If they do, Solzhenitsyn has indicated a desire to return to the Soviet Union. Even many who are optimistic about *glasnost* find such a scenario almost inconceivable.

It is too early to tell what will happen, but the next two or three years are critically important. Information is a dangerous commodity in a formerly totalitarian state, but it is the key to any meaningful evolution toward democracy.

Notes

1. John Stuart Mill, "On Liberty," in *Autobiography and Other Writings*, ed. Jack Stillinger (Boston: Houghton Mifflin, 1969), 366.

2. Serge Schmemann, "The Soviets Stop Years of Jamming of Radio Liberty," *New York Times*, 1 December 1988.

3. Mark Elliott, "A Typology of Western-Soviet Christian Contacts," (Unpublished manuscript, Institute for the Study of Christianity and Marxism, Wheaton College, Wheaton, Ill., 1988), 38-39. Earlier, published versions of this article appeared in the January 9 and 23, 1987 issues of *Pulse* (Wheaton, Ill.) and in *Eternity*, July-August 1986, 24-29.

4. Elliot, "Western-Soviet Contacts," 39.

5. A. A. Rotovsky, "Reactionary Religious Anti-Communist Radio Programming into the USSR: Ideological Functions, Political Calculations," *Questions of Scientific Atheism* (Voprosy Nauchnogo Ateizma), no. 36 (1987), 250-66.

6. Schmemann, "Soviets Stop Years of Jamming."

7. Michael Novak, "Climbing Up the Audience Chart," *The Washington Times*, 17 February 1989.

8. Mikhail Polivanov, introduction to *Memoirs* by Nadezhda Mandelstam, in "The *Glasnost* Papers: What the Soviets Are Saying about the Writers They Are Resurrecting," *New Republic*, 20 February 1989, 34.

9. Quoted in "The *Glasnost* Papers," 30.

10. Ibid., 28-30.

11. Ludmilla Alexeyeva, *Soviet Dissent: Contemporary Movements for National, Religious, and Human Rights* (Middletown, Conn.: Wesleyan University Press, 1987), 297; quotation in the introduction to Y. Kovalenko and E. Polianovsky, "Joseph Brodsky's Nobel Prize," *New Republic*, 20 February 1989, 38.

12. Kovalenko and Polianovsky, "Brodsky's Nobel Prize," 39.

13. Quoted in Felicity Barringer, "Stalin Victims Are Mourned by Throngs," *New York Times*, 28 November 1988.

14. Mikhail Heller and Aleksandr Nekrich, *Utopia and Power: The History of the Soviet Union from 1917 to the Present* (New York: Summit Books, 1986), 301, 306.

15. Vera Tolz, "The USSR This Week," *Report on the USSR*, Radio Free Europe/Radio Liberty, 17 February 1989, 27; 31 March 1989, 44; David Remnick, "Decades After Stalin, Shattering the Silence," *Washington Post*, 30 January 1989.

16. Quoted in Vera Tolz, *Report on the USSR*, 7 April 1989, 32.

17. Quoted in "Kremlin Had Trotsky Killed, Soviet Historian Reports," *Washington Post*, 5 January 1989; Vera Tolz, "Official Historian Says Hitler-Stalin Pact Was Mistake," *Report on the USSR*, 24 February 1989, 61.

18. Michael Scammell, "Anatoli Rybakov: Sons of the Revolution," *Christian Science Monitor*, 29 May 1988, 5. An English translation of *Children of the Arbat* was published by Little, Brown, and Company, 1988.

19. Michael Dobbs, "The Gulag Comes to the Stage," *Washington Post*, 17 February 1989. Ginzburg was a victim of eighteen years in the camps. Her *Into the Whirlwind* was first published in the West in 1967.

20. Barringer, "Stalin Victims Mourned"; Remnick, "Decades After Stalin."

21. Vera Tolz, "The USSR This Week," RL 529/88, 2 December 1988, 1.

22. Remnick, "Decades After Stalin."

23. Materials on the pending publication of Solzhenitsyn in the USSR, unless otherwise indicated, are taken from: Paul Quinn-Judge, "The Decensoring of Solzhenitsyn," *Christian Science Monitor*, 5 April 1989; and, David Remnick, "Soviet Journal to Publish 'Gulag'," *Washington Post*, 21 April 1989.

24. Quoted in Tolz, "USSR This Week," RL 529/88, 6.

25. Quoted in Tolz, "USSR This Week," 31 March 1989, 38.

CHAPTER 12

RELIGION IN
SOVIET CULTURE:

Stirrings of New Life

*I*n his 1986 short story, *Place of Action,* well-known Soviet writer Victor Astaf'ev describes a beautiful and moving spiritual celebration of Christ's resurrection as the author experienced it as a youth. He then describes this same occasion being "celebrated" in the present by a group of drunk and crude Soviet fishermen. The stark contrast troubles him:

> What has happened with us? Who and for which transgressions has plunged us into this abyss of evil and misfortunes? Who has extinguished the light of virtue in our souls . . . the sacred light of our consciousness. We used to live with light in our souls . . . without scratching out the eyes of our neighbors, without breaking our neighbor's bones. Why has all this been abducted from us, and replaced by godlessness. . . . To whom are we going to turn our prayers now . . . to ask forgiveness? . . . Yet, in the past . . . we used to forgive even our enemies.[1]

SOVIET LITERATURE

We do not expect to find such passages in contemporary Soviet litera-ture—and they are still rare. But they have cropped up with increasing frequency in recent years. The authors feel constrained to assure their readers (and the authorities) that they are faithful atheists, but their depictions of believers and religious questions are increasingly sympathetic, or at least not hostile.

One senses a genuine spiritual quest on the part of several Soviet writers who deal with religious themes. This trend predates the Gorbachev period by several years.

There has long been a debate among historians about whether history makes the individual or the individual makes history. In other words, did Thomas Jefferson, through the sheer force of his personality, fundamentally shape the direction of the United States with his Declaration of Independence, or did Jefferson only reflect the influences and conditions of his time? As in most dilemmas of this sort, the truth is firmly lodged between the two alternatives.

The same is true for Mikhail Gorbachev. *Glasnost* did not spring full-grown out of one person's vision for the future. Rather it was a product of many factors, including the deteriorating economic situation, a general and undeniable moral crisis in the society, and a widespread readiness to consider more honestly the role past Soviet mistakes have played in the problems that fester in Soviet society today.

Literature is a good example of where the signs of *glasnost* can be detected before Gorbachev took power. Since the late 1970s, there has been a more sympathetic treatment of religious believers in Soviet literature.[2]

These encouraging breakthroughs, however, have had to occur in the teeth of the deathly legacy of "Socialist Realism." Dating to at least the First Congress of Soviet Writers (1934), Socialist Realism was an attempt to bring artistic method into conformity with ideological purpose. Reality was not to be described as it was but as it ought to be according to Communist theory. Emphasis was placed on finding meaning in service to the socialist community; little attention was given to the private lives of individuals. Any serious treatment of religious questions was avoided, except perhaps when describing an early stage in the "natural" evolution of individual views from the darkness of religious superstition toward the light of scientific materialism and atheism.

Although the World War II era produced a few good novels and short stories, Soviet literature since the 1930s has been a desert compared with the century before the October Revolution. The tsars had their censors, but Russian literature was nevertheless a gold mine of social commentary and creative religious thought. Not so since the time of Stalin. The best writers have been constantly hounded or silenced.

Ironically, but not untypically for Russia, at the very moment Socialist Realism was officially introduced, one of the most unusual and daring twentieth-century Russian novels was being composed—a bizarre fantasy in which the devil visits Moscow. Mikhail Bulgakov completed the *The Master and Margarita* just a few months before his own death in 1940. He knew it was impossible for his book to appear in the Soviet Union in the foreseeable future.[3] It was not until 1967-1968 that *The Master and Margarita* finally appeared in a clumsily edited Soviet edition.

Bulgakov does not write as an orthodox believer, but the book teems with philosophical and theological discussions about Christ, Pilate, the Devil, and the nature of good and evil. At one point in the novel, Satan ridicules a character for his one-dimensional or narrowly "materialist" orientation:

> You spoke your words, as though you do not acknowledge the existence of shadows or of evil. Think now: where would your good be if there were no evil, and what would the earth look like without shadow? Shadows are thrown by people and things. There's the shadow of my sword. But shadows are also cast by trees and living beings. Do you want to strip the whole globe by removing every tree and everything alive to satisfy your fantasy of naked light? You are stupid.[4]

In dealing with the poverty of atheist ideology, talk of the Devil is as scandalous and potentially corruptive as talk of God.

Eight years before Gorbachev came to power, Moscow's avant-garde Taganka Theater premiered an adaptation of Bulgakov's novel. I was in Moscow during this period, and the play was the talk of the town. It was virtually impossible to get tickets, and there was a hushed awe in any conversation when the play was mentioned.

For several months one of the world's great directors, Yury Lyubimov, courageously continued the production. It was rumored that some patron in the Kremlin was protecting Lyubimov, but eventually the expected attack in *Pravda* occurred. Deciding that Lyubimov could be tolerated no more, he was dismissed as director of the Taganka Theater, expelled from the Communist party, and finally stripped of his citizenship. One of the sure signs of *glasnost* is that Lyubimov returned to direct two plays in the USSR during the Gorbachev era, and in May 1989 his citizenship was restored.[5]

If Soviet writers continue to insist that they are atheists, then how does their writing reflect a positive change in their treatment of religion? In the past, believers depicted in books or stories were expected to conform to certain stereotypes. Priests frequently were portrayed as drunkards living luxuriously off the gifts of their parishioners, and the suggestion of other moral problems was not unusual. The typical believer was invariably uneducated and superstitious. Believers were almost never productive members of society.

How different is the discussion of religion in the play *The Wood-Grouse's Nest* by Victor Rozov. The main character is the daughter of a leader in the Soviet peace movement. Her father comes home one day to their posh Moscow apartment and is shocked to find his daughter on her knees before his collection of icons. Her marriage in shambles, not even certain how to make the sign of the cross, she is praying: "Help me, God, help me."[6]

Vladimir Tendriakov is another Soviet writer who explored moral and religious themes many years before Gorbachev came on the scene. His short stories from the late 1950s until his death in 1984 reflect a gradual but perceptible shift from the perspective of a typical atheist to someone with considerable respect for religious faith. His 1987 posthumously published novel *An Attack on Mirages* is filled with quotations from Scripture, commentary on Paul and Christ, and discussions about the relationship between science and religion.[7]

Chingiz Aitmatov's *The Place of the Skull* is the novel with religious themes that has attracted the most attention in the Gorbachev period.[8] Aitmatov is a popular writer from the Kirghiz Republic, and his own religious background is Moslem, though he is a professing atheist. His novel appeared in three parts in the journal *Novyi Mir* during 1986 and 1987.

The hero of the novel, Avdy Kallistratov, is on a spiritual quest to find a new religion which avoids both traditional Russian Orthodoxy and scientific materialism. He is also dedicated to turning people away from evil and toward a religion of love. Thrown off a train by drug dealers, he is eventually left to die suspended on a tree by thugs who are destroying the local wildlife. The parallels with the life of Christ are unmistakable.

Though the main character of *The Place of the Skull* is a moral, even religious, figure, he is by no means an orthodox Christian. He asserts that Judas fabricated the doctrines of the Resurrection and the Second Coming. The author expanded his own views on Jesus in a 1987 interview.

> The legendary figure of Christ, which was very likely invented by men, is still a living figure to us today, one which teaches us a lofty and unforgettable lesson of personal courage and nobility. After Christ there were great men in all walks of life . . . but Jesus has outlived them all, appealing equally to men of the second and the twentieth centuries.[9]

Publication of just the first third of Aitmatov's book provoked a frontal attack by the atheist establishment. In July 1986 a senior Soviet authority on religion, I. Kryvelev, launched the offensive against Aitmatov and two other Soviet writers (Astaf'ev and Bykov) in the newspaper *Komsomol Pravda*. "To renounce a principled, consistent atheism," he contended, "is to renounce the very foundations of the scientific and materialistic world-view."[10] The title of Kryvelev's article contained the heart of his critique: "Flirtation with a Dear Little God," an intentional reminder of Lenin's attack on "God-Seeking."

All that is at stake in the debate over religious themes in Soviet literature is not generally understood. On the most superficial level, a dogmatic atheist might object to any mention of religious themes in other than the most pejorative of forms. Religious themes at this level might represent either Christian orthodoxy or heresy. The crude atheist simply hears the word *God* and he sees red, never bothering to find out if the word is used in a sacred or heretical way.

A distinction must be made between "God-Seeking" and "God-Building"—two early twentieth-century movements in Russia. "God-Seeking" refers to a genuine move toward a traditional notion of a transcendent God, separate from humanity. It is often associated with Nicolas Berdyaev and Sergei Bulgakov, former Marxists who became Orthodox Christians.

In contrast, "God-Building" is associated with Bolshevik Marxists Maxim Gorky and Anatoly Lunacharsky. The former was perhaps the best known early Bolshevik literary figure; the latter became the first Commissar of Education in the new Communist state. "God-Builders," recognizing the tremendous power religion has exercised in human history, wanted to harness religious language in the interests of a radically secular worship of humanity. In 1908, Gorky concluded his *Confession* with a prayer to "the almighty, immortal people!"

> Thou art my God and the creator of all gods, which thou hast fashioned from the beauties of the spirit in the toil and struggle of thy searchings!

> And there shall be no other gods in the world but thee, for thou art the one God that creates miracles! Thus do I believe and confess![11]

What at first glance appears religious is, in fact, a parody of true religion—with man, not God, the center of devotion.

Vladimir Lenin condemned both "God-Seeking" and "God-Building." Though the latter was but a pale, false shadow of true religion, Lenin considered it highly dangerous to play around with religious language in any form.[12] In the wake of Lenin's rebuke, Gorky and Lunacharsky moved away from their flirtations with "God-Building."

Though "God-Seeking" was what Kryvelev attacked in Aitmatov's novel, he would have been closer to the mark had he identified some of the novel's themes as "God-Building."[13] In a dream sequence encounter between Christ and Pilate, Christ does not identify himself with a transcendent God, but rather identifies the godhead with a perfected human consciousness. This sounds eerily like Ludwig Feuerbach, whose thought had such an impact on Karl Marx.

It is premature to make a final judgment on Aitmatov's spiritual odyssey. Though he may have some "God-Building" themes in his work, these may reflect more accurately the early stages of his spiritual quest than they do any Gorky/Lunacharsky notions. Since he seems fascinated with Jesus Christ as a creative and powerful historical figure, it is possible he will come to understand Christ in a more orthodox and traditional manner.[14]

It is important to separate the debate over the quality of the religious ideas being discussed in Soviet literature from the fact that there is discussion at all. It is encouraging, and indeed a sign of *glasnost,* that the dogmatic atheists' attack on Aitmatov was firmly met and turned back in the Soviet press by those who long for the fresh air of greater intellectual and cultural freedom.

This defeat of the doctrinaire atheists is very different from what happened in the early eighties. In 1982 Vladimir Soloukhin was strongly criticized in *Kommunist* for "religious and mystical ideas and moods" found in his "Pebbles in the Palm of a Hand." Soloukhin was brought to his knees, as was the journal *Nash Sovremennik* (Our Contemporary) which had published his story. He assured the Party committee of the Moscow Writers' Organization that he "had been and remained a convinced atheist, and that he had never engaged in god-building."[15]

In contrast to the 1982 affair, the 1986 attack on Aitmatov encountered the strongest of protests from some of the Soviet Union's literary lights. One of the USSR's leading poets, Yevgeny Yevtushenko, ridiculed the "dogmatism" of the critic in a letter published in the same journal that had attacked Aitmatov. "Our socialist state is a union of communists and non-party members, of believers and atheists. Atheism is a voluntary phenomenon, not something coercively thrust upon people," contended Yevtushenko. Ironically, Yevtushenko's letter appeared in print on International Human Rights Day, December 10, 1986.[16]

Yevtushenko also responded to Kryvelev's attack on the Bible as "an immoral book," insisting that it represented "a great cultural monument" and that Soviet youth could not understand the Russian classics of Pushkin, Gogol, Dostoevsky, and Tolstoy without a knowledge of the Bible.[17]

In all three of the published "round-table" discussions over the controversy surrounding Aitmatov's work, the intolerant attack on Soviet writers' use of religious themes was soundly condemned. One of the participants, E. Sidorov, asserted that it would have been better for the critic "to have thought about and tried to explain to the readers of a Komsomol paper why an interest in religion has been growing in the USSR among all ages and social strata." Sidorov contended that the reason for the clear spread of religion was "a spiritual vacuum, a crisis of faith" in the social and human values promoted in the Soviet Union.[18]

The vigorous discussion in the Soviet press about the use of religious themes in literature is in itself a positive sign. Without question the positive treatment of religious figures and themes in Soviet literature is on the increase. It should not surprise us that these references to religion span the entire range from "God-Seeking" to "God-Building" and that many of them (such as allusions to the cultural vitality of the Old Believers and to beautiful churches) may reflect as much a revival of cultural nationalism as of revived religious consciousness.

However, as long as religious themes in Soviet literature can be discussed only by sympathetic atheists and not by committed believers, we have a long way to go before the spiritual and literary riches of the Soviet peoples can be mined in full. Yet in the literary circles there is an air of expectancy, a sense of the possibility of more fully entering into the broad, impressive stream of the cultures of the Soviet Union—cultures permeated with religious themes. Though steps in this direction are still tentative, they are nonetheless real.

REVIVAL OF RELIGIOUS ARCHITECTURE

One of my hobbies during my graduate studies in the Soviet Union was to track down and photograph old churches. Novgorod, in northeast Russia, is one of the Soviet Union's medieval gems. After considerable searching, I managed to locate, well off the beaten track, a twelfth-century church. But something was not quite right. There were flower boxes in the upstairs windows and electrical wires coming from the roof. Finally the awful truth sank in. This architectural masterpiece had been turned into an apartment building.

Actually this church was one of the lucky ones. Tens of thousands of others were razed or turned into warehouses, concert halls, or whatever else the local authorities deemed appropriate for advancing the social needs of the post-religious Communist community.

This desecration is tragic, and yet it is ironic that some of the best restoration work in Europe has been done in the Soviet Union. The golden onion domes, whitewashed exteriors, and exquisite interiors of many churches have found their way into countless thousands of tourist slide shows.

Unfortunately, many more churches were destroyed than preserved, and it is against that destruction that many have actively protested during the *glasnost* era. In 1986 esteemed academician Dmitry Likhachev (not to be confused with the conservative Kremlin ideologue Ligachev) established a Cultural Fund. The presidium of the organization includes Gorbachev's wife, Raisa, and Metropolitan Pitirim, head of the Moscow Patriarchate's publishing department.[19]

The fund has raised millions of roubles to advance what Likhachev calls an "ecology of culture." He charges that Soviet culture is in a catastrophic state caused by moral nihilism. Before the Revolution, each church was a moral educator of the nation. In the wake of the destruction and massive closings of the churches, a moral vacuum remains where once were notions of good and evil, right and wrong.[20]

A graphic literary example of the contemporary protest against the Soviet destruction of culture is found in a short story by Victor Astaf'ev, published in the same year the Cultural Fund was set up. The author describes how invading Mongols in the fourteenth century set up camp in an ancient church. When they lit bonfires, lead in the dome of the church melted and poured down its molten judgment on the Mongols' heads. Reflecting on this scene, Astaf'ev writes:

Oh, if only a heavenly rain of molten lead, that final and punishing rain, would fall on the heads of all desecrators of churches, of all haters of mankind, of all persecutors of pure morals. . . .[21]

Considerable attention has been given in the Western and Soviet press to the "generosity" of the State in returning to the Russian Orthodox Church some of its most sacred and prized architectural treasures. In 1983 the Danilov Monastery in Moscow was given back to the Church and has become an important new center for the Russian Orthodox Patriarchate. In 1987 the keys to the well-known Optina Monastery and the Yaroslavl' Tolgsky Monastery were handed over to the Church as well.

On the occasion of the 1987 returns, Alexander Nezhnyi, one of the most notable Soviet correspondents on religious matters, wrote a superb article on the historical, cultural, and religious significance of Optina. Nezhnyi reported that when the monastery was returned to its original owner, it looked like it had been bombed in an air raid. He estimated that fifteen million roubles would be needed to restore it, but he had no doubt that the faithful believers would raise that amount, just as they had come up with the necessary funds to restore the Danilov Monastery a few years before.[22]

Nezhnyi also wrote an article on the Tolgsky Monastery. For six centuries the Church lovingly maintained the treasure, observed the correspondent, but after just sixty years in Soviet hands "the monastery presents a sorry sight . . . monks' cells are in ruin, doors and windows and their frames have disappeared . . . of the famous 160 giant cedars only twenty-seven have survived."[23]

What is particularly remarkable about Nezhnyi's 1988 article is his appeal to all Soviet citizens, believers and nonbelievers alike, to give funds for the restoration of the church. A bank account number is provided so that contributors will know where to send their donations.[24]

Soviet tourist guides are also being more honest about the fate of past architectural monuments. In the spring of 1988, our guide in Moscow showed us the site where Christ the Savior Cathedral had been dynamited in 1930 in order to construct a swimming pool.

At the recent Seventh Writers' Congress, one of the Soviet Union's most famous poets, Andrei Voznesensky, reminded those present of what had happened to Christ the Savior Cathedral and noted that the building of that cathedral had been a truly "national" affair, in contrast to the indifference with which contemporary Soviet citizens greet the building of monuments. "This indifference disfigures our whole present," Voznesensky asserted.[25]

It is impossible to miss the moral outrage that has emerged in recent months over the damage inflicted by the Communist authorities on the cultural treasures of the peoples of the Soviet Union. Nor is it just the physical buildings that are being defended by many of those involved in the restoration movement.

The head of the movement, Likhachev, has ridiculed atheist propaganda, calling it "ignorant . . . not only . . . of Church history, but of history as a whole . . . ignorant of culture, [particularly] the culture of democracy." He continued:

> We must stress, particularly now on the eve of the Millennium of Russia's Baptism, that we stand for the complete separation of Church from the State. Our State must be truly non-religious. It ought not to interfere in the affairs of the Church. . . . This is what the Council for Religious Affairs should guarantee! Alas, in the very recent past the CRA did interfere, and very actively so, in the life of the Church. And why should there be limits imposed on the church's right to publish books in the quantities needed by the believers, such as: the Bible, church calendars, works of the Holy Fathers, and other ecclesiastic literature?[26]

The "ecology of culture" movement is a strong force for religious freedom on the contemporary Soviet scene.

The stirrings of new life in Soviet literature, and in the cultural revival may represent phenomena which are being allowed by the regime for its own purposes. Nonetheless they also represent a genuine and significant new spirit of religious interest in the Soviet Union. In short, developments in the cultural sphere may prove to be deeper and more lasting than those in the public square or in the Council for Religious Affairs, topics we will take up in the next chapter.

RELIGIOUS THEMES IN SOVIET POPULAR MUSIC: "AQUARIUM"

In 1987, Soviet authorities allowed Aquarium, a previously underground Leningrad rock band, to release an uncensored album. Over half a million copies were sold in the first two releases. Boris Grebenshchikov's group has also been allowed to perform in some of the largest public facilities in the Soviet Union.[27]

What is unusual about Grebenshchikov's musical endeavors are the lyrics; they are full of religious sentiment and meaning. According to James E. Monsma,

> His songs speak of the comforting sight of Russian churches, of water which cleanses the soul, of bread and wine, of the need for forgiveness, of hope for the future age, of love as a straight and direct path home. Liberally sprinkled with exclamations to God, the songs are really prayers.[28]

In one song, Grebenshchikov almost prays: "Silver of my Lord, do I really have the words with which to speak to you? Silver of my Lord, silver of the Lord, higher than stars, higher than words, but equal to our longing." In another number, he challenges the listener: "At our spot in the sky there ought to be a star; you can feel a draft because that spot is empty." He seems to understand that this is a time of new awareness: "It's a natural shock when the moss falls off the nerves; and we question, why did we not live this way from the start. But who can know he's a wire until they turn on the current?"[29]

Though Grebenshchikov's music is filled with Christian symbols, they also include symbols from Celtic folklore and Taoism. He believes all three systems of thought can be traced back to one single ultimate divine source of life.[30] It is not clear to what degree the founder of Aquarium's religious ideas are orthodox in the traditional Christian sense of the term. Some of his lyrics may indicate that New Age thought is also at work here. Whatever the mix, the fact that he is exploring these religious themes in his music is another sign of *glasnost* in action.

Just a few years ago, the Leningrad Protestant rock composer Valery Barinov wrote a musical entitled *Trumpet Call*. His creative efforts were definitely not appreciated by the authorities. He was imprisoned before later being allowed to emigrate. One wonders if his rock evangelism today would be permitted without State interference, just as the wraps have been removed from the somewhat more ambiguous religious messages of Grebenshchikov.

Soviet Film: "Repentance"

To a believer, there can be no spiritual *perestroika* apart from confession and repentance. While much of Soviet society is talking about a kind of *glasnost* which acknowledges economic and political shortcomings, there are others who are exploring much more profound depths of the human soul. One such person is Georgian film director Tengiz Abuladze. His movie *Repentance (Pokaiane)* is perhaps the most moving cultural event thus far of the Gorbachev era, though the conception of the project itself predates the present general secretary's rise to power.

Beginning like a bizarre surrealistic comedy, the film thrusts itself into the viewer's imagination. A small-town Georgian mayor, Varlam Aravidze, has just been buried. However, his body keeps showing up in his relatives' backyard. We soon learn that an apparently crazy woman, Ketivan Barateli, is exhuming the body on a daily basis.

At her trial, it becomes obvious to the viewer that this is no ordinary comedy. What it is, in fact, is a devastating attack on Georgian-born Joseph Stalin—the Mussolini/Hitlerlike model for the deceased mayor. Ketivan's father, a Christlike artist, was one of Varlam's victims. The film contains graphic, emotional footage of family members seeking the names of loved ones carved into the ends of logs brought down from the forests. Indeed, this is how the victims of some of Stalin's forest gulags attempted to communicate with their wives and children.

Ketivan's sanity is questioned by the prosecution. After all, is it not both immoral and pointless to dig up the dead? But "Avaridze is not dead," exclaims the defendant. Moving in for the kill, the prosecutor pounces, "Then you believe he's alive?!" Ketivan fires back, "Yes he is! For as long as you continue to defend him, he lives on and continues to corrupt society."

But the movie is far, far more than an appeal to speak honestly about Stalin; it is a plea for spiritual soul searching. At the trial, Varlam Avaridze's son Abel, a respectable citizen who had always sought to defend his father's actions, drifts off into a dream sequence involving his own confession.

> I have come to confess my sins, Father. I have sinned, my soul is split in two. . . .

> It's as if I have a dual personality. I preach atheism, but wear a cross. Perhaps that's why my life is such a mess. . . .

> I'm worried because I'm gradually losing my moral principles. I no longer distinguish between good and evil. I've lost my faith. . . .

> I can forgive anything and justify any abomination, denunciation, treachery, deceit, baseness.

This confession, interspersed with comments by the unseen "priest," turns sour when Abel is accused of lying about his motives.

> Who are you deceiving, you hypocrite? You'll pulverize anyone who stands in your way. If someone strikes your left cheek, you'll not offer your right, you'll break his jaw. You care nothing for good or evil. It's not a split personality that bothers you, but fear.

Abel is stunned. "Fear of what?" he asks.

> Fear of our life. You always placed status above all else, gloating over your model family. Now everything is crumbling. . . .

> Your father's tossed out of his grave. You're losing your power. Your only son has rebelled. You'll be alone, weak and helpless. . . .

> You're afraid. You're terrified by the prospect of loneliness. An atheist thinks only of death when he is alone.

Abel finally recognizes his true motives, and is suddenly overcome by a terrible suspicion. "Who are you? Tell me who you are," demands Abel. Amidst malicious laughter, his confession becomes a nightmare. "Don't you recognize me, my son? Why you'd come to the devil to confess your sins?" Through breaking glass, Abel now sees the image of his father. When he comes to himself in the courtroom, Abel discovers he is holding the skeleton of a fish—the same fish that the unseen "priest" had been devouring during his confession.

Still, Abel cannot bring himself to face publicly the truth about his father and himself. Only after his teenage son commits suicide does the dam break and a soulful and genuine confession take place. He digs up his father's grave and throws the body over a cliff.

Undoubtedly the most moving lines of the movie are spoken at the end. In a flashback to the scene which opened the film, an old woman knocks on the window of the apartment where Ketivan is baking cakes.

"Is this the road to the church?"

Ketivan answers, "This is Varlam street. It will not take you to the church."

"Then what's the use of it," the old woman replies. "What good is a road if it does not lead to a church?"

A more eloquent statement about the importance of both religious freedom and the spiritual dimension of life would be difficult to find in any country. The fact that packed Soviet theaters in the largest cities of the Soviet Union have been allowed to view this powerful appeal for the spiritual dimension of life is an unmistakable sign of *glasnost*.[31]

Notes

1. Victor Astaf'ev, *Place of Action*, quoted in Dmitry Pospielovsky, "The Russian Orthodox Church in the Gorbachev Era" (Paper delivered at a conference sponsored by the Kennan Institute and the Library of Congress, Washington, D.C., 28 May 1988), 5-6.

2. Mary Seton-Watson, "Religious Themes in Recent Soviet Literature," *Religion in Communist Lands* 16 (Summer 1988):117-25.

3. Basic information on Mikhail Bulgakov is taken from Ellendea Proffer, "The Master and Margarita," in Edward J. Brown, ed., *Major Soviet Writers: Essays in Criticism* (London: Oxford University Press, 1973), 388-411.

4. Quoted in ibid., 409-10.

5. Megen Rosenfeld, "Lyabimov's Citizenship Restored," *Washington Post*, 24 May 1989.

6. Quoted in Seton-Watson, "Religious Themes," 124.

7. Ibid., 118-20. Other writers which the author cites as portraying believers in a positive light prior to Gorbachev coming to power include Georgy Semyonov ("The Ring Game," 1982) and Yury Bondarev ("The Game," 1985).

8. Chingiz Aitmatov, *The Place of the Skull* (New York: Grove Press, New York, 1989). The original Russian is entitled *Plakha*, literally, "executioner's bloc."

9. Chingiz Aitmatov, *Druzhba Narodov* (Friendship of the Peoples), no. 2 (1987), quoted in Seton-Watson, "Religious Themes," 117.

10. Quoted in John B. Dunlop, "The Controversy over 'God- Seeking': A Litmus Test for the Gorbachev Cultural Thaw" (Unpublished paper delivered at a conference on the millennium of Christianity in Kievan Rus', sponsored by the Kennan Institute and the Library of Congress, Washington, D.C., 28 May 1988), 1.

11. Quoted in James H. Billington, *The Icon and the Axe: An Interpretive History of Russian Culture* (New York: Random House, Vintage Books, 1970), 487. For further background on "God-Seeking" and "God-Building," see Billington, 486-92.

12. The *Bol'shaia Sovetskaia Entskiklopediia* [Large Soviet Encyclopedia], 1970, vol. 3, contains entries on both "God-Seeking" and "God-Building," which give Lenin's criticisms of both.

13. Irena Maryniak makes a strong case for the presence of "God-Building" elements in Aitmatov. See "Truthseekers, Godbuilders or Culture Vultures? Some Supplementary Remarks on Religious Perspectives in Modern Soviet Literature," *Religion in Communist Lands* 16 (Autumn 1988):227-236.

14. Dunlop believes "that Aitmatov is, in some sense, a religious believer," despite his claims of being an atheist, "Controversy Over 'God-Seeking,' " 6.

15. Quoted in ibid., 3.

16. Quoted in ibid., 7.

17. Ibid.

18. Quoted in ibid., 9-10.

19. See Pospielovsky, "Russian Orthodox Church," 5-6, 12, 14-15.

20. Ibid., 5.

21. Quoted in ibid., 6. The story is taken from a collection of three short stories entitled *Place of Action*.

22. Pospielovsky, "Russian Orthodox Church," 12.

23. Quoted in ibid.

24. Ibid.

25. Quoted in ibid., 4.

26. Quoted in ibid., 15.

27. James E. Monsma, "*Glasnost* and Religion: Meeting in the Popular Arts," *Christian Century*, 23-30 March 1988, 312. The author also discusses Aitmatov's book and the film *Repentance*.

28. Monsma, "*Glasnost* and Religion," 312.

29. Quoted in ibid., 313.

30. Ibid.

31. *Repentance* is now available for rent and sale at some American video stores.

CHAPTER 13

RELIGION IN THE PUBLIC SQUARE:

New Tactics, Same Goals?

*E*ven before our Millennium Tour group of twenty-one departed for the USSR in late March 1988, we were well aware of the Soviet religious and political leaders' new openness toward past "failures" in the treatment of its religious citizens. During the tour we had an excellent opportunity to experience firsthand the official Soviet views on religious *perestroika*.

The official Soviet tour agency Intourist arranged a session for us with three Moscow professors who belong to the voluntary organization *Znanie* (knowledge). We were told that the organization was forty-one years old and was dedicated to political education. What we were not told was that *Znanie* has been one of the chief State vehicles of official atheism and attacks on religion. On this occasion, however, *Znanie* academics had been dispatched to assure foreigners concerned about religion that there was no antagonism between Church and State.

Mikhail Lyubimov, history professor and now an editor at Novosti Press, chaired the session. His colleagues included Valentin Natalukha, an economics professor, and Alexander Dron, an English language teacher from the Academy of Sciences. They were silhouetted against an expansive stained-glass window picturing Vladimir Lenin. We were meeting in a large lecture hall in *Znanie* headquarters, located in the nineteenth-century Politechnical Library just a few blocks from the Kremlin.

The mood was upbeat, almost Western in tone. The three Soviets argued among themselves about the percentage of religious adherents in the Soviet Union (Dron's estimates were between 20 and 50 percent), and they differed somewhat on other issues as well. Lyubimov asserted that the Church was destined to "play a major role in *perestroika*."

In response to a question about the use of psychiatric hospitals to confine prisoners of conscience, Prof. Natalukha asserted that the Ministry of Foreign

Affairs had successfully pressed for shifting administration of those hospitals previously controlled by the State security to the Ministry of Health. He contended that new regulations governing the hospitals were the most advanced in the world and complained that Western propaganda had often unfairly criticized the Soviets in this area.

We were informed that prison regulations were now under review as was the mail delivery system to prisoners. When Natalukha charged that alleged violations of religious conscience by Soviet authorities were often nothing more than foreign propaganda, Prof. Dron exclaimed "there are more atheists than Christians jailed for unjust reasons in the Soviet Union." (It was unclear what comfort we were to take from his observation.)

The professors displayed surprising hostility toward Amnesty International, one of the most respected Western human rights monitoring organizations. Prof. Natalukha charged that Amnesty International was "very anti-Communist and very anti-Soviet."

The Soviet representatives sounded a call to return to "real socialism," to the ideas of Marx and Lenin. Prof. Dron noted the necessity of coming to terms with competition as a positive force in economics.

The warm winds of *glasnost* affected virtually every subject discussed except one—Jewish emigration. Here the conversation reflected the attitudes of a much earlier period. "We are solving the problems of refuseniks," contended Natalukha. It was pointed out that twice as many Jews had emigrated in 1987 as in 1986, though that was still much less than in the late 1970s. "But, fewer and fewer want to leave. They don't want to become part of the Western unemployed." (Much higher statistics for Jewish departures in 1988 and 1989 would seem to counter his claim.)

Other statements about the Jewish population also reflected less than complete openness. We were told that there were substantial security concerns represented by some of the would-be emigres. In addition, there was the serious problem of a "brain drain," in the words of Prof. Dron, if large numbers of Jews emigrated. The Americans depend heavily on Soviet Jewish emigrés to supply their need for qualified mathematicians. And we were informed that more and more Jews were interested in immigrating to, not from, the Soviet Union!

Another opportunity to detect the official Soviet perspective on religion came when we visited the largest museum devoted to atheism and (anti)religion in the Soviet Union. The museum is housed in the early nineteenth-century Kazan Cathedral in Leningrad. The visit was not part of the official tour, but our guide was willing, with some prodding, to arrange for us to visit this important site.

Our museum guide had been forewarned that he was dealing with a group of believers and to be on his best behavior; he was polite and helpful. He dutifully ushered us through the ages from prehistoric times to the present, painstakingly pointing out that religion was based on primitive superstitions and an antiscientific bias.

How has religion fared in a country where official State policy has repressed or limited religious ideas and practice? Many in the West have been determined to prove that religion is alive and well in the Soviet Union, and it is true that religion has survived and is in no danger of being stamped out in the foreseeable future. There is also considerable evidence in recent years of a growing interest in religion among the Soviet population, including the well educated.

But the impact of seventy years of militantly antireligious propaganda has taken its toll. In four trips to the Soviet Union, I have often talked to intelligent and well-educated Soviet citizens who have never been exposed to a positive view of religion; it invariably has been presented to them as fundamentally superstitious and antiscientific. To be sure, they knew there was some persecution and that not everything the government said about believers was true. But the lack of an opportunity to hear intelligent Christians describe and defend their beliefs had deprived these nonreligious Soviets of even a rudimentary knowledge of basic Christian beliefs.

Our Intourist guide during our two weeks in the Soviet Union illustrated this problem well. The idea that an educated person could seriously consider religious belief, let alone be a believer, was simply not something she had ever thought possible.

On the basis of these contacts with Soviet representatives in the spring of 1988, I concluded that the official Soviet line on Church/State matters had moderated, though it was not certain at that point that it had fundamentally changed. There was a greater willingness to acknowledge past "mistakes" by the government, to consider less restrictive new religious sect laws, to explore the possibility of believers contributing positively to the common good, and to support the release of prisoners of conscience (provided we could agree who they were). Nevertheless, there was little indication that the State had altered its basic philosophical hostility to religious belief. Religion still represented what any authoritarian or totalitarian State fears most—a competing source of ultimate allegiance.

However, before any more definitive judgments are proposed, we must supplement fragmentary firsthand interviews with a careful analysis of how religion is faring in the Soviet press.

RELIGION AND THE SOVIET PRESS

In November 1986, Mikhail Gorbachev, general secretary of the Communist party, demanded a "decisive and uncompromising struggle against manifestations of religion and a strengthening of political work with the masses and of religious propaganda."[1]

Just seventeen months later, in late April 1988, Gorbachev sounded remarkably more tolerant about the positive role of believers in Soviet society. During a reception at the Kremlin for the top leadership of the Russian Orthodox Church, he told a nationwide television audience, "Believers are Soviet people, workers, patriots, and they have the full right to express their conviction with dignity. *Perestroika* and democratization concern them too— in full measure and without any restrictions."[2]

How do we account for these apparently contradictory attitudes toward religion? A Soviet spokesman passed off Gorbachev's November 1986 comment as "just for party members."[3] But there seems to have been a deliberate and remarkable change in Soviet policy sometime between late 1986 and 1987.

There is strong evidence that a crude and typically negative treatment of believers in the Soviet press lasted at least until the end of 1986. As was noted in chapter 12, *Komsomol Pravda* launched an attack on religious themes in Soviet literature in late July 1986. It appears that Gorbachev's November 1986 comment came near the end of one last offensive initiated by the hard-line antireligious ideologues. One of the clearest signs of the lack of *glasnost* in the mid-1980s was the hysterical denunciations of Keston College (England), the foremost research center for the study of religion in Communist countries. The 1985 booklet *Argumenty 85,* with a press run of 150,000, accused Keston College general director Michael Bourdeaux of having connections with the CIA and of "fabricating and juggling the facts" to perpetuate the "dying myth" of "persecuted believers" in the Soviet Union. A few months later, the Soviets would publish materials that supported what Bourdeaux and Keston had been saying for years. Leningrad TV even interviewed Bourdeaux when he visited the Soviet Union in 1988—his first trip into the country in nine years!

The 27th Party Congress in Moscow in February 1986 depicted religion as old-fashioned, reactionary, and tied up with dangerous nationalist tendencies. Well into 1986 both national and local newspapers contained numerous attacks on believers of all denominations. Typical of these crude attacks is the June 1986 article in *Science and Religion,* which pictures the God of the Old Testament as a vengeful, bloodthirsty spirit.[4]

In short, the data is conclusive that at least until late 1986, it was "business as usual" with respect to the treatment of believers and religion in the Soviet press.

By the fall of 1987, however, change was in the wind. In Keston College's Annual Report (September 1987), the following assessment appeared:

> Anti-religious articles continue to be regularly published, but it is no longer taboo for *Pravda* to admit that religion is not only surviving but attracting new members, particularly among young people. The

interest shown in religious themes and Christian ethics by leading writers such as Aitmatov and Rasputin is certainly criticized but is nevertheless discussed in some detail.

Our earlier analysis of the defeat of the dogmatic atheists in the wake of the July 1986 attack on Aitmatov supports the contention that there was a strong shift away from the crude Soviet antireligious propaganda of the recent past.[5]

One of the most promising signs of change is the occasional defense of believers in the local press when they are the victims of vicious slander. Father Nikolai Sakidon, a thirty-three-year-old priest from near Kharkov in Ukraine was assaulted in the press (*October Dawn*) by local authorities who were zealous atheists. The matter came to the attention of Sergei Kiselev, a press correspondent, who then published an interview with the priest in the well-known national magazine *Literary Gazette*.[6]

The article is positive toward the young priest, who is credited with significantly increasing the giving at his church. He is warmly praised by his archbishop as "an honest and conscientious pastor . . . held in great respect by the clergy and by believers." Even Communist authorities are quoted as opposing the slander campaign conducted against him. N. Kolesnik, chairman of the Ukrainian Council for Religious Affairs, the government watchdog committee over religion, notes that slanderous articles reduce believers to "second-class" citizens and violate government regulations of atheist propaganda. The director of the Kiev branch of the Institute of Scientific Atheism, A. Onishchenko, describes the attacks in question as "primitivism" in atheistic propaganda.[7] Soviets themselves are pleased with the attitude shift in the press.

Five days before the Millennium Tour group I was directing arrived in the Soviet Union, a remarkable article appeared in *Leningrad Pravda* (March 22, 1988). The article was called "Is It Possible to Forbid Attending Church? *Perestroika* and Religion," and would have been unheard of ten years ago. The author, A. Ignatov, attacks local authorities for not knowing well the legislation dealing with religion. He reminds his readers that believers have the legal right to profess any religion and carry out the rites associated with it. Yet letters to the paper and his own investigations have confirmed that local authorities frequently harass believers.

A prominent example that Ignatov cites is the attempt to destroy churches. He tells of a letter from twelve Russian Orthodox believers from the Ukrainian village of Ilemnia reporting that their church was "temporarily" closed in 1961 and never reopened. In addition, for almost three years now they have had to protect the church from destruction. The letter went on to assert that in July 1985 the local authorities dissolved a church in the village of Luga and intended to tear it down. Only the believers' willingness to stand guard around the closed church prevented its demolition. However, the believers were fined, summoned before the authorities, and pressured to attend churches in other villages. Ignatov bristles: "What gives regional administrators the right to determine where citizens may or may not go to church?"

The Soviet journalist is not satisfied with listing a few examples of local administrative malfeasance. He documents that between 1962 and 1987 almost no new churches were opened, while many were closed. Ignatov observes: "It is no secret that official channels consider that 'religious prejudices ought to quickly die out' and that's why church buildings are not needed."

Ignatov does point out that "the situation today is changing" and that at the end of 1987 and during the early part of 1988 three new churches were opened in Ukraine; yet he is not convinced that the local authorities from the Council for Religious Affairs (CRA) are moving quickly in their study of the problem in Ilemnia. According to the CRA officials, there are 330 active religious communities in the Ukrainian province where Ilemnia is located. Ignatov claims, however, that dozens of requests for new registration have not received an answer from the CRA.

Ignatov charges that the local authorities view believers with suspicion. They see them as ideological enemies. "And this is what is paradoxical. We are learning how to converse in a normal human language with a real ideological enemy from the West, but with our own citizens—born and raised under socialism—we do not always follow the same humane laws." And it's not just local authorities who are heavy-handed. Ignatov scolds teachers who insensitively quiz the children of believers on why they believe in God.

But Ignatov is optimistic, though he admits the process of improving attitudes toward believers is slow. He cites as hopeful signs the increase in the output of religious literature and the return of important monasteries and churches to ecclesiastical control. According to the journalist, a similar change is occurring in government attitudes toward other religions as well as toward Christianity; it is not just a matter of the millennium celebrations scheduled for June.

Many articles in the Soviet press in recent months follow a similar pattern. The following problems are typically acknowledged: violation of laws or regulations, as well as arbitrary behavior, by local authorities; destruction of churches; serious delays or obstacles created by local authorities in registering churches; and rude, unfair treatment of believers by propagandists or teachers. The positive traits of believers are also more likely to be noted than in the past.

Not infrequently, officials connected with propaganda are involved in strong self-criticism. In the November 1988 issue of *Religion and Science*, A.G. Khmyrchik, the head of the propaganda section for the Kaliningrad Oblast (Province), asserts that the propaganda stereotypes of the Church are breaking down. Vulgar criticism of believers is likely to evoke a strong reaction from both believers and nonbelievers. "These days primitive atheism is not only ineffective, but harmful."[8] The propaganda official believes that many of the past problems with believers can be traced to the conduct of local authorities and that the April 1929 laws for controlling religious believers departed from Lenin's decree on the "freedom of conscience." He is convinced that the new laws being written will return to the spirit of the Soviet Union's first leader.

We have come a long way when the following can be published in an official Soviet journal:

> The time has come to put an end forever to suspicious and hostile attitudes to believers and to such ideals cherished by them as humanism, love, moral self- improvement. . . . The existence of millions of believers . . . is not an unfortunate error of history, but a reality. . . . The Church has succeeded in finding a place for herself in the socialist society without waiving her teachings, without deceiving either the believers or the state.[9]

The author does not reject atheism itself but rather the crude, intolerant form it has sometimes taken. The challenge is issued for atheism to appeal to the same inner instincts which draw people to religious belief. Indeed, commentary like this does have a "God-Building" character to it.[10] To the extent this is so, it will raise objections from both doctrinaire atheists and classical Christians mindful of the dangers of secular ideologies functioning like religions.

Concurrent with the positive signs in the press is considerable evidence that the older antireligious views remain powerful. An example of this is Dr. A. Okulov's analysis in the February 2, 1988 *Pravda* of the seventieth anniversary of Lenin's decree "On the Separation of Church and State." Though there are a number of signs in the article of a new tolerance, there are also strong indicators that traditional views are still prevalent. At one point the academic asserts that people turn to religion "because of the limited nature of human experience, its lack of development. Obviously it cannot be denied that the process of various social aberrations in society has had an appreciable effect on the maintenance of religiosity in the country." Okulov critiques the clumsy approaches atheist propagandists have sometimes taken, asserting that "atheistic work is a sensitive and delicate matter." It is an important job, he asserts, because its ultimate aim is "people's spiritual liberation from religious and other illusions."

In the quest to explain the resilience, and even growth, of religion, Soviet scholars have shown some willingness to note the role socialism's shortcomings may have played. Dr. Alexander Klibanov of the USSR Academy of Sciences' Institute of USSR History connects the growth of religious communities to the failure of socialism to live up to its ideals.[11] What is missing, of course, is any recognition that an individual's religious inclinations may be positive and innate rather than an escape from deficiencies in the social environment.

THE COUNCIL FOR RELIGIOUS AFFAIRS

If one had always been used to a wolf, and then one day is told the wolf is now a dog, one would make sure the statement is true before approaching.[12]

This is the unusually honest explanation given in July 1988 by the Soviet official in charge of all religious affairs in the Soviet Union as to why unregistered churches are still suspicious of him.

Believers in the Soviet Union, both registered and unregistered, have reason to be wary of the Council for Religious Affairs, the notorious State agency which has restricted and hounded their activities for many decades. But in an amazing change of posture, the CRA under Konstantin Kharchev has taken a radically different public stance towards believers and religion. In two of the most remarkable interviews on record, *Ogonek* correspondent Alexander Nezhnyi tenaciously questioned Kharchev about his views on religious believers in the Soviet Union.[13]

One of the most striking characteristics of Nezhnyi is the passion and power with which he addresses the issue of religious repression. In his May 1988 interview with Kharchev he quotes for millions of Soviet readers from the courageous and inspirational "Solovky Memorandum." The 1927 statement by the persecuted Russian Orthodox bishops in exile asserted that the Church "does not strive for the overthrow of the existing order . . . but it wants to preserve fully its spiritual freedom and independence, granted to it by the Constitution, and cannot become the servant of the state."[14]

That it was a secular journalist who had the spunk to quote these bishops underscores the great tragedy of the Russian Orthodox Church during the Soviet period. The tame and domesticated Orthodox hierarchy has been silent, and largely still is, about these great martyrs.

In the second of the *Ogonek* interviews, late in 1988, Kharchev went further than ever before in describing the situation in the Soviet Union:

I think we should extract ourselves as soon as possible from the 1929 legislation . . . a typically Stalinist, bureaucratic restriction of independent democratic activity, in this case of the church. . . . The law "On Religious Associations" [the 1929 legislation] appeared, which binds the church, figuratively speaking hand and foot, and thus they grossly violated and flouted the Decree on the Separation of Church and State [1918]! Virtually every line of the 1929 legislation emphasizes the total dependence of the church on the authorities. In these conditions any degree of tyranny could be perpetrated.[15]

When pressed by Nezhnyi, Kharchev acknowledged that the 1961 "Instructions on the Application of Legislation on Cults" was the source of even further suffering for the believer communities:

> It was these instructions that prohibited, for instance, religious associations and clergy from engaging in charitable activity. Moreover, in accordance with the instructions some religious communities could not be registered, including Jehovah's Witnesses, Pentecostals, True Orthodox Christians, the True Orthodox Church, Reformist Adventists. . . . To a significant degree we ourselves by our own hands created the so-called banned sects, membership in which was regarded as grounds for criminal proceedings.[16]

(In early spring 1989, *Moscow News* reported that the Khrushchev era decrees had been repealed.)[17]

Throughout the interview, Nezhnyi's commentary was stunning in its ability to cut to the heart of the issues:

> If we compare Article 17 of the . . . 8 April 1929 "On Religious Associations," which consists of numerous prohibitions, with the evangelical commandments that are moral duties for everyone who professes Christianity, we are forced to acknowledge that a Christian in our country cannot freely follow his doctrine without risk of being subject to proceedings for breaking the law. Bible study circles are banned, yet the Gospels instruct us to "follow the Scriptures"; works of charity and benevolence are banned, yet the Gospels say: "Love thy neighbor as thyself," and a Christian should show that love not in words but in energetic social action; any form of religious education of children or adults is banned, but Jesus Christ said: "Go ye into all the world and preach the Gospel to every creature. . . ."

> In 1929, in 1936, and again in 1977 [dates of religious legislation or new Soviet Constitutions] the creators of the Fundamental Law were not in the least concerned about real guarantees of freedom of conscience in the USSR. . . . It seems to me that there is a real need to review Article 52 of the existing USSR Constitution, and in the spirit of the current reforms of the Soviet political system to enshrine in it the right to freedom of both religious and antireligious propaganda.[18]

To suggest changing Article 52 of the Constitution is to touch a topic that has virtually been off limits. This article guarantees freedom of religion, but in fact represents one of the clearest legal embodiments of religious discrimination in Soviet law. It guarantees freedom of only "antireligious propaganda," with no mention whatsoever of "religious propaganda." The message could not be clearer; believers have no rights to public expression of their convictions. How would Kharchev respond to such a direct challenge to the Constitution itself? Surprisingly, the chief spokesman for religious affairs conceded the point:

> As for the present Constitution, it is true that its proclaimed guarantee of freedom of conscience has nothing to back it up. It is necessary, first, to amend Article 52 so that it grants equal rights to both atheists and believers in the expression of their views. . . . Drafts of the new version of Article 52 of the USSR Constitution and the "Law on Freedom of Conscience" should be submitted to the judgment of all the people.[19]

Numerous problems were acknowledged in the interview: the arbitrariness and illegal action of local authorities; the unjustified delays and rejections of church registrations; the need for more Bibles and expanded publication of theological works; the need for churches to have the status of legal entities; and the need to legalize the Church's right to organize religious education for its people.

Nor was the discussion confined to the theoretical. Real problems in the lives of real people are movingly described for the Soviet reader. Nezhnyi quotes from a letter from a woman in Brest:

> My grandparents, great-grandparents, and great-great grandparents all came from a poor peasant family and were all baptized and married in Shcherbinskaya Orthodox Church. It is more than 20 years since it was closed, the icons taken away, and the church was turned into a barn, with a huge lock on the doors.

A medical technician who helped in the cleanup of Chernobyl' expressed his thoughts in a poem:

> We have had enough of ravaged churches!
> To use them to store goods is a disgrace.
> The people's conscience says: "No more, we dare not!"
> Dire retribution we have had to face.[20]

Prior to December 1988 Kharchev had been making increasingly encouraging statements about religion in the Soviet Union,[21] but virtually no one expected him to go as far as he did in the interview with Nezhnyi.

Of course rhetoric is not the same as reality. For years, Soviet spokesmen have lied about conditions for believers in the Soviet Union; might they not now be lying about promises to improve the situation? Kharchev is right. Those who have been bitten repeatedly by the wolf will view with skepticism assurances that the wolf has become a dog.

And there are some reasons for doubt. In addition to reports of continuing serious problems for many believers in the Soviet Union, Kharchev's motives are not well known. Kharchev became the chairman of the Council for Religious Affairs in January 1985, just a couple of months before Gorbachev came to power. It was immediately noticed that he was more approachable than his predecessor, Vladimir Kuroedov. In May 1986 a delegation from the British Council of Churches had a two-hour discussion with Kharchev in Moscow. Upon their return, the secretary of the group, Canon Paul Oestreicher reported in a BBC broadcast:

> He is a remarkable figure, said to be one of the most uncorrupt Communist leaders. . . . We found him to be a man of great strength, of immense intellectual ability and quite aggressive in his attitude of defending Soviet policies. He didn't give away anything that suggested new policies. He was really a bit narked at these foreigners always coming and telling the Soviet Union what its religious policy ought to be, and socked it to us in many ways. . . . It was the kind of meeting that made us feel the Soviet Union is putting really significant people in charge of religious policy; and to be able to talk to those people as frankly as we did means that a dialogue has begun which may lead somewhere.[22]

Others in the group were less optimistic about Kharchev. For one thing, he has almost no knowledge of religion. His background is in engineering and economics; he has been a diplomat in Africa. One of the most experienced members of the delegation considered Kharchev to be a man of "vacillating words," willing to both bully and charm, and prone to hide his own ignorance behind aggressive talk. There is reason to believe he is personally hostile to religion. A person who met him on a trip to East Germany reported that when Kharchev was asked if he preferred dealing with the Protestant Church over the Orthodox Church, he responded: "The only thing I'd prefer would be not to have to deal with Christians at all."[23]

When the British Council of Churches delegation met with Kharchev in May 1986, a strong public antireligious stance was still the order of the day. Perhaps that accounts for Oestreicher's comment: "He didn't give away anything that suggested new policies." New policies may not have yet been approved by his superiors.

Of more concern in evaluating whether Kharchev means what he says is a disturbing report of a speech he gave to the teachers of the Senior Party School in Moscow at the end of March 1988. The speech was not intended for a Western audience, but notes of the address were taken by someone present who then managed to get them out of the country.[24] Western specialists on religion in the Soviet Union have noted certain errors in the speech but have not questioned the basic authenticity of the document.[25]

Kharchev frankly tells his colleagues that seventy years of efforts to eliminate the Church have failed:

The Church has not only survived, but has begun to experience a revival. And questions arise. Which is better for the Party? Someone who believes in God, someone who believes in nothing, or someone who believes in both God and communism? I think we must choose the lesser of two evils.[26]

According to Kharchev, though the Russian Orthodox Church has in general been successfully controlled, the Catholics and Protestants have been much more difficult to deal with. Kharchev expresses particular concern about those who go underground and "over whom we completely lose control."

His thinking is clear—since religion cannot be eliminated at present, every effort must be made to co-opt it for the uses of the government. Church influences in the government are going to become ever stronger, he warns.

We have got to look at this matter soberly. Whether by our will or against, religion is entering into socialism, and not just walking into socialism, but entering on rails. But since power belongs entirely to us, I believe that we can direct these rails in any direction that suits our interests.[27]

Kharchev says about church publications:

We practically have no church publishing organization. *The Journal of the Moscow Patriarchate* comes out in an edition of 30,000, which is like a drop in a bucket. Just beginning to come out is the *Messenger of the Moscow Patriarchate*. By the way, this is a beautiful publication, but it is purely published as advertisement, counterpropaganda for abroad.[28]

The Kharchev who emerges from this March speech is far more cynical and calculating than the one who meets with foreign Church leaders or even the one who does interviews with Soviet correspondents. Nevertheless, Kharchev is an enigma. His comments in 1989 (as will be seen from the analysis in chapter 14) are even more liberal than those of 1988. He asserted that religious communities need not seek registration if all they wanted to do was gather in a private home for Bible Study. He even suggested that the State ought not to subsidize atheistic propaganda.[29]

There are concerns that Kharchev is considered "too liberal" by some members of the Central Committee. Believers will have to hope that the April 1989 resignation of approximately one quarter of the more conservative members of the Central Committee has eliminated some of Kharchev's critics. The debate, however, is far from over. In May 1989, rumors became even more persistent that Kharchev was being relieved of his duties at CRA, and that he had been appointed as an ambassador.[30]

If the Kharchev who gave the private speech in March 1988 is the real Kharchev, then those unregistered believers who fear that he is still a wolf may be right; he may be a wolf whose tactic is no longer to attack the sheep openly, but rather to make sure they stay safely in the fold.

This is precisely what co-opting religion means. The fangs are drawn in and every effort is made to control rather than destroy the opponent. Given how ineffective Western observers, particularly Church activists, were in identifying open persecution, what chance do we have of dealing effectively with a more subtle and insidious form of oppression?

The Soviets are playing a dangerous game, however. The attempt to co-opt religion, if that is what they are up to, requires a high price; they must be willing to give a measure of religious freedom previously not allowed. The increased opportunities provided for the Church may overwhelm a cynical, atheist government's attempt to control it.

Only time will tell. The stakes are high for both the government and for Christians. Western observers will need to monitor the situation carefully if they expect to be in a position to help their co-believers in the Soviet Union.

Notes

1. Quoted in *Reform and Human Rights: The Gorbachev Record*, report submitted to the U.S. Congress by the Commission on Security and Cooperation in Europe (CSCE), May 1988, 49.

2. Quoted in ibid.

3. The Soviet spokesperson's comments were made to staff members of the Commission on Security and Cooperation in Europe, *Reform and Human Rights*, 49.

4. *Nauka i Religiia* (Science and Religion), June 1986.

5. See the end of chapter 16, however, for evidence of continuing problems of slander in the Soviet press—against Alexander Ogorodnikov in 1988, for example.

6. Sergei Kiselev, "Not Just by Any Means," *Literary Gazette*, 21 October 1987.

7. "Chronicle," *Religion in Communist Lands* (Autumn 1988):7. Other examples of positive press treatment of believers is given as well.

8. Interview with A. G. Khmurchik, "*Perestroika* and Atheism," *Nauka i Religiia*, November 1988, 3.

9. Quoted by Dmitry Pospielovsky, "The Russian Orthodox Church in the Gorbachev Era" (Unpublished paper delivered at a conference on the millennium, sponsored by the Kennan Institute and the Library of Congress, Washington, D.C., 28 May 1988), 26-27. The citation quoted originally appeared in *Kommunist*, March 1988.

10. Pospielovsky, "Russian Orthodox Church," 28.

11. *Sobesednik* (Conversationalist), no. 17 (April 1988). See *The Current Digest of the Soviet Press*, 11 May 1988, 5.

12. According to an unpublished trip memorandum by Scott Flipse, Konstantin Kharchev made this statement to Congressman Frank Wolf in Moscow during a 16-22 July 1988 trip to the Soviet Union.

13. *Ogonek*, no. 21 (May 1988); English translation in Joint Publications Research Service (JPRS), UPA-88-039, 20 September 1988, 37-43. *Ogonek*, no. 50 (December 1988); English translation in Foreign Broadcast Information Service (FBIS), SOV-89-006, 10 January 1989, 1-7. For an account of the December *Ogonek* interview, see David Remnick, "Key Soviet Official Urges New Rights for Religious Believers," *The Washington Post*, 23 December 1988.

14. Quoted in FBIS, 20 September 1988, 39. For more information on the Solovky bishops, see chapter 6.

15. Kharchev, as quoted in FBIS, 10 January 1989, 3-4.

16. Ibid., 4.

17. Michael Dobbs, "Kremlin Rescinds Antireligion Edicts," *Washington Post*, 7 April 1989.

18. Alexander Nezhnyi, in Kharchev interview, as quoted in FBIS, 10 January 1989, 5.

19. Kharchev, as quoted in ibid.

20. As quoted by Nezhnyi in ibid., 3.

21. For example, in September 1988 Kharchev made a surprise visit to the Geneva-based Ecumenical Center. The World Council of Churches, the Conference of European Churches, the World Alliance of Reformed Churches, and the Lutheran World Federation all have their headquarters there. Kharchev sought to communicate to these Western church leaders many of the key points of religious *perestroika* as he understood it. See "Soviet Official Makes Ecumenical Centre Visit," Ecumenical Press Service, 88.09.36; and *Christianity Today*, 21 October 1988, 48.

22. Canon Paul Oestreicher, BBC World Service broadcast, as quoted by Michael Bourdeaux, "BBC Team Escape Soviet Booby Traps," *Church Times*, 6 June 1986, 10.

23. Reported to me by Michael Bourdeaux, 8 September 1988.

24. The Russian text of the notes appeared on 20 May 1988 in the Paris-based Russian emigre paper *Russkaia Mysl'* (Russian Thought). Excerpts translated into English of Kharchev's speech can be found in *Religion in Communist Dominated Areas 27* (Spring 1988):36. The complete text will be published in *Samizdat Bulletin*, Summer 1989.

25. The Canadian Soviet specialist Bohdan Bociurkiw (Carleton University, Ottawa) believes that the transcriber made several errors in putting the speech in written form. Allegedly Kharchev said that 70 percent of the Soviet population were religious believers, whereas in the May 1988 *Ogonek* interview he said there were seventy million believers. The number of Russian Orthodox Churches left at the end of the Khrushchev period is listed as ten thousand, whereas in a November 1987 article (*Science and Religion*), Kharchev had put the number at about seventy-five hundred. And finally, allegedly Kharchev said there was no institute for the study of religion. There is. Phone interview with Bociurkiw, 24 March 1989.

26. Kharchev, "*Religiia i Perestroika*," (Religion and *Perestroika*) *Russkaia Mysl'*, 20 May 1989.

27. Ibid.

28. Ibid.

29. See interview with Konstantin Kharchev by Ezio Mauro, *La Republica*, 4 March 1989. English translation in Foreign Broadcast Information Service, 8 March 1989, SOV-89-044, 74.

30. *Keston News Service*, no. 325, 11 May 1989, 6-7.

CHAPTER 14

THE POSITIVE IMPACT
OF *GLASNOST*
ON CHRISTIAN BELIEVERS,
PART I

*T*he Soviet Union in the Mikhail Gorbachev era is a kaleidoscope of contradictory and competing realities.

There are many signs of a liberalized policy towards believers: releases from labor camp, more positive treatment of religion in the press, some admission of past government violation of religious freedoms, increased scope of activities allowed to believers, and permission to import or print large quantities of religious literature. There are also signs of serious continuing problems, which will be considered in more detail in chapter 16.

No one should expect that the damage done in three quarters of a century can be undone overnight. Nor can patterns of discrimination simply be decreed out of existence. Furthermore, the debate is only just beginning as to what role religion can or ought to play in Soviet society. No one knows which views will prevail.

But change is in the air, and in many ways Christians have benefited from developments in what has been called "religious *perestroika*." The purpose of this chapter is to outline the central features of positive changes during the Gorbachev era.

RELEASE OF RELIGIOUS PRISONERS

An unmistakable sign of *glasnost* has been the steady decline in the number of religious and political prisoners.

According to Keston College, the number of Christian prisoners in the Soviet Union rose from 180 at the beginning of 1979 to a high of 338 in late 1984.[1] It should be noted that Keston does not count Jehovah's Witnesses in its calculations of Christian prisoners, though they are of course included in the broader category of religious prisoners. From March 1985, when Gorbachev took over, to May 25, 1988, the number of Christian prisoners dropped by more than 300 to 19, while the number of religious prisoners overall was reduced from about 420 to 73.[2]

According to Leonid Sizov, the USSR's First Deputy Minister of Internal Affairs, as of early 1989 the Soviet authorities had released 356 persons considered by the West to be "prisoners of conscience." The Soviet official asserted that all prisoners serving time for violation of Article 227 of the Russian criminal code (or its equivalent in the legal statutes of the other republics: "infringement of the person and rights of citizens under the guise of performing religious rituals") were released during 1988. Many Soviet Christians, however, were never even sentenced under statutes referring to religious practices. This accounts in part for why Soviet and Western calculations of the number of religious prisoners do not coincide.[3]

Among those Christians released from labor camp or exile have been some of the most important cases monitored by Western human rights activists: Anna Chertkova (from psychiatric hospital in late 1987); Vasily Shipilov (released from psychiatric hospital in mid-1988, after almost half a century of internment in Soviet institutions); Father Alfonsas Svarinskas (July 1988); Viktor Walter (August 1988); Deacon Vladimir Rusak (October 1988); and Nikolai Boiko (October 1988). The latter will serve as a good example of what such releases mean in human terms.

Pastor Boiko had been away from his Odessa Baptist congregation for more than eight years when finally he was allowed to return from eastern Siberia. Unregistered pastors from throughout the country traveled to southern Ukraine for the long-awaited reunion. The service lasted several hours, there were many sermons and testimonies, and much singing. The theme of the day was taken from Christ's words as recorded in Matthew: "I will build my Church, and the gates of hell shall not prevail against it."

Finally the moment came for Boiko to address the gathering. He told of being reared in a family of non-believers, drafted into the Soviet Army, captured by the Nazis and taken to the Buchenwald concentration camp. On a work detail in Berlin he encountered the Lord's Prayer through a Polish prisoner. Eventually, belief in God was born and he began to pray.

Like many Soviet soldiers captured by the Nazis, upon his repatriation to the Soviet Union he was sent off to Siberia by Stalin as a "spy." It was in the far north that he became a dedicated Christian, and he was formally baptized in 1953 upon his release from labor camp.

He was arrested in 1968 after his church refused to register with the authorities. Four terms and twenty years later, having survived the deprivations and loneliness of labor camp and exile, Boiko testified to the faithfulness of God, as did his wife who stood with him through it all.[4] Such is but one of the human faces behind the decline in the number of Christians in prison, labor camp, or exile. There are many such stories.

There is no question that Gorbachev has tangibly reduced the suffering of those affected by the incarceration of Christian prisoners of conscience. It ought to be noted, however, that unlike many who were released by Khrushchev in the wake of Stalin's death, Gorbachev has not exonerated those who have been released. They still stand guilty of crimes against the State. But new convictions on the same charges are currently very rare.

FEWER CHRISTIANS IN PSYCHIATRIC HOSPITALS

Internment in Soviet mental institutions has been one of the most vicious forms of persecution endured by prisoners of conscience. Many fully sane Christians have been subjected to drugs and indefinite terms of confinement in an effort to break their spirits, and if necessary, their minds and bodies.

In the 1960s, but even more in the 1970s, the Soviets used psychiatric hospitals as confinement facilities. Medical authorities there reported directly to the Ministry of Interior. Andrei Snezhevsky invented the term "sluggish schizophrenia" to describe those dissidents in the Brezhnev era who possessed "an excessive desire for social justice." Vladimir Bukovsky smuggled information on this pernicious practice to the International Congress of Psychiatrists in 1971. In 1981, Dr. Anatoly Koryagin was sent to labor camp for refusing to diagnose a healthy dissident as insane, and for protesting against the abuse of psychiatry.

In 1983 when it became obvious that the Soviet Union was likely to be expelled from the World Psychiatric Association, the USSR withdrew its membership. Since Gorbachev, however, there has been a concerted effort to change conditions in order to regain membership.

In 1988 the "special" psychiatric hospitals were transferred from the Ministry of Interior to the Ministry of Health. And the Soviets themselves have begun to acknowledge abuses. Psychiatrist Mikhail Buyanov wrote an article for a Soviet publication in 1981 in which he praised Koryagin for exposing the abuse of psychiatry in the USSR. (In 1987 Koryagin was allowed to emigrate, and as late as November 1988 he contended that there were still sane dissidents in Soviet mental institutions.)

In late February 1989 a delegation of American psychiatrists and State Department officials went to the Soviet Union for two weeks to examine patients. The World Psychiatric Association was to consider later in 1989 whether the Soviet Union should be readmitted as a member.[5]

A NEW SEMI-OPENNESS TO FOREIGN CRITICS

One of the most tangible evidences of *glasnost* has been Soviet willingness to grant visas to those who have publicized the repression of religion in the USSR. Michael Bourdeaux, general director of Keston College,[6] was permitted two visits to the Soviet Union between June 1988 and February 1989. Even more unusual was the invitation from the Soviet Novosti Press

Agency for Bourdeaux to select a delegation of four associates of Keston College to come to the Soviet Union in April to discuss religious freedom and meet with government and religious figures. Unfortunately, just a few days before the trip, Novosti informed Keston that the trip had to be postponed for reasons beyond its control.[7]

That foreign critics, pilloried in the past as ''anti-Soviet'' because they documented religious repression in the Soviet Union, have been granted visas is firm evidence of considerable change.[8] But some experts remain locked out. Though the Soviets finally allowed Bourdeaux into the Soviet Union after a nine-year refusal to do so, efforts as late as 1989 to obtain a visa by Keston's senior authority on the Russian Orthodox Church, Jane Ellis, were fruitless.

Soviet response to foreign critics can only be described as highly unpredictable, even contradictory. For example, in 1988 while Bourdeaux waited in Kiev's airport he picked up a brochure in English titled: ''Prisoners of Conscience in the USSR and their Patrons.'' Published in 1988, the work slandered Keston College in a way as bad or worse than anything the Soviets had ever written. Keston College was charged with being involved since its founding in espionage with the CIA. At his next meeting with a Novosti Press official, Bourdeaux asked how it was possible that he could be invited to cooperate with the Soviets on meetings at the very moment he was being slandered in print. The response: ''The slander is a relic of the past. The brochure may have been published this year, but we will get rid of it.''[9]

Though Bourdeaux was allowed back into the USSR early in 1989, Andrei Bessmertny, an Orthodox Christian activist scheduled to meet him at the airport, was intercepted by the KGB and prevented from keeping his appointment with the English scholar.[10]

Why have some foreign critics been allowed more freely into the Soviet Union? One reason seems apparent. The positive reports of previous critics mean more than the words of witnesses who consistently exaggerated the amount of religious freedom during the pre-Gorbachev era. It is a risky venture, however—if the apparent liberalization is only skin deep or begins to unravel, authorities will have a big problem hiding that fact from experienced observers.

In early 1988 the East-West Conference on Human Rights (also called the De Burght Conference) met in Holland and brought together twenty-five men and women from East and West. Though Keston College was not invited to participate, members of the Western delegation were prepared and able to raise serious questions regarding the problems of believers in the USSR.[11]

As late as the spring of 1988, Soviet officials still criticized the reporting of Amnesty International. Yet in 1989 the Soviets invited Amnesty to visit the Soviet Union.

After fourteen years of being denied visas, Peter and Anita Deyneka of the Slavic Gospel Association were allowed to travel to the Soviet Union in

March 1989. They had productive meetings with evangelical Christians and discussed with government officials how Western Christians might help meet the religious literature and theological training needs of Soviet believers.

SHOWCASING THE MILLENNIUM

It is always an awkward moment when openly atheist Communist leaders must decide what to do about a commemorative occasion involving a nation's religious heritage. East German authorities had to face this problem in 1983— the five-hundred-year anniversary of Martin Luther's birth. They would no doubt have preferred to celebrate only the centennial of Karl Marx's death, also a 1983 event. But it was judged better to cooperate in the Luther year festivities than to interfere with them.

Nineteen eighty-eight marked the one-thousand-year anniversary of the formal baptism of the Eastern Slavs into Byzantine Christianity. Having sent emissaries to investigate a number of different religions, Prince Vladimir was most moved by the account of those who returned from Constantinople. An ancient Russian chronicler records that the traveling Slavs were overwhelmed by the beauty and mystery of the Orthodox worship service. Nor did it hurt that Vladimir stood to gain much closer ties with a prosperous trading partner if he converted to the religion of the Byzantine Christians.

Whatever the motives for Prince Vladimir's conversion, the religious influence of Byzantine Christianity on the history of Russia and Ukraine is incalculable. There can be no adequate understanding of the history of Russia and Ukraine apart from a firm grasp of the importance of Christianity in the shaping of the culture of the empire's Slavic peoples.

For more than seventy years Communist antireligious propagandists had sought to exorcise Soviet citizens of their ''reactionary'' religious ideas. What sense did it make to celebrate the coming of Christianity to the medieval Slavic state? And besides, this particular event was fraught with difficulties. Ukrainian nationalists might well try to use the occasion to highlight their own frustration at being absorbed into a larger, Russian-dominated Soviet empire.

Five years before Gorbachev took power, a government decision was made to commemorate the millennium; the State and the Russian Orthodox Church would play leading roles. From the beginning Ukrainians were wary that Russian religious and political nationalists were co-opting what many of them considered to be their rightful place of prominence.

There can be little question that the Soviets were interested in damage control: ''Better we be involved in organizing the celebration on our terms than genuinely independent religious groups on theirs.'' Still, what took place in 1988 represented important breakthroughs for religion in the Soviet Union.[12]

Even before the formal events in June and July 1988, the Soviet media, beginning in March 1987, adopted a much more positive stance toward the

Church. A series of favorable articles appeared in the Soviet press in the months preceding and during millennium activities. A particularly graphic example of this was a TV broadcast in May 1988 of portions of the documentary *Khram* (cathedral). The film showed the 1930s dynamiting of the Cathedral of the Saviour in Moscow in order to build an open-air swimming pool. Though the documentary was not widely advertised, it was also shown in Leningrad movie theaters earlier in 1988.

Another way in which *glasnost* positively affected the Church during the millennium year was the April 29 meeting at the Kremlin between Russian Orthodox leaders and Mikhail Gorbachev. It had been more than forty years since such a meeting had occurred. *Izvestiia* gave front-page coverage to the event and quoted Mr. Gorbachev as referring to the millennium as "a significant milestone" in the country's history and culture. Furthermore, he referred to Christians in the USSR as "Soviet people, working people, patriots," and reported that the legislation on religion was being revised.[13]

The main festivities were impressive and included an opening liturgy on June 5 at the Patriarchal Cathedral, attended by more than four hundred foreign church representatives. A special June 10 millennium commemorative concert at the Bolshoi Theater was attended by Raisa Gorbachev and President Gromyko. Two days later a Divine Liturgy was held for ten thousand people in the square in front of the Danilov Monastery Cathedral. Special events were also held in Kiev, Vladimir, Leningrad, and other cities within the USSR. In all, more than fifteen hundred official guests attended various celebrations.

Attempts by believers to hold unofficial millennium activities met with varying levels of success. Organizers in Leningrad fared the best, managing to get both dissidents and the rector of the Leningrad Theological Schools together for discussions covered by Leningrad television. Alexander Ogorodnikov's efforts in Moscow encountered more resistance. A longtime thorn in the side of the Soviets, Ogorodnikov fourteen years earlier had founded the Christian Seminar for intellectuals (including many new converts) interested in discussing their faith. For most of the decade preceding the millennium, Ogorodnikov had been in labor camp. Such was the price for pushing *glasnost* and religious *perestroika* before it became official Kremlin policy.

Even in the Gorbachev era Ogorodnikov is not popular with the authorities.[14] More than three hundred conferees attended the Ogorodnikov-organized June conference. Twice they encountered locked doors at halls they had rented. Participants were forced to conduct the twenty-two lectures in private apartments. Authorities did, however, allow the cramped meetings to proceed without further State interference.

Millennium events, despite their limitations and State attempts to control the agenda, reflected a new, more positive attitude toward the Christian community. Millions of Soviets became aware of the religious significance of the occasion, and though there were some negative articles in the press, many were positive. Ten years before, who could have imagined such celebrations?

SUCCESSES AT THE CHURCH COUNCIL

A *Pomestny Sobor* (Local Council) was allowed to convene from June 6 to 9. This was only the fourth time in Soviet history that the Orthodox were allowed to convene such a Council, and previously (1917-18, 1945, and 1971) it was always connected with the election of a new patriarch. But not in 1988. The main item of business was the approval of a new *Ustav* (Statute) to govern the internal affairs of the Orthodox Church. Here, too, the fresh breezes of *glasnost* were being felt.

The new Church statute rescinded State-imposed regulations of 1961 which deprived a local priest of financial and administrative control of his parish. The new statute also requires a Church Council to convene at least every five years; previously there was no such rule. Apparently, the Kremlin has decided to amend significantly the restrictive laws of 1929, since three of the new provisions conflict with existing State regulations. Church institutions now may buy property, give charity, and have the right of a juridical person (i.e. the right to defend itself in court).

While the *sobor* featured frank public dialogue regarding problems in the Church, *glasnost* was not allowed to extend to specific discussion of the myriad priests and other religious victims of previous antireligious decades. None of the nine new saints canonized during the Council belonged to the Soviet era. In an unusually candid reference to this neglect of the twentieth century, Metropolitan Mefodi declared at the Bolshoi Theater millennium celebration that "the time was not yet ripe" to take under consideration modern saints and martyrs.[15]

The Council represented an important, though still modest, step toward freedom. During the Gorbachev years there has been much talk about a return to the Leninist notion of "Church/State separation." The presence of the chairman of the Council for Religious Affairs sitting right next to the Orthodox leaders throughout the Council, however, was a sober reminder that a large gap between rhetoric and reality still exists.

RUSSIAN ORTHODOX HIERARCHS IN SOVIET PARLIAMENT

Three high-ranking Orthodox Church officials were elected in March 1989 to the Congress of People's Deputies: Patriarch Pimen, Metropolitan Pitirim, and Metropolitan Aleksy of Leningrad. Though there has been no specific legal prohibition against a Churchman being elected, it was always understood that such a thing was not permitted in the explicitly atheist Soviet government.

These elections certainly are a break with the past, but two points need to be understood. First, real power has never rested in the hands of the traditionally rubber-stamp parliament. And second, these religious leaders have no history of taking positions other than those espoused by the Kremlin.

On the other hand, Metropolitan Aleksy in his campaign program insisted that it was "inconceivable that a genuine renaissance in our society [could] occur without the inclusion of the Christian element," and insisted he would "strive to make the Soviet legal system more humane." One should not rule out the possibility that such men might recover their voices. At present, however, it is Gorbachev himself who is encouraging such statements.[16]

MORE LIBERAL RELIGIOUS REGULATIONS ON THE HORIZON

For decades the Soviet position was that full religious freedom was guaranteed by the Constitution and the laws of the USSR. This line was persistently maintained by registered Soviet Church leaders in dealing with their Western co-religionists, and in a distressing number of cases the tale was repeated to millions of Western Christians by their own leaders.

But the facts were quite different. As academician Igor Shafarevich put it in 1977, the Soviet regulations dealing with believers "cannot be regarded as conditions for the existence of religion; they are conditions for the death of religion."[17] A decade later, the Soviets themselves were saying as much.[18]

A 1989 interview between an Italian journalist and Konstantin Kharchev, the Soviet Union's senior official charged with handling religious matters, was unusually frank and revealing on the matter of believers and Soviet law. Kharchev was asked, "after sixty years, what is changing for religion in the country which is officially godless?" The Soviet official responded: ". . . the main thing is that believers of any faith will no longer be second-class citizens."

Kharchev went on to assert that the "constitutional discrimination between atheists and believers must end." In other words, Article 52 of the constitution ought to be amended, for it gives only atheists the right to propagate their views.

Even more startling was Kharchev's insistence that not only should religion be free to promote itself, but the State ought not officially to support atheism.

> The state must have nothing to do with religious belief, nor with atheism, and propaganda on the latter must not be financed by the state budget—this money belongs to everybody, including believers.[19]

The latter assertion goes well beyond liberalizing the laws governing religious associations. It would in effect put several hundred thousand religious propagandists out of work. If the State would not support the official propagation of atheism, who would?

The implementation of Kharchev's sweeping declaration, though of course consistent with true Church/State separation, is impossible to imagine in the foreseeable future. This cannot but make the observer more cautious about how seriously to take even the more modest promises of Kharchev.

In the West there has been a strong tendency to mistake rhetoric for reality. The Soviets admit the existence of a problem, declare their intention to correct it, and we rush to consider the promise an accomplished fact. Nevertheless, though the final draft of new religious regulations has yet to be promulgated, there seems little doubt that the new regulations will represent a marked improvement over the pre-Gorbachev legal status of believers.

Over the last two or three years, the following statements have been repeated innumerable times by Soviet spokespersons.

First: The Soviet Union ought to return to Lenin's 1918 decree on the separation of Church and State.

Second: The religious sect laws from 1929 to the present violate Lenin's 1918 decree and have made religious believers into "second-class" citizens.

Third: Local officials often restricted believers more than religious regulations required or allowed.

Although Kharchev claims that efforts toward new religious legislation began in 1979, he says work "in earnest" began only around the beginning of 1986. Many drafts of the legislation have circulated in both the Soviet Union and the West. One version, by the well-known Soviet jurist Yuri Rozenbaum, was published in the February 1989 issue of *Soviet State and Law*[20]

Registered religious organizations have had some input into the proposed Law on the Freedom of Conscience. The Council for Religious Affairs at the end of 1988 established a scientific-consultative commission, which included both religious figures and academic scholars, to discuss the new legislation. Kharchev called on those present at a February 14, 1989 commission meeting to propose amendments to the legislation. Participants were given one week to respond with suggestions and comments. The legislation was to be acted on in the spring by the Congress of People's Deputies but by May it had once again been delayed for redrafting.[21]

Among the twenty-seven draft articles are the following key provisions:[22]

1. *The Right to Spread Religious Ideas.* (Article 3) The right to determine one's own religious views and to *spread* either religious or atheist convictions is recognized. (Article 3 of the new law would thus contradict Article 52 of the USSR Constitution which gives no

such right to believers, meaning that changes in the latter are probably being planned.)

Religious services or rites may be performed without interference in buildings set aside for that purpose (and around them), in the residences of members of the group, and in cemeteries. Also, with the approval of the relevant authorities, they may be performed in hospitals, institutions for the elderly and in criminal facilities. Elsewhere they may be performed in conformity with regulations established by local authorities. (Article 20)

2. *The Right to Religious Literature.* "Every Soviet citizen has the right to possess and use religious literature in the language of his choice without interference." (Article 3)

3. *Parents May Provide Religious Education for Their Children.* (Articles 3, 7) This is not religious education instead of public education, but in addition to it, as arranged by the parents.

4. *Equal Rights for All Citizens Regardless of Religious Affiliation.* (Article 5) There is to be no discrimination against believers economically, politically, socially, or culturally. Official documents may not indicate religion.

5. *The Possibility of Alternative Service.* (Article 5) Although no citizen may escape his civic responsibilities on the basis of religious convictions, a court may substitute one civic obligation for another. Thus, refusal to serve in the military need not result in criminal prosecution.

6. *Internal Church Affairs Not Subject to Government Interference.* (Article 6) This is the Church/State separation article, and in theory this is nothing new. It has allegedly existed since 1918, though contradicted by the actions of Soviet officials and the laws governing religious associations.

7. *Believers Allowed to Participate in Society.* (Article 6) Although religious organizations are forbidden from interfering with government affairs, "they may participate in the societal dialogue," utilize the mass media, and maintain foreign contacts for the exchange of information.

8. *Religious Organizations Have the Status of Juridical Persons.* (Article 9) This gives believer organizations the right to defend themselves in court, something which Lenin's decree on the separation of Church and State had taken away.

9. *The Number Required to Register a Religious Community Reduced to Ten Adults.* (Article 11) Previously a petition for registration had

to be supported by not less than twenty members of the community, all of whom were eighteen years of age or older. Although the local authorities and Council for Religious Affairs may act on the request, the final decision rests with the USSR CRA.

10. *Religious Organizations May Own Buildings, Vehicles, and Property.* (Article 16) In addition, according to Article 15, registered religious organizations also have the right to utilize State property turned over to them by the local authorities.

11. *Personal and Group Religious Contacts within the Soviet Union and Abroad Are Guaranteed.* (Article 19)

12. *International Agreements Apply to Believers in the USSR.* (Article 27) "If international agreements which the USSR has signed are in conflict at some point with the Law on the Freedom of Conscience, then the international agreement takes precedence."

The right to perform charitable activities is not specifically included in the draft, but Kharchev and high officials in the Ministry of Justice have repeatedly said the new applicable principle is: "whatever is not forbidden is allowed."[23] In addition, Keston College analysis asserts that Article 20 (see point one above) may be understood to authorize Church activities outside the traditional four walls of the Church. Also, Article 24 provides that Church monies used for "charity" are exempt from taxation.

Further clues as to how the new statutes might function were provided by Kharchev a few days after this draft was released to the religious communities. Particularly noteworthy was the assertion that a religious group need not seek registration. The new law

will eliminate the obligation to seek "permission," and therefore also the state's discretionary power to grant it. The religious body—a circle, parish, or organization—will be created at will, without any need to request permission . . . . They will only have to inform the authorities of their existence if they want their organization to be registered and to secure the right to become a legal entity. If they want to do without registration, they are free to do so. But if they intend to construct buildings in which to hold services, if they need land, they must inform the state of their group's existence. But note that this is registration, not an application for permission. The law states that anybody can register his religious group and nobody can prevent him from doing so.[24]

If the situation Kharchev describes is actually implemented, it would be a tremendous step forward for religious freedom in the USSR. But as we will see in chapter 16, practice in the Soviet Union often lags considerably behind such assurances.

It is clear throughout this draft that believers must function within the framework of the laws and Constitution of the USSR. But Article 27, if honored, would appear to provide some assurance that religious freedom guarantees are real. Furthermore, Article 14, which deals with the reasons for dissolution of a religious organization, focuses on "self-liquidation" or a community failing to be faithful to its own founding purposes and regulations.

In the past, "de-registrations" often occurred when a KGB-controlled group within the religious community "voluntarily" dissolved that community. Law only works when there is a genuine commitment and willingness to apply it fairly. The long, painful legacy of persistent abuse by Soviet authorities makes believers and foreign observers wary about considering the battle won. Kharchev seems to recognize this when he observes,

> This is not an easy time. We still have a long way to go because I think we must reach a stage when the believer feels completely free in the USSR, freer under socialism than in any other system. Is it ridiculous to say this now? Listen carefully: It is only by doing this, and not by the old propaganda, that the believer will have reason to believe in socialism and will want to fight to defend it.[25]

Indeed, it can only be in the "doing," not in the "saying," that suspicions and fears can be laid to rest. Nevertheless, "saying" can be an important first step, and the draft law and Kharchev have said considerably more than has been said in the past.

Even in the absence of an officially-approved Law on the Freedom of Conscience, many of the above provisions have been implemented. Often, this amounts to non-enforcement of the old prohibitions, or at least to less harsh enforcement.

Revisions of the criminal code and the Constitution are necessary if they are to conform to the rights of believers detailed in the new Law on the Freedom of Conscience. For example, Article 142 (Russian Soviet Federated Socialist Republic, and its equivalent in other republic criminal codes) has been used against those who circulated religious literature, conducted unregistered religious services, and organized religious training for children. Article 227 has been used against conscientious objectors. Some Soviet officials have asserted that these laws would be repealed.[26]

An important measure of the depth of *glasnost* will be whether these changes in the law are formally approved, and then whether they are fully implemented. Administrative practice has often been very different from what the law provides.

RELIGIOUS LITERATURE STREAMS INTO THE SOVIET UNION

In July 1983, Gederts Melngailis, a Latvian Lutheran, was arrested for distributing unofficial religious literature. He was sentenced to an indefinite term in a psychiatric hospital.

Melngailis was freed in June 1988, and in that same year the *official* importation of Bibles to the Soviet Union was greater than all that had been legally imported to or printed there between 1945 and 1987.[27] Religious literature of all sorts is now flowing into the Soviet Union both officially and unofficially.

Only about 11 percent (450,000) of the estimated 4.1 million Bibles or New Testaments which reached Soviet believers between 1945 and 1987 were legally imported or printed in the USSR. The vast majority of Scriptures were smuggled in or printed without permission.[28] Between the late 1920s and 1956 there was an absolute ban on the printing of all Bibles in the Soviet Union.

Our group of American Christians visiting the USSR in the spring of 1988 was able to get some sense of the situation relative to the availability of and demand for religious literature. Everywhere we went, whether among the registered or unregistered Protestants, Catholics, or Russian Orthodox, the situation was the same—religious materials were becoming more available, but the needs far exceeded the supply.

Rev. Arnis Silis, pastor of a charismatic Baptist Church in Riga (Latvia), reported that fourteen new converts were baptized earlier in 1988 at his church. Unfortunately, he was able to give a Bible to only half of that group; the other half went home empty-handed.

Even in Leningrad, which boasts one of the two largest Baptist churches in the Soviet Union, the gift of a Bible by our delegation invariably was greeted with hugs and often tears—and this is a church which contains wall jacks for foreigners enabling them to listen to the service in their own languages. In churches off the tourist trail, the absence of Bibles is often a more serious problem.

For example, a young Methodist pastor in Estonia told us that in the last five years he had not had a single spare copy of the Bible to give to those who wanted to learn more about the Christian faith. He did say his church had a "loaner" Bible and most of his church families had a Bible.

On two separate occasions we were told—once by a believer, once by a Soviet official—that at least some Bibles legally imported to registered Russian Orthodox and Baptist churches had been sold for between thirty-five and one hundred roubles (approximately 55 to 160 U.S. dollars at the official exchange rates) by the denominations involved. It was not clear if this was to meet church funding problems, or if it was another manifestation that demand for Bibles outstrips supply.

Soviet officials often cited the recent granting of permission to import Bibles and commentaries as evidence of past problems being solved. At Moscow Sheremetevo airport, however, our delegation encountered another side of the story. Customs officials confiscated four copies of three different pieces of religious literature, including the Bible. The person from whom the materials were taken explained that the materials were gifts for members of churches he planned to visit during the millennium year celebration. But customs officials simply confiscated them as illegal contraband.

When we later reported the incident to Soviet officials at *Znanie* (Knowledge)—an organization specializing in propagating atheism for over four decades—we were told that decisions made at the center favoring greater openness were sometimes slow to reach customs officials. It is hard to believe, however, that if religious literature is no longer considered a threat to State security that a simple directive to customs officials would not settle the matter. Clearly, such an unequivocal directive had not been sent or was not being enforced.

According to a prominent Western authority, Soviet authorities approved the importation or Soviet printing of 1.25 million Bibles for 1987-88. Almost 80 percent were in Russian, and most were delivered by the end of 1988. This includes: a special edition of 100,000 Bibles printed by the Russian Orthodox Church in honor of the millennium; one third of a million each from the Slavic Gospel Association and the United Bible Society (the latter either directly provided the Bibles or helped other groups send Bibles in); 149,000 from the Vatican in cooperation with other groups; 100,000 New Testaments from Open Doors International; and 75,000 Lopukhin Bibles (a study Bible dating to the early part of the century) from the Institute for Bible Translation.[29] A Soviet source reports that 1.2 million Bibles arrived in 1988 alone,[30] while at the annual meeting of the German-speaking Protestant and Catholic Bible Societies, it was reported that 1.3 million Bibles were delivered in the millennium year.[31]

Permits are in hand or being solicited for almost six million Bibles for 1989 and 1990. Open Doors has permission to ship in 900,000; Door of Hope, 1,000,000; and Christian Solidarity International, 500,000. The authorities have agreed to a special Soviet Academy of Science's scholarly translation of the Bible (250,000).[32]

Beginning in November 1988, the Soviet monthly journal *V Mire Knig* (The World of Books) began publishing sections of the New Testament. The foreword to the first installment contained the following words of Professor Sergei Averintsev: "one cannot but rejoice that the triumph of common sense in our society has made this publication possible." With a print run of over 100,000, and assuming that each issue is read by several people, the potential impact of such a publication is great.[33] Unfortunately, the serialization abruptly stopped with the January issue. The editorial staff attributed the change "to circumstances which did not depend on them."[34]

In late 1988 an unusual meeting occurred between editors of the journal *Inostrannaia Literatura* (Foreign Literature) and some of its readers. The famous Soviet writer, Chingiz Aitmatov was asked: "Couldn't your editorial board take the bold step of publishing . . . the Bible? Four hundred thousand subscribers would thank you." Aitmatov responded that the journal was a member of an association called the "World of Culture" (part of the Cultural Fund), which is planning to publish the Bible with commentaries. "So if you are interested, it should appear soon, as . . . well, normal reading matter."[35]

The excitement displayed by members of a privileged Soviet church over a recent visitor's Russian Bible provides compelling evidence of the hunger for religious literature.[36] Even Konstantin Kharchev, head of the atheist-run religious watchdog committee, concedes that "the Bible should be printed in much larger quantities than it is at present."[37]

One problem with Bibles that *do* get printed is the archaic translation used. But recent developments suggest a more readable Russian Bible may be on the way. At an international Bible conference in the fall of 1988, the Georgian Orthodox Church communicated a request to the United Bible Society (UBS) for Western help in producing a more contemporary Russian translation. (The UBS is an umbrella organization representing 105 national Bible societies.)

As a result, Western Bible scholars are scheduled to meet in June 1989 with Soviet Orthodox leaders, Russian evangelicals, and Soviet Academy of Science linguists to consider what methods would be best for translating the Bible into modern Russian. This discussion is extremely important not only because it will bring together Orthodox and Protestants who must agree on which original texts should be used to make the translation, but because a successful project will yield a Russian Bible more understandable to the average person.[38]

As important as it is to provide Soviet believers with the Bible, another serious problem relates to the dearth of other religious literature: study materials, commentaries, concordances, Bible dictionaries, apologetic material. Here, too, there have been major breakthroughs. One of the most impressive and sensitive projects carried out by Western Christians involved choosing and translating a multi-volume commentary for the Soviet Protestant community. To determine which commentary would be most compatible with the needs of Russian Christians, translations were obtained of eight different Protestant commentaries of the Epistle to the Romans. The All-Union Council of Evangelical Christians-Baptists (AUCECB) studied the alternatives and decided that William Barclay's version was the most readable and practical, though at certain points there were interpretations which the Russian community deemed insufficiently conservative. It was decided simply to leave out the offending passages.[39]

From 1979 to 1986 British Baptist leader Dr. David Russell chaired the Barclay Commentary Committee. By late 1986, a fifteen-volume Russian edition of Barclay's New Testament commentary was complete, and by February 1987 final approval was announced by Kharchev for bringing the commentaries into the Soviet Union. Western sponsors of the expensive project included the Baptist World Alliance, the Mennonite Central Committee, and the European Baptist Federation.[40]

In 1987 and 1988, five thousand copies of the fifteen-volume commentary were delivered to the All-Union Council of Evangelical Christians-Baptists, and an additional five thousand copies are scheduled to be sent during the middle of 1989.[41] A translation is now underway of the Barclay Old Testament commentaries.

And this is not all. Religious literature is no longer getting into the country only through large, officially-approved Western shipments. On March 23, 1988, Soviet officials announced they would allow individual Soviet citizens to receive religious materials from the West. In 1988 the Slavic Gospel Association received thousands of letters from Soviet believers requesting religious materials.[42]

Requests for religious literature also are being generated by radio broadcasting into the Soviet Union. International Russian Radio (Finland), which beams its programs into the Soviet Union from a facility 200 miles west of the Soviet border, reports that up until 1986 it received approximately 250 letters annually from Soviet listeners. But in 1988 it received over 3,000, and in the single month of February 1989 more than 1,100 arrived. If the rate of increase continues, there may be as many as 30,000 to 40,000 letters for 1989. A fervent desire for religious literature is a central focus of the letters.[43] Many mission groups are scrambling to meet this dramatic increase in requests for literature.

The year 1988 also brought important changes in customs and postal regulations. As of September 1, customs tariffs were reduced on packages arriving from abroad, and many items may now be sent into the USSR without charge. The list of items which private citizens may receive from abroad has greatly expanded, according to Konstantin Kovalchuk, head of Soviet Customs and Excise in the Council of Ministers. "Religious literature and articles of religious practice" may now be received.[44]

The November 15, 1988 issue of *Izvestiia* contained further confirmation about sending in religious literature. A high-ranking customs official stated: "One may even send religious literature, which formerly was quite categorically forbidden."[45]

Though small packages of religious literature are getting through with high regularity, there have been difficulties with large shipments addressed to unregistered churches. Two shipments of 440 pounds each, sent in June 1988 to unregistered Baptist congregations in Leningrad and Makinsk (Kazakhstan), were not delivered for many months by Soviet authorities. In fact, the leaders of the churches in question were summoned by Council for Religious Affairs officials and told that they could not receive the shipments until they registered.[46] At least with respect to the Baptist church in Central Asia, Soviet officials finally relented and delivered the shipment.[47]

Slavic Gospel Association (SGA) provides an excellent example of a mission group taking advantage of the opportunities afforded by *glasnost* to send religious literature into the Soviet Union. In addition to truck loads of books, during much of 1988 SGA sent 440-pound pallets of Bibles and Christian books three times a week into the USSR. Such a shipment would typically include 100 Bibles and 500 Christian books.

In addition, thousands of seven-pound packages containing a study Bible and three or four apologetic books were shipped in. The materials in Russian included children's literature, Bible dictionaries and handbooks, and works by C.S. Lewis, F.F. Bruce, Francis Schaeffer, Josh McDowell, Joseph Stowell, and Warren Wiersbe. In addition to the third of a million Bibles which SGA shipped during 1988, an additional 177,000 Christian books were provided. The AUCECB has requested twenty tons of paper from SGA for printing Bibles inside the Soviet Union.[48]

Alexei Bychkov has recently reported that the AUCECB is arranging to receive or publish four books by Billy Graham.[49] Elsewhere in the Church world discussions are now in process which may result in joint-venture publishing between the Soviets and Westerners. Evangelical publishers were at the 1985 and 1987 Moscow Bookfairs, and will be present at the September 1989 fair as well.[50] At the 1987 bookfair, a Soviet publisher took interest in Ross Campbell's *How to Really Love Your Child,* a product of Scripture Press. The Soviet government permitted the publishing house to request permission to print a Russian translation of the book. Eventually Campbell received a contract for 500,000 copies of the book, which the Soviets intend to distribute in health centers. In addition to general information on raising children, the book includes information on how to become a Christian, and how to ensure that your child is a Christian.[51]

There is some indication that Soviet Christians themselves may be allowed to expand what they write and publish. The AUCECB hopes to publish a new magazine, possibly under the title *Gratitude,* and the young Soviet evangelicals (mainly associated with the AUCECB) have been publishing a new journal called *Protestant* since late 1988. Though the latter does not have official approval, it is not being shut down.

In March 1989, a Christian writers' conference was held in Kiev. Representatives of SGA and Media Associates International conducted writing seminars for pastors and Christian leaders.

The opportunities to provide religious reading materials have been so great in recent months that Western stockpiles of religious literature in Russian and other Soviet languages are exhausted.

SEMINARIES AND RELIGIOUS EDUCATION

The Orthodox Church in early 1989 received formal approval from the Council for Religious Affairs to open four new seminaries.[52] In the last week of February, permission was given for the All-Union Council of Evangelical Christians-Baptists to open a seminary in Moscow—the first evangelical seminary in the USSR since 1928. It may open as early as the fall of 1989, and the government has given permission for an enrollment of fifty. Fuller Seminary in California is seeking to provide guidance in establishing the interdenominational Protestant seminary.[53]

Baptist World Alliance executives have reported that permission has also been granted for the AUCECB to open seminaries in Tallinn and Riga. Eventually new buildings are hoped for, but initially, existing structures will be utilized. The three recently approved seminaries are the first ever allowed for the AUCECB. For a number of years, however, the Baptist World Alliance has been involved in setting up correspondence courses and in arranging for some theological training abroad for evangelical pastors.[54]

The Soviet news agency TASS reported that on December 2, 1988, a Seventh Day Adventist Center formally opened near Tula, about seventy-five miles south of Moscow. Present for the consecration of the main three-story building was Mikhail Kulakov (Soviet Adventist head), Neal Wilson (world Adventist leader), officials from the Council for Religious Affairs, and foreign journalists. When completed, other buildings at the site will house a seminary and publishing facilities. This represents the fruit of discussions dating to the beginning of the Gorbachev period.[55]

For a number of years Slavic Gospel Association has been developing materials for Theological Education by Extension. The first course in this program, on Galatians and Romans, was taught in several locations in the Soviet Union during 1988. Two more courses are ready for implementation, and another is in preparation.

It must be said that these strides toward religious freedom, as remarkable as they are, do not tell the whole story. In the next chapter we will see other developments which are at least as surprising.

Notes

1. "Freed," *Frontier*, March-April 1987, 3.

2. Michael Rowe, " 'Prisoners of Faith' in the USSR," *Frontier*, Keston College, July-August 1988, 22; phone interview, Keston College, 25 May 1989. The two largest groups in the broader religious category were Muslims (29) and Jehovah's Witnesses (21), while the Christian groups included: Pentecostals (6), Orthodox (3), Ukrainian Catholic (3), Seventh Day Adventists (1), Armenian Apostolic (1), and 5 whose denomination is unknown or nondenominational (4 may, in fact, belong to the Jehovah's Witnesses).

3. *Keston News Service*, "Soviet Prisoner Release," no. 319, 16 February 1989, 2. Henceforth, issues of the *Keston News Service* will be listed as *KNS*.

4. "Homecoming," *Frontier*, March-April 1989, i- 1.

5. Ludmilla Alexeyeva, *Soviet Dissent: Contemporary Movements for National, Religious, and Human Rights* (Middletown, Conn.: Wesleyan University Press, 1987), 311, 349; Michael Dobbs, "U.S. Psychiatrists Search for Soviet Abuses," *Washington Post*, 28 February 1989; Vera Tolz, *Report on the USSR*, "The USSR This Week," RL 518/88, 25 November 1988, 1.

6. The end of chapter 10 and appendix A contain more detailed information on the importance of the Keston College research center.

7. The trip was to include discussions in Moscow, Smolensk, and Suchumi (Georgia). As a member of the Keston, USA, board I have been invited to be a part of this delegation. There is concern that the postponement of this highly unusual trip may be connected to policy and personnel questions related to the senior leadership of the Council for Religious Affairs. Some on the Central Committee of the Communist Party are said to consider the chairman of the CRA, Kharchev, too liberal.

8. In the spring of 1988, the delegation of Christians I was leading to the Soviet Union in honor of the millennium year all received their visas, but mine was rejected. Only at the last moment, just hours before the plane was scheduled to depart, did the Soviets relent and issue me a visa.

9. Michael Bourdeaux, "Into the New Millennium," *Church Times* (London), 24 June 1988, 11.

10. Keston fax service, "Keston College Director in the USSR," 7 February 1989.

11. Congressman Frank Wolf, Congressman Chris Smith, George Weigel, Richard John Neuhaus, Brother Andrew (Open Doors, Holland), and Rosalyn Carter were some of the key Western participants. Keston College participation was evidently deemed too controversial by the organizers of the conference.

12. Unless otherwise indicated, discussion of the millennium activities is based on Helen Bell and Jane Ellis, "The Millennium Celebrations of 1988 in the USSR," *Religion in Communist Lands* 16 (Winter 1988):292-324.

13. Ibid., 295.

14. For more information on Ogorodnikov, see the section "The Slander of Believers Continues" near the end of chapter 16.

15. Bell and Ellis, "Millennium Celebrations," 296.

16. Oxana Antic, "Candidates in Cassocks for USSR People's Deputies," *Report on the USSR*, vol. 1, no. 11, 17 March 1989, 13-14; "The USSR This Week," vol. 1, no. 13, 31 March 1989, 33; John Lofton, "Soviet Churchman, Redefined," *Washington Times*, 12 April 1989.

17. Igor Shavarevich, in an interview with Gleb Yakunin, 1977 *samizdat* document, Keston College archives.

18. Particularly the Soviet correspondent Alexander Nezhnyi (see chapter 13).

19. Interview with Konstantin Kharchev by Ezio Mauro, *La Republica*, 4 March 1989, as quoted in Foreign Broadcast Information Service, 8 March 1989, SOV-89-044, 74.

20. For a comparative analysis of Rozenbaum's draft and the Kharchev draft, which is the one I discuss in this chapter, see John Anderson, *KNS*, no. 320, 2 March 1989, 18-20.

21. Oxana Antic, "USSR—Draft Law on Freedom of Conscience," Radio Liberty Report (Munich), 21 March 1989; *KNS*, no. 325, 11 May 1989, 7.

22. I worked from an original twelve-page Russian draft of the law in question as a basis for this section, which reached the West a week after it was given by Kharchev to the Soviet religious

communities for review. An English summary and analysis of this same document was distributed by Keston College England's fax service on 24 February 1989 under the title: "Draft of New Soviet Law on Religion."

23. This is the position USSR Deputy Minister of Justice Mikhail Vyshinsky took in meeting with reporters in Moscow in mid-1988. He connected it with the policy of *perestroika*. Radio Liberty Report 291/88, 1 July 1988, 5.

24. Interview with Kharchev, *La Republica,* 74.

25. Ibid., 75.

26. Assurances of this sort were given in July 1988 to U.S. Congressman Frank Wolf by Fedor Burlatsky, chairman of the Public Commission for Human Rights, and Yuri Rechestov, deputy director of the Department for Humanitarian and Cultural Affairs of the Foreign Ministry. *Congressional Record*, H6599, 8 August 1988.

27. Walter Sawatsky, "*Glasnost, Perestroika* and Religion: What Role for the Churches in Changing Soviet Society?" *Occasional Papers on Religion in Eastern Europe,* vol. 9, no. 2, April 1989, 9.

28. Walter Sawatsky, "Another Look at Mission in Eastern Europe," *International Bulletin of Missionary Research*, January 1987, 15.

29. Mark Elliott, "New Openness in USSR Prompts Massive Bible Shipments to Soviet Christians in 1987-1988, A Statistical Overview," *News Network International,* 20 March 1989, 28.

30. Konstantin Kharchev, *Ogonek*, no. 50, December 1988, 5.

31. *KNS*, no. 316, 5 January 1989, 13.

32. Elliott, "New Openness in USSR," 30. The only adjustment to Elliott's figures I have made is to drop the Christian Solidarity International (CSI) numbers to 500,000 to reflect a recent update on what the Soviets finally approved. The approval for the CSI request to import Bibles came as a direct result of a trip to the Soviet Union in July 1988 which included CSI representatives and U.S. Rep. Frank Wolf of Virginia.

33. Oxana Antic, "One Million Bibles for the Soviet Union," *Report on the USSR*, RFE/RL, vol. 1, no. 10, 10 March 1989, 17.

34. *KNS*, no. 322, 30 March 1989, 18.

35. Quoted in Antic, "One Million Bibles," 17.

36. Report by Steve Snyder on 16-22 July 1988 trip to the Soviet Union sponsored by Christian Solidarity International, in *News Network International,* 2 September 1988, 2.

37. Kharchev, *Ogonek*, December 1988, 5.

38. Robert Marquand, "The Good News of *Glasnost*," *Christian Science Monitor*, 17 November 1988.

39. Walter Sawatsky, "Barclay's Commentary for Russian Believers: A Translator's Reflections" (Lecture given on 30 November 1988 at Wheaton College [Illinois], sponsored by the Institute for the Study of Christianity and Marxism).

40. "Barclay Study Bible is First Protestant Commentary in Russian," Religious News Service, 13 October 1986, 9; David Russell, "William Barclay in Russian," *Frontier*, September-October 1987, 22.

41. Interview with Denton Lotz (General Secretary of the Baptist World Alliance) and Archie Goldie (Director of Baptist World Aid), Baptist World Alliance headquarters (McLean, Va.), 21 March 1989.

42. Alice Kalso,"New Year's Hope for Soviet Believers," interview with Peter Deyneka, *World*, 9 January 1989.

43. "International Russian Radio Receives Unprecedented Mail Response from Target Area," *National Religious Broadcasters 89 Convention News*, 31 January 1989.

44. *KNS*, no. 309, 22 September 1988, 8-9.

45. *KNS*, no. 315, 15 December 1988, 11.

46. *KNS*, no. 314, 1 December 1988, 19.

47. *KNS*, no. 317, 19 January 1989, 16.

48. Information provided by Anita Deyneka, 1-6 February 1989. Also see the 1988 Slavic Gospel Association annual report.

49. Interview with Lotz and Goldie. Bychkov reported this to the Baptist World Alliance Executive Committee on 3 March 1989 at BWA headquarters.

50. Information provided by A. Deyneka, 1-6 February 1989.

51. "Book on Christian Child Rearing to be Distributed in Soviet Union," *Religious News Service*, 20 January 1989, 4.

52. Information provided by A. Deyneka, 1 February 1989.

53. "Seminary Approved," *Christianity Today*, 21 April 1989, 48. That Soviet authorities still inform religious bodies how many students may enroll in their seminaries should serve as a reminder of the limits of the present religious *perestroika*.

54. Interview with Lotz and Goldie. As of this writing I have still been unable to confirm that permission has been granted for Kiev, but such permission has been sought for some time.

55. *KNS*, no. 315, 15 December 1988, 12.

CHAPTER 15

THE POSITIVE IMPACT
OF *GLASNOST*
ON CHRISTIAN BELIEVERS,
PART II

F or almost a quarter of a century before Mikhail Gorbachev came to power, the Council for Religious Affairs was headed by a man who wrote that "church charities have no practical value at all." Vladimir Kuroedov also asserted that:

> charity by the church is clearly absurd; charitable work by religious organizations in our country cannot be carried on because it has nothing whatsoever to do with satisfaction of the religious needs of people.

Gleb Yakunin quoted these words in an August 12, 1987 letter to Gorbachev. Yakunin went on to complain that it was "completely incomprehensible" why the Church, "the originator of charities," should be denied the opportunity to do charitable acts.[1]

In fact, one of the first appeals to appear in the Soviet press for a change in the official stance toward charity occurred in March 1987, more than a year before Baptist parishioners were allowed to begin volunteer efforts. The popular author Daniel Granin explained the demise of charity:

> Charity has not declined by accident; it was systematically obliterated during the time of the dispossession of the kulaks, when people were not allowed to help the victims, and sentiments like charity were regarded as suspect.[2]

The *kulaks* were wealthy peasants deliberately stripped of their wealth in the early 1930s in a State campaign to collectivize agriculture. Granin challenged Soviet citizens to become involved in charity once again.

THE HEALING TOUCH OF THE CHURCH

The Church was quick to pick up the challenge. At the end of March 1988, Professor Vladimir Sorokin, rector of the Leningrad Theological Academy, commented: "In the old days there existed church-based sisterhoods and brotherhoods, each of which adopted a particular hospital into its care. We must go back to that good old tradition."[3]

Patriarch Pimen emphasized the good that the Church could do, if only it were allowed to minister to society through compassionate volunteer work. Metropolitan Filaret of Kiev and Galicia echoed this offer of help. And Seventh Day Adventists also expressed interest in contributing to society in this way.[4]

In 1976 Russian Orthodox dissident Gennadi Shimanov wrote an open letter to Patriarch Pimen protesting the timidity of the Orthodox hierarchy in pressing for religious freedom. Near the end of his letter he made a remarkable prediction:

the elimination from Soviet legislation and Soviet practice of destructive points will lead to the moral health of Soviet society, because it will unite it with the thousand-year-old moral roots of Russia . . . . There are serious grounds for hoping that in the not too distant future the Soviet leaders will realize this and will go to meet their own best interests, and also world public opinion and the petitions of our Church.[5]

In a peculiar twist of fate, the mental hospital in which Shimanov himself was confined as a prisoner of conscience in the 1960s was the first hospital in which Baptist volunteers were allowed to serve during the Gorbachev era.

In early 1988 members of the Moscow Baptist Church approached Valentin Kozyrev, chief physician of the Kashchenko mental hospital, with an unusual proposal. Would he allow volunteers from the church to work in the hospital? Kozyrev immediately agreed, and in April 1988 fifty Baptist women began to visit the hospital daily to take care of patients, clean, and do other odd jobs.[6]

That such cooperation between a State hospital and a church is possible is a marked departure from the past. All charitable institutions have been nationalized since 1918, and since 1929 there has been a formal prohibition against all organized religious charitable activity. Though the prohibition is still on the books, its official abolition is anticipated in the near future and its practical abolition is already partially accomplished.

On September 24, 1988 Dr. Kozyrev and two of his staff attended a special thanksgiving service at Moscow Baptist Church, and the Soviet doctor was given a chance to say a few words:

Let me thank you for your invitation to come here. Had I been told several years ago that I, the chief physician of a major hospital, a communist, would stand here before you in a Baptist church, I would never have believed it.

Perestroika is under way in our country, the climate here has changed, and this symbiosis of cooperation between the hospital and church has become possible. The word charity itself was in oblivion for a long time, but it has emerged now, and we are assessing our life according to it . . . .

Some of our personnel doubted the success of this project, but after two or three days of our joint work every doubt disappeared. Our patients cannot be cunning, and their gratitude, likings, and impatient waiting for your nurses are the best testimony to the fact that we have chosen the right road. We feel that we ourselves are participating in the good work simply by granting you this opportunity.[7]

During the service thirty more women expressed interest in helping, bringing the total to eighty volunteers from this church. The hospital has now requested male workers for the men's ward. The Baptist Church gave the hospital officials Bibles and tapes of Christian music. Baptist leader Alexei Bychkov reported in March 1989 that the Baptists may even be allowed to build a hospital.[8]

In part, hospital authorities are simply responding to the desperate need for support personnel in hospitals. Kharchev put the shortfall at twenty thousand in a speech to party workers in 1988.[9] But some Soviet officials, at least, seem genuinely to recognize the unique value of religious volunteers. Dr. Kozyrev spoke of the necessity of "chemistry plus love" in the treatment of mental patients. And he went on to say:

And if we as doctors and scientists are able to fulfill the first part of this formula to some extent, we are virtually incapable of fulfilling the second part, which is love.[10]

The Soviet press in June 1988 even carried a story praising the Baptist volunteers.[11]

Beginning in June 1988, members of the Yelokhovsky Cathedral, the patriarchal cathedral, have been volunteers in the neurology department of Basmanov Hospital. The agreement to allow parishioners from the cathedral to help was reported June 17 on Soviet television.[12] One of the hospital officials exclaimed, "they're an absolute godsend."[13] Indeed, that is precisely how the Christian volunteers would like to be viewed.

A senior official in the USSR Ministry of Health signed a statement in June 1988 saying health authorities would accept volunteer help from believers in whatever form it was offered. There has been some concern, however, that at least until early 1989 Christian volunteers have been allowed only in facilities which care for the mentally ill or the aged. The Moscow

Baptists would gladly work in a hospital closer to their church, but permission has not been granted for that facility. Still, Christians are extremely gratified even to have the opportunities thus far been opened to them.[14]

Another sign of changed attitudes toward religious involvement in charity is how the press treats such activities. The March 1987 issue of *Science and Religion* included a moving account of a "cemetery church" which provides help to the homeless—former prisoners without residence permits and former prostitutes. Just a few years ago such church activities could only be presented in the most negative of colors; this article presented the young priest responsible for this compassionate work in an engaging and attractive manner.[15]

Following a visit to Moscow in December 1988, Mother Teresa sent four nuns from the Missionaries of Charity Order to Moscow to work in Burdenko Hospital. Four more nuns will work with earthquake victims in Armenia. It is hoped that their temporary stay will result in permission to stay indefinitely, and that eventually Soviet women will be allowed to join the sisters in their work.[16]

It would be a mistake to conclude that church charitable activities did not exist in the pre-Gorbachev era. They did—though they had to be done very quietly and there was always the threat of interference by the authorities. The Council for Religious Affairs frequently complained in the 1960s and 1970s that the churches were engaged in charitable activities.[17]

Charity is nothing new for Russian Christians. What is new are the opportunities openly to engage in it and the larger scale which is allowed.

NEW OPPORTUNITIES TO SPREAD THE GOSPEL

On a remarkable evening in the summer of 1988, ten thousand young people jumped to their feet at the Leningrad Sports Complex to cheer and clap their approval of a riveting American rock ballet. In a creative combination of mime, music, dance, and narration, a cast of thirty had just completed the last of eighteen performances in Moscow and Leningrad (August 31- September 14, 1988). This was not the first American show to visit this place; Billy Joel had performed there in 1987. But the 1988 production was very different.

The *Toymaker's Dream* is not just another rock opera. Its message is explicitly Christian and traces in unmistakable detail the biblical account of the creation of Adam and Eve, the Fall, the coming of Christ, His crucifixion, and His resurrection. The narration was in Russian.

Advertised with pictures in the local press, the production eventually played to a total of seventy-five thousand Soviet citizens. Some of the proceeds went to support a Soviet/American peace program. But the troupe was in the Soviet Union to perform, not make one-sided political statements about arms control. Enthusiastically received throughout their engagement, the Tulsa-based Impact Productions show has been invited to return to the

USSR for a three-week tour beginning the last week of August 1989. They will perform in Minsk, Kiev, Odessa, and Moscow.[18]

The Soviet Union is a land of anomalies. While customs agents at the Moscow airport still occasionally confiscate religious literature, night after night a Christian rock ballet downtown can blaze out the gospel message. There is indeed more openness under Mr. Gorbachev than under his predecessors.

But the openness is something like walking on an iced-over pond in springtime. Just when you think your footing is solid, you plunge into the chilly waters beneath the surface. New opportunities are sprinkled in unpredictably amidst the old restrictions and prohibitions.

Evangelism outside the four walls of a registered church traditionally has been forbidden. In April 1988, for example, Soviet officials arrested Christians for evangelizing in public.[19] Nevertheless, since Gorbachev, there have been some notable concessions.

Take for example the 1988 visit to the Soviet Union of the much-loved radio broadcaster Earl Poysti. The autonomous registered Baptist churches extended an invitation to Poysti to be a special guest speaker at several large baptismal services conducted in commemoration of the millennium. One drew between fifteen thousand and eighteen thousand people.[20]

In 1971 astronaut Jim Irwin was walking on the moon. Seventeen years later he was preaching in the Soviet Union. For many, the former is easier to imagine than the latter. Invited by the autonomously registered Baptists of Kiev, Riga, and Brest, Irwin in November 1988 preached the gospel in nine churches in ten days.

More than a thousand people came forward seeking salvation during Irwin's brief visit to the Soviet Union, and more than thirty thousand filled out requests for religious literature. Irwin also distributed ten thousand copies of his own testimony in Russian, prepared by Slavic Gospel Association. Irwin's trip was covered by Soviet TV and print media, and he met Soviet cosmonauts and scientists.[21]

These opportunities for evangelism demonstrate the possibility of preaching in the Soviet Union without becoming part of a Soviet-orchestrated disinformation campaign.

Not since the 1920s has it been possible to hold outdoor evangelistic services and openly invite nonbelievers to attend. In Kiev, however, local authorities permitted a Baptist church to host an evangelistic service attended by four thousand people. More than one hundred made a public commitment to Christ. Later that same day, other Baptist churches in Kiev held an outdoor revival service along the Dnieper River. Five thousand gathered to listen. When the local militia tried to interfere, the crowd insisted the service be allowed to continue, and the militia backed off. On the next day, Sunday,

Kievan believers conducted a baptismal service attended by more than ten thousand. Seventy-five were baptized.[22]

Slavic Gospel Association has received many reports from throughout the Soviet Union regarding open-air baptismal services and evangelistic meetings. One Soviet believer wrote to tell of a meeting on May 1-2 attended by 1,500 young people. He reported that 120 were converted. A Christian in Estonia reported meetings in local parks, but that there was often a shortage of Christian literature to give out.[23]

In the Baltic states in both Tallinn (Estonia) and Riga (Latvia), 10,000-seat capacity ice coliseums were rented in 1988 for evangelistic meetings. In Tallinn, Pentecostals and Baptists combined in mid-July to host a remarkable outreach effort. Thirty large posters advertised the event throughout the city. Because the arena was packed, a special announcement was made requesting believers to leave their seats to stand on the carpet-covered rink area. In this way, an additional 2,000 squeezed in. Canadian Victor Hamm preached, and reported that approximately 250 came forward to receive Christ. There were not nearly enough Bibles for those who wanted them. On October 16, Pentecostals hosting a similar meeting in Riga also reported a large number of converts.[24]

Victor Hamm's preaching itinerary in the Soviet Union in July 1988 stretched from the Baltic down through Brest and Kishinev to Odessa. A concert hall was secured in Kishinev and baptismal services were held on the banks of lakes and rivers. Particularly important for rebuilding ties within the Soviet Protestant community was the July 17 service in Brest in which leaders of the AUCECB, representatives of the autonomously-registered congregations, and members of the unregistered churches all sat together.[25]

In January 1989 the Moscow Baptist Church rented a hall for two evangelistic meetings. Two thousand attended and 120 made commitments to Christ. The AUCECB general secretary reported in March that within the last few months there were sixteen meetings like it. Furthermore, permission is anticipated for Billy Graham to preach in a large public setting in 1989.[26]

Dr. Luis Palau, the Argentine-born American evangelist, is scheduled for a series of preaching engagements in the Soviet Union during September 1989. He was invited by the AUCECB, the Russian Orthodox Church, and the autonomous Baptists to hold evangelistic meetings in Moscow, Leningrad, Riga, and Kiev. Kharchev himself gave permission for the sponsoring groups to apply to use public facilities for these meetings.[27]

Another form of evangelism is Christian apologetics as practiced in debates with atheists. In the past, genuine public dialogue between atheists and believers has been rare. A number of stimulating and fair debates, however, have occurred during the Gorbachev era.

In Donetsk, in south Russia north of the Sea of Azov, believers were allowed to stage a series of debates between pastors and professors of atheism.

Topics included the existence of God and the influence of religion on Russian culture. Up to one thousand attended each debate, and the pastors gave an excellent account of their side of the argument. Even some factory bosses have allowed discussions to occur between Christians and atheist teachers.[28]

Rev. Alexander Volokitkin, one of two principal pastors of the registered Leningrad Baptist Church, reported in the spring of 1988 that since 1986 his church had been in dialogue with local atheists. Discussions were conducted in a civil and respectful manner. Members of the Leningrad atheist clubs have visited the church, and Rev. Volokitkin chaired a public meeting outside the church. The session was well attended by both Christians and nonbelievers.

Atheists cordially asked many questions of the believers. Anatoly Morozov, the church secretary and an administrator in the AUCECB, thinks the new Soviet openness developed because the Church has not disappeared as was expected, and Communist authorities believe it is time to get on with establishing better relations. Besides, atheist lecturers on religion have recognized that they did not know their subject well. By September 1988, three such meetings for dialogue had occurred in Leningrad. A Leningrad Radio program entitled "For Believers and Unbelievers" covered the discussions.[29]

Dialogue sessions also occurred in 1988 in several cities in Soviet Central Asia. Local officials were particularly interested in why believers had more stable marriages and why their young people were able to avoid drugs and alcohol. The officials even noticed the young believers paid social visits on the elderly. Serious moral *perestroika* of Soviet society requires that the positive social fruits of a believer's lifestyle be considered seriously.[30]

The ingenuity and enthusiasm of Soviet Christians seeking to spread their faith and support their communities is quite unusual. Even the Soviet press has noticed this, as shown by a December 8, 1985 article in *Komsomol Pravda*.

Baptists in the Carpathian village of Olkhovskiye Lozy, in western Ukraine, are openly proselytizing in buses and on city streets. The correspondent reports that Christians are attracting many local villagers. Though not registered with the authorities, the Baptists erected a "summer kitchen" next to the pastor's house. This two-story "kitchen," in fact, has an auditorium, a stage, and is decorated with quotations and murals. There is a large pulpit, musical instruments, and religious books.

When local authorities realized what the "kitchen" really was, they decided to demolish it. But when Pastor Biben and his parishioners complained to higher officials, the decision to destroy was rescinded. When members of the Communist Youth League were asked their opinion about the Baptists, they replied that the Christians did not bother anybody, and they make a positive contribution to the community. Such an article would have been unheard of before the Gorbachev era.[31]

Video evangelism is also beginning to hit the USSR. In contrast to the U.S. where approximately half of all homes have a VCR and annual sales are about 13 million, the Soviet Union has between 350,000 and 1 million VCRs. The main producer of VCRs in the USSR, in Voronezh, can only turn out about 100,000 a year, far short of demand. The Soviet goal is to produce 2 million VCRs by 1995.[32] Requests for video equipment, blank videos (which cost up to $100 on the black market), and Christian videos are increasingly heard from contacts within the Soviet Union.

The authorities have reacted with considerably more tolerance in the Baltic states, Leningrad, and Moscow to the religious use of videos than they have in the Central Asian republics.

By early 1989 the All-Union Council of Evangelical Christians-Baptists reached agreement with the International Russian Radio of Finland to produce *Superbook,* a video Bible in Russian for children. Plans call for Soviet believers to travel to the recording studio in Finland to help in the preparation of a final product. Other videos are being planned as well.[33]

In addition, Slavic Gospel Association has prepared several of the Moody Science films in Russian. These and other tapes are already circulating within the Soviet Union.

REOPENINGS AND REGISTRATIONS OF CHURCHES

It was a glorious day for Lithuanian Catholics. Vilnius Cathedral was reconsecrated on February 5, 1989, with thirty thousand witnesses packed into the cathedral square and before a Lithuanian television audience. Seized by the authorities in 1949 and used as an art gallery since the 1960s, Vilnius Cathedral is now once again serving as a place of worship.

A particularly electric moment occurred when Nijole Sadunaite stepped forward to speak. A national symbol of courage and religious conscience, Sadunaite spent six years in prison, labor camp, and exile during the 1970s for her work on the longest running *samizdat* (self-publishing) publication in the Soviet Union—*Chronicle of the Lithuanian Catholic Church.* She addressed her fellow Lithuanians on behalf of all religious and political prisoners, especially those who had perished in labor camp or exile.[34]

Presiding at the reconsecration was Bishop Julijonas Steponavicius, him-self a victim of many years of internal exile. Michael Bourdeaux, the one major foreign guest to witness this historic moment, described the significance of the occasion as follows:

> If there is one dominant impression . . . it was the quiet dignity of the whole massive crowd. Bishop Steponavicius personified this dignity; never in private or public a word of self-pity. Only an indication . . . that a regime of more than a quarter of a century of reading and prayer during his time of enforced exile, with only minimal contact with the world outside, had strengthened his faith.[35]

Other congregations in Vilnius and Luga had their own special reasons for celebration.

Authorities in 1952 confiscated St. Casimir's Church in Vilnius and turned it into a Museum of Atheism. On March 4, 1989, they returned it to the Church. At approximately the same time, permission was given for Catholics to build a new church in a suburb of Vilnius. This is significant because it is unprecedented for a new church to be allowed into a new housing development.[36]

For the first time in fifty years, Baptists in the city of Luga (eighty-five miles south of Leningrad) are once again worshiping in their own building—a structure which predates the Bolshevik Revolution. The rededication of the building took place in the autumn of 1988.[37]

Even before the Gorbachev era, one architectural treasure of the Orthodox Church was formally returned. The Danilov Monastery in Moscow became church property once again in 1983. This structure was turned over to the Church in part to prepare for the 1988 millennium year and its anticipated great influx of foreign visitors. The Orthodox Church eventually moved its headquarters from Zagorsk (forty-five miles from Moscow) to Danilov in the heart of Moscow. A hotel for foreign guests is now under construction on the site.

Throughout the Gorbachev years, particularly beginning in 1987, Soviet and foreign coverage of *glasnost* has reported the return of many important cultural treasures to the Orthodox Church. In November 1987 the Optina Pustyn monastery was returned. Built at the end of the eighteenth century, this famous home of the legendary *startsy* (elders) was a well-known pilgrimage site for writers such as Gogol, Tolstoy, and Dostoevsky.[38]

The Monastery of the Caves in Kiev, founded in 1051, is considered one of the fountainheads of Slavic Christianity. Taken over by the secular authorities in 1961 and turned into a tourist attraction, parts of it were returned to the Church during millennium festivities.[39]

Facilities returned to the Church often are in need of extensive restoration. Typical of the kind of obstacles confronting believers even when Soviet authorities make concessions is the case of the St. Nicholas of Myra Church in Rzhavki (a few miles to the northwest of Moscow). At the end of 1987 it was decided that this old structure ought to become a museum dedicated to the defense of Moscow. When it was determined in 1988 that it would be returned to the Church, it was stipulated that the twenty-six-thousand-plus roubles spent on converting the facility into a museum be reimbursed by the Church to local authorities.[40]

Beyond the return of old churches, occasionally new Orthodox facilities are being built. A much-celebrated recent example is that of Orekhovo-Borisovo, on the outskirts of Moscow. Patriarch Pimen presided at the setting of the foundation stone of this church, intended to commemorate the millennium of Christianity. Kharchev stated that the church would serve as a symbol of *perestroika* in Church/State relations.[41]

Bychkov of the All-Union Council of Evangelical Christians-Baptists has reported that between 1981 and October 1988, more than 360 AUCECB churches were built in the Soviet Union, and he claims there are over 5,500 congregations in all which belong to the AUCECB.[42]

TASS reported that on November 16, 1988, Zaporozhe (Ukraine) witnessed the consecration of the city's first registered Pentecostal church. The church has three hundred members and was autonomously registered, which means it is not part of the AUCECB. The Soviet news agency also reported that three other Pentecostal churches had recently opened in the Ukraine.[43]

(It must be remembered there are several different groups of Protestants in the Soviet Union: the Baptists, Pentecostals, Lutherans, Reformed, Methodists, and Mennonites who are a part of the largest Protestant union (the AUCECB); the autonomously registered groups (Pentecostals, Baptists, Mennonites, who do not belong to the AUCECB, as well as the Seventh Day Adventists and others); and unregistered Protestants (a large group of Pentecostals, and the unregistered Baptist union which dates from 1965). The autonomously registered groups are frequently willing to come to some understanding with the Soviet State, but believe the AUCECB has been too submissive to Communist authorities.)

Within both the Russian Orthodox Church and the AUCECB there are those who believe the present leadership is too timid and too compromised by their past relationships to the authorities in the pre-Gorbachev era to provide the kind of strong guidance called for in the era of *glasnost*.

Drawing conclusions about the health of the Church on the basis of the number of registered religious communities is not as easy as it might first appear. On the one hand, it is clear there is a serious problem when the number of registered communities declines. For example, even the head of the Council for Religious Affairs, Vladimir Kuroedov, reported in a 1984 book that between 1977 and 1983 there was a net decline of 225 religious registered communities. During that time, 810 communities were registered with the CRA, but 1,035 were de-registered.[44]

We know from what Kharchev reported at the end of 1987 that the decline in the total number of registered religious communities ceased soon after Gorbachev arrived on the scene in the spring of 1985. He reports that between April 1985 and the end of 1987, 173 religious associations were registered, and 107 de-registered. Thus, a net gain of 66 registrations in 21 months. Kharchev associated the change with democratization, *perestroika,* and *glasnost*.[45] In 1988 the number of registrations climbed sharply; approximately 1,000 new registrations may have occurred.[46]

N. Kolesnik, chairman of the Ukrainian Council for Religious Affairs, asserts that in his republic alone almost 480 religious organizations or churches were registered, 430 of which were Orthodox (mainly in the western part of Ukraine).[47]

Several observations need to be made regarding what registration statistics do and do not tell us.

First, though Soviet statistics are not always accurate or even in agreement with each other, a gain of 1,000 registrations in 1988 would represent significant growth over recent years—an increase of about 7 percent in the total number of registered religious communities (which Kharchev said numbered just over 15,000 in 1986).[48] The Russian Orthodox Church asserted it had 6,893 churches in mid-1988.[49] If the reports for 1988 are reasonably accurate, the Orthodox Church may have had an increase of between 10 and 12 percent that year.

Second, there is concern about the meaning of Orthodox Church registrations in the western Ukraine. This is the area where Ukrainian Catholic churches have functioned illegally for many years. Are some of these newly-registered groups really Ukrainian Catholics who have been forced or persuaded to register as Orthodox?

Third, we must remember that often registrations do not mean the establishment of new religious communities, but only the legalization of previously underground ones or ones the authorities had refused to register. Thus, the increases may simply reflect a more accurate record of a long-term situation.

Fourth, Soviet registration—or in some cases "re-registration"—has often functioned as a control device or even a purge mechanism. In 1923 and in the 1960s the authorities sought to register groups in order to limit them or even close them down. The Gorbachev registrations may not be as sinister as the former ones, but there can be little doubt that even liberal reformers would prefer to have at least some control over religious communities.

Fifth, registration statistics cannot stand alone. They must always must be compared with de-registrations. Such statistics for 1988 are not yet available. Perhaps they are minimal for the millennium year, but we must be careful to watch this half of the figures in the coming years.

Sixth, even if the high figures of new registrations turn out to be accurate, a figure of even eight thousand Orthodox churches would represent only about one-seventh of the number of Orthodox churches which existed before the Communists took control in 1917. At the 1988 growth rates, it would take well over four decades to reach the number of Orthodox churches existing when the population was less than half that of today.

Another sobering way to get a sense of the paucity of the Soviet Union's religious communities is to compare New York City with Moscow. Moscow, with a population of more than eight million, has less than fifty Orthodox Churches and only a handful of Protestant, Catholic, or Jewish places of worship. In 1917, Moscow, with a population of less than two million, had seven hundred places of worship representing ten different faiths. By contrast, New York City with its more than a million fewer people had upwards of thirty-five hundred places of worship in the mid-1980s.[50]

EXPANDED EMIGRATION

For many years human rights activists in the West have pressed the Soviets to liberalize their emigration policy. Both Jews and Christians have sought emigration, but the former have been far more successful than the latter in achieving it.

Compared to Jewish emigration, Christian departures have usually been but a trickle. Why? First, the Jewish Western lobby has been forceful and committed in pressing its case. Christians have been far less organized and much more timid.

Second, the Soviets have shown more willingness to allow Jews to leave. In addition to responding to Western public pressure, there may well be an element of anti-Semitism involved in letting Jews emigrate. Russian anti-Semitism predates the arrival of the Bolsheviks. There is a real sense in which being ''Jewish'' is not even considered compatible with being ''Russian'' or ''Soviet.'' Thus, if you must let some go, let it be the Jews.

However, Jews in the Soviet Union, as throughout the world, are often well educated, highly motivated, and make significant contributions to society. They frequently leave holes that are not easily filled. In refusing to let more go, officials have sometimes talked about a Western-organized ''brain drain'' on Soviet intelligentsia.

Third, if it were made relatively easy for Christians (particularly Slavs) to emigrate, and many chose to do so, it would be concrete evidence that the Soviet Union did not, in fact, have the religious liberty which it always claimed to have. Furthermore, with the Slavic population declining each year relative to non-Slavs, Kremlin authorities have been extremely reluctant to allow widespread Slavic Christian departures.

Jewish emigration hit its peak in 1979 when more than 51,320 were allowed to leave. But then it steadily and rapidly declined: 21,471 in 1980; 9,400 in 1981; 2,700 in 1982; 1,315 in 1983; 913 in 1986. But in 1988 there was a dramatic change. In that year 19,233 Jews emigrated to the West, the vast majority choosing not to go to Israel. In the first four-and-a-half months of 1989, 15,462 left the Soviet Union. In April alone 4,557 Jews left the USSR—the highest monthly total since October 1979.[51]

But the biggest surprise of 1988 was the sharp increase in Christian emigration, particularly among Pentecostals. In previous years, only a few dozen Baptists or Pentecostals managed to leave the Soviet Union, and then only after extended waits and much anguish. In 1988, however, approximately 3,500 Pentecostals left the USSR. Already by mid-May 1989, the 1988 total was within a couple hundred of being reached. World Relief has projected that at least 10,000 Pentecostals may emigrate from the Soviet Union in 1989.[52]

Although most Pentecostals leaving the Soviet Union do come to the United States, others go to Canada, West Germany, and other Western countries. The vast majority of the approximate two hundred members of the Chuguyevka Pentecostal Church in the Far East have emigrated to West Germany. Their eight-year struggle to leave ended in November 1988, when the last of their group was permitted to emigrate.[53]

Ever since the late seventies it had been clear that large numbers of Pentecostals (mainly unregistered) wanted to leave; estimates have often ranged from thirty thousand to seventy thousand. Two factors have motivated this desire to emigrate. First, the unregistered Pentecostals (there is a registered group as well), like all unregistered Christians, have been subjected to considerable persecution. The issue of emigration became particularly pressing for many of them in the early 1960s during Khrushchev's antireligious campaign. In some cases, children were even taken away from Christian parents.

Second, many Pentecostals on the basis of Scripture and certain contemporary prophecies believe that a period of liberalization will be followed by a great persecution. They believe they must leave while they have the opportunity.

There is a serious misconception in the West that most unregistered Pentecostals want to leave. This is untrue. Most Pentecostals, like most other Christians in the USSR, would prefer to stay, and if *glasnost* continues to expand and does not follow the earlier, cyclical patterns of liberalization giving way to a new repression, the pressure to emigrate will undoubtedly lessen.[54] Even if seventy thousand did eventually leave the Soviet Union, that would be a relatively small number compared to the much larger group of Jews who have emigrated over the past decade.

Ironically, a few months after the Soviets began allowing more Pentecostals to emigrate, the United States Immigration and Naturalization Service (INS), which considers applications for refugee status, began in about mid-December 1988 to deny rather arbitrarily such status to a portion of the Pentecostal applicants. (The INS also rejected approximately the same percentage of Jewish applicants.)

World Relief (part of the National Association of Evangelicals) and the Institute on Religion and Democracy (Washington, D.C.) spearheaded efforts to correct the problem with the INS. On January 10, 1989, World Relief sent an investigative task force of eight (including lawyers, law students, and translators) to the processing center in Rome.[55] After reviewing all ninety-nine cases which had been rejected to that point, the head of the task force, Lynn Buzzard, on January 22 wrote a fourteen-page report. The task force findings were startling. As Buzzard later commented in an Institute on Religion and Democracy press release on February 2:

> We discovered numerous abuses of procedures and misapplications of legal standards in the INS processing of the Pentecostal emigres. Frankly, all of us were profoundly embarrassed by the arbitrary and insensitive treatment of refugee applicants that we witnessed.

Though the World Relief task force submitted detailed documentation on the cases explaining why the rejected applicants met the criteria for refugee status, more than forty were turned down once more.

Despite meetings with the INS and the presentation of materials documenting the severe persecution of unregistered Pentecostals in the USSR, the number of new rejections for refugee status continued to rise. By March 1989 at least 169 Soviet Christians had been rejected as refugees, 48 of whom were granted the status upon further review.

A major turning point in the situation occurred on March 17, 1989, when Michael Rowe from Keston College was invited to Rome to talk with INS officials. Rowe is perhaps the foremost expert in the world on Soviet Pentecostals, and his seven-hour session with INS was very productive. It is also likely that congressional pressure was beginning to mount.

By mid-April 1989 the vast majority (over 80 percent) of the cases originally rejected had been reconsidered and refugee status awarded. Virtually all Pentecostal cases are now granted refugee status when first considered.

In the meantime, however, the KGB was telling Pentecostals seeking emigration there was really no point in leaving— "the Americans won't accept you as refugees." This was a sad and confusing moment for American foreign policy. For years we had insisted that the Soviets ought to allow these people to emigrate since they were persecuted, and then when they were released, 169 were rejected because the criteria for refugee status—namely, persecution or a well-founded fear of persecution—allegedly was not met.

Several factors seem to have produced this three-month trauma for Soviet Christian emigrés: INS officers swamped with an increase in applicants, insufficient background in the history of the people they were working with, a failure to follow their own process guidelines for determining eligibility, and perhaps an unjustified assumption that the problems of the Soviet Union were now a product of the past. It ought to be noted that the INS never said a Soviet Christian could not come to the United States, only that some could not come as "refugees." The rejected could have come to the United States with a humanitarian parole status, which is more expensive for the sponsor and does not automatically lead to U.S. citizenship. To INS's credit, it seems to have taken some steps to correct the problem. Unfortunately the problems with the INS are not over. In May at least two dozen more Soviet Christian applicants were refused refugee status, including Baptists and Estonian Methodists, in addition to Pentecostals.[56]

It is interesting that in 1988, far more emigrants from the Soviet Union and Eastern Europe went to West Germany than to the United States. At least 292,000 arrived, including 48,000 (three times the 1987 figure) from the Soviet Union. The Soviet emigrants were mainly ethnic Germans who have been guaranteed a home in West Germany.[57]

The increase in emigres from the Soviet Union is straining existing U.S. government programs. The number of applicants for permanent residency in the U.S. increased dramatically between 1987 and 1988. The total number of applicants for 1989 will undoubtedly be much higher. In early 1989, President Bush raised the ceiling on Soviet-bloc refugees from 18,000 to 24,500. He has since proposed that Congress increase the number to 47,000. In addition, a new U.S. emigration category has been proposed between refugee status and humanitarian parole. This would put an emigre on a citizenship track (five years), but shift more of the financial burden from the U.S. government onto the shoulders of the emigrant's sponsor. The quota for this category would be separate from that allowed for refugee status.[58]

The Soviet Union has been permitting another group to emigrate— Armenians. In 1988, 10,864 Armenians left the Soviet Union and most came to the United States.[59] Most observers do not believe the majority of Armenians seeking to emigrate have the same claim to refugee status that Jews and Christians do. In fact, Soviet Armenians rarely claim to have been the victims of religious persecution or discrimination, and approximately 75 percent of those who were applying for refugee status were being denied it as of April 1989. The proposed new emigration category would be of particular help to Armenians.

There can be little doubt, however, that the Pentecostals currently seeking emigration *do* meet the criteria for refugee status. Here it is not a close call.

A Soviet joke from the 1970s explains part of the Soviet fear of unlimited emigration:

> "Let's rip down the Iron Curtain and open the borders of our country!" Kosygin declares to Brezhnev.
>
> "We can't do that," retorts Brezhnev, "everyone would leave except you and me."
>
> "Speak for yourself," responds Kosygin.

Opening the gates of a nondemocratic country is a dangerous step, for it allows people to vote with their feet when they can't with a ballot.

Emigration figures have fluctuated for Soviet Jews before, so there is a wariness about predicting how long the more open emigration policy will last. For Christians, the uncertainty is even greater, since the present emigration is definitely the exception to the rule.

It is likely that the liberalized emigration policy of Gorbachev is a calculated risk. It rids the country of the most unhappy groups and individuals, while at the same time promoting the image abroad of a more humane Soviet Union. But ultimately, the success of *glasnost* will be measured, in part, by whether the desire to emigrate significantly lessens. Most individuals opt to stay in their homeland unless driven out by repression or serious economic problems. And among Christians, many more will want to stay if they see even modest progress in achieving the religious freedom they desire for themselves and their children.

While the future of *glasnost* is not certain, to the extent that emigration continues to be more open, the reality of the present *glasnost* cannot be questioned.

CONCLUSION

It has been said that the most dangerous moment for a bad government is when it begins to reform. Pent-up anger is unleashed, expectations rise faster than they can be fulfilled, and there is a general sense of unease.

On the other hand, there can be tremendous bursts of energy, excitement, and enthusiasm when genuine changes are allowed. With respect to religious believers, it is fair to say there is convincing empirical evidence confirming the reality of *glasnost*.

Improvements are uneven and incomplete, but they are real. Opportunities exist for the Church today, in the great majority of its denominational varieties, which were unheard of even five years ago.

Nevertheless, we now must turn our attention to an analysis of the problems which remain. This is necessary, because without a sober look at the darker side of Soviet life we will be unable to make an intelligent assessment about the prospects for *glasnost* in the years ahead.

Notes

1. Quoted in *Occasional Papers on Religion in Eastern Europe*, vol. 8, no. 4, August 1988, 21-22.

2. Quoted in Oxana Antic, "The Charity Program and the Role of the Churches," Radio Free Europe/Radio Liberty, RL 516/88, 22 November 1988, 3. Granin's comments appeared originally in *Literaturnaia Gazeta* (Literary Gazette), no. 12, 1987.

3. Quoted in Antic, "Charity Program," 2. Taken from *Izvestiia*, 9 April 1988.

4. Antic, "Charity Program," 1-3.

5. Quoted in Jane Ellis, *The Russian Orthodox Church: A Contemporary History* (Bloomington: Indiana University Press, 1986), 372-73.

6. "The Quality of Mercy," *Frontier*, March-April 1989, 12-15.

7. Ibid., 15.

8. Interview with Denton Lotz (General Secretary of the Baptist World Alliance) and Archie Goldie (Director of Baptist World Aid), 21 March 1989. Reporting on March 3 meeting with AUCECB leaders at the Baptist World Alliance headquarters.

9. "Quality of Mercy," 15.

10. Quoted in ibid.

11. *Moskovskie novosti* (Moscow News), late June 1988. Reported by Religious Liberty, 291/88, 1 July 1988, 6.

12. Jim Forest, "Church and Hospital," *One World*, December 1988, 9.

13. Quoted in Antic, "Charity Program," 5.

14. Ibid., 5-6.

15. Dmitry Pospielovsky, "The Russian Orthodox Church in the Gorbachev Era" (Unpublished paper delivered at a conference on the Millennium co-sponsored by the Kennan Institute and the Library of Congress, 28 May 1988), 22.

16. *Keston News Service*, no. 322, 30 March 1989, 17.

17. Dmitry Pospielovsky, *The Russian Church Under the Soviet Regime: 1917-1982* (Crestwood, N. Y.: St. Vladimir's Press, 1984), 2:419.

18. Letter and press release from Tom Newman, president of Impact Productions, 29 September 1988; letter from Tim Ramseier, tour coordinator, 12 May 1989.

19. "Reforms and the Church in Russia," *Break Through*, Slavic Gospel Association, March-April 1989, 10.

20. Information provided by Anita Deyneka, Slavic Gospel Association, 1 February 1989.

21. "Many Respond to Gospel as Irwin Visits Churches," *Break Through*, January-February 1989, 2-3.

22. "New Opportunities for Evangelism," *Break Through*, November-December 1988, 1.

23. "Public Evangelism Explosion," *News Wire*, Slavic Gospel Association, December 1988-January 1989, 2.

24. Phone conversation with Victor Hamm, Mennonite Brethren Communications (Manitoba, Canada), 10 April 1989.

25. Victor Hamm, "Report on the Visit to the Soviet Union." Description of the July 1988 preaching trip was provided by Hamm in April 1989.

26. Interview with Lotz and Goldie.

27. Information provided by David Jones, executive vice president of the Luis Palau Evangelistic Association, in a phone interview in April 1989 and a news release from the Luis Palau Evangelistic Association, 14 April 1989.

28. "New Opportunities for Evangelism," 2.

29. *KNS*, no. 309, 22 September 1988, 8.

30. Walter Sawatsky, "*Glasnost, Perestroika* and Religion," *Occasional Papers on Religion in Eastern Europe*, vol. 9, no. 2, April 1989, 16.

31. V. Panov, "Assignment Based on a Worrisome Letter: Mutual Protection," *Komsomolskaya Pravda*, 8 December 1985, reported in *The Current Digest of the Soviet Press*, 22 January 1986, 21-22.

32. "USSR Liberalizes Policy on VCRs: Increases Production, Allows More Imports," *Soviet East European Report*, RFE/RL, vol. 6, no. 10, 1 January 1989.

33. Bulletin from the International Russian Radio, Finland, early 1989.

34. For more information on Sadunaite's experiences, see her autobiography *A Radiance in the Gulag* (Manassas, Va.: Trinity Communications, 1987).

35. *KNS*, no. 319, 16 February 1989, 7. Also see *KNS*, no. 312, 3 November 1988, 6-8.

36. *KNS*, no. 322, 30 March 1989, 2.

37. *KNS*, no. 316, 5 January 1989, 7.

38. Michael Bourdeaux, *Opium of the People* (London: Mowbrays, 1965), 36-37; *KNS*, no. 303, 23 June 1988, 5.

39. *KNS*, no. 303, 23 June 1988, 4-5.

40. *KNS*, no. 307, 25 August 1988, 2-3.

41. *KNS*, no. 303, 23 June 1988, 9.

42. James Scherer, "Interviews with Soviet Religious Officials and Dissidents," *Occasional Papers on Religion in Eastern Europe*, April 1989, 22, 27.

43. *KNS*, no. 316, 5 January 1989, 15.

44. Cathy Henry, "Registration of Churches in the Soviet Union," *Religion in Communist Dominated Areas* 26 (Winter 1987):19.

45. "Guarantees of Freedom," *Nauka i Religiia* (Science and Religion), November 1987, 23. An English translation of this article is available in *Religion in Communist Dominated Areas* 26 (Fall 1987):115-20.

46. Patriarch Pimen in a 1 January 1989 interview with TASS reported an increase of seven hundred Orthodox parishes in 1988. On January 16, the German newspaper *Die Welt* published an interview with Metropolitan Filaret, chairman of the Moscow Patriarchate Foreign Church Relations Department, in which Filaret reported that one thousand registrations occurred in 1988, eight hundred of which were Orthodox. On the same day, a TASS interview with Professor Yuri Rozenbaum of the Institute of State and Law also contended that one thousand registrations had occurred the previous year, though he placed the number of new Orthodox registrations at six hundred. (Oxana Antic, "*Die Welt* Interview with Metropolitan Filaret," *Report on the USSR*, vol. 1, no. 4, 27 January 1989, 17-18.)

In an interview published 4 March 1989, Kharchev claimed there were fourteen hundred new registrations since Mr. Gorbachev's meeting with Patriarch Pimen (29 April 1988) and the time of the interview (*La Republica*, 13, reported in Foreign Broadcast Information Service, SOV-89-044, 8 March 1989, 75.) In mid-November 1988 Kharchev had asserted in London that during the first ten months of that year 650 religious associations had been registered (Oxana Antic, "Increase in Number of Orthodox Parishes," *Report on the USSR*, vol. 2, no. 2, 13 January 1989, 9).

Even if we assume that the great majority of the 650 registrations Kharchev mentioned in November had occurred after the Pimen meeting with Gorbachev on 29 April, it appears that between eight and nine hundred registrations were recorded between 1 November 1988 and 1 March 1989. Based on the statistics given earlier in the year by Pimen and Filaret, registrations must have averaged at least two hundred per month beginning in November 1988. This would put Kharchev's total registrations for 1988 at over one thousand, and mean that perhaps another 350 to 400 registrations may have occurred in the first two months of 1989. But it is much too early yet to determine the reliability of these statistics.

The 6 April 1989 issue of *Moscow News* reported 1,610 new registrations last year, including: 1,244 Russian Orthodox churches, 72 Georgian Orthodox churches, 71 Roman Catholic churches, 36 Baptist churches, and 48 mosques. (Michael Dobbs, "Kremlin Rescinds Anti-religion Edicts," *Washington Post*, 7 April 1989.) It is difficult to know what to make of these numbers since they are significantly higher than the other three sources listed above.

47. "Bells Over the Desna: More Than 430 Churches Consecrated in the Ukraine Last Year," *Izvestiia*, 2 February 1989, 6, as reported in Foreign Broadcast Information Service, SOV-89-027, 10 February 1989, 67.

48. Konstantin Kharchev, "The Soviet Government and the Church," *Nauka i Religiia* (Religion and Science), November 1987. Kharchev's figures for the total number of religious communities are approximate at best. He has considerably underestimated the number of registered evangelical churches and listed the Jehovah's Witnesses which have never been registered.

49. Antic, "Increase in Orthodox Parishes," 8. For information on the conflicting Soviet reports on the number of Russian Orthodox parishes for the period up to about the middle of 1988, see Helen Bell and Jane Ellis, "The Millennium Celebrations of 1988 in the USSR," *Religion in Communist Lands* 16 (Winter 1988):326-27.

50. Marshall Winokur, review of three books on Russian church architecture, *St. Vladimir's Theological Quarterly* 26, no. 1 (1982):58; and information provided by Prof. Winokur to me in mid-November 1985.

51. Peter Reddaway, "Soviet Policies on Dissent and Emigration: The Radical Change of Course Since 1979," Occasional Paper No. 192, 28 August 1984; Kennan Institute for Advanced Russian Studies (Washington, D.C.), 24; World Relief News Release, 31 January 1989; Ari Goldman, "4,000 Soviet Jews Migrated in March," *New York Times*, 5 April 1989; telephone interview with Brenda Schaefer, Hebrew Immigrant Aid Society (HIAS), New York City, 25 May

1989. "57,000 Permits So Far This Year Show Soviets Serious About Exits," Associated Press story, *Washington Times,* 15 May 1989.

52. Telephone interview with Schaefer, HIAS, 25 May 1989; World Relief News Release, 31 January 1989. The State Department says 3,442 Pentecostals and Baptists left the USSR in 1988 (*U.S. News and World Report*, 30 January 1989, 16). According to Ambassador Richard Shifter, 3,500 Pentacostals left the USSR in 1988 ("57,000 Permits," *Washington Times,* 15 May 1989.

53. The difference between Christian communal living and forced communism can be seen by studying the unusual Chuguyevka community. They shared everything in common, and their fellowship was strong and vibrant, but the Soviets persecuted them mercilessly. Between 1984 and 1988, ten of their leaders spent time in labor camp. (*Break Through*, November-December 1988, January-February 1989; "The Right to Believe," Keston College, no. 1, 1989, 3.)

54. Much of my information on unregistered Pentecostals comes from a series of conversations with Boris Perchatkin between August 1988 and April 1989. Perchatkin is a Soviet Pentecostal who emigrated to the U.S. in July 1988 and maintains close contacts with unregistered Pentecostals throughout the Soviet Union. He now lives in Massachusetts.

55. Although organized by World Relief, Church World Service, Episcopal Migration Ministries, and Lutheran Immigration and Refugee Services also supported the World Relief task force investigation. All of these groups have been involved in helping to settle Soviet Pentecostals in the United States. The actual processing of the Pentecostals in Rome until December 1988 was done by the World Council of Churches, and was then picked up temporarily by the International Catholic Migration Commission. A proposal is now under consideration whereby as of September 1989, World Relief and the three sister relief organizations listed above would collectively process arriving Christians from the USSR.

56. Phone interview with Serge Duss, World Relief, 24 May 1989.

57. Robert J. McCartney, "Thousands From East Bloc Drawn by Westward Hopes," *Washington Post*, 31 March 1989. Many of the ethnic Germans are from religious communities which have experienced discrimination and persecution, just as other Soviet religious groups have. Twenty-seven thousand of the 57,000 exit permits granted by May 1, 1989, by the Soviet government are to ethnic Germans. ("57,000 Permits," *Washington Times,* 15 May 1989.)

58. Elizabeth Shogren, "Soviet Armenians Allowed to Leave but Are Kept Out by U.S.," *Washington Post*, 31 March 1989. Telephone interview with Serge Duss, World Relief, 14 April 1989.

59. Telephone interview with Dr. Sidney Heitman, Colorado State University, an expert on Soviet emigration, 17 April 1989.

CHAPTER 16

WHERE *GLASNOST* HAS
YET TO REACH

"What do you think about the future of *glasnost*?" I asked an elderly Baptist believer. A slow smile crept over his wrinkled face. "We are very grateful for the opportunities of today." Not wanting to be impolite but still desiring an answer to my question, I tried again. "But what do you think about tomorrow?" His words were soft and measured. "We are very grateful for the opportunities of today."

Gaining the trust of believers in the USSR will be some of the last and most difficult terrain for the architects and practitioners of *glasnost* to take. The legacy of distrust and fear spawned by over seventy years of Communist state abuse of the Church will not soon be laid to rest.

Although virtually everyone acknowledges some significant positive changes, there are serious concerns where *glasnost* has not become a reality, where it remains business as usual. Problems continue to plague Soviet Christians: the lack of structural, institutional guarantees of religious freedom; the refusal to legalize the Ukrainian Catholic Church; the continued fining (and occasional jail sentences) of believers for holding unregistered church services; and the very existence (even if in a substantially liberalized form) of laws regulating religious communities.

In a political system based on arbitrary rule rather than law, a shift toward meaningful and secure constitutional and legal guarantees of believers' rights will not come easily. And if legal changes are made during the present era of greater toleration, will they survive into a post-Gorbachev period?

In particular, *glasnost* has found rough going in the provinces and in some of the non-Russian nationalist areas. As in previous periods, there can be considerable variance in policy from one area to another. This too is a legacy of a system where personality, not law, is frequently the most important factor.

And the questions go well beyond pitting reactionary provincial Party officials against progressive Moscow reformers; many do not accept at face value the intentions of Gorbachev himself.

TAKING THE SKEPTICS SERIOUSLY

While some skeptics in the West must be ignored because they have made a prior ideological commitment to the view that change in the Soviet Union can never be anything but an illusion, there are skeptics in the USSR who deserve to be taken far more seriously.

Father Vladimir Shibaev is such a person. Interviewed in a Russian emigré paper following his arrival in the West early in 1988, he expressed the following doubts about the sincerity of Gorbachev's reforms:

> I think the changes are tactical and do not only concern the State's attitude to the Church. It is a temporary pause in the terror tactics. Gorbachev needs this pause. However, the most important thing is that all measures which are undertaken allegedly for the benefit of the Church are, on the contrary, directed towards the tightening of the screws.[1]

For example, though it is no longer required that passports be submitted to obtain a baby's baptism, a birth certificate with the names of the parents still is, and this information is passed on to the authorities, according to Shibaev. Others have expressed a concern that Church registrations are a potentially dangerous phenomenon, for it can increase State control over what were previously totally independent organizations.

Cardinal Vincentas Sladkevicius of Lithuania is concerned about the West's tendency to become enamored of attractive personalities. While acknowledging that there are changes about which to rejoice, he warns: "I am afraid they may not last long. As long as you have a one-party government, there is a danger of dictatorship. Stalinism is dormant, but it is not dead." He cautions that the great majority of Lithuanians would oppose the Pope recognizing the incorporation of Lithuania into the USSR.[2]

WILL IT TAKE MORE THAN GLASNOST
TO HEAL THE REGISTERED HIERARCHY?

Father Shibaev contends that the Orthodox hierarchy has been weakened spiritually by its decades of servility to State authorities. These concerns are raised not by an outsider but by a priest who lived and worked within the Church. Shibaev comments:

> There is the Church, there are genuine Orthodox people there. There is the Church "against which the gates of hell shall not prevail." But one is hardly able to see this externally. Everything that shines and

sings is usually under the full control of Soviet authorities, particularly in central cities with large populations. Every church warden is a protege of the KGB or a Regional Executive Committee; he is simply a Soviet representative discharging certain functions.[3]

He reports that many young people are disillusioned with the Orthodox Church leadership. Shibaev firmly believes in the vibrancy and survivability of Christianity in the Soviet Union, but he is convinced the authorities' prolonged tactics have effectively damaged the hierarchy. "Acts of terror prevailed earlier, now the Church is being destroyed—all Churches are being destroyed—from within."[4] Once the chains are taken off a broken prisoner, his captors need not fear that he will depart from the restricted path he has trod for years.

Shibaev is not alone in expressing concern about the health of the Church hierarchy. Solzhenitsyn, Yakunin, Poresh, Ogorodnikov, and many others have sounded the same warning through the years.[5] Because the registered Church, both Orthodox and Protestant, has been significantly beat down through the decades, the critics assert that the leadership is anemic and passive, incapable of taking full advantage of the opportunities the *glasnost* era offers.

Rhetoric is cheap and can be changed in any number of directions depending on the political currents of the day. Some fear that the registered Churches are defending *glasnost* for the same reason they once defended the myth that there was no religious repression—that is what they are told to do. If this is true, should the present openness turn out to be but a brief interlude, we can expect their responses to once more conform to whatever political line the Communist authorities demand.

Prominent observers have suggested that perhaps the healthiest part of the Soviet Protestant world is not represented either by the All-Union Council of Evangelical Christians-Baptists (AUCECB) or their unregistered antagonists but by the growing number of independently registered Baptist and Pentecostal groups. They have not been compromised nearly so much as the AUCECB or the Orthodox hierarchy. (Among the Orthodox, it must be remembered, there is the decades-old Catacomb Church and a definable and vocal group of dissidents.)

Unfortunately, there is still strong evidence that important figures within the Russian Orthodox hierarchy are seriously compromised. A Western delegation to the Soviet Union met recently with Father Theopan, deputy chairman of the Russian Orthodox Church's Department of External Ecclesiastical Relations. Surprisingly, Theopan's conduct and comments were not those that many have come to associate with the *glasnost* era.

Theopan argued that there were no problems in the relationship between the Orthodox Church and the State. He insisted there were no religious prisoners in the USSR. When asked about the great shortage of religious literature, he launched into an attack on the pointlessness of Americans placing Bibles in hotel rooms when obviously no one uses them. He told the American visitors that they ought to be concerned about empty American churches, not packed Soviet churches. The delegation later learned that Father Theopan had laughed about the stories he had told the Americans and called them ''Western idiots.''

In the months ahead we can expect considerable debate within both the Protestant and the Orthodox worlds as to who is best suited to take advantage of the openings of the present moment: those with a history of subservience or those who are fresh faces on the scene and are willing to push for more independence. This struggle will occur within the registered church bodies as well as between the large registered groups and the autonomous or un-registered alternatives.

On Implementing Legal Guarantees of Freedom of Religion

The official Soviet position is that it is a criminal offense to ''refuse to give a citizen a job or to admit him to an educational establishment, to dismiss him from work or expel him from an educational establishment, to deprive him of benefits or advantages laid done by the law, or impose other significant restrictions on citizens' rights because of religious attitudes.''[6]

Surely there is some comfort to be taken from such a direct and uncom-promising defense of believers' rights. This is what we have come to expect from the Gorbachev era. But the statement does not date to the era of *glasnost* at all. It is a resolution from the Russian Soviet Federated Socialist Republic's Supreme Soviet Presidium, issued some nineteen years before Gorbachev took power (March 1966).

The existence of this resolution and similar constitutional guarantees did not prevent the systematic and widespread violation of every guarantee listed. And during the Gorbachev era, significant evidence exists that in many parts of the USSR the rhetoric of legal guarantees has not been matched by the reality of religious freedom.

A believer from Novgorod wrote to the editors of *Izvestiia* in early March 1989 to complain that what believers in Leningrad and Moscow are allowed, believers in the provinces are not. In his case, he was dismissed from his duties as a teacher for reading his Bible during lunch break. He decided to abandon a career in education.

A high official in the Council for Religious Affairs responded with a frank admission that the CRA itself receives similar letters. He conceded that for years ''obstacles have secretly been placed in the way of believers,'' resulting in them being treated as ''second-class citizens.'' He assured the former teacher that such discrimination ought not to occur because legal guarantees are in place to protect him.[7]

But religious *perestroika* is going to have to come to terms with precisely this great discrepancy between paper guarantees and concrete realities.

GLASNOST HAS NOT BEEN TRANSLATED INTO GERMAN

Ethnic Germans in the Soviet Union have experienced little of *glasnost*. Indeed for many Westerners it is a great surprise to discover there are significant German communities in the Soviet Union.

Since the time of Catherine the Great in the second half of the eighteenth century there have been sizable German-speaking communities in what is now the Soviet Union. As many as 1.4 million Germans may have been living in the Soviet Union at the time Hitler attacked in June 1941. Between August and October of that year over 650,000 Germans were deported to Siberia and Central Asia from the autonomous Republic of the Germans of the Volga and from other German settlements in the Caucasus and southern Ukraine. An additional 250,000 would eventually follow them into involuntary exile. The communities also have Baltic and Polish deportees.[8]

Of the German deportees, 60 percent are Lutheran, 30 percent Catholic, and the rest Mennonites and Baptists. There are many unregistered Catholic religious groups, since the authorities are rarely willing to approve of their priests.

Glasnost is not faring well in the hinterlands. In anticipation of foreign German guests in 1988, German-speaking religious groups in Central Asia were summoned and told by the Council for Religious Affairs: "You know what you have to say: that you are fine and that *perestroika* is going well." The religious leaders were to discourage contact with the religious community members, and after the guests left, the leaders had to render a full report on all that had occurred.

When the foreign guests met with the CRA in Dushanbe (Tadzhikistan), there was the all-too-familiar litany of lies long associated with the CRA in the pre-Gorbachev period. Although the Latvian Catholic Church is recognized to have authority over the Catholic communities outside of the Baltic states, until recently visits to them have rarely been allowed.

The continuing problem for the German ethnic communities in the Soviet Union is a major factor in their large emigration to West Germany in recent years.

HARASSMENT OF UKRAINIAN CATHOLICS CONTINUES

In Ukraine, as in Lithuania, religion and nationalism are often inseparable. This is why the authorities have continued to lash out at independent religion in Ukraine for fear that it could become an even more powerful focal point of resistance to continued Soviet hegemony in that region. Approximately four million Ukrainian Catholics and over half of the existing Russian Orthodox Churches are located in Ukraine.[9] The problem is that many of these

"Russian" Orthodox churches in Ukraine would prefer to be either Ukrainian Catholic or Ukrainian Orthodox.

The Ukrainian Catholic Church has six bishops, several hundred priests, approximately a thousand parishes (located in apartments and houses), an underground seminary, and a publication—*The Chronicle of the Catholic Church in Ukraine.*[10]

Pope John Paul II is committed to the "catacomb" Ukrainian Catholic Church. Within the Soviet Union, prominent non-Catholic human rights activists such as Alexander Ogorodnikov, Father Georgy Edelshtein, and Vladimir Poresh have called for the legalization of the Catholic Church in Ukraine. In early June 1988 Andrei Sakharov threw his prestige behind the campaign, noting that it was long overdue to end the "archaic" ban on the Ukrainian Catholic Church.[11] And Ukrainian Catholics themselves have become more bold since informing Gorbachev and the pope in August 1987 that they intended to emerge from the underground and exist openly in public life.

If Kharchev's views (discussed in the previous chapter) are implemented, unregistered "house" churches, whether they seek registration or not, would immediately cease to be illegal. This ought to mean their pastors and the hosts of the meetings should cease being fined. However, Ukrainian Catholics, Pentecostals, and Baptists have continued to suffer this tangible discrimination at the very time Kharchev has talked of greater liberalization.

Bohdan Bociurkiw, the prominent Canadian specialist on Ukraine, believes that in the summer of 1988, Moscow authorities yielded to pressure from hard-liners in the Ukrainian Communist party, the KGB, and the Russian Orthodox hierarchy, and decided, at least for the time being, against legalization of the Ukrainian Catholic Church.[12]

In some ways the situation with fines has worsened. It used to be that the host and/or the pastor of an unregistered religious service held in a private home would be fined fifty roubles. But thanks to a new Gorbachev-era decree, the fines can be much higher.

In July 1988 the Presidium of the Supreme Soviet issued a decree "On the Procedure for Organizing and Holding Meetings, Rallies, Street Processions and Demonstrations in the USSR." It was immediately feared that the authorities might apply this to unregistered believer meetings, and indeed the next day a Ukrainian Catholic priest was told the new decree covered unregistered liturgies.[13]

Ivan Hel' of L'vov (Lviv), one of the leaders of the illegal Ukrainian Catholics, reported that when church services in July 1988 attracted several thousand people, the authorities decided to take action. Services were physically broken up, rural residents were prevented from reaching villages where services were scheduled, and large fines were levied. First offenders were assessed a fine of 300 roubles ($480) and as much as 1,000 roubles ($1,600) for a second infraction. In addition, there were arrests of leaders in August.[14]

The Orthodox Christmas Day masses on January 7, 1989 were prevented in seven villages in Ukraine. At the same time, one of the prominent leaders of the Ukrainian Catholic Church, Bishop Pavlo Vasylyk, informed Western correspondents of a new wave of repression directed against the Ukrainian Catholics, which included fines of up to two hundred roubles and fifteen-day prison sentences for priests who celebrated unsanctioned masses.[15]

In March 1989 Ukrainian Catholic priest Mykhailo Volshyn was sentenced to a six-month army detail for taking part in an unsanctioned requiem service in L'vov in February.[16]

Early in 1989, Bishop Vasylyk sent a disturbing letter to Archbishop Theodore E. MacCarrick of the United States describing the great pressure exerted by the Russian Orthodox Church, the State, the KGB, and the militia on the Ukrainian Catholics. He reports the seizure of their churches, fines, and fifteen-day jail terms. Then he notes:

> One can justifiably say that our government is playing a dual game: one for export—full of smiles, demagogic declarations about democratization, the signing of documents in the field of human rights—while domestically there is a brutal persecution of Ukrainian Catholics under the guise of *perestroika* and *glasnost*.[17]

The extreme conservatism of the political leaders of the Ukrainian Republic and their hostility toward Gorbachev accentuates the problems for believers there. A joke is told about Vladimir Shcherbitsky, the Party leader in Ukraine, which expresses well the attitude of the old guard toward recent changes.

Shcherbitsky goes to the barbershop for a haircut, and his barber launches into a discussion of *glasnost*. The Party boss quickly changes the topic. Three weeks later he is back for a trim, and once again the barber raises the issue of *glasnost*. Irritated, Shcherbitsky steers the conversation in another direction. A month later Shcherbitsky returns, and sure enough, the barber begins to praise the changes in Moscow. Exasperated, the politician flies into a rage. "Why do you keep bringing this topic up? You know I can't stand *glasnost*!" "Of course I know," replies the barber. "But it makes your hair stand on end, which makes my job much easier."

Unfortunately for Christians in Ukraine, especially unregistered Catholics and Protestants, the reactionary character of the local leadership is no laughing matter. An increase in Church registrations in Ukraine is not a sign of *glasnost* for Ukrainian Catholics. So long as the Ukrainian Catholics are not a recognized religious group, registrations of Russian Orthodox Churches may be simply another way the local authorities are suppressing the Catholics by forcing them to register as a Russian Orthodox community or taking their buildings over and turning them into registered Orthodox communities. Simultaneous with this increased registration of "Russian" Orthodox parishes has been a clampdown on nonregistered Ukrainian Catholic groups.[18]

To make matters worse, the new June 1988 Church Statute returning administrative parish authority to the local priest is only a positive change in those places where the priest really represents his parish. But in many parishes in Ukraine (particularly the western part), the new Statute actually makes it easier for a newly registered "Russian" Orthodox parish to resist the pressure of a congregation which would prefer to be Catholic. This situation arises because the newly registered Orthodox parishes have often been hastily organized by the secular authorities in collusion with the Russian Orthodox Church to displace existing Ukrainian Catholic communities.

Other factors related to registration must also be considered. Periods of increased registrations in the past have often been done to gain more effective control over the Christian communities.[19]

In January 1989 Stepan Khmara, one of the activists pressing for legalization of the Ukrainian Catholic Church, was arrested. As in the previous December, he was sentenced to fifteen days in jail. On this occasion, his wife and daughter were distressed to overhear a police official attempting to secure a medical diagnosis that would permit them to incarcerate Khmara in a psychiatric hospital.[20]

In the non-Russian republics it is difficult to know where the religious freedom issue leaves off and political nationalism takes over. They are often inextricably mixed. But one thing is certain: Khmara's outspoken call for legalization of the Ukrainian Catholic Church is much resented.

CAMPAIGN FOR A UKRAINIAN AUTOCEPHALOUS ORTHODOX CHURCH

An independent Orthodox Church existed in Ukraine for approximately a decade after the Bolshevik Revolution. But at the end of the twenties Stalin had it forcibly swallowed up by the Russian Orthodox Church. Sentiment against this involuntary incorporation has long existed, but in recent years has become more vocal. In the 1970s Father Vasyl' Romanyuk called for the creation of an independent Orthodox Church, but he did so from prison.

In February 1989 the formation of the Initiative Committee for the Restoration of the Ukrainian Autocephalous Orthodox Church was announced. The founding members proclaimed that the Russian Orthodox Church "is not capable of satisfying the needs of Ukrainian Orthodox believers."[21]

An unusually courageous statement was made by Father Bohdan Mykhailechko at a Ukrainian Language Society conference less than a week before the Initiative Committee's formation was announced.

. . . instead of conducting ecumenical work in the world, the Russian

Orthodox Church fights against the Ukrainian Catholic Church and the Ukrainian Autocephalous Orthodox Church, which exists in the underground. We do not see in this an expression love.[22]

Less than a week later church authorities forced Mykhailechko to sign a statement giving up all his pastoral duties.

As the founders of the Initiative Committee put it in their inaugural declaration: "We want, like all civilized people, to communicate with God in our own native language."[23] There is little chance that religious *perestroika* will respond favorably to this new plea for independence. This is not what Gorbachev means by "democratization," nor is the Russian Orthodox Church anxious to lose over half its parishes.[24]

HARASSMENT OF UNREGISTERED BAPTISTS CONTINUES

In May 1988 an analyst for Radio Free Europe gave this grim assessment of conditions for unregistered believers in the Soviet Union:

> The situation of "unregistered" religious groups . . . has not improved in recent years. The policy of harassment adopted by the Soviet state several decades ago continues to be applied with full force.[25]

Though there have been some remarkable signs of progress in certain areas, this analyst accurately notes that much remains distressingly the same.

The July 1988 decree on demonstrations has been used as a weapon against the Baptists, just as it has been against the Ukrainian Catholics. The first known instance of this took place in early September in the unregistered church in Listopadovo (125 miles south of Kiev). The church had been registered until 1986 when local officials revoked its registration and confiscated the church building because its members did not cooperate closely enough with the authorities.

Later, local militia broke up a church service meeting in a private home and threatened the owner of the house with a fine of one thousand roubles. Young people who continued to sing while the police dispersed those present were threatened with fines of up to three hundred roubles. (The average salary in the USSR is about two hundred roubles a month.)[26]

Thus the 1988 Gorbachev-era decree is considerably harder on believers than the earlier regulations which stipulated more modest fines.

The authorities harassed unregistered Baptists in at least twenty different locations during 1988. They broke up services, destroyed meeting houses, levied heavy fines, and attempted to recruit informers. In February local authorities destroyed the home of a believer in Tashkent (Uzbekistan) who hosted religious services, and in June the same fate was inflicted on the new meeting place. (The same thing happened to a meeting house in Odessa in December 1987, and the destruction began even while a service was in progress.)[27] A tent used for meetings in Rostov on the Don was ordered torn down. A summer children's camp in Shakhty, a few miles from Rostov, was forcibly broken up twice and the children sent home. In July the authorities disrupted a baptismal service in the Prut River near Chernovtsy (southwestern Ukraine). The next day in Bryansk (two hundred miles southwest of Moscow) authorities went to a service at a new convert's home, confiscated religious literature, took the young people to the police station, and handed out fines. A persistent question was: "Do you belong to the CEBC or the AUCECB?"[28] Their refusal to be a part of the latter, the registered group, angered the authorities.

In 1988 in Svetlogorsk (Belorussia), Baptists held a testimony meeting in a public park. As a result two believers were fined one hundred roubles each. Keston College has reports of fines occurring in many other cities as well.[29]

While Kharchev assured Soviets and foreigners alike that religious *perestroika* was fully underway and the ways of the past were over, 1988 ended on a very different note in Fergana (Central Asia). There on December 4, sixty Christians gathered for a baptism when thirty militia (both uniformed and in street clothes) rushed in, broke up the service, took the leaders to the police station, and threatened those present with fines ranging from three hundred to one thousand roubles. All of this was done in accordance with the 1988 decree on registering demonstrations and gatherings.

In Vinnitsa, about 115 miles southwest of Kiev, the authorities have resorted to more drastic tactics. The Mashnitsky family has been fined almost two thousand roubles for holding services in their home. The services have continued up to the present even while members of the family were in prison. By September 1988, unidentified persons had thrown explosives into the house seven different times. It is not difficult to understand why the unregistered are more skeptical about *glasnost* than the registered.

But even the unregistered acknowledge some changes. As of mid-December 1988, all Baptist prisoners had been released from labor camps or exile. Unregistered Baptists in Kiev in the spring of 1988 told me that though the authorities still kept them under surveillance, for the time being they were doing little to interfere with their activities. When our visit together ended and I emerged onto the nearly empty suburban street, a car with four men in it immediately drove away from in front of the house. The Baptists just smiled. They were used to this.

HARASSMENT OF UNREGISTERED PENTECOSTALS CONTINUES

Unregistered Pentecostals have also faced continued persecution and discrimination during the era of religious *perestroika*. Like the Baptists, the Pentecostals are divided into three different groups. A relatively small number are part of the All-Union Council of Evangelical Christians-Baptists. Shatrov, their leader, is not trusted by large groups of Soviet Pentecostals. There are a large number of autonomously registered Pentecostal groups, and there is a significant group of unregistered, most of them in the Moscow fellowship (which includes the Baltic and other areas of the USSR as well) headed by Bishop Ivan Fedotov.[30]

It is difficult to determine the number of Pentecostals in the USSR, but estimates range between 500,000 and 700,000.[31] Unlike the Baptists, a much larger group are unregistered or independently registered than are registered with the AUCECB.

The West learned much about the Pentecostal situation during the Siberian Seven drama. In fact, the quest for emigration had begun in the early 1960s. The protracted attempt of the Chuguyevka community on the Pacific Coast to emigrate during the 1980s also captured some publicity among foreign observers.

One of the most intolerant cities in which Pentecostals have lived is Nakhodka, not far from Vladivostok. Members of the unregistered communities in this Far Eastern city have endured over eighty trials and have served a collective time in labor camp or exile of 350 years. Seven have died during imprisonment.[32]

One of the most unusual documents to have surfaced during the Gorbachev era comes from Nakhodka. Unregistered Pentecostals in that city managed to obtain an official document passed by the City Council which outlined specific actions planned against four unregistered Pentecostal congregations and groups of unregistered Jehovah's Witnesses and Seventh Day Adventists. Dated October 6, 1987, the document explains that it contains "measures to regulate the network of religious associations, to curtail the activities of religious extremists and to increase educational work with believers within the city of Nakhodka for the years 1987-89."[33]

According to the document, during 1988 the Nakhodka City Council was to sponsor a city-wide seminar with lectures on atheism. In 1988 and 1989 special attention was to be paid to atheist education in the schools where children of believers were studying. Steps were to be taken to "eliminate religious influence on students from believing families." Educational work was to be stepped up in the places of work where believers were employed. A "thorough study" was called for in 1988 of all the unregistered congregations in order "to register them or to curtail their activities."

One of the best known Pentecostal figures of Nakhodka is Boris Perchatkin. At the age of twenty-three Perchatkin felt called by God to help Pentecostals who sought to leave the USSR. In 1976 he became acquainted with human rights activists Yuri Orlov, Anatoly Sharansky, and Alexander Ginzburg. Twenty times between 1970 and 1980, Perchatkin covered the 13,000-mile round trip between his home town and Moscow. Despite threats from the authorities, he documented and sent to the West information on the repression of believers.[34]

In 1980 Perchatkin was elected Secretary of the Moscow-based all-union unregistered Pentecostal group led by Bishop Fedotov, who had been in prison since the late 1960s and who would not be released until well into the Gorbachev era—after nineteen years in confinement.

In August 1980 it was Perchatkin's turn to go to labor camp. His first stop was the prison in Vladivostok where his grandfather, a Pentecostal minister, had died in 1933. During most of the next five years Perchatkin suffered horrors that many incorrectly think ended with Stalin's death. Beatings and constant threats, both physical and psychological, were a regular occurrence. His mother and wife were also subjected to criminal trials and were under virtual house arrest throughout much of the early Gorbachev era.

Following his release Perchatkin was selected by Fedotov in 1987 to help strengthen contacts with foreign Christians. In early 1988 the KGB summoned Perchatkin and threatened him with a third prison sentence if he did not leave the country. After consulting with Fedotov, it was decided that Perchatkin should emigrate and become their official representative abroad. In late May 1988 Perchatkin found himself in Moscow, one of a number of Soviet dissidents President Reagan had wanted to meet. Sitting next to Nancy Reagan, Perchatkin heard words from the First Lady which must have sounded unbelievable after the lonely, torturous years in labor camp: "You're here [Moscow] because we are worrying about you."

Upon his emigration in late July, Perchatkin soon discovered a bitter truth. Leaders in the Assemblies of God, the largest U.S. Pentecostal denomination, were nervous about contacts with the unregistered, fearing it would harm their relations with the registered Soviet Pentecostals or involve them in politics. They failed to understand that the autonomously registered and the unregistered Pentecostals represented many times more Pentecostals than those with whom they were being so careful to keep contacts. Nor did they seem to understand that it might be possible to maintain relations with all of them. In contrast, the smaller and more independent Pentecostal denominations and groups in the West have been far more willing to become actively involved in helping.[35]

Reports from Pentecostals throughout the Soviet Union during 1988 and into 1989 indicate that they are being fined and on occasion even jailed for a few days for holding unregistered religious gatherings. In addition, Grigory Kushin, editor of an underground Pentecostal religious journal (*Khristianin*), was threatened with violence if he did not cease his activities. In December 1988 he was involved in a serious car accident near Rostov. The threat evidently had been carried out.[36]

In the Vinnitsa region of the Ukraine, 1989 is turning out to be a much rougher year than 1988. Between November 1987 and late 1988 the authorities ceased fining the unregistered Pentecostals and contented themselves with sending regular visitors to their services. This improved situation ended, however, in December 1988 when the fines were renewed; it took a dramatic turn for the worse in mid-February when leaders of the key unregistered churches were called in and warned by the authorities that they would now be fined under the provisions of the July 1988 decree on meetings and demonstrations. Fines for unregistered religious meetings were previously fifty roubles. Now the first fine would be three hundred roubles; the second six hundred; and the third one thousand. A maximum sentence of six months in prison could then be imposed.[37]

This continuing harassment well into the Gorbachev era is a major factor in the desire of many Pentecostals to leave the Soviet Union. In mid-September 1988 a congress of unregistered Pentecostals convened in Khotkovo, just a few miles to the northeast of Moscow. Though the authorities were not happy about the gathering, the more than two hundred Pentecostal delegates from throughout the Soviet Union were allowed to meet. The purpose of the conference was to encourage greater unity among Soviet Pentecostals. A second conference is being planned.

Registered Protestants are not immune to difficulties. At the end of August 1988, registered Pentecostals in Bataisk (near Rostov) were holding a meeting for young people on the outskirts of the city. The meeting was dispersed and the preacher forced to sign a document agreeing not to hold such a meeting in the future.[38]

PROBLEMS IN REGISTERING CHURCHES OR CLOSING EXISTING ONES

A constant concern, which even the Council for Religious Affairs acknowledges, is the continuing difficulties experienced by believers who seek registration. Konstantin Kharchev reported in March 1988 that the CRA had received over three thousand complaints from believers in 1987 alone, mostly related to frustrated attempts to register.[39]

At the end of May 1985, just a couple of months after Gorbachev became general secretary, local authorities demolished a Ukrainian Catholic church in Grabivka. Earlier attempts to close the church had been frustrated by parishioners standing guard round the clock. With the help of the police, however, the State officials finally succeeded. The iconostasis was destroyed, and three trucks hauled away all items of value. Several people were arrested and fined. Several other churches were also closed down in the area during 1987.[40]

Just before the millennium celebrations in June 1988, the Council for Religious Affairs turned down an appeal by fifty-four Orthodox Christians to reopen the Church of the Archangel Michael in a Moscow suburb. The church, it turns out, was close to the Academy of Social Sciences and other higher education institutes. An official of the CRA explained: "If the church was opened, the students would start to visit it. We have no intention of facilitating church attendance by the students."[41]

A good example of the obstacles faced by local believers can be found in Kerch (Crimea). An Orthodox community has been seeking to locate themselves in the unused Church of St. John the Baptist. In May 1988 the regional CRA refused to register the group on the grounds that there were already two active churches in Kerch (a city of over 150,000). The disappointed applicants appealed to Kharchev in Moscow, pointing out that in one of the existing churches alone 4,000 who wish to attend must make do with a chapel that can only seat 150. Moscow failed to overturn the refusal to register, and plans to turn the church into a museum were still underway at the end of the year.[42]

Glasnost has encouraged some to pursue the recovery of their church buildings more energetically. In October 1988, two thousand demonstrators in Batumi called for a local Orthodox church being used as a factory to be turned back over to the Church.[43]

On March 6, 1989, in the Ukrainian city of Rovno, five elderly women carrying icons began a hunger strike in quest of the return of their Orthodox Church which was confiscated in 1962. Currently used as a museum of atheism, the Cathedral of Resurrection has since the strike seen as many as three thousand people and an Orthodox Choir show up on a single day to demonstrate solidarity with the stubborn women.[44]

On March 19, 1989, 300 people gathered in the town square of Ivanovo (150 miles northeast of Moscow) to demand the return of their church. The church was confiscated by the authorities in 1935 and turned into a repository for State archives. Two days later, four women began a hunger strike, and on March 30 the secretary of the town soviet told the strikers, "If there were a God, then we would open the Church, but under the circumstances no one is prepared to open it for you."

A number of students who sought to help the women in the town square were beaten and fined ninety roubles each. On April 1 the women were forcibly hospitalized and fed intravenously. The women's protest attracted the attention of human rights activists elsewhere in the Soviet Union, and they pledged to join the hunger strike. On April 11 the women ended their strike after receiving a promise from the local government head that the fate of their church would be decided within a month.[45]

While the hunger strike in Ivanovo was continuing, authorities bulldozed an unregistered Baptist church in Rostov-on-Don. The Church had been warned in February that if it refused to register, the church building would be destroyed.[46]

PROBLEMS IN OBTAINING RELIGIOUS LITERATURE

Leading Soviet officials and literary figures are now saying that religious literature is no longer considered dangerous and is, in fact, allowed. Actual events do not always bear this out.

Seven days after Gorbachev took power, N. Tolstykh was arrested and sentenced for "anti-Soviet agitation and propaganda." Among the books confiscated from him were a New Testament and a book for children on the Old Testament. When Tolstykh was released in February 1987, he sought to recover his two books, but discovered they had been destroyed. The official reason, according to the head of the Investigative Section of the Leningrad KGB: "They were publications that are prohibited from being brought into the USSR and distributed."[47]

Though Soviet authorities insist that policies governing the availability of religious literature have been greatly liberalized, it is obvious they want to continue controlling access to such literature.

In September 1988 a delegation of almost one hundred Roman Catholic priests and parishioners from West Germany visited leaders of the Ukrainian Catholic Church, whose existence the Soviets refuse to recognize as lawful. The German Catholics brought three hundred Bibles to give to their fellow believers. Shortly after the delegation left the Soviet Union, Council for Religious Affairs' officials arrived at Archbishop Serniuk's home in L'vov and forced him to sign a statement "donating" the Bibles to the Council. In all, the CRA was able to confiscate one-third of the Bibles.[48]

On November 14, 1988 the militia intercepted a consignment of eighty thousand copies of John's Gospel, which had been produced by the clandestine Protestant press of *Khristianin*. One person arrested was later released, but the confiscated Gospels were not.[49]

Though officially the ban on bringing in religious literature has been lifted, word of this has not always reached the borders. Russian Orthodox Christian Vladimir Ryabokon found this out the hard way on December 18, 1988 when he returned to the Soviet Union after visiting Paris. Among the many books confiscated by border authorities in Brest were twenty Bibles with concordances, ten New Testaments, and six illustrated Bibles for children. When the frustrated Ryabokon reminded the customs agent of assurances published in *Izvestiia* on November 15, 1988 that the ban on religious literature had been abolished, the Brest official responded:

> They write lots of things in *Izvestiia,* and how can you tell how much it can be believed? All I know is that I have my orders from my boss, and I'm carrying them out. And in any case, you ought to be grateful that you can ask—three years ago I was the only one who would have been asking questions here, not you. . . . I'm all for *glasnost* and *perestroika* and democratization, but there are still plenty of class enemies around—you know who I mean—and we mustn't relax our vigilance.[50]

The attempt to control information has deprived the public of access to copy machines until recently. Around January 1989, however, two photocopy shops opened in Moscow. Unfortunately the requirement that they not print anything "anti-Soviet" rules out much religious literature. When Alexander Ogorodnikov sought to use the new establishments to print his *Christian Community Bulletin,* he was refused. On April 14, Soviet customs officials confiscated a printing machine being brought to Ogorodnikov by an English priest. The machine was to be used for producing the *Christian Community Bulletin.*[51]

COOPERATIVES NOT PERMITTED TO PRODUCE RELIGIOUS GOODS

In June 1988 a new law opened up the possibility of more private business in the Soviet Union. However, in December 1988 the USSR Council of Ministers passed a decree containing restrictions on what the Gorbachev-instituted private cooperatives may manufacture. On the forbidden list are "the production and restoration of icons, objects used in religious worship, articles with religious symbolism and attribution." Candles may be produced so long as they are for secular and not religious use.[52]

RELIGIOUS PRISONERS OF CONSCIENCE

There has been some discussion of how pacifists or conscientious objectors will be treated in the era of Gorbachev. Kharchev has spoken approvingly of the alternative, nonmilitary service permitted under Lenin. And on June 13, 1988 the deputy director of the USSR Institute of State and Law said in London that discontinuing criminal prosecutions of conscientious objectors was under consideration. The Council for Religious Affairs' draft of the new Law on Freedom of Conscience may allow for a court to permit alternative service for someone who refuses to bear arms.

However, in 1987, 1988, and 1989 the majority of new religious prisoners were prosecuted for their refusal to serve in the military. For example, Mikhail Karmanov, a Jehovah's Witness from near Krasnoiarsk, was sentenced in early November 1988 to three years in labor camp. Authorities placed a request in a local Zagorsk (near Moscow) newspaper seeking information on a young Orthodox Christian who had refused military service on the grounds of his religious convictions.[53]

In March 1989, Vasyl Prizhok was sentenced to two years of labor camp for refusing to serve in the military. Earlier in 1989 Alexander Timchuk was arrested and charged with desertion from the Soviet army for leaving a psychiatric hospital in which he had been confined by military authorities. While in the army, he was persecuted for his faith. Both men are Pentecostals from western Ukraine.[54]

In late March 1989, Amnesty International reported that the USSR still commits sane dissidents to mental institutions, but Western criticism has cut the number of such occurrences. Amnesty also said that reforms in Soviet psychiatry have not been effectively implemented.[55]

THE SLANDER OF BELIEVERS CONTINUES

In spite of marked improvement in the treatment of believers in the press, there are still graphic signs that the politics of government slander and intimidation are utilized in the Gorbachev era.

The State's venom has been particularly aimed at Alexander Ogorodnikov, one of the leading Russian Orthodox dissidents. Raised by committed Communists, Ogorodnikov did not come to faith until he was an adult. The emptiness of atheist materialism drove him to the deep wells of Russian religious thought to find meaning. A key factor in Ogorodnikov's coming to God was seeing the Italian film *The Life of Christ According to the Gospel of Matthew*. Pasolini's film overwhelmed him with the truth of the Gospel. His appetite whetted for religious truth, Ogorodnikov threw himself into a study of late nineteenth- and twentieth-century figures such as Dostoevsky, Berdyaev, and Florovsky.[56]

Reasons for the State's ire against Ogorodnikov are not hard to come by. As a well-educated former Marxist committed to spreading the faith, he is an ever-present reminder of the failure of the official Soviet ideology to inspire and hold on to its young. In 1974, at the age of thirty-four, Ogorodnikov and his friend Vladimir Poresh founded the Christian Seminar. Deliberately emulating earlier religio-philosophical circles of the pre-Revolutionary period, intellectuals from several major Soviet cities formed a nucleus of spiritual vitality—a vitality new converts often could not find in the timid official Church with its severely restrained religious activities.

The intimidation and persecution of Christian Seminar members was fierce beginning in 1976. They lost their jobs, were subjected to surveillance and arbitrary searches, and were sent to labor camp. Ogorodnikov was arrested and condemned to labor camp in 1978 for parasitism, anti-Soviet agitation, and propaganda. He suffered greatly while in confinement, deprived of the two things he treasured most on this earth: the opportunity to read and write. He had an indomitable will and at one point maintained a modified hunger strike for two years. He was finally released in 1987.[57]

It has long been Soviet policy to coerce religious figures to recant.[58] This was still going on in 1986. In April of that year, Boris Razveyev, a Russian Orthodox Church member of the Christian Seminar (earlier imprisoned for participating in private religious discussion groups and one of Ogorodnikov's friends) denounced his own "anti-Soviet" behavior and made the absurd charge that Ogorodnikov was a rapist and a sexual pervert. The slander was later repeated on national television. The KGB had circulated these allegations since Ogorodnikov's first arrest in 1978.

The timing of the Razveyev recantation was clearly orchestrated by the Soviet authorities. Five days before, Ogorodnikov had been sentenced to three additional years in prison for allegedly breaking camp regulations. (This tactic of resentencing represents a insidious form of oppression since prisoners can be held indefinitely regardless of the original sentence.)[59]

But surely this sort of public slander has ended several years into *glasnost*. In fact, it has not. The KGB pressured dissidents and intellectuals into writing fourteen derogatory letters against Ogorodnikov which were published in *Krokodil, Pravda,* and *Izvestiia* during July and August 1988. Capitalizing on the pain of his wife divorcing him when he refused her demands to emigrate, the Soviet authorities have sought to convince foreigners that Ogorodnikov wishes to break all contacts with Westerners. This is not true, and he is as committed as ever to freeing the Orthodox Church from its subservience to the State.[60]

The Soviet press in the Gorbachev era has slandered other unregistered religious groups. In September 1986 Pentecostal leaders were charged with "holding children in a deadly grip" and "adding narcotic substances to believers' food." Unregistered Baptists who were on trial in March 1987 were pilloried by the press as "ringleaders of schismatics," "obscurantists," and "parasites." And in Estonia late in 1987, it was charged that the activities of Jehovah's Witnesses were incited by foreign contacts.[61]

EDUCATIONAL, ECONOMIC, AND POLITICAL DISCRIMINATION

Both before and during *glasnost* the official position has been that believers have not and are not discriminated against. But as the Soviets are now admitting, Christians have been "second-class citizens" in many ways and only achieved that ranking by cooperating with the authorities in agreeing to restrict their religious activities and register with the government.

Though important officials and the press have made assuring statements that this discrimination is part of the past, to date no major evidence that the situation has tangibly changed has reached the West. Mark Elliott's 1989 assessment needs to be kept clearly in view:

> Perhaps the greatest single disability facing Christians in the USSR today is the ongoing, widespread, and systematic exclusion of them from higher education and preferred employment. Party membership, entailing an atheist oath, is a route to economic and social advancement not open to Christians.[62]

CONCLUSION

The Russian Empire before the Revolution and the Soviet Union after has always been a land of contradictions and anomalies. The one who dares examine it is a bit like the blindfolded Indian boy who thought he had felt four different animals when he touched an elephant's trunk, ear, tusk, and leg.

In assessing the meaning, depth, and breadth of *glasnost,* it is necessary that we take into account all the available data, both positive and negative, about the conditions of believers in the Soviet Union.

Of course, whether religious liberty expands or contracts in the Soviet Union depends in part on whether *glasnost* and *perestroika* can be sustained and expanded. It is to that topic that we now turn our attention.

Notes

1. Vladimir Shibaev, *Russkaya Mysl', La Pensée Russe* (Russian Thought), Paris, 29 April 1988; English translation printed in *Samizdat Bulletin*, San Mateo, Calif., no. 180 (Winter 1988), 14.

2. Quoted in the ELTA Information Bulletin, Washington, D.C., no. 3 (363), March 1989, 16.

3. Shibaev, *Russian Thought*, 12.

4. Ibid., 16.

5. For further information on Yakunin, see the end of chapter 8. Details on the role of Ogorodnikov and Poresh in founding in the 1970s the important Christian Seminar are discussed at the end of this chapter, in the section dealing with continuing problems with slander.

6. "Editor's Mailbag," *Izvestiia*, 9 March 1989, as quoted in Foreign Broadcast Information Service SOV-89-056, 24 March 1989, 79.

7. *Izvestiia*, 9 March 1989, in FBIS, 24 March 1989, 79.

8. Information on the ethnic Germans is taken from Gerd Stricker, "Little *Glasnost* Beyond the Urals," *30 Days*, San Francisco, no. 7, November 1988, 35-37.

9. Bohdan Nahaylo, "Ukrainian Catholic Issue Overshadows Start of Moscow Patriarchate's Millennial Celebrations," Religious Liberty 230/88, 6 June 1988, 6. The chairman of the Ukrainian Supreme Soviet Presidium stated in the middle of 1988 that there were 4,022 Russian Orthodox Churches in the Ukraine. (News from Ukraine, no. 26, June 1988.)

10. "Press Conference of the Representatives of the Committee for the Defence of the Ukrainian Catholic Church," 22 December 1987, in *Occasional Papers on Religion in Eastern Europe*, vol. 9, no. 1, February 1989, 43.

11. Nahaylo, "Ukrainian Catholic Issue," 1-5.

12. Bohdan R. Bociurkiw (Carleton University, Ottawa), "Gorbachev's Religious and Nationality Policies in Ukraine" (Unpublished paper delivered in Rome at an international conference on "Ukraine: A Negated Nation," 3 March 1989), 18. Tangible evidence of the hardening of the policy against this large illegal church can be found at the end of 1988 when the Ukrainian Communist Party Central Committee journal attacked the Vatican for working to support the Ukrainian Catholics (Bociurkiw, 19).

13. *USSR News Brief*, Munich, 31 July 1988, 5, 9-10. The full text of the decree can be found in *Current Digest of the Soviet Press*, vol. 40, no. 30 (1988), 15.

14. Bohdan Nahaylo, "Lvov Authorities Resort to Old Methods in Breaking Up Unauthorized Meetings and Religious Services," Radio Liberty 355/88, 13 August 1988, 3.

15. "Harassment of Ukrainian Catholics," *Keston News Service (KNS)*, no. 319, 16 February 1989, 4.

16. *KNS*, no. 322, 30 March 1989, 17.

17. Letter from Bishop Pavlo Vasylyk to Archbishop Theodore E. MacCarrick (Newark, N. J.), 7-8 February 1989. Used by permission of the Ukrainian Congress Committee of America.

18. *KNS*, no. 319, 16 February 1989, 3-4.

19. See the section on reopenings and registrations of churches in the previous chapter for more information on the possible implications of church registrations.

20. "Ukrainian Catholic Activist Detained," *KNS*, no. 319, 16 February 1989, 2-3.

21. Bohdan Nahaylo, "Initiative Group for Restoration of Ukrainian Autocephalous Orthodox Church Founded," *Report on the USSR*, Radio Liberty, vol. 1, no. 9, 3 March 1989, 24.

22. Ibid., 26.

23. Quoted in ibid., 26-27.

24. For more information on this topic see Frank E. Sysyn, "The Ukrainian Orthodox Question in the USSR," Millennium Series, Harvard University Ukrainian Studies Fund, 1988.

25. Oxana Antic, "Unofficial Religious Groups in USSR are Vilified in Press, Harassed by Officials," *Soviet East European Report*, RFE/RL, vol 5, no. 22, 1 May 1988, 1.

26. *KNS*, no. 311, 20 October 1988, 6; no. 322, 30 March 1989, 7.

27. *USSR News Brief*, 31 July 1988, 12.

28. *Prisoner Bulletin*, International Representation for the Council of Evangelical Baptist Churches of the Soviet Union, Winter/Spring 1989, 25-27. Unless otherwise indicated, reports on the unregistered Baptists come from this source.

29. *KNS*, no. 321, 16 March 1989, 5.

30. Boris Perchatkin, personal interviews from August 1988 to April 1989. Perchatkin emigrated from the USSR in July 1988. He lives in West Springfield, Massachusetts, and heads up the Slavic Refugee Relief Committee which seeks to help both those Pentecostals who remain in the USSR and those who emigrate.

31. Michael Rowe of Keston College puts the number at about half a million (telephone interview, 19 April 1989), while Boris Perchatkin estimates closer to 700,000 (testimony before the Commission on Security and Cooperation in Europe, Washington, D.C., 4 August 1988, 1).

32. Perchatkin testimony before the Commission on Security and Cooperation in Europe, 1.

33. In the fall of 1988, I was given a copy of both the original Russian and an English translation of the document by Perchatkin.

34. Biographical data supplied by Perchatkin in late 1988.

35. Though I have noted that the present Assemblies of God leadership is "somewhat nervous" about contacts with other than registered Pentecostals, there may be more openness in the late 1980s to expanding their Soviet Pentecostal contacts.

36. Numerous personal conversations with Perchatkin. I have been supplied with copies of the notifications of fines and other documents related to the continuing problems of Pentecostals in the USSR.

37. *KNS*, no. 322, 7.

38. Letter from a Soviet Christian to Congressman Frank Wolf, received 8 November 1988.

39. Oxana Antic, "Increase in Number of Orthodox Parishes," *Report on the USSR*, Radio Liberty, vol. 1, no. 2, 13 January 1989, 8.

40. "Chronicle," *Glasnost*, English edition of nos. 7-9, November 1987, 73; *USSR News Brief*, no. 14, 31 July 1988, 5.

41. Quoted in *Break Through*, September-October 1988.

42. *KNS*, no. 315, 15 December 1988, 7-8.

43. "Georgian Demonstrations Reported," Radio Liberty 485/88, 4 November 1988, 13.

44. *KNS*, no. 322, 3.

45. Keston College fax service, "Hunger Strike for Return of Russian Orthodox Church," 22 March 1989; "Protest Widens Against Refusal to Hand Back Russian Orthodox Church," 3 April 1989; *KNS*, no. 322, 30 March 1989, 3; Vera Tolz, *Report on the USSR*, vol. 1, no. 16, 21 April 1989, 38-39.

46. Keston fax service, "Soviets Demolish Church in Rostov," 5 April 1989.

47. N. Tolsykh, "The New Testament in the Incinerator of the KGB," 9 October 1987, in *Glasnost*, no. 12 (1987), 24-25.

48. *KNS*, no. 310, 6 October 1988, 5.

49. *KNS*, no. 317, 19 January 1989, 16.

50. *KNS*, no. 316, 5 January 1989, 5.

51. *KNS*, no. 321, 16; no. 324, 27 April 1989, 4-5.

52. *KNS*, no. 316.

53. *KNS*, no. 303, 23 June 1988, 7-8; no. 316, 14.

54. *KNS*, no 324, 7-8.

55. Vera Tolz, *Report on the USSR*, vol. 1, no. 14, 7 April 1989, 40.

56. Information on Ogorodnikov, unless otherwise indicated, is from Jane Ellis, *The Russian Orthodox Church: A Contemporary History* (Bloomington: Indiana University Press, 1986), 381-88.

57. James Scherer, "Interviews with Soviet Religious Officials and Dissidents," *Occasional Papers on Religion in Eastern Europe*, vol. 9, no. 2, April 1989, 33.

58. See the beginning of chapter 8 for an account of the sad story of Father Dudko.

59. The Razveyev/Ogorodnikov affair was covered in the Soviet press in *Trud* (Labor), 8 July 1986, and in *Zaria Vostoka* (Dawn of the East), 4 July 1986.

60. Scherer, "Interviews," 33-34.

61. "Unofficial Religious Groups Vilified," 1.

62. Mark Elliott, "Church and State under Gorbachev: What has Continued? What has Changed?," *World Perspectives, News Network International*, vol. 2, no. 4, 14 April 1989, 2.

CHAPTER 17

ON PYRAMIDS AND PARTHENONS:

Reflections on the Future of *Glasnost* and *Perestroika*

... the Soviet system is made up of massive, heavy blocks. It is well suited to the suppression of human freedom, but not to revealing, nourishing and stimulating it. On the whole, it resembles an Egyptian pyramid built out of colossal stones, carefully assembled and ground to fit together. ...

Can you rebuild a pyramid into the Parthenon? The ancient Egyptian pyramids are rightly considered the most enduring of architectural forms—much more durable and solid than the Parthenon. And the legitimate question arises: Do pyramids lend themselves to *perestroika*?[1]

These haunting words are those of Andrei Sinyavsky, one of the most famous dissidents of the early Brezhnev era. After fifteen years of living in the West, in early 1989 he was allowed to return to the Soviet Union for five days following the death of his good friend and fellow dissident Yuly Daniel.

Sinyavsky was struck by the changes he observed. Clearly there was less fear and people talked far more openly than in the past. But the shadow of the KGB was still ever present, and he could not shake a basic skepticism that past problems were a long way from being solved. As Sinyavsky put it, it is "a lot easier to print Boris Pasternak's novel *Doctor Zhivago* than to produce salami. And if there's no salami, little by little *glasnost* will die away as well."[2]

Without doubting Gorbachev's sincerity, Sinyavsky still believes the general secretary can best be understood as a pragmatist, not a liberal. As for the political changes, the Russian emigre points to a sobering reality. "Democracy is being introduced by order of the authorities, who at any moment can expand it or restrict it at will."[3]

A number of questions are fundamental to any serious reflection on the future of reforms in the Soviet Union. Can democracy mandated from above be truly secure? Is economic recovery compatible with the continuance of Marxist communism? And of particular importance for believers, can communism genuinely disengage itself from militant atheism?

ARE COMMUNISM AND DEMOCRACY COMPATIBLE?

Gorbachev, like previous Soviet leaders, has often preferred to talk of "socialism" rather than "communism." This has caused considerable confusion in the West, where Scandinavian brands of "socialism" seem quite harmless.

But it is critical that we sharply distinguish between the "socialism" of Sweden and that which has evolved in the Soviet Union. The former is close to what is generally understood as capitalism, and allows for considerable individual, political, and economic freedom. The latter may call itself "socialist," but it is sufficiently different that we ought to use a different term to describe it. Communism is the traditional term to describe Marxist socialism in action.

Gorbachev seeks to connect the notion that "socialism and democracy are indivisible" with Vladimir Lenin. Western socialism (or rather capitalism with a generous "social net" policy for dealing with the unemployed, the aged, and the disadvantaged) is indeed compatible with democracy, but communism has not yet proven its ability to coexist with democracy.

Gorbachev's hero is a perfect case in point. The general secretary makes no mention in his book on *perestroika* of how Lenin dealt with democracy when he had the opportunity. In all the history of the Soviet Union there has been only one multi-party national democratic election—a few weeks after the Bolsheviks took power in October 1917. Despite Lenin's strong reservations, the election (which had been scheduled by the Provisional government before the Bolsheviks took over) was held and did not give the Bolsheviks the largest number of delegates.[4]

How did Lenin respond to this disturbing development? On January 4, 1918, the day before the Constituent Assembly was to have its first meeting, Lenin joked: "Since we made the mistake of promising the world that this talk shop would meet, we have to open it up today, but history has not yet said a word about when we will shut it down."[5] When the Constituent Assembly would not go along with what Lenin wanted, he simply refused to let it meet the next day. It was Lenin who abruptly ended the Bolsheviks' one-day experiment with democracy.

So when Gorbachev asserts that for Lenin "socialism and democracy are indivisible," there is some cause for concern. The true test of one's commitment to democracy is whether one allows to stand a people's decision at variance with the Party line.

The test for Gorbachev's commitment to democratization will be whether he allows rival political parties to form and the will of the people to prevail if they reject certain sacred economic or political tenets of communism. Thus far, Gorbachev has given no serious indication that democratization would be allowed to go this far.

In a remarkable week in April 1989, just a day after an unprecedented Gorbachev-engineered loss of power by almost one-quarter of the Central Committee's more conservative members, a whole series of statements were made demonstrating just how much resistance there still is to genuine democracy. Bemoaning the decline of Party prestige and influence during the Gorbachev years, and the rise of independent political groups and publications, one speaker warned that the nation was in danger of losing its immunity to "ideological AIDS."[6] Though the most strident speeches came from those who were soundly defeated in elections a few weeks before, there can be little doubt that Gorbachev is as nervous about the proliferation of independent groups as are the conservatives.

On February 10, 1989, a *Pravda* editorial expressed concern that among the estimated sixty thousand independent groups which recently have sprung up in the Soviet Union, were many which "under cover of democratization, *glasnost,* and national self-assertion" overtly criticize the Soviet system.[7]

To the extent that full democracy really is important for unleashing the economic and moral resources of a population, interference with its development can only frustrate and impede the ultimate success of *perestroika.* In other words, if democratization is not allowed to develop, *perestroika* may well flounder. If genuine democracy is allowed to evolve, communism as we have known it will cease to exist.

Although Communist revolutionaries have often talked about the "will of the people" and egalitarianism, the record conclusively demonstrates that they do not believe the masses know what is best for them. Marx and Lenin looked down on the vast majority of the population—the peasantry—considering them to be hopelessly conservative or reactionary. It was the proletariat, the urban workers (and even here, only the socially-conscious workers) who were slated in theory to lead the revolution. And in the Bolshevik version of Marxist social democracy, a small, elite party was expected to lead. Marxists have never really trusted the world's poor to know how to make themselves happy.

In 1978 a Communist party member from Moscow State University explained to me that if the people were given a choice "they would go back to capitalism, and we can't have that." Will Gorbachev really let the people decide what sort of economic and political system they want? If his public and written statements are accurate, the answer is no. When he talks of democracy, he means choosing between candidates committed to a Communist program firmly set at essential points.

If, however, Gorbachev subsequently proves capable of valuing democracy above that of protecting the ideological mainstays of communism, then Soviet society can be expected to evolve in ways yielding greater and greater religious freedom. But if democracy runs into an immovable ideological stone wall, previous gains in religious liberty may be endangered.

HOW FUNDAMENTAL ARE THE ECONOMIC REFORMS?

There is the view that [perestroika] has been necessitated by the disastrous state of the Soviet economy and that it signifies disenchantment with socialism and a crisis for its ideals and ultimate goals. Nothing could be further from the truth. . . .

Those who hope that we shall move away from the socialist path will be greatly disappointed. Every part of our program of perestroika— and the program as a whole, for that matter—is fully based on the principle of more socialism and more democracy.[8]

Or to put it as the skeptical Vladimir Bukovsky does, "Gorbachev does not want to change the system; he wants to save it, together with his skin."[9] If Gorbachev's words are sincere and not motivated by the need to pacify conservatives at home, then the ultimate success of perestroika on the economic front is in grave jeopardy.

In sorting through the commentary concerning perestroika, the reader invariably runs into a wall of confusion. On the one hand, Gorbachev says that although the Soviet economy is in considerable trouble and has been stagnating since the late 1970s, perestroika is aimed at perfecting socialism, not replacing it.

On the other hand, many Western commentators insist the Soviet economy is in terrible shape and its problems are directly tied to its fundamental economic structures. Jean-Francois Revel, for example, goes so far as to declare that "the socialist economy is everywhere in a state of collapse."[10] (What the French writer has in mind would be better termed "communism," as explained above.)

An absolutely critical question in all this is whether Gorbachev and the Soviets are willing to face openly the most basic and profound issue of all: Is communism (Marxist-Leninist socialism) itself really the core of the problem? Revel gets to the heart of the matter:

. . . Communist leaders go on affirming that socialism itself remains blameless and all-good. But how is it, then, that from a principle so satisfactory there have evolved nothing but execrable results? Initiatives like Gorbachev's have always been undertaken in the name of the "true" socialism and against the false. Then how is it, again, that even by the testimony of its partisans, there has never been anything but false socialism?

This potentially would lead *glasnost* to a depth that Gorbachev has shown no willingness to approach.

> And what if the so-called false socialism should turn out to be identical with the true? A terrible question—but real *glasnost* will not have come about until the contradiction is acknowledged and somehow overcome.[11]

The French newspaper *Le Monde* once summarized Soviet reform efforts and potential as including greatly increasing the autonomy of economic enterprises, revamping management structures nationally, overturning the whole Soviet system of planning, moving toward greater democracy as a means of achieving economic reforms. At one point the French paper went so far as to assert: "One cannot minimize the scope of this reform. By every available measure, it is without doubt of the first importance."

The French reporting in question, however, is not about the second half of the 1980s under Gorbachev. It is about the first few months of Brezhnev's regime twenty years earlier.[12] To be sure, Brezhnev did not implement such changes, but the point is that it is not unique to talk about the problems of centralization, lack of incentives, and the need for basic reforms. Many Soviet leaders have done so, but none have been willing to use the sharp knife of analysis on their most sacred beliefs. At least in rhetoric, Gorbachev, too, has sought to keep certain sacred cows out of the public discussion: Marx, Lenin, socialism, and communism.

Thus far, the Chinese have shown themselves somewhat more willing than the most senior Soviet officials to depart from recent past. But even here, there has been strong reluctance to acknowledge the possible source of their problems. Zhao Ziyang, general secretary of the Communist party, has commented:

> We intend to take everything that is good from foreigners, to be inspired by it and to absorb it . . . but the basis of our regime remains and will remain socialism.[13]

If, to save face, Communist leaders implement capitalist techniques and simply call them advanced socialism, that is one thing; but if they do not understand the empirical advantages to incentive-driven, market-driven economic forces, and they simply play around the edges at basic changes, the fundamental restructuring so desperately necessary for economic and social recovery will remain as elusive as ever.

In light of this, the words of Revel are well worth considering.

> . . . the only real way to reform socialism is to shake free of it. So long as Communist rulers insist on restructuring the system *in order to save it,* they are on a false trail.[14]

Revel compares trying to mix socialism and competition with attempts to drive a boat up a tree or a bicycle across the ocean.[15] Until Gorbachev shows a greater sense of the fundamental tension between the economic dogmas of communism and the measures it would take to cure the ills such dogma spawns, there is little hope *perestroika* can succeed.

So far, the impact of *perestroika* on the Soviet economy has been disappointing. After an initial growth of 4 percent in the 1986 economy, the rate dropped significantly the next year and was only 1.5 percent in 1988. Living standards not only have failed to improve, but in some ways have gotten worse. The rationing of sugar began in Moscow in May 1989. Gorbachev has responded by slowing the pace of his economic reforms, including delaying plans to deregulate retail prices at least until 1992.[16]

The basic question is whether Gorbachev really has the desire or the will to make the kind of changes required to revive the economy. In the view of the well-known Soviet dissident Yuri Orlov,

> . . . removing the food deficit and the notorious inefficiency of both agriculture and industry requires more than the half-measures currently proposed under *perestroika*. It requires a virtual renunciation of party control over the economy and a significant expansion of the scope and influence of the free market.[17]

A Soviet joke well illustrates this problem. But first, remember that in Russian, *perestroika* means both "to restructure" and "to rebuild." This gives the joke more punch in the original.

Stalin, Khrushchev, Brezhnev, and Gorbachev all end up outside the Pearly Gates at the same time. Stalin, in a fit of honesty, confesses to St. Peter: "I must admit, I really did not build anything solid during my years as leader." Khrushchev, also overcome by a desire to tell the truth, says, "I, too, did not build anything during my time as general secretary." Brezhnev, without a moment's hesitation, chimes in: "I certainly built nothing."

Before Gorbachev can open his mouth, St. Peter turns to him and demands: "Then what in the world did you *re*build?"

Reform is not needed, for that implies something solid to return to; what is needed is revolution. It doesn't matter what the Soviet leaders choose to call it, whether capitalist or socialist. Whatever the name, it had better be closer to what fuels the Western countries than what is behind the failed experiments of the Soviet Union since the Bolshevik Revolution. Otherwise, economic breakthroughs will remain nothing but dreams.

ECONOMIC *PERESTROIKA* AND RELIGIOUS FREEDOM

Is there a connection between *perestroika* and religious freedom? Definitely.

If a strong economic system evolves in the Soviet Union, it will be because the Communist party has decided to allow *significant* decentralization of the economy. Such a shift will not only break the Party's monopoly on the wealth of the country, but its monopoly on power and ideas as well.

Such a revolutionary move towards pluralism, if buttressed by structural changes in the legal system making it difficult to reassert unitary control, would create the conditions necessary for religious freedom to flower.

CAN ATHEISM BE DISENGAGED FROM COMMUNISM?

This is a critical question to which there is no easy answer. If one takes seriously what Karl Marx, Vladimir Lenin, Joseph Stalin, Nikita Khrushchev, and Leonid Brezhnev repeatedly said, atheism is not an optional belief for true communists. It is an absolutely essential tenet of their worldview.

It is essential because a religious orientation fundamentally threatens the classical Marxist notion that human beings are the masters of their own fates and the creators of their own values. In the Soviet context, religion is a practical threat because to the degree genuine religion exists, there remains an obstacle to absolute State power. Totalitarianism is incompatible with genuinely independent religion.

Certainly the Church can be "useful" to a secular Marxist state. It can be a focal point of nationalism and patriotism during war. If properly domesticated and controlled, it can even provide good and sober workers. It can function as a major arm of disinformation, hiding, for example, the degree to which religion is not free.

But genuinely independent religion is always a threat to an atheist state.

In order for religious freedom to be secure in the Soviet Union, for the improvements under *glasnost* to remain, there must be a fundamental and public renunciation of all antireligious elements. There must be a commitment to genuine separation of Church and State—the Church should not dictate policy to the State, nor should the State interfere with the internal affairs of the Church. Nor should the State disallow religious involvement in its affairs. Like any other citizen, a religious citizen must have the right to elect officials and be elected to public office. There must be fundamental, legal, and constitutional guarantees of religious freedom.

If this state of affairs came into being, atheistic communism as we have known it would no longer exist. A socialist state, with a wider "social net" even than those currently found in the West, might take its place. But such a state would not represent a threat to religious liberty. It might not function well economically, but its failings would not constrain it to interfere with religious freedom.

Full religious freedom will not be secure in the Soviet Union until the antireligious (not necessarily atheist) pretensions of Marxism are abandoned. There may need to be a transitional phase where the antireligious (or atheist) points continue to be rhetorically affirmed, while the practice of hostility to religion is quietly laid to rest. But there will be danger until the rhetoric from top to bottom in the Communist party, from Moscow to Vladivostok, formally matches the behavior which to date is only found in certain places within the Soviet Union.

The struggle between the ideology of atheism and the existence of religion is much more deadly and basic than the empirical discussion over what works economically. The *perestroika* debate about the latter is not sufficient to deal with the former.

Anyone who thinks that men's minds can be changed simply by making a convincing case regarding the superiority of one form of economic organization over another, has not studied history. The compelling case against collectivized agriculture has been known in the Soviet Union for many years; private plots are many times more productive than their collectivist counterparts, yet there has been a systematic refusal by the Party to dismantle collectivization. Ideology is much more powerful than we often imagine. Fidelity to a particular ideology for helping the masses can be much stronger than fidelity to the masses themselves.

When it comes to the struggle between a religious world view and a secular one, more is going on than meets the eye. For the uncommitted person, belief systems are like clothes put on and off at will; it really doesn't much matter what one wears. But Christians have always believed more was at stake then just a struggle between human beings. As St. Paul expressed it:

> . . . our struggle is not against flesh and blood, but against the rulers, against the authorities, against the powers of this dark world and against the spiritual forces of evil in the heavenly realms.[18]

To look deep into the well of Christian suffering during the last seventy years in the Soviet Union is not to encounter a "disagreement" between reasonable people about the proper relationship between Church and State. It is to come face to face with forces not of the human dimension. Such sentiments are not fashionable in the sophisticated analyses of the present century, but then the evils wrought by Hitler and Stalin soar beyond our pathetic human attempts at comprehension.

This is no simplistic attempt to turn the Soviet Union into an "evil empire." Rather, it is a recognition that forces of evil do manifest themselves in a compulsive antireligious form of atheism. You don't argue someone out of such hostility by talking about the benefits to society which a religious person offers. At this level, the hostility springs from one thing and one thing only: a hatred of everything connected with the notion of a sovereign, divine being.

But of course, there is another possible scenario. What if Mikhail

Gorbachev is not an atheist at all? What if he is, in some sense, a believer? "Preposterous idea!" many will exclaim—but it is a possibility getting some play in the press. Is there any justification for it?

It is well known that Gorbachev's mother is a fervent Russian Orthodox believer, and it has long been rumored that Gorbachev himself may have been baptized as an infant. His grandparents on his father's side are said to have hidden religious icons behind pictures of Lenin and Stalin hanging on the wall.

According to Mark Helprin in the *Wall Street Journal*, Larry Speakes, press secretary to former President Reagan, comes very close to asserting that Gorbachev told Reagan he was, in fact, a believer.[19] Further evidence that Gorbachev may believe in God is taken from some of his public statements. In 1985, Gorbachev told *Time*, "surely, God on high has not refused to give us enough wisdom to find ways to bring us an improvement in our relations." After beginning his first American visit, Gorbachev commented to former Secretary of State George Shultz: "The visit has begun, so let us hope. May God help us."[20]

Skeptics, of course, have good grounds for suspicion. If Gorbachev is a secret believer, he has had to lie about it in Party circles for decades. Nor can I forget one of Khrushchev's offhand remarks: "Thank God I'm an atheist." The colloquial reference to God in exclamations, whether in the Soviet Union or in the West, tells us little about the speaker's ultimate belief about a divine being.

On the other hand, what Gorbachev truly believes may be considerably more than the skeptics think is possible. And if he is not, in fact, a doctrinaire atheist, he may be less inclined to moral relativism and belief in the perfectibility of human beings than his classical Marxist predecessors. He seems to have few illusions about how difficult it will be for the Soviet Union to get back on track. "This is the edge of the abyss," Gorbachev commented when describing the strength of his opponents. "One more step and it's the abyss." As Helprin concluded, "Given the correlation of forces, it may be a task fit only for a believer."[21]

Even if it turns out Gorbachev is not a secret believer, Jews and Christians have long believed that in the providence of God, nonbelievers can be used to fulfill God's will. The example of the Persian king Cyrus may offer an interesting parallel to the contemporary Soviet situation. At least such a possibility should not be ruled out.

And even if Gorbachev is neither a closet believer nor a King Cyrus, it is still possible that *perestroika* and *glasnost* may unleash forces able to challenge the grip of atheism on the ideology of the ruling party of the Soviet Union. That, in any event, must be the prayer of the religious communities.

THE LANDMINE OF NATIONALISM

An irreconcilable conflict exists between democratization and the maintenance of the Soviet Union as we have known it. The USSR is not a country in the twentieth-century sense of the term; it is an empire made up of many subject nationalities who greatly resent their absorption into the USSR.

The Baltic states were all independent countries between the World Wars; Ukraine has always coveted its fleeting moments of independence; and the Caucasian and Central Asian republics do not appreciate Russian hegemony, either. The problem comes when these groups interpret Gorbachev's rhetoric regarding democratization as a signal to express more independence. Few doubt that expressions of independence will continue to explode into demands for autonomy. This is what Gorbachev's critics on the Right have long argued, and they may be right.

What will Gorbachev do? It may prove impossible to both honor the pledge to democratize—to allow the people to decide their own fate—and to continue the empire. If the empire dissolves or breaks apart, religious liberty may expand. If, however, there is a backlash against the expression of non-Russian nationalism, religious liberty in outlying republics will decrease.

But there is another possible scenario. Narrow Russian chauvinists may connect Gorbachev's policies with nationalist unrest. According to Bohdan Bociurkiw, a prominent authority on religion in Ukraine,

> . . . it is not impossible that the threatening disintegration of the Soviet empire may force the Gorbachev regime—in order to counter a conservative Russian nationalist backlash against *glasnost* and *perestroika*—to seek the good will of the so-called "extreme nationalists" supporting Gorbachevite political reforms in Ukraine; should this happen, legalization of the Ukrainian Catholic—on terms analogous to those applied to the Roman Catholic Church in Lithuania—would be a logical concession to West Ukrainians and a policy much more consistent with Gorbachev's stated objectives than the continuation of the Stalinist repression of the Uniates [Ukrainian Catholics].[22]

Some fear that Gorbachev will compromise with Russian nationalists bent on not losing the empire before he will make broad concessions to the nationalities. However, the June 1, 1989 decision of the Congress of People's Deputies to set up a commission of inquiry into the 1940 annexations of the Baltic states is unprecedented and was supported by the general secretary.

What makes the matter so complicated is the mixture of nationalist and religious motivations. In Eastern Europe and in the Soviet Republics, loyalty to the dominant religion of one's native area may genuinely reflect religious conviction, but it is also likely to be a tangible expression of nationalism as well. On the other hand, clamping down on a nationalist religious group may be motivated as much by political considerations than by atheistic ones.

Events in April 1989 are a sober reminder that a crackdown on nationalist dissidents may be ahead. For many months, human rights activists had been looking forward to changes in the criminal code that would replace Articles 70 and 190-1 (of the Russian republic's criminal code). These clauses dealt with the crimes of anti-Soviet agitation, illegal propaganda, and slandering the Soviet state.

On April 8, the Presidium of the USSR Supreme Soviet issued a decree amending the 1958 law "On Criminal Liability for Crimes Against the State." Though Soviet commentators have sought to argue that the new regulations do not make private criticism of the State illegal, the wording is ambiguous enough to raise concerns. For example, Article 7 is concerned with "calls for the overthrow or alteration of the Soviet State and social system" by means not in conformity with the Constitution.[23] If the point of this article is really to deal with violent calls for overthrow of the government, why is the word "violent" missing? It would appear the door is left open for labeling "illegal" even those statements which do not call for violence.

Article 11 of the new decree deals with "insulting or defaming state bodies or public organizations" and "infringement of national or racial equality." To the degree that those campaigning for greater religious freedom in the non-Russian republics are perceived to be agitating for increased independence of the republics, the new decrees may be applied. Sentences of three to ten years in prison are stipulated in the decree. Organizing, receiving financial aid from abroad, and disseminating materials considered to violate the new decree are punishable by long jail sentences—in some cases longer than what the previous law allowed.

On April 11, *Pravda* charged that law enforcement bodies are failing to do their duty in dealing with those who violate the laws against "anti-Soviet" behavior. In particular, the Party newspaper criticized activists in Armenia, Azerbaijan, the Baltic Republics, Moldavia, and Georgia for masking their illegal behavior under cover of support for *perestroika*.[24]

There is no more explosive issue Mikhail Gorbachev must face than that of nationalism. And just as in the issues involving the economy, there is no certainty that Gorbachev understands how this time bomb can be defused. Bohdan Nahaylo's analysis here is instructive.

> Mr. Gorbachev himself now acknowledges that the success of *perestroika* depends on the solution of the national question, but he is still avoiding grappling with the root of the matter. The longer he continues to pretend that harmony would prevail in the "common Soviet fatherland" if not for those "nationalist" trouble-makers, the more serious the national problem is likely to become.[25]

Glasnost in the religious sphere has frequently had a much tougher time in the provinces than in the Russian centers precisely because of this complicating factor of nationalism. Religious freedom will definitely be affected by this tug of war between nationalism and democratization.

MARXISM: A SACRED COW NO LONGER

We still adhere to Marxist theory, but much of this theory should be adjusted because many of the conclusions of Marx have failed to stand the test of time.[26]

What is particularly startling about these words is their source. They belong to Oleg Bogomolov, the director of the Institute of the Economics of the World Socialist System, and they were spoken on February 8, 1989 at a press conference of the Soviet Foreign Ministry.

Bogomolov also asserted that the USSR's decision to ban private property had undermined the farmer's concern for the land. He predicted that changes in Soviet law would legalize family farms and allow the farmer to select his own crops and sell them at market value. He also conceded that "the Stalinist system . . . was imposed on other countries," and he suggested that the time had come for each country to find its own way to recover from the damage done.[27]

Other scholars from this important Soviet economics think tank have gone even further than their director. Alexander Tsipko, an expert on socialism, in a four-part article published in *Science and Life* asserts that the roots of Stalin's purges ought to be sought in the Bolshevik terror immediately following the October Revolution. He charges that it is the flaws of Marxist theory which produced Stalinism.[28]

Tsipko even goes so far as to contend that Marxist attacks on the marketplace inevitably result in "totalitarianism, in the violation of the rights and dignity of individuals, and in the creation of an omnipotent administrative and bureaucratic apparatus."[29] Tsipko ridicules the position long maintained by moderates and liberals in the Soviet Union (and the West) that the problem with Stalin was simply the methods he used to achieve worthwhile ends. According to this Soviet scholar, Stalin was no aberration from Marxism; his hostility to the individual, independent peasant was basic to classical Marxism. Then Tsipko poses the question which many thought could never appear in print in the USSR: Was collectivism even a good idea?

When the ideas about the goals of socialism are wrong . . . if they contradict the laws of normal civil life, it is useless to argue about the pace or methods by which they are achieved. When you are dealing with an unrealistic goal, it does not matter whether you try to achieve it by cavalry methods or gradually—the result will be the same.[30]

A revealing measure of the depth of *glasnost* will be whether Tsipko's trailblazing analysis will be allowed to continue. Just a few years ago the expression of such ideas was considered "anti-Soviet slander," and could have resulted in an extended period in labor camp.

CONCLUSION

A number of serious issues will have to be resolved before *glasnost* and *perestroika* become permanent features on the Soviet landscape.

Democratic institutions must be allowed to undermine the power base of the Communist party and to set up institutional and structural guarantees protecting inalienable human rights.

Economic rethinking must be allowed to question the fundamentals of Marxist and Communist economic creeds, and fresh ideas must be given an opportunity to unleash the creativity and power of the Soviet people.

The continuation of *glasnost* and *perestroika* depends in part on granting the non-Russian republics either independence or meaningful autonomy within a truly federal system. If this does not occur, then religious freedom (to say nothing of political freedom) of non-Russians will be in great jeopardy.

And finally, before religion can ever be secure, antireligious ideology must be publicly and firmly renounced as incompatible with a progressive, socially just, modern Soviet State. This means nothing less than a conscious and public departure from the convictions of the German and Russian founders of Marxist communism.

Notes

1. Andrei Sinyavsky, "Would I Move Back?," *Time*, 10 April 1989, 129.

2. Ibid., 132.

3. Ibid.

4. Mikhail Heller and Aleksandr Nekrich, *Utopia in Power: The History of the Soviet Union from 1917 to the Present* (New York: Summit Books, 1986), 47.

5. Quoted in ibid.

6. Michael Dobbs, "Gorbachev Purges Central Committee," *Washington Post*, 26 April 1989; David Remnick, "Soviet Party Chiefs' Speeches Show Anxieties," *Washington Post*, 28 April 1989.

7. Vera Tolz, *Report on the USSR*, vol. 1, no. 7, 17 February 1989, 38-39.

8. Mikhail Gorbachev, *Perestroika: New Thinking for Our Country and the World*, updated ed. (New York: Harper and Row, 1988), xii, 23.

9. Vladimir Bukovksy, "Reforms Will be Reversed," in *Perestroika: How New is Gorbachev's New Thinking?* (Washington, D.C.: Ethics and Public Policy Center, 1989), 217.

10. Jean-Francois Revel, "Is Communism Reversible?" *Commentary*, January 1989, 18.

11. Ibid., 19.

12. Ibid., 20. The *Le Monde* articles in question date to 1964 and 1965.

13. Quoted in Revel, "Is Communism Reversible?" 21.

14. Ibid., 20-21.

15. Ibid., 21.

16. Don Oberdorfer, "Snags Hit Gorbachev Economics," *Washington Post*, 23 April 1989; Francis X. Clines, "Moscow Rations Sugar, a First Since '45," *New York Times*, 13 April 1989; Martin Feldstein, "Why *Perestroika* Isn't Happening," *Wall Street Journal*, 21 April 1989.

17. Yuri Orlov, "The Meaning of Gorbachev's Reforms," in *Reform and Human Rights: The Gorbachev Record*, report to the U.S. Congress by the Commission on Security and Cooperation in Europe, May 1988, 87.

18. Ephesians 6:12 (New International Version).

19. Mark Helpren, "The Russian Reformation," *Wall Street Journal*, 28 April 1989.

20. Quoted in ibid.

21. Ibid.

22. Bohdan R. Bociurkiw (Carleton University, Ottawa), "Gorbachev's Religious and Nationality Policies in Ukraine" (Unpublished paper delivered in Rome at an international conference on "Ukraine: A Negated Nation," 3 March 1989), 22.

23. Keston Fax service, "New Articles of Soviet Criminal Law: A Blow Against *Glasnost*?" 19 April 1989, 1; Vera Tolz, *Report on the USSR*, vol. 1, no. 16, 21 April 1989, 39-40.

24. Tolz, *Report on the USSR*, 21 April 1989, 38.

25. Bohdan Nahaylo, "Soviet Nationalities in Gorbachev's Blind Spot," *Wall Street Journal*, 24 April 1989. In November 1989 Nahaylo's book *Soviet Disunion* is scheduled for publication in London by Hamish-Hamilton.

26. Quoted in Tolz, *Report on the USSR*, 17 February 1989, 34.

27. Ibid.

28. Vera Tolz, "Soviet Scholar Sees Roots of Stalinism in Bolsheviks' Terror and Marxist Theory," *Report on the USSR*, vol. 1, no. 8, 24 February 1989, 1. Tsipko's multi-part article appeared in *Nauka i zhizn'*, nos. 11 and 12 (1988); nos. 1-2 (1989). Tsipko has repeated his central points in *Nedelia Week*, no. 11. Further information is available here on Tsipko's career and his ideas. See Tolz, *Report on the USSR*, vol. 1, no. 14, 7 April 1989, 33.

29. Tolz, *Report on the USSR*, 24 February 1989, 2. The connection Tolz makes between a market economy and human rights is remarkably similar to that advanced by Peter Berger and Michael Novak. See Berger, *The Capitalist Revolution* (New York: Basic Books, Inc., Publishers, 1986) and Novak, *The Spirit of Democratic Capitalism* (New York: Simon & Schuster Publication, 1982).

30. Quoted in Tolz, *Report on the USSR*, 24 February 1989, 3.

CHAPTER 18

A CHRISTIAN RESPONSE TO *GLASNOST*

*I*n the Vatican hangs a well-known sixteenth-century painting by Raphael titled *School of Athens*. The work depicts both the "other world" and "this world" sides of Greek philosophy. Plato stands pointing to the heavens, while the practical Aristotle gestures towards the earth as if cautioning those present not to forget the ground on which they stand.

In a very real sense, it is that sort of "both/and" attitude that Christians ought to have about recent developments in the Soviet Union. It is a time to utilize fully both our hearts and our heads. It is a time to both rejoice and to be sober. To do either to the exclusion of the other is to badly misunderstand the dynamic of this moment—and in so doing, fail to understand the opportunities to be grasped.

On the one hand, there are tangible signs of positive change for believers: releases from labor camp and exile; greater availability of religious literature; the opportunity to contribute to society in the form of charity; wonderful, new possibilities for evangelization; the possibility of legally organizing religious education for children; a new, more open, positive attitude toward religion in the Soviet press and literature; the promise of more liberal laws and regulations dealing with religious organizations; and a generally more lenient attitude toward believers by the authorities.

On the other hand, serious problems remain: foremost of these, the liberalizations of *glasnost* have yet to be enshrined in legal structures and institutional guarantees such that future leaders would be compelled to respect the rights of believers. Juridical statutes on the rights of believers will not be secure until they exist within a genuinely democratic context—that is, one which has real political checks and balances and separation of powers. The Soviet Union need not emulate Western forms of democracy, but it will have to find a way to obtain the essential feature: a genuine dispersal of power among the people and among the diverse non-governmental groups within Soviet society.

Practice has yet to fully conform with rhetoric. Many Soviet commentators have acknowledged this fact. Throughout the Gorbachev era there have been many accounts of continued problems: fines and short jail sentences for holding unregistered religious gatherings, as well as longer sentences for refusing to serve in the military; interference with the reception, printing, and spread of religious literature; and a continuing harassment of some unregistered religious activities. To be sure, these problems have been less serious than in the past. But for certain groups and in certain parts of the USSR, the warm winds of *glasnost* have yet to melt the icy past.

Western experts on the Soviets, including many religious ones, are quick to point out some of the more obvious reasons for the changes they see. Kremlin pragmatists recognize that a more open society is necessary to revitalize a stagnant economy. Antireligious activities are unnecessary, waste State resources, antagonize some of the best workers in the Soviet Union, and irritate Western world opinion at a time when the USSR is in particular need of foreign investment and good will. Believers in the Soviet Union are needed: They provide a model of moral life—good marriages, honesty, and a means of dealing with drug and alcohol problems.

But while we analyze these changes in the Soviet Union and ponder the likely economic and political causes of a more liberal environment, we run the risk of missing a key point. As one Canadian evangelist has put it: "*God* is behind *glasnost* and *perestroika*. The people in the Soviet Union are waking up from the opiate of atheism and are turning to God."[1]

Although we ought not to declare a full-fledged religious revival in the USSR, the signs of response by the Soviet people to the gospel are unmistakable. In religious terms, *glasnost* must be understood, in part, as "repentance." Indeed, that is the title of the major *glasnost*-era Soviet film.

In the fall of 1988, in the city of Rostov on the Don River in southern Russia, a man approached an evangelist and pleaded for forgiveness. The Pentecostal preacher, Joseph Bondarenko, did not understand what the man was talking about. Then the stranger reached into his pocket and pulled out his KGB identification: "I am the one who put you behind bars. Please forgive me!"

At another service, a young man came forward, accepted Christ, then turned to the congregation and made the following remarkable statement: "I am the editor of an atheist paper. People, I have been deceiving you. Please forgive me. God *is* real!"[2]

It should be obvious that millions of Soviet citizens—reared in an atheist country, unconnected to the Church and without religious convictions—remain unaware and untouched by the several thousand recent conversions. But that is how it has always been in the history of the Church. A committed minority comes to believe and in turn becomes the catalyst for much larger groups coming to know and accept Christian truths.

Even among atheists who show no interest in converting, there is noticeable irritation and boredom with the clumsiness and narrowness of atheism, particularly in its militant forms. Atheist Marxism has had many decades to create a cohesive, committed, "new" society. It has utterly failed to do so. Nationalism is a much more powerful force in all its manifestations than the idea of communism.

But nationalism, particularly non-Russian nationalism, is precisely what may spell the greatest political danger for the continuation of Gorbachev's reforms. It is unlikely Gorbachev would preside over the dismantling of the Soviet empire. But that is what hundreds of thousands, perhaps millions, of Soviet citizens would want in the Baltic states, Ukraine, Georgia, and other republics. They believe Gorbachev's rhetoric of "democratization" must mean "self-determination," or else it is just another version of the worn-out propaganda of the past.

The other reality which could spell the end of Gorbachev is economic. If he really does not grasp how fundamental the economic changes must be (that is, that basic Marxist-Leninist assumptions must be challenged), then economic *perestroika* will not produce enough tangible economic benefits to maintain a support base among the people.

But what do people living in an undemocratic state have to do with who rules the Kremlin? It would be difficult to argue with economic successes which strengthen the country internally, enhance its reputation internationally, and enjoy the enthusiastic support of the population. On the other hand, those who are nervous about Gorbachev's reforms are looking for pretexts to use against him in interparty struggles. Nationalist unrest and economic failure would provide valuable ammunition for Gorbachev's enemies.

Perhaps Gorbachev can work out something with the constituent republics short of total independence, yet involving greater autonomy—a kind of genuinely federal system. And perhaps he understands, or will come to understand, how radical the economic changes must be if he is to unleash the economy. And perhaps Gorbachev, through careful control of political appointments and clever internal alliances, can hold on to power during difficult years when there may be little to show for his policies.

Perhaps. But the West must neither underestimate the obstacles ahead nor rule out the possibility they can be hurdled. Western analysts would be well advised to understand the cyclical nature of Soviet history and the powerful forces which must be neutralized before it can break free.

The Soviet Union today is something like a spaceship circling the earth. From time to time it fires its engines in an attempt to develop sufficient thrust to escape the gravitational pull of earth. But though it occasionally ventures out a few miles beyond its normal orbit, it is invariably drawn back toward the ground.

The challenge of *glasnost* and *perestroika,* from a political and economic standpoint, is to find the power necessary to break out of the orbit of stagnation and repression endemic to Marxist, atheist communism. Part of the tension of the present is that Soviet leadership either will not or cannot fully acknowledge the connection between breaking out of its problems and abandoning the ideological commitments of the past.

The world watches as this dramatic experiment in political and economic liberalization takes place. The final outcome is not known, though it is difficult to imagine that the Soviet Union will not emerge as quite a different entity than it was in 1985 when a new ruler arrived on the scene. Even should the forces of reaction win out, they will likely be unable to put the genie completely back in the bottle.

Soviet power has historically rested on two things: the control of the military and the control of information. Of the two, the latter is at least as dangerous as the former. In recent months there has been an explosion of information illuminating ''blank spots'' in Soviet history, and ''blank spots,'' once filled in, cannot be made blank again. The historical memory of the Soviet people has been publicly altered, and it is beyond the power of the Communist party to restore the earlier picture.

Every day that passes with more information on the loose is a further guarantee that there cannot be a full return to the way things were. That does not mean there cannot be a reaction of considerable proportions; there can. The Soviet people are used to such reversals, and that is why they are considerably more temperate than we in the West when asked to predict the future of *glasnost.*

ADVICE FOR WESTERN CHRISTIANS

In light of the preceding analysis, how ought Western believers respond to this critical moment in Soviet history?

1. We must celebrate the power of God to sustain his people in the Soviet Union for more than seventy years under incredibly difficult circumstances.

Even before *glasnost* the Church was alive and vibrant, though significantly decreased in size from its pre-Soviet period. Indeed, its resiliency was part of what compelled authorities to realize that apart from physically exterminating every believer, there would be no way to rid society of the Church. It is true that parts of the Church have been badly compromised; but even where compromise appears to be the greatest, there are remarkable signs of life. And where compromise failed to gain a foothold, a fresh group of martyrs has gone forth to join those of other times and other places to provide models of faithfulness for future generations.

2. We ought to acknowledge fully the positive changes which have occurred and are occurring.

It is dishonest and counterproductive to allow the bitterness of the past to blind us to the very real changes of *glasnost*. Though some in the Soviet Union see the present changes as little more than a pragmatic necessity until communism can again get on its feet, many others genuinely desire a more free and open society, a society which has no need to persecute or discriminate against religion.

3. We must firmly resist the temptation to enfold ourselves in the euphoria of the present while denying the major problems which remain.

So long as one prisoner is confined for his or her religious commitments, so long as believers are not allowed the full rights of other citizens, so long as full religious freedom is denied, so long as talk continues of "revising" rather than "abolishing" laws regulating religious communities, there is much left to do. So long as the four-million-strong Ukrainian Catholic Church and the millions in the Ukrainian Orthodox Church are not allowed to legally exist, there is cause for protest.

We must never forget that rhetoric is not reality, though it can be an important first step toward achieving it. Those who respond to every statement of the Soviets with a long list of broken promises are only half-correct. Their warnings ought to serve as a check on the many Westerners dazzled by promises of change. But skeptics must understand that much being said by Soviet authorities today would never have even been said in the past. It is hard to see how they could bring themselves to lie about much of this. It is extremely dangerous to make sweeping statements that, in the court of world opinion, may one day prove to be lies. To be shown a liar is much more humiliating than never to have made the promises at all.

Thus, while we must be sober and measure words by deeds, we must realize that words can be an important first step to actions. It is a time to use our heads, not our hearts or our desires. We must do our homework and let the chips fall where they may.

4. Now, more than ever, we must fully support those research institutions which have a track record of providing accurate information on religion in Communist countries.

Places like Keston College in England and the dozens of responsible parachurch mission and information groups which provide millions of people with reliable information deserve our generous support.[3]

The focus of many such groups has already shifted dramatically from the problem of prisoners and their families to describing the remaining problems and the unique opportunities of the present time. Resources are being redirected to tangibly help Christians in the Soviet Union who are starved for religious literature and contact with their co-religionists abroad.

It would be a major tragedy if Western support for these missions and information groups faded precisely at the moment when they are most needed. It would be like returning a kickoff ninety-five yards, then walking off the field five yards short of the goal line. The opportunities available today are unprecedented. Research institutions like Keston College can provide the roadmap, the guidebook, to what help can be given.

5. We must respond generously and quickly to the opportunities now available for helping fellow Christians in the Soviet Union.

While many groups have permission from the Soviet Union to supply large quantities of Bibles, commentaries, and other religious materials, they do not have the funds to print these materials. Christian churches in the Soviet Union have requested and need tape recorders, video equipment, tapes (recorded and blank), and other supplies which would help their ministries. Much of this can be mailed or shipped in under existing Soviet laws.

Given the personal and Church resources of Western Christians, it would be irresponsible not to respond to these opportunities with unusual generosity. Churches and individuals could include in their missions budget groups like Keston College, Slavic Gospel Association, Open Doors, the American Bible Society, and many other fine groups which are working hard to meet these unique needs.

There is no guarantee the present opportunities will long exist. Even if they do last for some time, the possibility of sharing the gospel, of nurturing the Church, is not something we can delay even for a single day. The budgets of the parachurch mission groups—and one would hope the church mission groups—ought to expand dramatically in the coming months.

We Western Christians do not render help because we are spiritually superior, but because we have it within our power to meet real needs. We must pray that out of the vitality of the Soviet Church may come a revival in their society which may in turn touch off a religious reawakening in the Western Church. We, too, exist in a secular society, and our churches are often anemic and apathetic. How many of us would have been faithful had the price of our faith been the persecution and discrimination suffered by fellow believers in the Soviet Union? Most of us would not have mustered the strength to become a member of a registered Church, let alone an unregistered one.

6. We need to expand dramatically our written and personal contact with fellow believers in the Soviet Union.

Never have the opportunities for such contacts been greater. Believers from the West ought to travel to the USSR *and* bring religious literature and other supplies when they go. This can be done legally. In addition to supplying Christians with literature and materials desperately needed and wanted, the fellowship between believers will tremendously help and inspire all concerned. We have much to learn from the vitality and vibrancy of Christians in the Soviet Union.

7. We must reassess critically our past contacts with believers in Soviet Union.

Too often in the past, the Western Church—from ecumenical church organizations right through to evangelicals—has played directly into the hands of the architects of Soviet disinformation. This was surely one of the great Soviet foreign policy successes from the early 1960s on. The Soviets succeeded in silencing Western Christian leaders in ways far exceeding what they were able to accomplish with Western Jews, psychiatrists, scientists, literary figures, and political leaders.

Why did so many Western Christians fail to portray accurately the plight of believers in the Soviet Union? Their motives varied. Some appear really to have believed what they were told by Soviet and Church authorities. Others believed only part of what they were told, but incorrectly assumed that speaking out about problems would endanger their co-religionists in the Soviet Union. Others were more attracted to the foreign policy agenda of the Kremlin than to that of the White House, and their fear of nuclear war kept them silent on human rights violations in Communist countries. Still others maintained silence because they believed this to be the price for opportunities to evangelize Communist areas.

Some Western believers overreacted to this silence and inaccurate reporting by focusing exclusively, and sometimes sensationally or inaccurately, on the plight of the persecuted. It was good, of course, that those ignored or neglected by Western religious leaders should be defended; but it was unfair that any Soviet Christian who was part of the registered Church world should be vilified. While it is true that registered Church leaders frequently misrepresented their situation, it should have been recognized that the situation was exceedingly complex, involving a full spectrum of appropriate and inappropriate Church actions.

There have always been those across denominational lines who have understood the unique problems and challenges of both the registered and the unregistered Churches. There have always been those who were willing, in the same speech, to talk favorably about both groups, about those who felt they must make concessions to the authorities and those who believed they could not. There have always been those who believed it was possible to maintain contacts with both registered and nonregistered, to utilize both public and silent diplomacy in the defense of believers in the USSR. There have always been such people—but there have been far too few, and the views and politics of less balanced approaches have too often set the agenda.

A CALL FOR WESTERN CHRISTIAN UNITY

One consequence of our fallen humanity is that we find it exceedingly difficult to heal past divisions between Christian brothers and sisters.

This is the case in the Soviet Union no less than in the West. Divisions between the registered and the unregistered, between the Russian Orthodox hierarchy and dissidents within that Church, are deep, frequently bitter, and cultivated by Soviet authorities. We ought not to be too quick to judge. The unregistered have felt, quite rightly, that they have often been betrayed and abandoned by their registered counterparts. On the other hand, the registered have frequently felt, quite rightly, slandered and misrepresented by the unregistered. As one registered Baptist told me, "God put Daniel in the lion's den, but he didn't ask him to pull the lion's tail." Time and God will have to sort out the truth on both sides, and I suspect there will prove to be saints (and villains) in both camps.

Part of the healing in the Soviet Church for which we must pray is that forgiveness and reconciliation can restore unity to the Body of Christ.

In the West, we too have our battle scars, and feelings often run deep. Those who believe the conduct of Western religious leaders toward believers in the USSR has been inadequate (and even shameful) have been swift to label such leaders as unwitting accomplices of Communist propaganda. On the other side, those who have confined themselves to the registered world have too often dismissed as political pawns of anti-Communist Western ideology those who have talked more forthrightly about religious repression in the Soviet Union. Goodwill is not often encountered under such circumstances. This book itself reflects a perspective which some will reject.

But as raw and sensitive as are all of our egos, as inclined as each of us is to defend ourselves against unjust and perceived unjust attacks, we must work to put aside our differences and seek a new unity in Christ. As strong as is the temptation to settle old political and religious scores, the opportunities of the present and the call of God compel us to work together in common cause.

There are fine, reflective, and sensitive Christians in *all* Western Christian groups and denominations who are willing to join hands in seeking more effective ways to help our fellow Christians in the USSR. Yes, we do need to deal with the "blank spots" of our own history, our own failings—but more importantly, we need to commit together to do better in the future. We need to do this for two reasons.

First, millions of dollars need to be raised quickly to take advantage of current opportunities. We all hope the doors remain open, but we have no guarantee that they will.

Second, we must learn from our past mistakes so that if *glasnost* does end and a new period of persecution and discrimination begins, we will be a more effective and coordinated Christian community working on behalf of those who suffer. Learning these lessons will serve us well in dealing with all Communist countries; indeed, in dealing with all countries lacking full religious freedom.

We are entering a new phase of Marxist treatment of religion featuring a strong trend toward backing away from frontal attacks on religion. Some believe this represents a fundamental change in attitude toward religion. Others believe it is simply a new tactic to control and co-opt religion for State purposes—and a co-opted, domesticated, and controlled Church is one of the most insidious forms of religious persecution in existence. Given the Western Church's past inability to perceive or deal with direct persecution, there is real cause for concern that we will be unable to handle this more subtle and developed form of discrimination.

All the more reason to utilize this period of *glasnost* to reexamine our own pasts, just as the Soviets are beginning to come to terms with theirs.

CONCLUSION

Westminster Abbey's contribution to the millennium celebrations of the Soviet Union was the world premiere of a new choral work on November 21, 1988. But this was no ordinary performance.

The forty-four-year old British composer, John Tavener, was himself a convert to Russian Orthodoxy. His work, "Akathist of Thanksgiving," was based on a poem written by Archpriest Grigory Petrov shortly before his death in a Siberian prison camp.

Some of Father Petrov's last words are contained in Tavener's hymn of gratitude.

> What is my praise before you? I have not heard the cherubim singing, that is the lot of souls sublime, but I know how nature praises you. In winter I have thought about the whole earth praying quietly to you in the silence of the moon, wrapped around in a mantle of white, sparkling with diamonds of snow. I have seen how the rising sun rejoiced in you, and choirs of birds sang forth glory. I have heard how secretly the forest noises you abroad, how the winds sing, the waters gurgle, how choirs of stars preach of you in serried motion through unending space.[4]

There is no more poignant testimony to the difference between Marxism and Christianity than that a Christian martyr would end his earthly existence in a spirit of praise to God rather than in bitterness towards his oppressor. Indeed, another English writer, G.K. Chesterton, has observed that the origin of theology is gratitude.

Soviet television was on hand to film the final rehearsal, and many members of the Soviet Embassy in London were present for the performance.

For the sake of all Soviet citizens, we must pray that their leaders come to understand fully the truth of Gleb Yakunin's words:

> Religion is like salt which protects humanity from decomposition

and disintegration. Any attempt to banish it from social life invariably leads to a degradation of society.[5]

Indeed, the success of *glasnost* and *perestroika* will depend largely on Soviet leaders coming to terms with the practical consequences of recognizing the fundamental inalienability of religious freedom.

But far more important for the Christian community is what it believes about the faithfulness and ultimate victory of God over anything this world can assemble against his existence or that of his people. As St. Paul put it in Romans:

> Who shall separate us from the love of Christ? Shall trouble or hardship or persecution or famine or nakedness or danger or sword? As it is written: "For your sake we face death all day long; we are considered as sheep to be slaughtered." No, in all these things we are more than conquerors through him who loved us. For I am convinced that neither death nor life, neither angels nor demons, neither the present nor the future, nor any powers, neither height nor depth, nor anything else in all creation, will be able to separate us from the love of God that is in Christ Jesus our Lord.[6]

In the final analysis, the fate of Christians in the Soviet Union depends on God, not Gorbachev or *glasnost*. But in the providence of God, *glasnost* may represent the crude, punched-out windows through which the fresh winds of religious truth may blow into the stale confines of a narrow ideological prison.

May our thankfulness be expressed in deeds, for it is in that unique combination of divine providence and human response that the will of God is done on this earth.

Notes

1. Viktor Hamm, Mennonite Brethren Communications, April 1989 radio commentary.

2. These last two episodes were described in a Viktor Hamm radio commentary in April 1989.

3. See Appendix A for a listing of such groups. Information is also provided on how to mail materials to believers in the Soviet Union.

4. Quoted in Michael Bourdeaux, "A Hymn of Radiant Faith," *Frontier*, March-April 1989, 17.

5. Gleb Yakunin, 30 May 1988, Spasso House (Moscow), as quoted by Warren Zimmermann, speech on religious freedom at the Vienna Conference on Security and Cooperation in Europe, 10 June 1988.

6. Romans 8:35-39 (New International Version).

APPENDICES

WHAT WESTERN CHRISTIANS CAN DO TO HELP

*N*ever during the Soviet period have the opportunities been as great for Christians in the West to help their co-believers in the USSR. This appendix is intended to be a resource guide for responding to this unique, and perhaps only temporary, open door.

There is a serious shortage of religious literature in the Soviet Union. In addition to a tremendous demand for more Bibles in many languages, there is a great need for theological works, training materials for preparing ministers and priests, and religious literature for children. Churches' ministries could also be aided considerably if they had video players, video tapes, computers, religious goods, and audio cassettes. (According to *Izvestiia*, November 15, 1988, tourists may bring in one item each of such equipment duty free; nor is there a limit on the number of trips per year.)

Section I deals with organizational resources. Effective involvement depends on reliable information and a willingness to help in some concrete way. Individuals and churches interested in ministry to the Soviet Union (and Eastern Europe) should subscribe to one or more periodicals provided by several research centers. I particularly recommend *Keston News Service* and other fine publications from Keston College. (Subscriptions to Keston materials can be arranged through Keston, USA—the American affiliate of the English research center.)

Christians also ought to support one or more of the fine parachurch mission organizations which provide support for believers in the USSR. Slavic Gospel Association, Open Doors, and Christian Solidarity

International are three excellent groups involved in supplying religious literature to Christians in the Soviet Union. Other fine mission groups are also listed, though there is not space to list every group involved in ministry to the Soviet Union.

Section II is a guide for providing religious literature and other items to Soviet believers. Some Western Christians may want to send materials directly to the USSR or provide materials in a specific language for a particular denomination. Changes in postal and customs regulations now make it possible to supply legally more literature than at any time in the past. This appendix contains a detailed guide to fifteen different organizations in six countries where materials in a variety of languages can be obtained. There is also information on how to send literature and to whom it can be sent.

Contact with Christians in the USSR is strongly recommended. Section III gives suggestions for writing letters and taking advantage of travel opportunities to the Soviet Union. Churches ought to consider establishing direct contact with a specific church in the Soviet Union. One of the mission organizations could perhaps help facilitate such a relationship.

Section IV is a guide to advocacy on behalf of Soviet Christians. Although the situation for believers is much better in many respects than in years past, some serious problems remain unresolved and old problems could reoccur. To whom should our concerns be expressed? This section provides several dozen government and church addresses which will prove useful for expressing concern about continuing problems or appreciation for problems resolved.

Emigration from the Soviet Union is sharply on the rise. For those who wish to be involved in this ministry, to open their homes and churches to families arriving from the USSR, contacts for further information are provided in Section V.

A number of different levels of involvement are possible. Some will want to write letters, send literature, and travel to the Soviet Union. For others whose time commitments do not allow additional mission activities, financial gifts can be given to those organizations providing information and ministering to Christians in the USSR. Often these groups do not have adequate resources to respond to the growing needs. There ought to be an outpouring of support from churches and Christians in the West.

Finally, we must never forget that human efforts alone are never sufficient for sustaining and supporting the Church. We are ultimately dependent on God and his providential care. We have been instructed to pray daily for one another, and as individuals and as churches we ought to pray for those who suffer for their faith and who have unusual opportunities to proclaim their faith.

I. Organizational Resources

A. *British and American Research Organizations*

Keston College
Heathfield Road
Keston, Kent BR2 6BA
United Kingdom
(0689) 50116

Keston, USA
P. O. Box 1310
Framingham, MA 01701
(617) 247-7071
Exec. Sec.: David Ziomek

General Director: Rev. Michael Bourdeaux

Keston, USA is the American affiliate of Keston College in England, the foremost organization in the world for study of religion in Communist countries. Keston was founded in 1969 by Michael Bourdeaux. Its chief function is "to gather, assess and publish the facts about religious communities of many faiths in Eastern Europe." Keston maintains vast archives recording the experiences and history of believers. It provides up-to-date information through *Keston News Service,* Keston FAX Service, several periodicals, and the publication of books.

Keston News Service is a biweekly news bulletin providing current, comprehensive, and reliable news of religious people and organizations in Communist lands. Subscriptions are available from Keston, USA, for $50 per year.

Religion in Communist Lands (RCL) is Keston's quarterly scholarly journal, containing in-depth analysis of a range of subjects, including Church/State relations and accounts of personal and corporate experiences from believers, often from *samizdat* (unofficial or "self-published" publications). Available from Keston, USA, for $30 per year.

Frontier is Keston's bimonthly popular magazine providing news and commentary on religion in the Communist world. Available for $15 per year.

The Right to Believe is a quarterly newsletter offering updates on Keston activities and focusing on current issues.

Keston FAX Service provides approximately two news releases a week. Available for $125 per year.

Institute for the Study of Christianity and Marxism (ISCM)
Wheaton College
Wheaton, IL 60187
(312) 260-5917

Director: Dr. Mark Elliott

Founded in 1986, the ISCM has a two-fold purpose: (1) to articulate in a variety of forums a clear understanding of the Marxist challenge to faith, (2) to assist ministries and Christians in academia both in comprehending the nature of Marxist Church-State relations and in acting on behalf of Christians in socialist countries. The ISCM is actively involved in formal and informal education and training. It sponsors seminars and tours, produces reference materials, and serves as a consultant and resource for a variety of ministries.

Research Center for Religion and Human Rights in Closed Societies
475 Riverside Drive
New York, NY 10115
(212) 870-2481 or 2440

Executive Director: Blahoslav Hruby

Established in 1962 with support of the National Council of Churches (NCC), the Center was required to become independent in 1972 when the NCC withdrew its financial support. The Center continues to hold conferences and publish information, including its quarterly journal, *Religion in Communist Dominated Areas (RCDA)*. This journal offers analysis of current information on the attitudes and practices of Communist governments toward the life, work, and vital concerns of religious believers. Particular attention is given to the violation of religious freedom and other human rights in all closed societies. *RCDA* is available to individuals for $20 per year ($35 for two years) from the Center.

Freedom House, Inc.
48 East 21st Street
New York, NY 10010
(212) 473-9691

USSR Specialist: Ludmilla Thorne

Freedom House is a forty-six-year-old humanitarian organization that monitors political rights and civil liberties worldwide. Its bimonthly publication, *Freedom-at-Issue,* reports on the freedom and progress of democratic institutions around the world. This is available for $20 per year.

B. *Advocacy Organizations*

1. *The Coalition for Solidarity with Christians in the USSR* was formed in 1987. Its first activity was on May 1 at a rally on the steps of the U.S. Capitol. The rally organizers, thirteen organizations at the time, called for the release of imprisoned Christians. More importantly, it signaled a new day of unified and continued work by Orthodox, Protestants, and Catholics on behalf of Soviet Christians.

Dr. Kent Hill, chairman of the Coalition, laid out the Coalition's mandate at this rally: "We must not rest until *glasnost* means liberty to all who are captive and an end to discrimination against all religious believers. We will not rest until that day comes. That is our solemn pledge."

Keston, USA, and Freedom House (both described in the previous section) serve as research consultants to the Coalition, which has the following eighteen organizations as members:

All-Ukrainian Evangelical Baptist Fellowship
6751 Riverside Drive
Berwyn, IL 60402
(312) 788-0999

Director: Rev. Olexa Harbuziuk

The Fellowship advocates the rights of Ukrainian Baptists, a community hit hard by imprisonment and harassment for religious activities. Many Ukrainian Baptists went underground after they refused to abide by 1960s statutes which revived restrictions against teaching religion to children, proselytizing, and organizing study groups. The Fellowship also carries out important work in support of evangelical Baptist emigres in the United States.

Christian Rescue Effort for the Emancipation of Dissidents (CREED)
787 Princeton Kingston Road
Princeton, NJ 08540
(609) 497-0224

President: Dr. Ernest Gordon

CREED, founded in 1980, supports the witness of persecuted Christians in the Eastern bloc by maintaining communication and personal contacts and encouraging fellowship between Christians in Western and Communist countries. CREED calls for the defense of religious freedom and publishes regular updates regarding oppression of religious dissidents. Its work includes direct contact with church leaders across the United States through "CREED Fellowships."

Christian Solidarity Internationales Christian Solidarity International (CSI)
Sekretariat   P.O. Box 24042
Forchstrasse 280   Washington, D.C. 20024
Postfach 52   (301) 989-0298
CH-8029 Zurich   U.S. Director: Steven Snyder
Switzerland
President: Hans Stuckelberger

CSI is a worldwide, interdenominational organization (based in Zurich, Switzerland) working for freedom of faith around the world, and particularly in the Eastern bloc. Emphasizing solidarity with Christian prisoners and dissidents, CSI provides legal, material, and spiritual assistance to Christians who are arrested, persecuted, or tortured. Through its U.S. office and twelve others around the world, CSI promotes public awareness, initiates government intervention, and often provides assistance to Eastern bloc emigrés.

Committee for the Defense of Persecuted Orthodox Christians (CDPOC)
P.O. Box 9669
Washington, D.C. 20016
(202) 755-4232

President: Father Victor Potapov

The CDPOC was formed in 1977 in response to appeals for support from the Christian Committee for the Defense of Believers' Rights—the initiative begun by Russian Orthodox priest Gleb Yakunin who was imprisoned for his activities. The Committee coordinates financial support for religious prisoners of conscience and their families. It also coordinates public advocacy work on behalf of Russian Orthodox communities.

Concerned Women for America
370 L'Enfant Promenade, SW, Suite 800
Washington, D.C. 20024
(202) 488-7000

President: Beverly LaHaye

CWA, which is active in a broad range of social and political issues, plays an important role in promoting grassroots programs on behalf of persecuted Christian believers. CWA also organizes Christian women in united prayer networks to support religious prisoners of conscience.

Door of Hope International
P. O. Box 303
Glendale, CA 91209
(818) 956-7500

International President: Paul Popov

Since its inception in Europe in 1968, and then in the United States in 1972, Door of Hope International (founded by Bulgarian minister Haralan Popov) seeks to "eliminate the tragic shortage of God's Word in Communist countries." DOHI prints Bibles and portions of Scripture in many languages; it also produces teaching materials and songbooks and offers relief help to those in need.

DOHI offers many opportunities for ministry. It encourages family-to-family correspondence whereby Christian families in the West can contact Soviet families. The exchange of letters, postcards, and greeting cards help sustain the Soviet believers. DOHI also publicizes news from Communist lands through prayer and action committees locally and internationally. It publishes the magazine *Door of Hope*. For these and other opportunities, contact Door of Hope.

Holy Trinity Fathers
P. O. Box 5719
Baltimore, MD 21208
(301) 486-5764

Religious Liberty Director: Father Stan DeBoe

Founded in 1198 the Trinitarian Order is a Roman Catholic community of priests dedicated to ministry for those persecuted for their faith. The Trinitarians were founded to ransom Christians and Moslems pressed into slavery during the Crusades. Today they work actively to gain the release of religious prisoners, offer educational programs, and organize prayer and action groups.

Institute on Religion and Democracy
729 15th Street, NW, Suite 900
Washington, D.C. 20005
(202) 393-3200

Executive Director: Dr. Kent Hill

The Institute on Religion and Democracy was founded in 1981 to promote spiritual renewal within the Church and a more balanced church involvement in foreign policy questions. The IRD places a special emphasis on expanding religious liberty, the cornerstone of all human rights. It conducts research on the state of religious freedom and publicizes the plight of persecuted peoples of all faiths worldwide. The IRD encourages U.S. churches to give priority attention to religious freedom in their social action work.

Lithuanian Catholic Religious Aid
351 Highland Boulevard
Brooklyn, NY 11207
(718) 647-2434

Director: Ginte Damusis

LCRA provides spiritual, material, moral and other support to the Church in Lithuania, which suffers from a shortage of many things: food, clothing, medical supplies, technology, and publications of all sorts. While recent developments in Lithuania caught many unprepared, they found LCRA ready and able to make the most of the increased demand, particularly for religious literature.

Mission Possible
P. O. Box 2014
Denton, TX 76202
(817) 382-1508

President: W. Ralph Mann

Since 1975 Mission Possible Foundation has provided the evangelical church of the Soviet Union, Romania, Bulgaria, and Czechoslovakia with material and spiritual assistance. Annually, Scripture/literature distribution, church leadership training programs, and children's ministries become a reality for thousands of Soviet bloc Christians. MPF also promotes church-to-church sponsorship programs and individual support for Soviet churches and families.

National Association of Evangelicals
1023 15th Street, NW, Suite 500
Washington, D.C. 20005
(202) 789-1011

Executive Director: Billy Melvin
Project Coordinator (religious liberty contact): Brian O'Connell

Representing some forty-five thousand churches from more than seventy denominations, the NAE takes an active role in advocating religious liberty worldwide. NAE encourages and assists its member churches in programs to publicize and lend support to Christians suffering persecution and discrimination.

National Committee to Commemorate the Millennium
of Christianity in Ukraine
30 Montgomery St.
Jersey City, NJ 07302
(201) 451-2200

Chairman: Dr. George Soltys

The National Committee promoted the 1988 millennial anniversary of Eastern Slavic Christianity and sought to counter Soviet attempts to "russify" the millennium. The Committee publishes materials emphasizing that the baptism in 988 of Prince Vladimir took place in Kiev in Ukraine. A major thrust of the Committee's work is to publicize the tragic fact that both the Ukrainian Orthodox Church and the Eastern-rite Catholic Church in Ukraine have been outlawed by the Soviet government, and so were forced to celebrate their thousandth anniversary underground.

National Interreligious Task Force
1307 S. Wabash, Room 221
Chicago, IL 60605
(312) 922-1983

Executive Director: Sister Ann Gillen

NITF brings together believers of all denominations and human rights activists to work for emigration, religious freedom, and related human rights in the USSR, Eastern Europe, and elsewhere. It seeks to combine the powers of prayer, publicity, and political pressure.

Open Doors   Open Doors/USA
P.O. Box 318   P. O. Box 27001
3850 AH Ermelo   Santa Ana, CA 92799
Netherlands   (714) 531-6000
President: Brother Andrew   U.S. Director: Robert Hawley

Open Doors/USA is the U.S. office for the international missions organization Open Doors, which was founded by the Dutch missionary Brother Andrew in 1955. Open Doors correspondents from around the world report on the conditions of persecuted Christians, providing a voice for them in the world Christian community. Its primary work is to advance the Christian faith by providing religious literature, active support, and training to Christians in all countries where government-sponsored persecution exists or is emerging. Open Doors conducts radio broadcasts worldwide.

Puebla Institute
910 17th Street, NW, Suite 409
Washington, D.C. 20006
(202) 659-3229

Executive Director: Nina Shea

Founded in 1983 as a lay Catholic group focusing on the Church in Nicaragua, the Puebla Institute broadened its focus in 1986 to a worldwide concern for the human and religious rights of Christians. The Institute disseminates information on the victims of government-sponsored persecution.

Slavic Gospel Association
P. O. Box 1122
Wheaton, IL 60189
(312) 690-8900

Director: Peter Deyneka, Jr.

SGA is a worldwide organization founded in the United States in 1934, making it one of the oldest Eastern bloc missions. SGA maintains several different ministries that support Christians in the Soviet Union and Eastern Europe. The mission broadcasts radio programs, disperses literature for theological education and training, and spearheads prayer and letter-writing campaigns to offer support and to apply pressure for believers' rights. SGA is involved in ministering to emigres in Western Europe and operates a training center—the Institute of Soviet and East European Studies—which offers courses at Wheaton College and elsewhere on Church/State relations in the USSR and Eastern Europe.

Society of St. Stephen
231 E. Carroll Street
Macomb, IL 61455
(309) 833-4249

General Director: Father Keith Roderick

With a focus on spiritual concerns, the Society of St. Stephen encourages prayer, letter-writing to religious prisoners and their families, and "bridge-building" among Christians around the world. Prisoner adoption programs—predominantly for Soviet and Eastern European Christians—have been a major part of the Society's work since it was founded in 1982. Though interdenominational, St. Stephen emphasizes work with the Orthodox and Catholic communions. Over two hundred individuals, churches, or groups are affiliated with the Society, which is affiliated with Aid to Russian Christians, a mission based in England.

Ukrainian Congress Committee of America
203 Second Avenue
New York, NY 10003
(212) 228-6840

President: Ignatius Billinsky

The Ukrainian Congress Committee defends the Orthodox, Catholic, and other religious communities in Ukraine that have been outlawed or forcibly incorporated into the Russian Orthodox Church. Through the publications of its Ukrainian National Information Service, including the *Ukrainian Quarterly,* the Committee provides news updates and insights into political, cultural, and religious developments in Ukraine.

CONGRESSIONAL LIAISON FOR THE COALITION

Congressional Human Rights Caucus
U.S. House of Representatives
House Annex 2, Room 552
Washington, D.C. 20515
(202) 226-4040

Co-chairmen: Rep. Tom Lantos (D-Calif.) and Rep. John Porter (R-Ill.)

The Congressional Human Rights Caucus, founded by its present co-chairmen in 1983, plays an important role in addressing human rights concerns in the U.S. Congress and making the violation of human rights, including religious persecution, a more visible issue.

2. *Other Advocacy Organizations*

Amnesty International/USA
322 8th Avenue
New York, NY 10001
(212) 807-8400

Executive Director: John Healey

Amnesty International is a worldwide movement independent of any government, political faction, ideology, economic interest, or religious creed. Its activities focus strictly on prisoners. It seeks the release of prisoners who have been detained for their beliefs, color, sex, ethnic origin, language, or religion. It is the world's largest human rights organization.

International Representation, Inc.
(Full title: International Representation for the Council of Evangelical Baptist Churches of the Soviet Union, Inc.)
P. O. Box 1188
Elkhart, IN 46515
(219) 522-3486

General Director: Georgi Vins

Founded in 1980, International Representation represents, defends, and aids unregistered Baptists in the Soviet Union. Its publications, including the quarterly *Prisoner Bulletin,* seek to "echo the voice of the persecuted church."

International Society for Human Rights, Inc.
P. O. Box 90
Toms River, NJ 08754
(201) 341-1441

President: Serge Padukov

ISHR's U.S. branch was founded in 1982 as an independent section of the worldwide organization based in Frankfurt, West Germany. It is the second largest human rights organization in the world with no political or religious affiliations. ISHR also has advisory status with the European Parliament.

Slavic Refugee Relief Committee
P. O. Box 503
West Springfield, MA 01090
(413) 562-9932

President: Rev. Boris Perchatkin

Upon Perchatkin's immigration to the United States in 1988, the Slavic Refugee Relief Committee was founded. The goals of the SRRC are to secure letters of invitation for those wishing to leave the Soviet Union, to publicize the current situation of the Soviet Pentecostals, to improve contacts between the underground Church and Western Christians, particularly Pentecostals, to aid the transmittal of more religious literature, and to work to unify the scattered Pentecostal brotherhood into one strong, recognized body.

3. Government-Related Groups

Bureau of Human Rights and Humanitarian Affairs
Department of State
2201 C Street, NW, Room 7802
Washington, D.C. 20520
(202) 647-2126

Commission on Security and Cooperation in Europe
(Helsinki Commission)
House Annex 2, Room 237
Washington, D.C. 20515
(202) 225-1901

Commission Chairman: Senator Dennis DeConcini (D-Ariz.)

Created as an independent agency in 1976, the Helsinki Commission is composed of twenty-one legislative and executive branch officials whose mandate is to monitor compliance with the Helsinki Final Act, signed in August 1975 by the United States, the USSR, and more than thirty other countries. The Helsinki accords provide for the protection of fundamental freedoms, including freedom of thought, conscience, religion, or belief. The Commission actively documents violations of the Final Act, promotes public awareness of implementation of its provisions, and helps formulate and execute U.S. government policy on these issues.

United Nations Special Rapporteur on Religious Intolerance
The Honorable Angelo Vidal d'Almeida Ribeiro
Provedor de Justica
Avenue 5 de Outubre 38
1094 Lisbon
Portugal

U.N. Special Rapporteur: Dr. Angelo Vidal d'Almeida Ribeiro

The United Nations Human Rights Commission adopted a resolution in March 1986 providing for appointment of a Special Rapporteur—a "reporter" to monitor incidents of governmental actions in all parts of the world inconsistent with the provisions of the 1981 U.N. "Declaration on the Elimination of All Forms of Intolerance Based on Religion or Belief." Dr. Ribeiro of Portugal, a longtime human rights advocate, was appointed to the office in August 1986. In his second report, issued in January 1988, he identified specific examples of religious discrimination in seven countries, including the USSR. His reports are based on information received from U.N. member nations, specialized agencies, interested nongovernmental organizations, and private individuals.

II. Providing Religious Literature, Equipment, and Supplies to Christians in the USSR

A. *Where to Get Materials to Send into the USSR*

American Bible Society
1865 Broadway
New York, NY 10023
(212) 408-1499

ABS is a nonprofit, interdenominational organization which is a member of the United Bible Society. Its purpose is to bring the Scriptures, without doctrinal note or comment, to people everywhere. The Society has translated the Scriptures into many languages and makes them available at a low cost, enabling Christians in the West to purchase them and mail them to the Soviet Union.

To order by phone using a credit card (Visa or MasterCard), you may call a twenty-four-hour toll-free service: (800) 543- 8000. Orders must total $20 or more, and there is a $1.95 handling charge on all orders. For mail orders, use the form that comes with the catalog, which can be obtained from the above address or any ABS center.

ABS sells its Scriptures at cost, without profit (usually between $5 to $7). No quantity discounts are given. Please allow four to six weeks for delivery.

Bibles for the World
1300 Crescent Street
Wheaton, IL 61087
(312) 668-7733

Founded in 1971, Bibles for the World has distributed over 600,000 Bibles in the Soviet Union; it also has available Russian New Testaments. The organization pays for the printing of Russian Bibles and provides them to churches and individuals who wish to mail them to believers in the Soviet Union. If needed, Bibles for the World will even provide the names of Soviet believers. Ask for current prices at the time of ordering.

Christian Broadcasting Network
CBN Publishing
Virginia Beach, VA 23463
(804) 424-7777

CBN has two VHS video tapes (in English) of animated stories of the Bible suitable for children: "Superbook" (Old Testament stories) and "Flying House" (New Testament stories). They are partially fictionalized in that they place modern-day children into the biblical age so that they may observe the stories as they unfold. The tapes cost $19.95 plus tax and shipping and may be ordered by calling the toll-free number: (800) 288-4769. Tapes may only be compatible with American-made cassette players.

Credence Cassettes
115 East Armour Boulevard
P. O. Box 419491
Kansas City, MO 64141-6491
(800) 333-7373

Credence Cassettes is a service of the National Catholic Reporter. They have available a ten-set series (in English) of animated Bible stories that focus on heroes of the Bible "whose lives we look to for inspiration as models." These videos are for children ages four to twelve. Videos may be purchased individually ($29.95 or $39.95) or as an entire set ($269.00). Tapes may only be compatible with American-made cassette players.

Door of Hope International
P. O. Box 303
Glendale, CA 91209
(818) 956-7500

One of the main tasks of DOHI is to help overcome the shortage of Bibles in the Soviet Union; a main priority is the printing and distribution of Bibles and other Christian literature in native languages of people in the Soviet Union. Translations of Bibles, hymnals, Christian poetry, and *Halley's Bible Handbook* are currently available. A translation of the *Open Bible Study Bible* is being prepared to meet the needs of training and supporting pastors. Literature is sent to the Soviet Union by way of couriers who also take with them clothing, food, medical supplies, and money. Donations are especially needed for the translating and printing of materials.

Foyer Oriental Chretien
206, Avenue de la Couronne
B-1050 Bruxelles
Belgium

This excellent organization has been in ministry for forty years. Besides making Bibles and religious literature available, it also publishes journals that are sent into the Soviet Union. It monitors the distribution of these materials and maintains extensive contact with individual believers in the Soviet Union. Most books available through them are of interest primarily to Catholic believers, although some material is useful to Orthodox and Protestants as well. Extensive lists of philosophy, theology, patrology, catechisms, spirituality, ecumenism, Mariology, and ecclesiology make up the catalog. There is a good selection of classic religious literature as well as many books by Russian theologians.

Holy Trinity Monastery
P. O. Box 36
Jordanville, NY 13361
(315) 858-0940

This Russian Orthodox monastery publishes their own Christmas and Easter cards in Russian for sale at nominal prices. They also publish many Orthodox theological titles and children's books. All literature is in Russian. Catalogs are available in Russian and English.

Les Editeurs Reunis
11, Rue de la Montagne Sainte Genevieve
75005 Paris
France

This YMCA press based in France has an extensive catalog of Russian-language literature in the areas of Russian philosophy and theology and Russian art and icons. The catalog is printed entirely in Russian, but they will provide French translations of titles. Books would be of most interest to Orthodox believers and are scholarly and theological in nature, rather than devotional.

If large quantities of books are ordered, discounts of 33 percent to 40 percent may be available on books published by their own presses. A 10 percent discount may be given to large quantities of books not printed by Les Editeurs Reunis.

Licht im Osten   Light in the East
Postfach 1340   184 Mars Hill Road, NW
7015 Korntal Munchingen 1   Powder Springs, GA 30073
West Germany   (404) 424-0419

Light in the East is a fellowship of Christians of different backgrounds whose aim is to help Christians in Eastern Europe. Literature is available in several languages suitable for the Soviet Union (Russian, Latvian, Central Asian languages). Literature is sent free of charge to believers in Eastern Europe and at printing cost to believers in the West who wish to mail literature into Eastern Europe.

All resources are now being utilized to send books and Bibles into the Soviet Union, and little is available for purchase by Western Christians. Christians interested in assisting Light in the East may do so by sending tax-deductible contributions to the U.S. office, and the monies will be sent to the West German offices.

Light in the East has many titles that are beneficial for pastors and Bible students. There is also an extensive list of materials for children. Currently, Light in the East has several thousand parcels of religious literature ready to mail to the Soviet Union. Their need is for Christians to make the funds available to mail them. The total cost for one parcel, including postage, is $44.50.

Lithuanian Catholic Religious Aid
351 Highland Boulevard
Brooklyn, NY 11207
(718) 647-2434

LCRA ships religious books to people involved in the spiritual and cultural revival in Lithuania: religious and educational leaders, independent publishers, libraries, unofficial movements and clubs, charitable groups, and youth organizations. Books for Lithuania are provided free to visitors traveling to Lithuania and groups wishing to ship the books themselves. Donations to help defray the postage and printing expenses are greatly appreciated. Target addresses in Lithuania are available upon request.

Open Doors/USA
P. O. Box 27001
Santa Ana, CA 92799
(714) 531-6000

Post Project: Upon request, Open Doors provides three Russian New Testaments (free of charge), mailing instructions, and the address of a church or individual who has agreed to receive Bibles. Individuals and groups can participate by mailing these packages to the Soviet Union from their local post office. Approximate postal cost is $13.50 per package of three New Testaments.

St. Sophia Religious Association of Ukrainian Catholics in Canada
85 Lakeshore Drive
St. Catherines, Ontario L2N 2T6
Canada

St. Sophia supports the recognition of the Ukrainian Catholic (Uniate) Church and provides Bibles, religious literature, theological works, spiritual writings, and icons to Catholic believers in Soviet Ukraine. They translate and publish literature and make it available for distribution and can provide the names and addresses of people in Ukraine who are willing to receive such literature. Books can be purchased by writing the St. Sophia Religious Association at the above address.

Slavic Gospel Association
P. O. Box 1122
Wheaton, IL 60189
(312) 690-8900

SGA translates, produces, and distributes large quantities of Bibles and Christian literature for the Soviet Union and Eastern Europe. Resources include training materials for Russian and Eastern European pastors, and they are one of the few sources for Sunday school materials and for apologetical materials for non-Christians. SGA is shipping large amounts of literature into the Soviet Union at present. Small packages prelabeled by SGA consisting of a Bible and two or three books are available to be mailed by individuals from the West.

Slaviska Missionen
P. O. Box 15037
S-161 15 Bromma
Sweden
010-46 8 252875

Slaviska Missionen prints Ukrainian and Russian Bibles, hymnbooks, dictionaries, and children's literature. Their Bibles do not appear to have been printed abroad, which is useful during those periods when religious literature from abroad is forbidden. Please contact them for current availability and prices.

Ukrainian Family Bible Association
P. O. Box 3723
Palm Desert, CA 92261-3723
(619) 345-4913

The Ukrainian Family Bible Association was founded in 1988. Its mission is to make Bibles available to Christians of all denominations in Ukraine. The organization is concerned with the Soviet government's longstanding efforts to destroy the unique culture of the sixty million Ukrainians.

With the financial support of Christians in the West, the UFBA prints and delivers Ukrainian Bibles to churches and individuals in the Soviet Union. (They have obtained a Soviet permit in recent months for importing Bibles.) Voice of America and Radio Free Europe-Radio Liberty broadcast the offer to the Ukrainian people, and the Association responds to their needs.

At present, a Ukrainian language children's Bible is being prepared at the request of Ukrainian families. Christians may participate in this ministry by sending donations to help offset the cost of printing and bulk distribution.

B. *How to Send Materials into the USSR*

In recent months, the Soviets have been allowing large numbers of packages of religious literature and other goods to reach their destinations by mail. The following are some guidelines for mailing such materials into the USSR:

Religious Literature:

- Obtain Bibles and other religious literature from the organizations listed above.

- Do not send more than three books in one package. It is preferable if all three books are of different titles.

- Wrap the parcel firmly, and write your return address on the package. Seal it with brown paper tape. Do not use any kind of plastic tape (because of U.S. and Soviet postal regulations).

- Send a package that weighs *two pounds or less* by *registered mail* (white form #3806), International Air Parcel Union, *small package rate*. Ask for "return receipt requested" (pink form #2865) from the U.S. Post Office, which requires someone to sign for the package before receiving it. Though this method of mailing the package will cost more than if it were sent "surface book rate" (described below), the package will reach the Soviet Union more quickly. A customs form is required (green form #2976). Write "books" (not "Bibles") in English, and *religioznoe izdanie* (which means "religious publications.") The declared value is the price you paid for the materials.

- You may include a cover letter. If you do, mention your delight at being able to send these packages into the USSR, ask for confirmation of receipt of these packages, and ask for addresses of others who would like to receive similar packages. Write your name and address on this cover letter.

- A package that weighs *eleven pounds or less* may be sent *surface book rate*. This is a slower but less expensive method of mailing. A customs declaration is *not* required because the package consists of only books. Do *not* include a cover letter if sending a package book rate. We recommend that you send a separate card or letter indicating that you have sent a package.

- It may take ten to twelve weeks before receipt of the package is acknowledged (or longer if you send the package by surface mail).

- *Note*: It is reported that various U.S. post offices in the past have interpreted the *International Mail Manual* (USSR Section K3) differently with regard to questions of customs declarations and Cyrillic lettering on packages. What is listed above should be standard for most post offices.

Nonreligious materials:

Video cassette recorders, video cameras, radios, musical instruments, personal computers, and so on are now being allowed to be sent from the West. Printing equipment was still being confiscated as late as April 1989. Please contact Slavic Gospel Association or another member of the Coalition for Solidarity with Christians in the USSR for further information on requests from Soviet Christians, postal arrangements, customs duties, and other details.

C. *Whom to Send Religious Literature and Support To*

Many of the members of the Coalition for Solidarity with Christians in the USSR have lists of contacts, both registered and unregistered, for Western Christians who wish to send materials into the Soviet Union or visit with fellow believers while on a trip to the Soviet Union.

The following information from Keston, USA, lists some prominent religious leaders (lay and clergy) who are key contacts throughout the Soviet Union.

Group for Free Distribution of Religious Literature in the USSR:

Latvian SSR
Riga
Pr. Siguldas, d. 3, kv. 2
BOMBIN, Mikhail
USSR

Lithuanian SSR
Vilnius
ul. Arkhitektu 27, kv. 2
SADUNAITE, Nijole
USSR

RSFSR
Moscow
Ulansky pereulok 14, kv. 54
SENDEROV, Valeri
USSR

Soviet Christians who have undertaken to distribute religious literature to those who need it:

RSFSR
Kostroma
ul. Osypnaya 3, kv. 58
EDELSHTEIN, Fr. Georg
USSR

RSFSR
Moscow
ul. Dubenko, d. 30, korp. 1, kv. 45
YAKUNIN, Fr. Gleb
USSR

RSFSR
Leningrad 197349
Komendantsky pr. 27
Korp. 2, kv. 8
PORESH, Vladimir
USSR

RSFSR
Moscow 117513
ul. Bakuleva d. 6, kv. 135
AKSYUCHITS, V.V.
USSR

RSFSR
Moscow 111250
1 - Krasnokursantskii proezd.
d. 3/5, korp. 10, kv. 9
ANISHCHENKO, G.A.
USSR

It is possible to donate money directly to registered churches in the Soviet Union. Many of the churches and monasteries that have been returned to the religious communities need considerable restoration work. The Russian Orthodox Church has set up a fund for overseas contributions. You may send funds to:

Moscow 113191
Danilovsky Val 22
Danilov Monastery
DECR (Department of External Church Relations)
Metropolitan Filaret of Minsk
USSR

You may send contributions to the large registered Protestant Union:

AUCECB (All-Union Council of Evangelical
Christians-Baptists)
Moskva
Glavpochtamt PYa 520
Vsesouzny Sovet Yevangelskikh Khristian Baptistov
BYCHKOV, Alexei Mikhailovich
USSR

III. Contacts with Christians in the USSR

A. *Letters*

In the previous section there was a listing of a number of contacts. For more names and suggestions, contact some of the members of the Coalition such as Slavic Gospel Association, Keston, USA, and Open Doors.

Guidelines for writing to Soviet Christians:

- Write in simple English.

- Keep your message brief.

- Mention your own faith and copy Scripture verses.

- Artistic, colorful cards are especially valued.

- Avoid mentioning politics or the Soviet government.

- If there is a problem, express your concern and awareness of their situation.

- Do not type on the envelope. Write the address by hand. Write your return address on the back flap.

- Send the letter airmail: 45 cents per one-half ounce. A card or letter usually weighs one ounce. Write "AIRMAIL" on the envelope.

- Persist in sending your letters even if you receive no reply; however, most letters are being delivered to addressees at the present time.

The following Russian phrases, greetings, and Scripture verses may be copied onto letters or cards:

Dear Brother in Christ
Дорогой брат

Dear Sister in Christ
Дорогая сестра

Christ is risen!
Христос Воскрес

Merry Christmas!
С Рождеством Христовым!

Happy New Year!
С Новым годом!

Happy Birthday!
С днем рождения!

The Lord be with you!
Господь с Вами.

God is love.
Бог есть любовь.

We are praying for you.
Мы молимся о Вас.

May God bless you and strengthen you.
Бог да благословит и укрепит Вас.

Be strong in the Lord and in the power of His might.
Укрепляйтесь Господом и могуществом силы его.

Everyday we ask our Heavenly Father to help you and give you strength.
Каждый день мы просим Отца нашего Небесного Вам помогать и Вам давать силу.

And the Lord, it is He who goes before you; He will be with you, He will not fail you, neither forsake you: fear not, neither be dismayed.
Господь сам пойдет пред тобою, сам будет с тобою, не отступит от тебя и не оставит тебя: не бойся и не ужасайся.

B. *Travel*

For a first-time traveler to the Soviet Union who is interested in good preparatory material, we suggest that you contact Slavic Gospel Association (listed under ''Organizational Resources'') and request their *Handbook for Christian Travelers to the USSR,* available for $5.00.

If you are interested in establishing personal contacts with Soviet Christians, bringing in Bibles and other religious literature, VCRs, video tapes, and so on, then we suggest you contact member organizations of the Coalition for further information.

Slavic Gospel Association and other Coalition members arrange tours to the Soviet Union. The National Council of Churches through its Travel Seminar Office (475 Riverside Drive, Room 851, New York, NY 10115) also sponsors tours.

IV. Advocacy on Behalf of Christians

A. *Why Write?*

Though the situation has improved for believers there are still prisoners of conscience and numerous examples of continuing harassment of unregistered believers (Baptists, Pentecostals, Ukrainian Catholics, and others). Keston College maintains a prisoner list, as does the Institute on Religion and Democracy. The IRD runs an "Adopt-a-Prisoner" program on behalf of the Coalition for Solidarity with Christians in the USSR.

So long as serious problems remain for believers in the USSR, Western Christians need to express their concern to American and Soviet officials, their own Church leaders, as well as the Soviet believers and their families.

It is also important that we write to Christians in the USSR in order to be in contact with fellow believers. We should further be willing to write letters of appreciation to the appropriate officials when conditions for believers improve.

B. *Addresses*

Writing to government and church officials:

1. *U.S. Senators and Representatives.* (Be as specific as you can in your letter.)

Your Senator/Representative
U.S. Senate/U.S. House of Representatives
Washington, D.C. 20510/Washington, D.C. 20515

Salutation: Dear Senator (name) or Representative (name)

2. *U.S. Administration officials.*

The President
The White House
1600 Pennsylvania Avenue, NW
Washington, D.C. 20500

The Vice President
U.S. Senate
Washington, D.C. 20510

Secretary of State
U.S. Department of State
Washington, D.C. 20520

Assistant Secretary of State for Human Rights and
Humanitarian Affairs
U.S. Department of State
Washington, D.C. 20520

Salutation: Dear Mr. President, Mr. Vice President, or Mr. (name)

3. *Political and Religious Soviet officials.* (Provide them with as many details as possible. Urge compliance with the Helsinki Accords and other international human rights covenants the USSR has signed, and ask them to grant greater religious liberty within their land. Commend them for improvements but be specific about the serious problems that remain unresolved.)

His Excellency, Mikhail S. Gorbachev
General Secretary of the Central Committee
Communist Party of the Soviet Union
The Kremlin
Moscow 103132
USSR

Konstantin M. Kharchev, Chairman
Council for Religious Affairs
Smolensky Bul'var 11/2
Moscow 119121
USSR

Fodor M. Burlatsky, Chairman
Public Commission for Human Rights
Soviet C.S.C.E.
Kropotkinskaia 3
Moscow
USSR

Ambassador Yury Dobrynin
Embassy of the USSR
1125 16th Street, NW
Washington, D.C. 20036

General Secretary (Alexei M. Bychkov) or
President (Vasily Logvinenko)
All-Union Council of Evangelical Christians-Baptists
P.O. Box 520
Moscow
USSR

His Holiness Patriarch Pimen
Moscow Patriarchate of the Russian Orthodox Church
113191 Moscow
Danilovsky Val 22
USSR

4. U.N. Special Rapporteur on Religious Intolerance.

Honorable Angelo Vidal d'Almeida Ribeiro
Provedor de Justica
Avenue 5 de Outubre 38
1094 Lisbon
Portugal

5. Officials of the World Council of Churches, the U.S. National Council of Churches, and your denomination. (Urge public statements of support and strong private initiatives. When possible, address your letters to the current leader of the organization you are writing.)

Headquarters, World Council of Churches
150 route de Ferney, (P.O. Box 66), 1211
Geneva, 20, Switzerland

Office of the Executive Director
World Council of Churches
475 Riverside Drive, Room 1062
New York, NY 10115

Office of the General Secretary
National Council of Churches
475 Riverside Drive
New York, NY 10115

Office of the General Secretary
Baptist World Alliance
6733 Curran Street
McLean, VA 22101

Office of the Secretary
Department of Social Development and World Peace
U.S. Catholic Conference
3211 4th Street N.E.
Washington, D.C. 20017

Office of the President
National Conference of Catholic Bishops
4445 Lindell Boulevard
St. Louis, MO 63108

Office of the President
Council of United Methodist Bishops
P.O. Box 6006
Pasadena, CA 91102

Office of the Presiding Bishop
Episcopal Church Center
815 Second Avenue
New York, NY 10017

Office of the Stated Clerk
Presbyterian Church
100 Witherspoon Street
Louisville, KY 40202-1396

Office of the President
United Church of Christ
105 Madison Avenue
New York, NY 10016

Office of the Bishop
Evangelical Lutheran Church in America
8765 West Higgins Road
Chicago, IL 60631

Office of the General Superintendent
Assemblies of God
1445 Boonville Avenue
Springfield, MO 65802

6. *Organize a local conference on religious liberty.* (Several groups have materials and speakers available. See listing of the members of the Coalition for Solidarity with Christians in the USSR. Another valuable activity is to organize prayer vigils within your community. Arrange to show videos available from various missions organizations and monitoring groups.)

C. *Millennium Appeal: An Example of Advocacy*

The Millennium Appeal was signed by over 450 prominent Americans from various fields and religious backgrounds, including members of Congress, church leaders, and religious liberty activists. The James Madison Foundation in Washington, D.C., sponsor of the project, delivered copies (in Russian and English) to the Soviet embassy on April 25, 1988. President Reagan personally received the Appeal on the same day. The Appeal will continue to be circulated throughout the United States and in the Soviet Union. The Millennium Appeal's specific concerns are modeled after a September 1987 watershed appeal from religious activists in the Soviet Union, including members of the Russian Orthodox, Protestant, and Catholic communities. Fortunately some, though certainly not all, of the problems raised by this appeal were being dealt with in 1988 and 1989.

AN APPEAL FOR RELIGIOUS FREEDOM IN THE SOVIET UNION ON THE OCCASION OF THE MILLENNIUM OF CHRISTIANITY IN KIEVAN RUS'

To Mikhail Sergeyevich Gorbachev
General Secretary of the Communist Party of the Soviet Union

I. 1988 MARKS THE MILLENNIUM OF CHRISTIANITY in Kievan Rus'. While this anniversary has special meaning for the Christian community throughout the world, it also provides an occasion for all men and women of goodwill to celebrate the great and varied spiritual heritages carried by the peoples of the Soviet Union—Orthodox, Catholic, Protestant, Jewish, Muslim, Buddhist.

Religious freedom has been acknowledged as a fundamental right in such landmark steps towards the growth of international law as the United Nations Charter, the Universal Declaration of Human Rights, the International Covenant on Civil and Political Rights, the International Covenant on Social, Economic and Cultural Rights, the Conventions Against Discrimination in Education, the Helsinki Final Act, and the U.N. Declaration Against All Forms of Religious Intolerance—agreements to which the Soviet Union has solemnly pledged its adherence. The international community recognizes that respect for such fundamental human rights as religious freedom is an essential building block of peace, within and among nations.

Unhappily, present state policy in the USSR puts pressure on religious believers of all faiths, and circumscribes the activities of religious communities. We join with believers in the Soviet Union who hope that this remarkable anniversary, the Millennium of Christianity in Kievan Rus', can become the occasion for fundamental change in Soviet state policy and practice toward religious communities.

We the undersigned, Americans of many different creeds and political persuasions, joined by a common concern for human rights and peace, appeal to you, General Secretary Gorbachev, to honor your nation's commitments to international agreements on the fundamental human right of religious freedom.

We are heartened by the progress our two countries have made in the area of arms reduction, and by your call for a new era of openness in the Soviet Union.

We note the resolution of a number of individual emigration and prisoner cases.

But we urge deeper, more permanent change, commensurate with your commitment to *glasnost, perestroika,* and democratization. Thus we urge you to redress the continuing pattern of discrimination and harassment against religious believers in your country.

We believe that significant progress in the matter of human rights, and especially on the fundamental right of religious freedom, will contribute to a new pattern of relationships between our countries, and thereby enhance the prospects of peace.

II. WE JOIN IN SOLIDARITY WITH BELIEVERS OF all faiths in the Soviet Union, urging you to undertake immediately the actions necessary to effect these specific constitutional and legal steps toward full religious freedom in the USSR:

- We urge that Article 52 of the Soviet Constitution be amended so that citizens of the USSR are guaranteed the right, not only to "religious worship," but also to "form religious associations and disseminate religious beliefs" on terms of full constitutional equality with atheistic organizations and atheistic propaganda. We urge you to restore to all religious associations the full status of "juridical person" under Soviet law.

- We urge that the Decree of the All-Russian Central Executive Committee and the Council of People's Commissars of the RSFSR of April 8, 1929 (and its equivalents in other Soviet republics, as amended by decree of the RSFSR Supreme Soviet Presidium of June 23, 1975), and the equivalent laws "On Religious Associations" adopted subsequently in other Union republics, be repealed. In particular, we urge you:

  — to return to individual religious groups the houses of worship, religious artifacts and religious books which have been expropriated by the authorities;

  — to restore the right to construct and own new houses of worship;

  — to allow religious instruction of children, young people and adults outside the public school system;

  — to lift the ban against charitable activities by religious groups;

  — and to end the requirements of preliminary state "registration" of religious associations and the clergy.

- We urge that Articles 142 and 227 of the RSFSR Criminal Code (and their equivalents in other republican criminal codes), as well as the March 18, 1966 Decrees of the RSFSR Supreme Soviet Presidium "On the Application of Article 142 of the RSFSR

Criminal Code'' and ''On the Administrative Liability for the Violation of the Legislation on Religious Cults'' (and the equivalent decrees adopted by the Supreme Soviet Presidia of the other Union republics), be repealed as contrary to the constitutional separation of church and state.

- We urge you to publish and submit for public reconsideration, with the participation of religious believers, all hitherto secret or only partially published decrees and instructions setting the structure, powers, and procedures of the Council for Religious Affairs (CRA) attached to the USSR Council of Ministers, its republican and oblast branches and commissioners. We urge that you assure representation on the CRA at all government levels, of representatives of religious believers, and that the activities of the Council for Religious Affairs be guaranteed full legality and publicity (*glasnost*).

- We urge you to legalize the Greek Catholic (Uniate or Ukrainian Catholic) Church and other religious 361 groups (such as, for example, the Ukrainian Autocephalous Orthodox Church) that were banned by the Stalin government, and to restore to these religious groups the churches, houses of prayer, religious artifacts, monastic and seminary buildings, and other confiscated property necessary for their religious activities.

III. THE FUNDAMENTAL RIGHT OF RELIGIOUS freedom, as codified in the U.N. Declaration Against All Forms of Religious Intolerance, has many concrete expressions in daily life. Therefore we urge the following:

- A general amnesty should be declared for all religious prisoners of conscience.

- Religious believers should be able to practice their faith without interference, harassment, or persecution. The requirements for compulsory state ''registration'' or religious congregations and the clergy, prior to their starting their activities, should be abolished, along with the prerogative of state authorities to veto any members of congregations' executive and auditing committees. Membership on these committees (including chairmanship) should be open to the clergy.

- Religious communities should enjoy freedom to preach, to publish, and to disseminate their teachings through the mass media. Independent religious publishing institutions should not be hindered in their work.

- Parents should be able to transmit their faith to their children without being harassed or discriminated against on this account. Religious organizations should be able to conduct institutions of religious education without state interference. Clergy should be allowed, with parental permission, to provide religious instruction to children. School children and students at secondary or university levels should not be pressured to join organizations espousing atheism; punished for declining to do so; or otherwise be denied equality of educational opportunity and advancement on account of their religious beliefs and practices.

- The state should not interfere in the appointment of seminary faculties, and should relinquish its control over the appointment of candidates to seminaries.

- Religious believers, including children, should be able to absent themselves from work or from school on religious holidays.

- Believers who wish to emigrate from the Soviet Union on religious grounds should be allowed to do so.

- Believers, clergy, and religious groups in the Soviet Union who wish to maintain contacts with fellow-believers and religious institutions throughout the world should be free to do so.

- Religious communities should enjoy the full rights of social organizations in the Soviet Union. Religious communities should be able to solicit funds for charitable activities, to engage in works of charity, to own property, and to participate in organizations such as temperance societies.

- Religious services should be permitted in hospitals, prisons, and homes for the aged. Religious believers should be able to wear religious symbols, and to have access to religious literature, while they are in hospitals, prisons, and homes for the aged.

IV. ESTABLISHMENT OF THESE BASIC GUARANTEES of the fundamental right of religious freedom is an important measure of the status of human rights in the Soviet Union. We call on you, Mr. General Secretary, to demonstrate your commitment to peace by assuring all the peoples of the Soviet Union the right of religious freedom, which is an essential guarantor of peace. We appeal to you, on this occasion of the Millennium of Christianity in Kievan Rus', to join with us in working for an international community committed to defending the dignity of human beings as a fundamental requisite of peace.

V. HELPING SOVIET CHRISTIANS WHO LEAVE THE USSR

A. *Sponsor a Refugee Family*

World Relief is the international humanitarian assistance arm of the National Association of Evangelicals. While there are ten national organizations contracted to sponsor and resettle refugees, World Relief is the only organization responsible for working primarily with the evangelical Christian denominations in resettling refugees in the United States.

The chief objective of the sponsor is to help the refugee to integrate quickly and successfully into American society. World Relief encourages sponsors to help the refugees to become self-sufficient as soon as possible. The responsibilities of sponsoring a family include meeting their initial material needs (housing, clothing, food) as well as their spiritual and emotional needs (adjusting to the Western Church, for example). The time commitment and responsibilities will be high, but so will be the rewards of the sponsor. If your church or community is interested in getting involved in a direct ministry to aid Soviet refugees, contact World Relief:

Mr. Serge Duss
Soviet Refugee Project
World Relief
P.O. Box WRC
Nyack, NY 10960
(914) 268-4135

Other organizations do good work providing information on refugee resettlement. You may also wish to contact them:

Boris Perchatkin
Slavic Refugee Relief Committee
P.O. Box 503
West Springfield, MA 01090
(413) 739-3153

Mr. Dennis Ripley
EXODUS World Service
P. O. Box 7000
West Chicago, IL 60185-7000
(312) 733-8433

SOVIET LAWS ON RELIGION:

1918-1988

*T*he importance of this section in part lies in its historic value. On the basis of these laws and regulations, Christians for many decades have been persecuted and discriminated against.

The religious sect laws are being revised at the time of this writing, and may even be approved by the end of 1989. The Council for Religious Affairs draft version was discussed in chapter 14.

Article 52 of the Soviet Constitution also may be revised so as to allow both believers and atheists the right to propagate their views.

An April 1989 decree modified criminal statutes 70 and 190-1, according to which religious believers have often been convicted. Unfortunately, the changes are ambiguous and are not the clear step forward that had been anticipated.

DECREE OF THE SOVIET COMMISSARS CONCERNING SEPARATION OF CHURCH AND STATE, AND OF SCHOOL AND CHURCH (JANUARY 23, 1918)

1. The Church is separated from the State.
2. Within the confines of the Republic it shall be prohibited to issue any local by-laws or regulations restricting or limiting freedom of conscience, or establishing privileges or preferential rights of any kind based on the religious creed of citizens.
3. Every citizen may profess any religious belief, or profess no belief at all. All restrictions of rights, involved by professing one or another religious belief, or by professing no belief at all, are canceled and void. Note: All reference to the professing or non-professing of religious creeds by citizens shall be expunged from all official documents.

4.   State or other public functions binding in law shall not be accompanied by the performance of religious rites or ceremonies.

5.   Free performance of religious rites is permissible as long as it does not disturb public order, or interfere with the rights of the citizens of the Soviet Republic. The local authorities shall be entitled in such cases to adopt all necessary measures for maintenance of public order and safety.

6.   Nobody is entitled to refuse to perform his duties as a citizen on the basis of his religious belief. Exceptions to this rule, on the condition that one civic duty be replaced by another, may be granted in each individual case by the verdict of the People's Court.

7.   The official taking or administering of religious oaths is canceled. In necessary cases merely a solemn promise is given.

8.   Births, marriages, and deaths are to be registered and solemnized solely by civic (secular) authorities: marriage and birth registration offices.

9.   The School is separated from the Church. Instruction in any religious creed or belief shall be prohibited in all State, public, and also private educational establishments in which general instruction is given. Citizens may give or receive religious instruction in a private way.

10.   All Church and religious associations are subject to the ordinary legislation concerning private associations and unions. They shall not enjoy special privileges, nor receive any subsidies from the State or from local autonomous or self-governing institutions.

11.   Compulsory collection of imposts and taxes in favor of Church and religious associations, also measures of compulsion or punishment adopted by such associations in respect to their members, shall not be permitted.

12.   No Church or religious associations have the right to own property. They do not possess the rights of juridical persons.

13.   The property of all Church and religious associations existing in Russia is pronounced the property of the People. Buildings and objects especially used for the purposes of worship shall be let, free of charge, to the respective religious associations, by resolution of the local, or Central State authorities.

Signed: President of the Soviet Commissars, ULIANOV (LENIN) and eight People's Commissars.

* * * *

SELECTIONS FROM
THE RSFSR LAW ON RELIGIOUS ASSOCIATIONS OF 1929
(AS AMENDED BY DECREE OF THE PRESIDIUM
OF THE SUPREME SOVIET OF THE RSFSR ON JUNE 23, 1975)

1.   Churches, religious groups, sects, religious movements, and other cult associations of all denominations, are governed by the Decree of the

Council of People's Commissars of the RSFSR of January 23, 1918, on the Separation of Church from State, and of School from Church (SU RSFSR 1918 No. 18 item 203).

2.   Religious associations of believing citizens of all denominations shall be registered as religious societies or groups of believers.

A citizen may be a member of only one religious association (society or group).

3.   A religious society is a local association of not less than twenty believers who are eighteen years of age or over and belong to the same cult, faith or sect, who have united for the common satisfaction of their religious needs. Believers who are not numerous enough to organize a religious society may form a group of believers.

Religious societies have the right to acquire church-plate, articles of the religious cult and means of transport, and to rent, build and buy buildings for their own needs in the procedure established by law.

4.   A religious society or group may start its activities only after the decision to register the society or group of believers has been taken by the Council for the Affairs of Religions of the Council of Ministers of the USSR. . . .

6.   In order to register a group of believers, the request, undersigned by all believers of that group, is submitted [to district or city authorities and, ultimately (section 7) to the USSR Council for the Affairs of Religions]. . . .

8.   The Council for the Affairs of Religions of the Council of Ministers of the USSR keeps a register of religious associations, prayer houses and buildings. . . .

9.   In the list of members of religious societies or groups of believers may be included only those believers who expressed their consent thereto.

12.   The general assemblies of religious societies and groups of believers (except prayer meetings) may [only] be held with permission of [district or city authorities].

13.   . . . The religious associations elect, by open ballot, at their general assemblies, executive bodies from among their members. . . .

14.   The registration agencies are entitled to remove individual members from the executive body of a religious society or the representative elected by a group of believers.

17.   Religious societies may not:

a) create mutual credit societies, cooperatives or commercial undertakings, or in general use property at their disposal for other than for the satisfaction of religious needs;

b) give material support to their members;

c) organize special prayer or other meetings for children, young people and women, nor general Bible, literary, handicraft, work, catechetical and other similar meetings, groups, circles and departments, nor organize excursions and children's playgrounds, nor open libraries and reading rooms, nor organize sanatoriums and medical help.

Only prayer books necessary for the performance of the relevant cult may be kept in the prayer buildings and premises.

18.   The teaching of any kind of religious cult in educational institutions is inadmissible. . . .

19.   The activities of the ministers of religion, religious preachers, teachers and the like shall be restricted to the place where the members of the religious association which they serve reside and where the prayer premises are located. . . .

20.   Religious societies and groups of believers may convene religious congresses and conferences only with the permission, issued separately for each case, of the Council for the Affairs of Religions of the Council of Ministers of the USSR. . . .

25.   Property necessary for the performance of the cult . . . are nationalized and shall be registered at [the district or city authorities] . . . .

28.   The building of the cult and the property in this building shall be received under a contract from the representative of the [district or city authorities] by no less than twenty members of the religious society in order to put the said property at the disposal for the use of all believers.

41.   Prayer buildings, which are subject to closure and which are not under state protection as monuments of culture, may be used and reequipped for other aims or torn down only by the decision of the Council for the Affairs of Religions of the Council of Ministers of the USSR. . . .

57.   Prayer meetings of believers who have formed a group of society may be held, without notification to or permission of the authorities, in buildings of the religious cult or specially adapted premises which comply with the technical and sanitary regulations.

Prayer meetings of believers may be performed in premises not specially adapted for these purposes, if notification [is made] in villages to the executive committee of the village Soviet of workers' deputies, in cities to the executive committee of the district or city Soviet of workers' deputies.

58.   The performance of any kind of religious ceremonies or rites or the location of objects of the cult in the buildings belonging to the State, public or cooperative institutions or enterprises is prohibited.

Such prohibition does not apply to the performance of religious rites in hospitals and places of confinement in specially isolated rooms, if requested by dying or seriously ill persons, or to the performance of religious ceremonies in cemeteries and in crematoria.

59.   Religious processions, performance of religious rites and ceremonies in the open air, and also in the apartments and houses of believers are allowed

only with a special permission, for each separate case, of [the district or city authorities].

The request to give permission for a religious procession and a performance of religious rites in the open air has to be handed in at least two weeks before the ceremony is to take place.

The performance of religious cult rites in apartments and houses of believers on the request of dying or seriously ill persons may take place with permission or notification of the [district or city authorities].

60.   Special permission or notification of the authorities is not required for religious processions which are an inevitable part of the divine service and are made around the buildings of the cult whether they are located in cities or villages, provided they do not disturb the normal street traffic.

64.   Supervision of the activities of religious associations, as well as of the maintenance of buildings and cult property handed over to religious associations on the basis of a contract, shall be exercised by the agencies in charge of registration, and in rural areas, additionally, by village Soviets. [Complete text can be found in *Review of Socialist Law*, Vol. 1 (September 1975), 223-234.]

* * * *

EXTRACTS FROM THE 1977 CONSTITUTION OF THE USSR

Article 6

The Communist Party of the Soviet Union (CPSU) is the leading and guiding force of Soviet society and the nucleus of its political system, of all state and public organizations. The CPSU exists for the people and serves the people.

Armed with the Marxist-Leninist teaching, the Communist Party shall determine the general perspective of society's development, give guidance to the great creative endeavor of the Soviet people and place their struggle for the triumph of communism on a planned, scientific basis.

Article 25

In the USSR a uniformed system of education shall exist and be developed, which shall serve the communist education and cultural and physical development of young people, their training for work and social activity.

Article 34

Citizens of the USSR shall be equal before the law, irrespective of origin, social and property status, race or nationality, sex, education, language, attitude to religion, type or character of occupation, domicile or other particulars.

Equality of rights of citizens of the USSR shall be ensured in all fields of economic, political, social and cultural life.

Article 52

Freedom of conscience, that is the right to profess any religion or not to profess any religion, to perform religious rites or to conduct atheist propaganda shall be guaranteed for all citizens of the USSR. Incitement of hostility and hatred on religious grounds shall be prohibited.

The church in the USSR shall be separated from the state and the school from the church.

* * * *

Articles of the Russian (RSFSR) Criminal Code

(Equivalent articles for most offenses exist in the criminal codes of other Soviet republics. Compiled from resources of Keston College, England, and United States Department of State documents [Religion in the USSR: Laws, Policy, and Propaganda," *Foreign Affairs Note*, May 1982; "New Soviet Legislation Restricts Rights, Strengthens Internal Security," *Foreign Affairs Note*, July 1984]. Explanations [in brackets and quotation marks] at the end of each criminal code article are based on Keston College [commentary as found in Michael Bourdeux and Michael Rowe, eds. *May One Believe—in Russia? Violations of Religious Liberty in the Soviet Union*, (London: Darton, Longman and Todd, 1980) and *Religious Prisoners in the USSR* (Keston College: Greenfire Books, 1987)].)

Religious Offenses

Article 142. Violation of the laws on the separation of church and state and of school and church.

   1.   . . . is punishable by correctional tasks for a period not exceeding one year or by a fine not exceeding fifty roubles.

   2.   The same actions committed by a person previously sentenced for violating the laws on the separation of church and state and of school and church, and likewise organizing activity directed at the commission of such actions are punishable by deprivation of freedom for a period not exceeding three years.

["Under Article 142 it is an offense to organize any activity of an unregistered church and to teach religion to children (except one's own)." (Bourdeaux, *May One Believe?*, 16.)]

Article 227. Infringement of the person and rights of citizens under the guise of performing religious rituals.

   1.   Organizing or leading a group whose activity, carried on under the guise of preaching religious doctrines and performing religious rituals, is connected with causing harm to citizens' health or with other infringements of the person or rights of citizens, or with inciting citizens to refuse to do social

activity or to fulfill obligations, and likewise with enticing minors into such a group, is punishable by deprivation of freedom for a period not exceeding five years or exile for the same period with or without confiscation of property.

2.   Active participation in the activity of a group such as described in the first part of this article, and likewise, systematic propaganda directed at the commission of the acts described therein, is punishable by deprivation of freedom for a period not exceeding three years or exile for the same period or correctional tasks for a period not exceeding one year.''

[''Article 227, introduced in 1959, was initially directed mainly at Pentecostals. It was soon, however, also applied to Baptists who left the officially recognized Church and has been applied to Christians of almost all denominations, and even to Buddhists. The essential features are 'causing harm to health' (frequently stated to result from speaking in tongues by Pentecostals) and 'inciting citizens to refuse to do social activity,' for example, urging members not to take part in secular cultural activities.'' (Bourdeaux, 16.)]

MILITARY OFFENSES

Article 80. Evasion of regular call to active military service.
. . . is punishable by deprivation of freedom for a period of one to three years.
[''Refusal to be drafted into the armed forces is likely to bring an automatic conviction under Article 80, and the military authorities might subsequently repeat the call-up.'' (Bourdeaux, 17.)]

Article 198-1. Evasion of training courses or musters and of military registration by person subject to military service.
. . . is punishable by deprivation of freedom for a term not exceeding one year.
[''People who have become conscientious objectors subsequent to completing military service may refuse to do reservist training and are punished under Article 198-1. Christians and Jews wishing to emigrate may fear that reservist training may block their emigration on the grounds that they have had recent access to military secrets.'' (*Religious Prisoners*, 16.)]

Article 249. Evasion of military service by maiming or any other method.
(a) The evasion by a person in military service of performance of military duties by causing himself any kind of injury (maiming) or by malingering, forgery of documents or any other deception, or a refusal to perform military duties is punishable by deprivation of freedom for a period of three to seven years.
(b) The same acts committed in wartime or in a combat situation are punishable by death or by deprivation of freedom for a period of five to ten years.

["Under Article 249(a), refusal to swear the military oath—which is unacceptable to many Christians—can be construed as refusal to perform military duties, on the grounds that many duties cannot be performed by soldiers who have not sworn the oath. However, prosecution is not automatic and Christian soldiers are often transferred to units engaged in construction projects."(*Religious Prisoners,* 16.)]

POLITICAL OFFENSES

Article 64. Treason
["Offenses under this article include escaping from the country and 'conspiracy for the purpose of seizing power'. Maximum sentence fifteen years plus five years exile or death." (*Religious Prisoners,* 16.)]

Article 70. Anti-Soviet agitation and propaganda.
1.   Agitation or propaganda carried on for the purpose of subverting or weakening Soviet authority or of committing particular, especially dangerous crimes against the state, or circulating for the same purpose slanderous fabrications which defame the Soviet state and social system, or circulating or preparing or keeping, for the same purpose, literature of such content, is punishable by deprivation of freedom for a period of six months to seven years, with or without additional exile for a period of two to five years, or by exile for a period of two to five years.
2.   The same actions committed using monetary means or other material resources received from foreign organizations or from foreign individuals acting on behalf of such organizations, or committed by a person previously convicted of especially dangerous crimes against the state . . . are punishable by deprivation of freedom for a period of three to ten years with or without additional exile for a period of two to five years.

Article 190-1. Circulation of deliberately false concoctions, slandering the Soviet state and social order.
The systematic circulation in an oral form of knowingly false fabrications which defame the Soviet state and social system and, equally, preparation or circulation in written, printed, or in any other form of works of such content, is punishable by deprivation of freedom for a period not exceeding three years, or by correctional tasks for a period not exceeding one year, or by a fine not exceeding one hundred roubles.
["Article 70 and especially Article 190-1 are frequently applied to believers who have written or spoken of religious persecution or been involved in the circulation of documents detailing violations of religious freedom and other human rights. . . . Both articles specify that information slandering the Soviet Union disseminated by the accused must have been known by the accused to be false. In practice the courts regularly fail to investigate the truth of statements made either by the accused, or in confiscated material. They do not

even consider whether they were *known* to be false. Article 70 covers a wider range of 'subversive' propaganda.'' (*Religious Prisoners*, 17.)]

Article 162. Engaging in a prohibited trade.

2.   Engaging in a trade concerning which there is a special prohibition, if such act does not entail administrative liability or if it is committed after imposition of an administrative penalty for such act, is punishable by correctional tasks for a term not exceeding one year or by a fine not exceeding two hundred roubles.

. . . [if] committed on a significant scale, or by using hired labor, or committed by a person previously convicted of engaging in a prohibited trade, [it] is punishable by deprivation of freedom for a period not exceeding four years with or without confiscation of property.

["The unofficial printing or distribution of religious literature is considered a prohibited trade." (*Religious Prisoners*, 18.)]

Article 188-3. Malicious disobedience to the requirements of the administration of a corrective labor institution.

[Violation of camp regulations] . . . by a person serving a sentence of punishment in places of deprivation of liberty, if that person has in the course of a year been punished by transfer to the cells [solitary confinement] or to a prison, is punishable by deprivation of liberty for a period of up to three years.

The same acts, if committed by an especially dangerous recidivist or by a person convicted of a serious crime, are punishable by deprivation of liberty for a period of one to five years.

["This article, introduced in the RSFSR on October 1, 1983, enables the Soviet authorities to impose an additional period of imprisonment solely on the evidence of camp officials. Acts of disobedience can include helping other prisoners." (*Religious Prisoners*, 20.)]

Article 190-3. Organization of, or active participation in, group actions which disrupt public order.

Organization of and, equally, active participation in group actions which violate public order, or which are attended by clear disobedience of the legal demands of representatives of authority or which entail the violation of the work of transport or of state and social institutions or enterprises, is punishable by deprivation of freedom for a period not exceeding three years, or by correctional tasks for a period not exceeding one year, or by a fine not exceeding 100 roubles.

["This article can be applied when believers assemble in public, for example when locked out of a church or conducting an open-air baptism." (*Religious Prisoners*, 22.)]

Article 191. Resisting representative of authority or representative of public fulfilling duties of protection of public order.
   . . . is punishable by deprivation of freedom for a term not exceeding three years, or by correctional tasks for a term not exceeding one year, or by a fine not exceeding 60 roubles.

Article 191-1. Resisting policeman or people's guard (Druzhinnik).
   1.   . . . is punishable by deprivation of freedom for a term not exceeding one year, or by correctional tasks for the same term, or by a fine not exceeding 100 roubles.
   2.   . . . the same acts committed with violence or the threat of employing violence . . . are punishable by deprivation of liberty for a period of one to five years or by corrective labor for a period of one to two years.
[''These charges are used to justify the breaking up of religious meetings or peaceful demonstrations and unprovoked assault on believers.'' (*Religious Prisoners,* 22.)]

Article 206. Hooliganism.
   Hooliganism, that is, intentional actions violating public order in a coarse manner and expressing a clear disrespect toward society, is punishable by deprivation of liberty for a period of six months to one year. . . .
   Malicious hooliganism, that is, the same actions committed by a person previously convicted of hooliganism or connected with resisting a representative of authority or representative of the public fulfilling duties for protection of public order, or distinguished in their content by exceptional cynicism or impudence, is punishable by deprivation of freedom for a period of one to five years.
   Petty hooliganism committed by a person to whom measures of social or administrative pressure for petty hooliganism have been twice applied in the course of a year is punishable by correctional tasks for a period not exceeding one year or by a fine not exceeding 50 roubles.
[''Peaceful demonstrations and other non-violent actions may be considered malicious hooliganism.'' (*Religious Prisoners,* 22.)]

Article 209. [Parasitism] Malicious evasion of fulfillment of decision concerning arrangement of work and discontinuance of parasitic existence.
   Systematically engaging in vagrancy or in begging, continued after warning given by administrative agencies, is punishable by deprivation of freedom for a period not exceeding two years or by correctional tasks for the same period.
[''Some religious believers cannot work because of discrimination; others are supported unofficially by fellow believers. In either case prosecution is possible under this article if work is not found within one month of an order to that effect.'' (*Religious Prisoners,* 23.)]

INTERNATIONAL LAWS CONCERNING FREEDOM OF RELIGION

*T*he following are international laws to which the USSR is a signatory. Emphasis throughout is mine.

* * * *

CHARTER OF THE UNITED NATIONS
(SIGNED ON JUNE 26, 1945)

Article 1

The Purposes of the United Nations are:

3. *To achieve international co-operation* in solving international problems of an economic, social, cultural, or humanitarian character, and in promoting *and encouraging respect for human rights and for fundamental freedoms for all without distinctions* as to race, sex, language, or *religion.*

Article 2

2. *All Members,* in order to ensure to all of them the rights and benefits resulting from membership, *shall fulfill in good faith the obligations assumed by them in accordance with the present Charter.*

* * * *

UNIVERSAL DECLARATION OF HUMAN RIGHTS
(APPROVED BY THE GENERAL ASSEMBLY OF THE UNITED NATIONS
ON DECEMBER 10, 1948)

Article 2

Everyone is entitled to all the rights and freedoms set forth in this Declaration, without distinction of any kind, such as race, colour, sex, language, *religion,* political or other opinion, national or social origin, property, birth or other status.

Article 7

All are equal before the law and are entitled without any discrimination to equal protection of the law. *All are entitled to equal protection against any discrimination in violation of the Declaration* and against any incitement to such discrimination.

Article 8

Everyone has the right to an effective remedy by the competent national tribunals for acts violating the fundamental rights granted him by the constitution or the law.

Article 9

No one shall be subjected to arbitrary arrest, detention or exile.

Article 13/2

Everyone has the right to leave any country, including his own, and to return to his country.

Article 18

Everyone has the right to freedom of thought, conscience and religion; this right includes freedom to change his religion or belief, and freedom, either alone or in community with others and in public or private, to manifest his religion or belief in teaching, practice, worship or observance.

Article 19

Everyone has the right to freedom of opinion and expression; this right includes freedom to hold opinions without interference and to seek, receive and impart information and ideas through any media and regardless of frontiers.

Article 20

Everyone has the right to freedom of peaceful assembly and association.

Article 26/2

Education shall be directed to the full development of the human personality and to the strengthening of respect for human rights and fundamental freedoms. *It shall promote understanding, tolerance and friendship among* all nations, racial or *religious groups,* and shall further the activities of the United Nations for the maintenance of peace.

Article 26/3

Parents have a prior right to choose the kind of education that shall be given to their children.

Article 30

Nothing in this Declaration may be interpreted as implying for any State, group or person any right to engage in any activity or to perform an act aimed at the destruction of any of the rights and freedoms set forth herein.

* * * *

INTERNATIONAL COVENANT ON CIVIL AND POLITICAL RIGHTS

(APPROVED BY THE GENERAL ASSEMBLY OF THE UNITED NATIONS ON DECEMBER 16, 1966; IN FORCE SINCE 1976.)

Article 2

1. *Each State Party to the present Covenant undertakes to respect and to ensure to all individuals within its territory* and subject to its jurisdiction *the rights recognized in the present Covenant, without distinction of any kind, such as* race, colour, sex, language, *religion,* political or other opinion, national or social origin, property, birth or other status.

Article 18

1. *Everyone shall have the right to freedom of thought, conscience and religion.* This right shall include freedom to have or adopt a religion or belief of his choice, and freedom, either individually or in community with others and in public or private, to manifest his religion or belief in worship, observance, practice and teaching.

2. *No one shall be subject to coercion which would impair his freedom to have or to adopt a religion or belief of his choice.*

3. Freedom to manifest one's religion or beliefs may be subject only to such limitations as are prescribed by law and are necessary to protect public safety, order, health, or morals or the fundamental rights and freedoms of others.

4. *The States Parties to the present Covenant undertake to have respect for the liberty of parents* and, when applicable, legal guardians *to ensure the religious and moral education of their children in conformity with their own convictions.*

Article 20

2. *Any advocacy of* national, racial or *religious hatred* that constitutes incitement to discrimination, hostility or violence *shall be prohibited by law.*

Article 21

The right of peaceful assembly shall be recognized. No restrictions may be placed on the exercise of this right other than those imposed in conformity with the law and which are necessary in a democratic society in the interests of national security or public safety, public order . . . , the protection of public health or morals or the protection of the rights and freedoms of others.

Article 25 c

Every citizen shall have the right and the opportunity, without any of the distinctions mentioned in article 2 and without unreasonable restrictions to have access, on general terms of equality, to public service in his country.

* * * *

FINAL ACT OF THE CONFERENCE ON SECURITY AND CO-OPERATION IN EUROPE (CSCE)
(APPROVED BY ALL STATES OF EUROPE AND BY THE USA AND CANADA IN HELSINKI ON AUGUST 1, 1975)

VII. *Respect for Human Rights and Fundamental Freedoms, Including the Freedom of Thought, Conscience, Religion or Belief.*

The Participating States will respect human rights and fundamental freedoms, including the freedom of thought, conscience, religion or belief, for all without distinction as to race, sex, language or religion.

They will promote and encourage the effective exercise of civil, political, economic, social, cultural and other rights and freedoms, all of which derive from the inherent dignity of the human person and are essential for his free and full development. *Within this framework the participating States will recognize and respect the freedom of the individual to profess and practice, alone or in community with others, religion or belief acting in accordance with the dictates of his own conscience.*

The participating States recognize the universal significance of human rights and fundamental freedoms, respect for which is an essential factor for the peace, justice and well-being necessary to ensure the development of friendly relations and co-operation among themselves as among all States.

They will constantly respect these rights and freedoms in their mutual relations and will endeavor jointly and separately, including in co-operation with the United Nations, to promote universal and effective respect for them.

They confirm the right of the individual to know and act upon his rights and duties in this field.

In the field of human rights and fundamental freedoms, the participating States will act in conformity with the purposes and principles of the Charter of the United Nations and *with the Universal Declaration of Human Rights.* They will also fulfill their obligations as set forth in the international declarations and agreements in this field, including *inter alia, the International Covenants on Human Rights,* by which they may be bound.

2. Co-Operation in Humanitarian and Other Fields

    A. Human contacts:

        d) Travel for personal or professional reasons

        The participating States intend to facilitate wider travel by their citizens for personal or professional reasons and to this end they intend in particular:

            —gradually to simplify and to administer flexibly the procedures for exit and entry;

            —to ease regulations concerning movement of citizens from the other participating States in their territory, with due regard to security requirements. They confirm that *religious faiths,* institutions and organizations, practicing within the constitutional framework of the participating States, and their representatives *can,* in the field of their activities, *have contacts and meetings among themselves and exchange information.*

    B. Information:

        a) Improvement of circulation or access to, and exchange of, information

            i. Oral Information—To facilitate the dissemination of oral information through the encouragement of lectures and lecture tours by personalities and specialists from the other participating States, as well as exchanges of opinions at round table meetings, seminars, symposia, summer schools, congresses and other bilateral and multilateral meetings.

            ii. Printed information—To facilitate the improvement of the dissemination, on their territory, of newspaper and printed publications, periodical and nonperiodical, from the other participating States.

3. Co-operation and Exchanges in the Field of Culture

    Extension of relations:

        To expand and improve at the various levels co-operation and links in the field of culture, in particular by:

        —contributing to the development of direct communications and co-operation among relevant State institutions and non-governmental organizations, including, where necessary, such communication and co-operation carried out on the basis of special agreements and arrangements.

* * * *

DECLARATION ON THE ELIMINATION OF ALL FORMS OF INTOLERANCE AND DISCRIMINATION BASED ON RELIGION OR BELIEF

(ADOPTED BY THE GENERAL ASSEMBLY OF THE UNITED NATIONS ON NOVEMBER 25, 1981)

Article 1

1. *Everyone shall have the right to freedom of thought, conscience and religion. This right shall include freedom to have a religion or whatever belief of his choice, and freedom, either individually or in community with others and in public or private, to manifest his religion or belief in worship, observance, practice and teaching.*

2. No one shall be subjected to coercion which would impair his freedom to have a religion or belief of his choice.

3. Freedom to manifest one's religion or beliefs may be subject only to such limitations as are prescribed by law and are necessary to protect public safety, order, health or morals or the fundamental rights and freedoms of others.

Article 2

1. No one shall be subject to discrimination by any State, institution, group of persons or person on the grounds of religion or other beliefs.

2. For the purposes of the present Declaration, the expression ''intolerance and discrimination based on religion or belief'' means any distinction, exclusion, restriction or preference based on religion or belief and having as its purpose or as its effect nullification or impairment of the recognition, enjoyment or exercise of human rights and fundamental freedoms on a equal basis.

Article 3

Discrimination between human beings on the grounds of religion or belief constitutes an affront to human dignity and a disavowal of the principles of the Charter of the United Nations, and shall be condemned as a violation of the human rights and fundamental freedoms proclaimed in the Universal Declaration of Human Rights and enunciated in detail in the International Covenants on Human Rights, and as an obstacle to friendly and peaceful relations between nations.

Article 4

1. All States shall take effective measures to prevent and eliminate discrimination on the grounds of religion or belief in the recognition, exercise and enjoyment of human rights and fundamental freedoms in all fields of civil, economic, political, social and cultural life.

2. All States shall make all efforts to enact or rescind legislation where necessary to prohibit any such discrimination, and to take all appropriate measures to combat intolerance on the grounds of religion or other beliefs in this matter.

Article 5

1. The parents or, as the case may be, the legal guardians of the child have the right to organize the life within the family in accordance with their religion or belief and bearing in mind the moral education in which they believe the child should be brought up.

2. Every child shall enjoy the right to have access to education in the matter of religion or belief in accordance with the wishes of his parents or, as the case may be, legal guardians, and shall not be compelled to receive teaching on religion or belief against the wishes of his parents or legal guardians, the best interests of the child being the guiding principle.

3. The child shall be protected from any form of discrimination on the grounds of religion or belief. He shall be brought up in a spirit of understanding, tolerance, friendship among peoples, peace and universal brotherhood, respect for freedom of religion or belief of others, and in full consciousness that his energy and talents should be devoted to the service of his fellow men.

4. In the case of a child who is not under the care either of his parents or of legal guardians, due account shall be taken of their expressed wishes or of any other proof of their wishes in the matter of religion or belief, the best interests of the child being the guiding principle.

5. Practices of a religion or beliefs in which a child is brought up must not be injurious to his physical or mental health or to his full development, taking into account article 1, paragraph 3, of the present Declaration.

Article 6

In accordance with article 1 of the present Declaration, and subject to the provisions of article 1, paragraph 3, the rights to freedom of thought, conscience, religion or belief shall include, *inter alia,* the following freedoms:

a)   To worship or assemble in connection with a religion or belief, and to establish and maintain places for these purposes;

b)   To establish and maintain appropriate charitable or humanitarian institutions;

c)   To make, acquire and use to an adequate extent the necessary articles and materials related to the rites or customs of a religion or belief;

d) To write, issue and disseminate relevant publications in these areas;

e) To teach a religion or belief in places suitable for these purposes;

f) To solicit and receive voluntary financial and other contributions from individuals and institutions;

g) To train, appoint, elect or designate by succession appropriate leaders called for by the requirements and standards of any religion or belief;

h) To observe days of rest and to celebrate holidays and ceremonies in accordance with the precepts of one's religion or belief;

i) To establish and maintain communications with individuals and communities in matters of religion and belief at the national and international levels.

Article 7

The rights and freedoms set forth in the present Declaration shall be accorded in national legislations in such a manner that everyone shall be able to avail himself of such rights and freedoms in practice.

Article 8

Nothing in the present Declaration shall be construed as restricting or derogating from any right defined in the Universal Declaration of Human Rights and the International Covenants on Human Rights.

* * * *

RESOLUTION ON RELIGIOUS INTOLERANCE

(ADOPTED AT THE 42D SESSION OF THE UNITED NATIONS COMMISSION ON HUMAN RIGHTS [GENEVA, 1986])

The Commission on Human Rights,

Recalling the Declaration on the Elimination of all Forms of Intolerance and of Discrimination Based on Religion or Belief, which was proclaimed without a vote by the General Assembly on 25 November 1981,

Bearing in mind that the General Assembly has, most recently in Resolution 40/109 of 13 December 1985, repeatedly requested the Commission on Human Rights to continue its consideration of measures to implement the Declaration,

Seriously concerned by frequent, reliable reports from all parts of the world which reveal that, because of governmental actions, universal implementation of the Declaration has not yet been achieved,

Determined to promote full implementation of the existing guarantees under the relevant international instruments of the right to freedom of thought, conscience and religion, including the freedom of everyone to have a religion or whatever belief of his choice without fear of intolerance or discrimination,

Recognizing the value of constructive dialogue on the complex and serious questions of intolerance and of discrimination based on religion or belief, and that the problem of such intolerance and discrimination requires sensitivity in its resolution,

Recognizing the valuable nature of the study undertaken by Mrs. Odio Benito, the Special Rapporteur of the Sub-Commission on Prevention of Discrimination and Protection of Minorities, on the root causes and current dimensions of the general problems of intolerance and of discrimination on the grounds of religion or belief, including recommended educational and other specific measures to combat these problems,

Convinced also of the need to deal urgently with questions of intolerance and of discrimination based on religion or belief by promoting implementation of the declaration:

1. Expresses its deep concern about reports of incidents and governmental actions in all parts of the world which are inconsistent with the provisions of the declaration on the elimination of all forms of intolerance and of discrimination based on religion or belief,

2. Decides therefore to appoint for one year a Special Rapporteur to examine such incidents and actions and to recommend remedial measures including, as appropriate, the promotion of dialogue between religious communities and their governments,

3. Requests the Chairman of the Commission, after consultations within the bureau, to appoint an individual of recognized international standing as the Special Rapporteur,

4. Decides further that the Special Rapporteur in carrying out this mandate shall seek credible and reliable information from governments, as well as specialized agencies, intergovernmental organizations, and non-government organizations, including religious communities and groups of believers,

5. Requests the Secretary-General to appeal to all governments to cooperate with and assist the Special Rapporteur in the performance of his duties and to furnish all information requested,

6. Further requests the Secretary-General to provide all necessary assistance to the Special Rapporteur,

7. Invites the Special Rapporteur, in carrying out his mandate, to bear in mind the need to be able to respond effectively to credible and reliable information that comes before him and to carry out his work with discretion and independence,

8. Requests the Special Rapporteur to submit a report to the Commission at its forty-third session on his activities regarding questions involving implementation of the declaration, including the occurrence and extent of incidents and actions inconsistent with the provisions of the declaration, together with his conclusions and recommendations,

9. Decides to consider this question again at its forty-third session under agenda item "Implementation of the Declaration on the Elimination of all Forms of Intolerance and of Discrimination Based on Religion or Belief."

* * * *

CONCLUDING DOCUMENT OF THE
VIENNA MEETING (1986-1989) OF
CONFERENCE ON SECURITY AND CO-OPERATION IN EUROPE
(JANUARY 19, 1989)

Principle 3. . . . [T]hey confirm that . . . they [the CSCE participating States] will ensure that their laws, regulations, practices and policies conform with their obligations under international law and are brought into harmony with the provisions of the Declaration on Principles and other CSCE commitments.

Principle 11. They confirm that they will respect human rights and fundamental freedoms, including the freedom of thought, conscience, religion or belief, for all without distinction as to race, sex, language or religion.

Principle 13g. [They will] ensure human rights and fundamental freedoms to everyone within their territory and subject to their jurisdiction, without distinction of any kind such as race, color, sex, language, religion, political or other opinion; national or social origin, property, birth or other status.

Principle 16. In order to ensure the freedom of the individual to profess and practice religion or belief the participating States will, *inter alia,*

a) take effective measures to prevent and eliminate discrimination against individuals or communities, on the grounds of religion or belief in the recognition, exercise and enjoyment of human rights and fundamental freedoms in all fields of civil, political, economic, social and cultural life, and ensure the effective equality between believers and non-believers;

b) foster a climate of mutual tolerance and respect between believers of different communities as well as between believers and non-believers;

c) grant upon their request to communities of believers, practicing or prepared to practice their faith within the constitutional framework of their states, recognition of the status provided for them in their respective countries;

d) respect the right of religious communities to
    —establish and maintain freely accessible places of worship or assembly,
    —organize themselves according to their own hierarchical and institutional structure,
    —select, appoint and replace their personnel in accordance with their respective requirements and standards as well as with any freely accepted arrangement between them and their State,
    —solicit and receive voluntary financial and other contributions;
e) engage in consultations with religious faiths, institutions and organizations in order to achieve a better understanding of the requirements of religious freedom;
f) respect the right of everyone to give and receive religious education in the language of his choice, individually or in association with others;
g) in this context respect, *inter alia,* the liberty of parents to ensure the religious and moral education of their children in conformity with their own convictions;
h) allow the training of religious personnel in appropriate institutions;
i) respect the right of individual believers and communities of believers to acquire, possess, and use sacred books, other articles and materials related to the practice of religion or belief;
j) allow religious faiths, institutions and organizations to produce and import and disseminate religious publications and materials;
k) favorably consider the interest of religious communities in participating in public dialogue, *inter alia,* through mass media;

Principle 17. The participating States recognize that the exercise of the above-mentioned rights relating to the freedom of religion or belief may be subject only to such limitations as are provided by law and consistent with their obligations under international law and with their international commitments. They will ensure in their laws and regulations and in their application the full and effective implementation of the freedom of thought, conscience, religion or belief.

Principle 32. They will allow believers, religious faiths and their representatives, in groups or on an individual basis, to establish and maintain direct personal contacts and communication with each other, in their own and other countries, *inter alia,* through travel, pilgrimages and participation in assemblies and other religious events. In this context and commensurate with such contacts and events, those concerned will be allowed to acquire, receive and carry with them religious publications and objects related to the practice of their religion or belief.

SELECT BIBLIOGRAPHY
ON RELIGION IN
THE SOVIET UNION

Alexeev, Wasslij, and Theofanis Stavrou. *The Great Revival: The Russian Church Under German Occupation.* Minneapolis: Burgess Publishing House, 1976.

Alexeyeva, Ludmilla. *Soviet Dissent.* Middletown, Conn.: Wesleyan University Press, 1987.

Anderson, Paul B. *People, Church, and State in Modern Russia.* Westport, Conn.: Hyperion Press, 1981.

Beeson, Trevor. *Discretion and Valour: Religious Conditions in Russia and Eastern Europe.* Rev. ed. London: Collins, Fount Paperback, 1982.

Berdyaev, Nicolas. *The Origin of Russian Communism.* Ann Arbor, Mich.: University of Michigan Press, 1960.

Billington, James H. *The Icon and the Axe: An Interpretive History of Russian Culture.* New York: Random House, Vintage Books, 1970.

Bociurkiw, Bohdan R. *Ukrainian Churches Under Soviet Rule: Two Case Studies.* Cambridge, Mass.: Harvard University Ukrainian Studies Fund, 1984.

Bourdeaux, Michael. *Opium of the People.* London: Mowbrays, 1965.

_____. *Patriarch and Prophets: Persecution of the Russian Orthodox Church.* London: Mowbrays, 1975.

_____. *Religious Ferment in Russia: Protestant Opposition to Soviet Religious Policy.* London: Macmillan, 1968.

_____. *Risen Indeed: Lessons in Faith from the USSR.* Crestwood, N. Y.: St. Vladimir's Seminary Press, 1983.

Bordeaux, Michael and Michael Rowe, eds. *May One Believe—in Russia? Violations of Religious Liberty in the Soviet Union.* London: Darton, Longman and Todd, 1980.

Brandenburg, Hans. *The Meek and the Mighty.* London: Mowbrays, 1974.

Bulgakov, Sergei. *Karl Marx as a Religious Type*. Belmont, Mass.: Nordland Publishing International, 1979.

Buss, Gerald. *The Bear's Hug: Christian Belief and the Soviet State, 1917-86*. Grand Rapids, Mich.: Wm. B. Eerdmans Publishing Co., 1987.

Carlson, Gordon William. "Russian Protestants and American Evangelicals Since the Death of Stalin: Patterns of Interaction and Response." Ph.D. diss., University of Minnesota, 1986.

Chmykhalov, Timothy. *The Last Christian: The Release of the Siberian Seven*. Grand Rapids, Mich.: Zondervan Publishing House, 1986.

Communism and Christianity in Theory and Practice: Doctrines/Facts/Conclusions. United Kingdom: Aid to the Church in Need, 1978.

Conquest, Robert. *The Great Terror: Stalin's Purge of the 1930s*. Rev. ed. New York: Collier Books, 1973.

——————. *The Harvest of Sorrow: Soviet Collectivization and the Terror-Famine*. Oxford: Oxford University Press, 1986.

Deyneka, Peter, Jr., and Anita Deyneka. *A Song in Siberia*. Elgin, Ill.: David C. Cook Publishing Co., 1977.

Dudko, Father Dmitrii. *Our Hope*. Crestwood, N. Y.: St. Vladimir's Press, 1977.

Durasoff, Steve. *Pentecost Behind the Iron Curtain*. Plainfield, N. J.: Logos International, 1972.

Ellis, Jane. *The Russian Orthodox Church: A Contemporary History*. Bloomington: Indiana University Press, 1986.

Fletcher, William C. *Religion and Soviet Foreign Policy*. London: Oxford University Press, 1973.

——————. *The Russian Orthodox Church Underground, 1917-1970*. London: Oxford University Press, 1971.

——————. *Soviet Believers: The Religious Sector of the Population*. Lawrence, Kans.: Regents Press of Kansas, 1981.

——————. *Soviet Charismatics*. New York: P. Lang, 1985.

——————. *A Study in Survival: The Church in Russia, 1927-1943*. New York: Macmillan Publishing Co., 1965.

Florinsky, Michael T. *Russian: A History and an Interpretation*. 2 vols. New York: Macmillan Publishing Co., 1968.

Gorbachev, Mikhail. *Perestroika: New Thinking for Our Country and the World*. New York: Harper and Row Publishers, 1988.

Goricheva, Tatiana. *Talking about God Is Dangerous*. New York: Crossroad, 1987.

Hebly, Hans. *Eastbound Ecumenism: A Collection of Essays on the World Council of Churches and Eastern Europe*. Lanham, Md.: University Press of America, 1986.

——————. *Protestants in Russia*. Belfast: Christian Journals, 1976.

Heller, Mikhail and Aleksandr M. Nekrich. *Utopia in Power: The History of the Soviet Union from 1917 to the Present*. New York: Summit Books, 1986.

Hollander, Paul. *Political Pilgrims: Travels of Western Intellectuals to the Soviet Union, China, and Cuba, 1928-1978*. New York: Oxford University Press, 1981.

House, Francis. *Millennium of Faith: Christianity in Russia, 988-1988 A.D.* New York: St. Vladimir's Seminary Press, 1988.

Lefever, Ernest. *Amsterdam to Nairobi: The World Council of Churches and the Third World*. Washington, D.C.: Ethics and Public Policy Center, 1979.

_____. *Nairobi to Vancouver: The World Council of Churches and the World, 1975-87*. Washington, D.C.: Ethics and Public Policy Center, 1987.

_____ and Robert D. Vander Lugt, eds. *Perestroika: How New is Gorbachev's New Thinking? Mikhail Gorbachev and His Critics*. Washington, D.C.: Ethics and Public Policy Center, 1989.

McLellan, David. *Karl Marx: His Life and Thought*. London: Macmillan Publishing Co., 1973.

Nesdoly, Samuel. *Among the Soviet Evangelicals*. Carlisle, Penn.: The Banner of Truth Trust, 1986.

Pollock, John C. *The Faith of the Russian Evangelicals*. New York: McGraw-Hill Book Co., 1964.

_____. *The Siberian Seven*. Waco, Tex.: Word, Inc., 1979.

Pospielovsky, Dmitry. *The Russian Church Under the Soviet Regime: 1917-1982*. 2 vols. Crestwood, N. Y.: St. Vladimir's Seminary Press, 1984.

Ratushinskaya, Irina. *Grey is the Color of Hope*. New York: Alfred A. Knopf, 1988.

Reform and Human Rights: The Gorbachev Record. Report submitted to the U.S. Congress by the Commission on Security and Cooperation in Europe, May 1988.

Religious Prisoners in the USSR. Keston College: Greenfire Books, 1987.

Sadunaite, Nijole. *A Radiance in the Gulag*. Manassas, Va.: Trinity Communications, 1987.

Sawatsky, Walter. *Soviet Evangelicals Since World War II*. Scottdale, Penn.: Herald Press, 1981.

Shirley, Eugene B. and Michael Rowe, eds. *Candle in the Wind*. Washington, D.C.: Ethics and Public Policy Center, 1989.

Simon, Gerhard. *Church, State and Opposition in the USSR*. London: C. Hurst, 1974.

Solzhenitsyn, Aleksandr I. *The Gulag Archipelago, 1918-1956*. Abridged by Edward E. Ericson, Jr. New York: Harper and Row, 1985.

_____. *Lenin in Zurich*. New York: Farrar, Straus and Giroux, 1976.

Spinka, Matthew. *The Church in Soviet Russia*. Westport, Conn.: Greenwood Press, 1980.

Steeves, Paul D. *Keeping the Faiths*. New York: Holmes and Meier Publishers, 1989.

Suziedelis, Saulius. *The Sword and the Cross: A History of the Church in Lithuania*. Huntington, Ind.: Our Sunday Visitor, Inc., 1988.

Szczesniak, Boleslaw, ed. *The Russian Revolution and Religion: A Collection of Documents Concerning the Suppression of Religion by the Communists, 1917-25*. Notre Dame: University of Notre Dame Press, 1959.

Vermaat, J. A. Emerson. *The World Council of Churches and Politics: 1975-1986*. New York: Freedom House, 1989.

Walters, Philip, ed. *World Christianity: Eastern Europe*. Monrovia, Calif.: Missions Advanced Research and Communication Center, 1988.

INDEX